D1224138

Interpersonal Processes in the Anxiety Disorders

Interpersonal Processes in the Anxiety Disorders

Implications for Understanding Psychopathology and Treatment

Edited by

J. Gayle Beck

American Psychological Association

Washington, DC

Copyright © 2010 by the American Psychological Association. All rights reserved. Except as permitted under the United States Copyright Act of 1976, no part of this publication may be reproduced or distributed in any form or by any means, including, but not limited to, the process of scanning and digitization, or stored in a database or retrieval system, without the prior written permission of the publisher.

Published by
American Psychological Association
750 First Street, NE
Washington, DC 20002
www.apa.org

To order
APA Order Department
P.O. Box 92984
Washington, DC 20090-2984
Tel: (800) 374-2721; Direct: (202) 336-5510
Fax: (202) 336-5502; TDD/TTY: (202) 336-6123
Online: www.apa.org/books/
E-mail: order@apa.org

In the U.K., Europe, Africa, and the Middle East, copies may be ordered from
American Psychological Association
3 Henrietta Street
Covent Garden, London
WC2E 8LU England

Typeset in Goudy by Circle Graphics, Inc., Columbia, MD

Printer: Edwards Brothers, Inc., Ann Arbor, MI
Cover Designer: Minker Design, Sarasota, FL

The opinions and statements published are the responsibility of the authors, and such opinions and statements do not necessarily represent the policies of the American Psychological Association.

Library of Congress Cataloging-in-Publication Data

Interpersonal processes in the anxiety disorders : implications for understanding psychopathology and treatment / edited by J. Gayle Beck. — 1st ed.
    p. ; cm.
Includes bibliographical references and index.
ISBN-13: 978-1-4338-0745-9 (print)
ISBN-10: 1-4338-0745-9 (print)
ISBN-13: 978-1-4338-0746-6 (electronic)
ISBN-10: 1-4338-0746-7 (electronic)
1. Psychology, Pathological. 2. Anxiety disorders. I. Beck, J. Gayle.

RC480.1586 2010
616.89—dc22
                    2009039858

British Library Cataloguing-in-Publication Data

A CIP record is available from the British Library.

Printed in the United States of America
First Edition

To Bruce—my partner, friend, and husband.

CONTENTS

CONTRIBUTORS

Lynn E. Alden, PhD, University of British Columbia, Vancouver, Canada
Steven R. H. Beach, PhD, University of Georgia, Athens
J. Gayle Beck, PhD, University of Memphis, Memphis, TN
Kristy E. Benoit, Virginia Polytechnic Institute and State University, Blacksburg
Catherine M. Caska, University of Utah, Salt Lake City
Dianne L. Chambless, PhD, University of Pennsylvania, Philadelphia
Natalie M. Costa, PhD, Virginia Polytechnic Institute and State University, Blacksburg
Joanne Davila, PhD, Stony Brook University, Stony Brook, NY
Rachel Dekel, PhD, Bar-Ilan University, Ramat-Gan, Israel
Thane M. Erickson, PhD, Seattle Pacific University, Seattle, WA
Steffany J. Fredman, PhD, VA National Center for PTSD, Boston, MA
Molly F. Gasbarrini, Texas A&M University, College Station
Stephen N. Haynes, PhD, University of Hawaii at Manoa, Honolulu
Richard E. Heyman, PhD, Stony Brook University, Stony Brook, NY
Kevin D. Jordan, University of Utah, Salt Lake City
Annette M. La Greca, PhD, University of Miami, Coral Gables, FL

Ryan R. Landoll, University of Miami, Coral Gables, FL

Candice M. Monson, PhD, Ryerson University, Toronto, Ontario, Canada

Michelle G. Newman, PhD, Pennsylvania State University, University Park

Thomas H. Ollendick, PhD, Virginia Polytechnic Institute and State University, Blacksburg

Keith D. Renshaw, PhD, George Mason University, Fairfax, VA

Camila S. Rodrigues, Boston University, Boston, MA

Timothy W. Smith, PhD, University of Utah, Salt Lake City

Douglas K. Snyder, PhD, Texas A&M University, College Station

Lisa R. Starr, Stony Brook University, Stony Brook, NY

Gail Steketee, PhD, Boston University, Boston, MA

Charles T. Taylor, PhD, McGill University, Montreal, Quebec, Canada

Mandy Uliaszek, Northwestern University, Evanston, IL

Mark A. Whisman, PhD, University of Colorado at Boulder

Paula G. Williams, PhD, University of Utah, Salt Lake City

Richard E. Zinbarg, PhD, Northwestern University, Evanston, IL

Interpersonal
Processes
in the Anxiety
Disorders

INTRODUCTION

J. GAYLE BECK

Traditionally, the study of anxiety and anxiety disorders has focused on intrapersonal factors. As exemplified by Freud's (1894/1940) original conceptualization of anxiety, most theoretical frameworks have highlighted cognitive, affective, behavioral, physiological, and genetic processes that establish and maintain anxiety. Although exceptions can be found, these theories have traditionally emphasized factors within the individual, leaving open to question the role of interpersonal factors in the genesis and maintenance of anxiety. Yet those of us who treat and conduct research with anxious individuals know that their interpersonal world is shaped in part by the nature of their symptoms and vice versa. How can we begin to reconcile our research and clinical experiences with our current theoretical accounts to develop a thorough and accurate understanding of interpersonal processes in the anxiety disorders? This volume is a beginning step toward answering this question.

In organizing this book, it was important to first provide an overview of conceptual and assessment tools in Section I. Chapter 1 orients the reader to models for understanding interpersonal influences on anxiety disorders. In particular, one must begin to include reciprocal, bidirectional influences between the anxiety-disordered individual and friends, family, and romantic partners into any interpersonally based conceptual model. Although social influences may constitute part of the psychopathology of a given anxiety disorder (as is the case with social anxiety disorder), this is not always the case. Thus, Chapter 1 provides an overview of current theoretical approaches to conceptualizing interpersonal processes, with a review of models that allow flexibility in conceptualizing how close relationships might influence the psychopathology and treatment of an anxiety-disordered individual. Chapter 2 outlines the current state of measurement approaches within both of these domains. As recognized by Snyder and colleagues, our understanding of the interpersonal context of anxiety-related problems is constrained by measurement properties of instruments to assess both of these arenas. Chapter 2 is designed to provide a user-friendly overview of assessment strategies in these two areas, with the intent of benefiting both clinical and research activities. Together, these two chapters provide a foundation for the balance of the volume.

Section II is organized around specific topics under the broad umbrella of anxiety disorders. Each of the eight chapters in this section reviews the available literature on interpersonal processes, divided into specific age groups or disorders. Chapters 3 and 4 cover interpersonal processes pertaining to anxiety disorders in children and adolescents, respectively. The remaining chapters discuss interpersonal processes pertaining to various specific disorders in adults: social anxiety disorder (Chap. 5), obsessive–compulsive disorder (Chap. 6), posttraumatic stress disorder (Chap. 7), panic disorder and agoraphobia (Chap. 8), generalized anxiety disorder (Chap. 9), and health anxiety and hypochondriasis (Chap. 10). The chapters in Section II are intended to provide the reader with a critical overview of the current knowledge about interpersonal processes within a specific condition, including a clinical description, review of etiological formulations, summary of research about interpersonal processes, and information pertaining to comorbidity and treatment. Clinical material is included to help readers to bridge the gap between clinical and research work.

In designing this book, my primary goal was to integrate available knowledge on the topic, with a longer term goal of stimulating additional clinical and research work in this domain. It is hoped is that this book will begin a series of dialogues between individuals from somewhat disparate fields and motivate young scholars and clinicians to focus their energies on a closer examination of how relationships function within the anxiety disorders. The pages of this book offer many intriguing ideas for future study, and these ideas could easily become the basis of tomorrow's treatment advances. If this volume accomplishes its goals, we will witness a growth in our clinical and empirical knowledge of how interpersonal processes influence the development, maintenance, and treatment of anxiety disorders. This new knowledge will allow us to hone our assessment and case conceptualization skills, and refine treatments, in an effort to improve the effectiveness of available interventions.

As noted across the chapters of this volume, a considerable amount of basic information is beginning to accumulate concerning interpersonal processes in the anxiety disorders. This knowledge base challenges us to integrate it, to draw together basic interpersonal processes as they apply to maladaptive fear learning. In accepting that challenge, we need to reach out to related areas of study to use the broader knowledge base. It is an exciting time to be working in this area, as enumerated by the authors of this book's chapters.

REFERENCE

Freud, S. (1940). The justification for detaching from neurasthenia a particular syndrome: The anxiety-neurosis (J. Rickman, Trans.). In *Collected papers* (Vol. 1, pp. 76–106). New York, NY: Basic Books. (Original work published 1894)

I

CONCEPTUALIZATION
AND ASSESSMENT

1

MODELS FOR UNDERSTANDING INTERPERSONAL PROCESSES AND RELATIONSHIPS IN ANXIETY DISORDERS

MARK A. WHISMAN AND STEVEN R. H. BEACH

Relationship

The drive to form and maintain strong, stable interpersonal relationships has been identified as a fundamental human motivation (Baumeister & Leary, 1995). Likewise, close relationships are often identified as a key concern for those entering therapy (e.g., Shumway, Wampler, Dersch, & Arredondo, 2004), and relational conflict is associated with immunological down-regulation and proinflammatory response (Kiecolt-Glaser et al., 2005; Kiecolt-Glaser, Malarkey, Chee, & Newton, 1993). Interpersonal functioning and interpersonal relationships, therefore, should be intricately intertwined with mental health and well-being. Indeed, there is a growing body of research indicating that poor relational functioning is associated with a variety of mental and physical health outcomes (Beach et al., 2006).

Interpersonal processes and relationships have been shown to be important for understanding the onset and course of anxiety disorders. For example, marital quality at baseline has been shown to predict first (i.e., new case) and total incidence of anxiety disorders occurring between 1 and 3 years later (Overbeek et al., 2006). Interpersonal processes have also been shown to be important for outcome following treatment for anxiety (e.g., Borkovec, Newman, Pincus, & Lytle, 2002). However, the literature detailing the involvement of interpersonal processes in anxiety disorders is not yet well developed.

In this chapter, we provide an overview of several frameworks for studying interpersonal processes in anxiety disorders. The review is divided into three sections: (a) conceptual tools to guide the construction of systemic interpersonal models, (b) the potential importance of positive social relationships in interpersonal models of anxiety, and (c) genetic and epigenetic processes. In the section on conceptual tools, we begin by describing the circumplex model because it may provide a useful foundation for hypotheses about repetitive, interpersonal transactions occasioned by the onset of an anxiety disorder or that may maintain symptoms once the disorder is underway. We then discuss the interpersonal stress model because of the important role typically assigned to stress in models of etiology or maintenance of anxiety disorders, particularly when these are considered from a broad developmental biopsychosocial perspective. Finally, we describe the stress generation model to further illustrate the potential for iterative processes to connect symptoms with problematic interpersonal transactions in a manner that can become self-sustaining. In the second section of the chapter, we briefly review the role of attachment relationships, social support effects, and interpersonal skills on anxiety. In each case, well-documented effects connect particular positive interpersonal processes (or their absence) to anxiety disorders. As a result, it appears likely that positive interpersonal relationships and processes will also be useful in constructing specific interpersonal models of anxiety disorders. In the third section, we briefly review the potential for genetic and epigenetic models to help elaborate interpersonal models of anxiety and perhaps clarify individual variation in response to interpersonal events and processes. We conclude the chapter with some suggestions for future research.

We make no attempt to provide a single, integrated model of interpersonal processes in the anxiety disorders. Rather, the models we review are meant to provide a flexible set of tools and building blocks to allow theoretical and conceptual advances as researchers construct specific models in which the relative importance of particular processes varies across disorders. We make no attempt to be exhaustive, but we do hope to illustrate the range of findings that are relevant for researchers studying the anxiety disorders. In addition to describing each model, we highlight illustrative studies that have applied this model to the etiology, course, or treatment of anxiety disorders; specific research findings regarding interpersonal processes in specific anxiety disorders are provided in the remaining chapters of this volume.

CONCEPTUAL TOOLS FOR ITERATIVE, SYSTEMIC MODELS

In this section, we describe three general models that may be useful as conceptual and theoretical foundations for building systemic interpersonal models of anxiety disorders. Specifically, we review the circumplex model, the interpersonal stress model, and the stress generation model, highlighting how research based on each of these broad models may help to increase our understanding of anxiety.

Interpersonal Circumplex Model

The interpersonal circumplex model of interpersonal functioning has its roots in the writings of Harry Stack Sullivan (1953). Rather than adhering to Freud's focus on internal processes within an individual, Sullivan emphasized interpersonal processes that occur between individuals. This interpersonal focus is captured by his oft-cited definition of personality as "the relatively enduring pattern of recurrent interpersonal situations which characterize a human life" (pp. 110–111) and by his definition of psychological problems as "patterns of inadequate and inappropriate action in interpersonal relations" (p. 314).

Sullivan's (1953) theory and ideas were operationalized by Leary (1957), who conducted an ordinary language analysis of clinicians' observations of the things that patients did to each other in group psychotherapy. What resulted from this work was a taxonomy of interpersonal behaviors represented by a circular, or circumplex, arrangement of interpersonal behaviors. The interpersonal circumplex, which has been revised several times (e.g., Kiesler, 1983), depicts a variety of interpersonal behaviors in terms of a circular continuum. The vertical axis, referred to as *dominance* (vs. submissiveness), is a dimension marked by problems with domineering interpersonal behavior at one pole and by problems with unassertiveness at the other pole. The horizontal axis, referred to as *love–nurturance* (vs. coldness), is a dimension marked by problems with excessive concern for others at one pole and by problems with inability to feel love and concern for others at the other pole. On a metatheoretical level, it may be helpful to consider the dominance and nurturance axes in terms of Bakan's (1966) concepts of agency and communion, respectively (Wiggins, 1991). The interpersonal circumplex can be divided into smaller units, usually between eight and 16 segments, which refer to different interpersonal behaviors. An example of the interpersonal circumplex is provided in Figure 1.1.

Unlike traditional assessment methods, circumplex measures of interpersonal behavior are interpreted with reference to the geometric principles of a circle (for a detailed description of scoring the interpersonal circumplex, see Gurtman, 1994). For example, behaviors measured in a particular segment (e.g., octant) display moderate positive correlations with adjacent segments, and the correlations decrease in magnitude with each successive segment, ending with negative correlations with behaviors measured in the segment on the opposite side of the circle. Interpretation of the interpersonal circumplex has traditionally emphasized predominant interpersonal trends and the intensity of those interpersonal trends. Specifically, scores on the dominance and nurturance axes

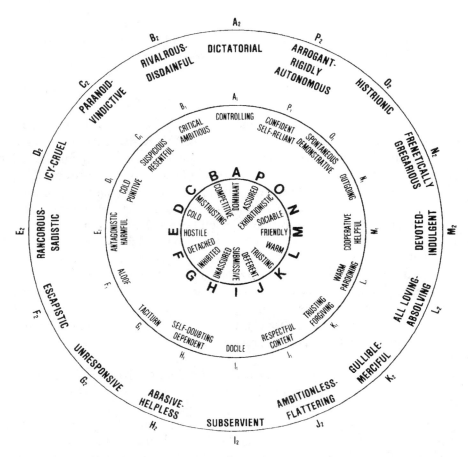

Figure 1.1. The 1982 Interpersonal Circle. From "The 1982 Interpersonal Circle: A Taxonomy For Complementarity in Human Transactions," by D. J. Kiesler, 1983, *Psychological Review, 90,* p. 189. Copyright 1983 by the American Psychological Association.

are used to plot the location of a person or group in two-dimensional interpersonal space, which is the *typological* category (i.e., the prevailing interpersonal style) of the person or group. Furthermore, the vector length reflects the degree of interpersonal rigidity (vs. flexibility): Greater vector length suggests extreme or unwavering interpersonal style and inflexible adaptations to different interpersonal situations. For example, as can be seen in Figure 1.1, submissive behavior is the mild level of the interpersonal behavior represented by the submissive end of the dominant–submissive axis, whereas docile behavior is a moderate level of this axis and subservient behavior is an extreme level of this axis.

According to the tenets of interpersonal theory, understanding the location of a person or group in interpersonal space can provide useful information regarding the kinds of interpersonal transactions the person or group is likely to experience and the impact that they are likely to produce in others on the basis of the theory of complementarity or reciprocity, introduced by Sullivan (1953) and expanded by Kiesler (1983). Although a full review of complementarity is beyond the scope of this chapter, we highlight what we believe are some of the most relevant of these propositions for anxiety. First, a person's interpersonal behavior is believed to elicit or pull restricted classes of behavior from other people that lead to a repetition of the person's original behavior in a self-sustaining fashion. This is known as the *interpersonal principle of complementarity*. Specifically, complementarity is hypothesized to occur on the basis of reciprocity with respect to the dominance axis (e.g., dominance pulls for submission, submission elicits dominance) and correspondence with respect to the nurturance axis (e.g., friendliness pulls for friendliness, hostility elicits hostility). Furthermore, it is hypothesized that complementarity operates at the same level of intensity: Interpersonal behaviors performed at one level of intensity will pull for complementary responses at the same level of intensity. For example, as seen in Figure 1.1, dominant behavior pulls for submissive behavior, whereas dictatorial behavior pulls for subservient behavior.

Interpersonal theory was developed to understand the interpersonal functioning related to personality, psychopathology, and psychotherapy. As such, it holds considerable appeal for scholars interested in understanding anxiety disorders from an interpersonal perspective. Several studies have been conducted on interpersonal circumplex models of anxiety disorders. For example, Alden and Phillips (1990) examined differences among socially anxious, depressed, and nondepressed individuals. They found that compared with nondepressed control individuals, socially anxious individuals differed on dimensions of unassertiveness and social avoidance; depressed individuals did not differ from control individuals. More recently, Kachin, Newman, and Pincus (2001) evaluated whether subgroups of people with social phobia could be identified on the basis of interpersonal problems. Results suggested the presence of two subtypes of social phobia: one with interpersonal problems relating to hostile, angry behavior and the other with interpersonal problems relating to friendly, submissive behavior. These findings suggest that the interpersonal circumplex model may provide useful information for understanding anxiety disorders.

Interpersonal Stress in Development

Another potentially useful model in the study of anxiety is the severe interpersonal stress model, a model that may be particularly useful when focused on events occurring during childhood and adolescence but that may also play a role in adulthood. When stressors are viewed as being intentionally inflicted, they are more likely to produce an effect on mental health outcomes (Kessler et al., 2005), suggesting that interpersonal stressors have the potential to be more tightly linked to mental health relative to noninterpersonal stressors. Likewise, severe interpersonal stressors produce higher levels of subjective distress than do noninterpersonal stressors, leading to greater toxicity (Frans, Rimmo, Aberg, & Fredrikson, 2005). More important, severe childhood stressors may sensitize individuals to the experience of later stressors, rendering them more vulnerable to adult internalizing disorders (Andrews, Brewin, Rose, & Kirk, 2000; Brewin, Andrews, & Valentine, 2000). Similarly, childhood stressors may accumulate such that experience of several early childhood traumas or stressors may be linked to internalizing problems later in life (e.g., Chapman et al., 2004). As a consequence, severe interpersonal stressors, which accumulate across childhood, may be worse in their effects than severe but transitory stressors or severe, noninterpersonal stressors. This difference provides justification for examining the effects of severe interpersonal stressors separately from the effects of other severe stressors (for an extended discussion, see Charuvastra & Cloitre, 2008) and underscores the importance of careful description of key relational processes as they relate to diagnosis and intervention (Beach et al., 2006). At the same time, animal models have suggested the possibility that a moderate level of stress may induce resilience, whereas more severe stress may create vulnerability to startle and anxiety responses (e.g., Cirulli & Alleva, 2003).

Gender

Several considerations also suggest the possibility of differential impact of severe interpersonal stressors, such as child abuse, as a function of gender. For example, several authors have reported that the symptoms of sexually abused boys and girls differ along the dimension of internalizing and externalizing behaviors (e.g., Bolton, Morris, & MacEachron, 1989; Finkelhor, 1990). These authors found that boys tend to display more externalizing behaviors (such as acting out aggressively, limit testing, and antisocial behavior), whereas girls tend to display more internalizing behaviors (such as fear, social withdrawal, depression, and inhibition). According to Bolton et al. (1989), boys also display a greater degree of inappropriate sexualized behavior. At the same time, rates of different types of child abuse may vary by gender. Compared with males, females report greater prevalence and severity of childhood sexual abuse (Ullman & Filipas, 2005), whereas physical abuse in childhood is more prevalent among men than women but may have greater impact for women than for men (Thompson, Kingree, & Desai, 2004). Similarly, the results of the Third National Incidence Study of Child Abuse and

Neglect (Sedlak & Broadhurst, 1996) indicated that whereas girls are sexually abused three times more often than boys, boys are at a greater risk of serious injury and emotional neglect than are girls. These considerations suggest that gender may be an important moderator of the behavioral impact of severe interpersonal stressors in childhood. With regard to anxiety disorders, one might suspect that sexual abuse in childhood and adolescence would be a more prominent risk factor for anxiety disorders for girls than for boys, both because it is more common for girls and because it may more typically predispose girls than boys to internalizing disorders.

Developmental Stage

Several considerations from both clinical and basic research frameworks suggest that developmental stage may be important in understanding the impact of severe interpersonal events. When the severe stressor is produced by a parent, as in the case of child abuse for young children, there is also the potential for disruption of basic attachment processes, a point we return to later. In addition, children may be particularly sensitive to severe interpersonal stress at key developmental transitions or when they are not buffered by support from a secure attachment figure. Similarly, adolescents may be at increased risk of negative impacts of severe interpersonal stressors because of the developmental processes characteristic of adolescence (Gunnar & Quevedo, 2007; Spear, 2000). More specifically, it may be that at puberty children develop adultlike patterns of responsiveness to stress (e.g., Spear, 2000), leading to increased vulnerability to the emergence of anxiety disorder at this time of social and biological change. Each of these considerations suggests the importance of adopting a developmental framework in examining the impact of interpersonal stress on vulnerability to anxiety disorders.

Stress Generation

Historically, stressful life events have generally been viewed as events that happen to unfortunate people, who in turn were seen as the victims of these events. Over time, however, this view has changed because research has shown that people not only react to their environments but also rather actively shape these environments. These models emphasize the bidirectional effects of people and environments in general and life stress and psychiatric disorders in particular. Much of this work has focused on stress generation associated with depression (Hammen, 1991, 2006). The stress generation perspective posits that compared with nondepressed individuals, depressed individuals experience more stressful life events that are the result, in part, of their own enduring cognitions, traits, and behaviors. Although the stress generation perspective holds that individuals actively contribute to the occurrence of some types of stressful events (i.e., events involving interpersonal conflict), it is important to note that the theory does not suggest that this process is intentional. The experience of stressful environments, in turn, is likely to result in continuing or recurrent symptoms, perhaps further increasing the propensity for future stress-generating behavior. This creates a vicious cycle in which symptoms and stress-inducing behavior may become mutually sustaining.

Although originally developed as a model for understanding interpersonal processes associated with depression, preliminary evidence has suggested that this model may also be important for understanding anxiety. For example, Hankin, Kassel, and Abela (2005) found that baseline anxiety predicted interpersonal stress generation during a 2-year follow-up. However, we know of no research that has evaluated the association between diagnosed anxiety disorders and dependent stressful life events that might be at least partly caused by the person. It remains for future research to evaluate whether stress generation is associated with more severe forms of anxiety. If individuals with anxiety disorders (or individuals prone to develop anxiety disorders) are actively contributing to stressful environments, including the generation of interpersonally stressful events, then the stress generation model may provide important insights regarding the onset, maintenance, or recurrence of anxiety disorders.

BUILDING BLOCKS FOR INTERPERSONAL MODELS OF ANXIETY DISORDERS

In this section, we focus on specific types and qualities of social relationships that may be important for understanding interpersonal aspects of anxiety. Specifically, we provide an overview of interpersonal relationships (romantic relationships, familial relationships, expressed emotion), attachment and social support, and interpersonal social skills, and discuss their relevance for understanding anxiety.

Interpersonal Relationships

How people function in their interpersonal relationships is likely to influence and be influenced by their level of anxiety. In this section, we focus on two important relationships—romantic relationships and familial relationships—and one particular relationship process—expressed emotion—and discuss how each may be important for understanding anxiety.

Marriage and Close Relationships

Demographic data have indicated that more than 90% of the population of the United States will marry at least once in their lifetime (Kreider &

Fields, 2001) and that many people who do not marry form cohabiting relationships (Seltzer, 2000). Furthermore, the relationships that people form with their romantic partners are most often among the most, if not the most, important and long-standing interpersonal relationships formed during their lifetime. Therefore, an individual's mental health and well-being is likely to influence, and be influenced by, interpersonal processes within romantic relationships. For example, mental health problems such as anxiety may negatively affect a person's role functioning, resulting in lower satisfaction in close relationships. Alternatively, relationship problems may act as a social stressor or lead to loss of social support, increasing the likelihood of anxiety and other mental health problems.

Much of the research on close relationships and mental health has focused on respondents' global evaluations of their relationship, described by terms such as *satisfaction* and *discord*. Furthermore, most of the research on close relationships has focused on married individuals. These studies have suggested that marital satisfaction is lower among people with psychiatric disorders, including anxiety disorders. For example, in population-based samples of married individuals in the United States, people with anxiety disorders reported lower marital satisfaction than people without anxiety disorders (Whisman, 1999, 2007). Marital quality has also been shown to prospectively predict the onset of anxiety disorders. For example, in a population-based sample of 3,383 people in the Netherlands, lower marital quality at baseline was associated with increased risk for first (i.e., new case) and total incidence of anxiety disorders (generalized anxiety disorder, panic disorder, social phobia, agoraphobia) occurring between 1 and 3 years later (Overbeek et al., 2006).

In addition to examining global relationship functioning, researchers have begun to study specific relationship processes that are associated with mental health problems, including anxiety disorders. Much of this research has focused on marital interaction (i.e., communication). Communication has been identified as the most common reason why people seek couple therapy (Whisman, Dixon, & Johnson, 1997), and marital interaction is associated with relationship satisfaction and stability (for a review, see Kelly, Fincham, & Beach, 2003). In studying the association between marital interaction and psychopathology, much of the existing research has focused on couples' self-reports of their interactions or on observational studies of couples' problem-solving interactions. In observational studies of problem-solving interactions, couples are asked to solve one or more problems in their relationships, and these interactions are videotaped and subsequently coded by trained observers. Chambless et al. (2002) provided an example of research on marital interaction and anxiety disorders in a study that used both self-report and observational methods to evaluate women with agoraphobia. Results indicated that couples in which the wife was agoraphobic were less likely than control couples to engage in positive problem solution. Furthermore, compared with husbands in control couples, husbands of wives with agoraphobia were more critical of them; husbands of agoraphobic wives did not, however, differ from husbands in control couples in terms of supportiveness. Additional research evaluating other interaction behaviors (e.g., demand–withdraw communication), other types of communication tasks (e.g., social support interactions), and other anxiety disorders could increase understanding of the specific relationship processes that are associated with anxiety.

Family Functioning

Similar to research on couple relationships, investigators have evaluated the association between family functioning and anxiety disorders on the basis of the assumptions that family relationships may influence and be influenced by the presence of psychopathology. As with the global quality of couple relationships, it has been shown that anxiety disorders are associated with global measures of family functioning. For example, compared with control families, families in which one person has an anxiety disorder report poorer overall functioning (Friedmann et al., 1997). Similarly, researchers have examined specific family processes that are associated with anxiety disorders. For example, compared with nonclinical control families, the families of patients with anxiety disorders report greater impairment in communication (i.e., indirect and vague communication) and problem solving (i.e., impairments in their ability to resolve problems within and outside of the family; Friedmann et al., 1997).

Expressed Emotion

One particular interpersonal process that has been studied in the context of couples and families is expressed emotion (EE). *Expressed emotion* refers to the extent to which family members express criticism of, hostility toward, and emotional overinvolvement with patients with psychiatric disorders to a researcher during a private interview. The benchmark instrument for the assessment of EE is the Camberwell Family Interview (Vaughn & Leff, 1976), a semistructured interview with the patient's partner or relative. The interview generally lasts between 1 and 2 hours, is recorded on audiotape, and is coded by trained raters. Research has demonstrated adverse effects of high-EE interactions between psychiatric patients and a relative or partner. Negative effects of high-EE relationships with someone who is in regular contact with the patient have been noted for schizophrenia, depression, anxiety, posttraumatic stress disorder, and eating disorders (see Butzlaff & Hooley, 1998; Hooley, 2007). Moreover, when viewed in the context of nonpsychiatric medical disorders (Wearden, Tarrier, Barrowclough, Zastowny, & Rahill, 2000), high-EE relationships continue to have predictive value for the course of a number of medical conditions (e.g., asthma, diabetes, epilepsy). In terms of predictive power, the dimension of criticism is considered to be the strongest component of EE.

In addition to measuring actual criticism expressed by family members toward a patient, researchers have also studied patients' subjective reports of how critical they believe their partner or family member is of them. This phenomenon has come to be called *perceived criticism* (Hooley & Teasdale, 1989). Early research on perceived criticism evaluated the association between it and relapse rates for depression. Hooley and Teasdale (1989) measured perceived criticism with a 10-point Likert-type scale reflecting how critical depressed patients considered their spouses to be of them. They found not only that perceived criticism was highly correlated with spouses' overall EE ratings as assessed by the Camberwell Family Interview but also that perceived criticism was a better predictor of relapse than EE and marital discord. Perceived criticism also appears to be associated with the course and treatment outcome for anxiety disorders. For example, perceived criticism has been associated with poorer outcome following treatments for obsessive–compulsive disorder (Chambless & Steketee, 1999) and panic disorder with agoraphobia (Renshaw, Chambless, & Steketee, 2003). Moreover, perceived criticism was not associated with concurrent symptom severity (Renshaw et al., 2003) and remained a significant predictor of outcome when controlling for major depression (Renshaw, Chambless, & Steketee, 2001), suggesting that this association is not just an artifact of the association between perceived criticism and anxiety severity or comorbidity with other disorders. Taken together, these findings suggest that future research on understanding of the role of couple and family functioning on treatment outcome may want to consider actual criticism from the partner and family (i.e., EE) as well as perceptions of such criticism.

Attachment Relationships and Social Support

Attachment theory, first introduced by Bowlby (1969) and expanded on by Ainsworth, Blehar, Waters, and Wall (1978), has proven important in guiding human and nonhuman research, again pointing to an important role for positive interpersonal processes in protecting against the short- and long-term effects of severe stressors. Young children who are in the presence of a secure attachment figure, typically the mother, show reduced physiological response to potentially distressing events (e.g., Spangler & Schiecke, 1998), leading to decreased production of stress hormones and better regulation of affect (see also Gunnar & Quevedo, 2007). Similarly, better social support during the aftermath of natural disaster may predict level of posttraumatic stress disorder symptoms in adolescence (Bokszczanin, 2008) and perhaps in adulthood. Converging evidence from animal models has suggested that maternal behavior is critical in understanding development of the stress response (Meaney & Szyf, 2005) and the cumulative effects of stress. Similarly, in humans attachment processes appear to influence whether stressors result in increased cortisol production (Gunnar & Donzella, 2002) and so longer term effects on the stress response and the propensity for development or worsening of an anxiety disorder.

The importance of positive, protective interpersonal processes extends beyond childhood. The best way to characterize and assess key attachment processes and more general, positive interpersonal processes in adulthood (e.g., social support), however, remains a point of some debate. Recent progress in assessing adult attachment styles provides an important extension into adulthood. Results from a factor analysis of existing self-report measures of adult attachment have suggested the presence of two global factors underlying measures of attachment: anxiety and avoidance (Brennan, Clark, & Shaver, 1998). Furthermore, results from taxometric analyses—statistical methods that examine the covariation among indicators (such as test scores) to seek patterns that are diagnostic of either latent categories (i.e., taxa) or dimensions (Waller & Meehl, 1998)—have suggested that these two factors are best conceptualized as continuously distributed rather than as reflecting categories or typologies (Fraley & Waller, 1998).

Research has shown that adult attachment is predictive of longitudinal changes in anxiety. For example, Hankin et al. (2005) found that anxious attachment, but not avoidant attachment, predicted prospective changes in anxiety symptoms during a 2-year follow-up. Additional research is needed to see whether adult attachment is prospectively associated with the onset and course of specific anxiety disorders.

Social support research has also suggested that transactions within adult romantic relationships may be linked to positive mental and physical health (Cunningham & Barbee, 2000), relationship stability (Bradbury, Fincham, & Beach, 2000), and effective coping (Cutrona, 1996). The findings suggest considerable relevance of social support processes for anxiety-related symptoms. In some cases, it appears that spouses play a central role in support provision (Cutrona & Suhr, 1994; Reiss, 1990), and perhaps a unique role in that receiving support outside the marriage may not be sufficient to compensate for lack of support within the marriage (Julien & Markman, 1991). However, support in adulthood has been conceptualized as complex, consisting of multiple forms that may be associated with differential outcomes. Weiss (1974) distinguished among six functions potentially served by support: attachment, social integration, reassurance of worth, guidance, reliable alliance, and opportunity to provide nurturing. It is not clear to what extent one or more of the various dimensions of social support is central in the context of understanding anxiety. However, it is clear that perceived availability of support, a construct rather similar to secure attachment, may be particularly important. Cutrona (1996) proposed a potentially useful distinction between *action-facilitating support* and *nurturant support* that may also be useful. Nondirective, nurturant forms of support and the perceived availability of support from a partner are reliably associated with positive emotional outcomes, whereas the impact of directive, action-facilitating support appears to depend on the goals of the support recipient (Cutrona, Cohen, & Igram, 1990). The distinction between action facilitating and nurturant suggests that some supportive interactions are important because they affirm the adult attachment relationship (i.e., are nurturant), whereas some are important because they enhance the individual's efficacy (i.e., are action facilitating).

Gender and Social Support

As with the impact of social stressors, clear gender differences in receipt of social support may influence interpersonal models. In particular, men in heterosexual relationships rely more heavily on their wives as their central source of nondirective support than vice versa (Antonucci & Akiyama, 1987). It was found that 82% of husbands reported confiding in wives compared with only 63% of wives who reported confiding in husbands. Similarly, 74% of husbands said they talked to their wives when they were upset, whereas only 56% of wives listed their husband as their greatest source of emotional (nondirective) support (Huston-Hoburg & Strange, 1986). To the extent that gender differences are present in key dimensions of social support, this suggests the potential need for gender-specific models of the link between interpersonal processes and anxiety. Likewise, husbands with agoraphobic wives may be more critical but not less supportive than are community comparison husbands (Chambless et al., 2002), suggesting the need for greater attention to the manner in which spousal support is provided in this and other anxiety disorders.

Interpersonal Social Skills

Another interpersonal model that has offered insight into the anxiety disorders is an interpersonal social skills model. According to this model, people with anxiety disorders display less well-developed interpersonal or social skills in comparison with people without anxiety disorders, and these interpersonal behaviors, in turn, evoke negative responses from other people. The interpersonal social skills model has most commonly been used to study social anxiety and social phobia, anxiety disorders that are defined in part by the core feature of fear of negative evaluation. For example, as reviewed by Alden and Taylor (2004), social anxiety is associated with low social skill, non-assertiveness, and visible anxiousness. Furthermore, following a behavioral "getting acquainted" discussion, other people are less likely to desire future interactions with socially anxious people than with people without social anxiety. Poor interpersonal behavior is particularly likely to occur in situations involving social evaluation (i.e., the interpersonal threat of negative evaluation). Over time, the expectation of negative reactions from others causes people with social anxiety to fear and avoid social interactions, which may in turn create a self-fulfilling prophecy, resulting in a dysfunctional interpersonal cycle. As predicted by this model, people with social phobia have fewer and more negative social relationships throughout life.

GENETIC AND EPIGENETIC EFFECTS

As can be seen from the data supporting the various interpersonal models reviewed earlier, there are many important interpersonal processes to be captured both in terms of negative, or stressful, interpersonal interactions and positive, or supportive, interpersonal events. In addition, a number of measurement traditions can be helpful in selecting measurement tools. Adding to the potential complexity of interpersonal models related to anxiety, however, is the potential for genetic effects to influence not only interpersonal behavior and symptoms of anxiety but the relationship between them as well. As interpersonal models of anxiety are developed, it will be important to consider potential sources of genetic influences and to integrate findings with the emerging literature on genetic effects. With this in mind, and because this is a new area for many researchers, we briefly review the basis for expecting genetic effects on symptoms of anxiety and then draw out several implications for interpersonal models of anxiety.

Anxiety is traitlike for many individuals, suggesting that once established, it is relatively persistent. Using genetically informed designs, it has been shown that 30% to 40% of variation in level of anxiety can be attributed to genetic variability, and there is substantial heritability for both panic disorder (0.43) and generalized anxiety disorder (0.32; Hettema, Neale, & Kendler, 2001). Therefore, we should expect attention to genetic predispositions to enhance our understanding of etiology and maintenance of anxiety symptoms as well as specific anxiety disorders. It is important to note that not all the contribution of genes to anxiety symptoms is direct. It is likely, for example, that there may be a genetic predisposition to experience particular severe stressors (Kendler, 2001), and this genetic effect may contribute indirectly to the level of anxiety symptoms. This type of finding suggests that genetic contributions to anxiety are complex and may potentially inform interpersonal process models of anxiety in a variety of ways (i.e., through direct and indirect pathways). To deal with this complexity and also relate genetic predispositions to more familiar traits, a number of researchers have proposed that genes may directly affect certain traits, or endophenotypes, that in turn produce a vulnerability to anxiety symptoms, disorders, or both. To provide a framework for the integration of interpersonal models with genetic influence models, we briefly discuss the potential for genes to influence endophenotypes (i.e., the developmentally intermediate behavior patterns that may be more directly linked to genes and to which psychologists more readily relate). We also discuss the potential interaction of genes with social stressors and sources of social support and the likely mechanisms of epigenetic regulation of genetic effects (i.e., ways in which the environment may change the long-term expression of a particular gene). By doing so, we hope to provide a useful set of conceptual tools for models that may increasingly integrate biology and genetics along with interpersonal dynamics as explanations of the etiology and maintenance of anxiety disorders. However, we do not assume familiarity of the reader with genetic effects or genetic terminology.

Genes and Endophenotypes

It is increasingly accepted that one way in which genes may come to be associated with symptomatic outcomes is through their effect on endophenotypes, that is, intermediate phenotypes that are more proximal to genes and that precede and confer risk for disorder but that are not, considered alone, indicative of disorder (Gottesman & Gould, 2003). The range of potential endophenotypes in anxiety is broad and beyond the scope of the current review. In addition, different authors use the term somewhat differently. However, there are several possible endophenotypes that are intuitive, have clear relevance to anxiety, and provide useful examples in illustrating this approach. Of these useful examples, neuroticism is the best known. Other, more specific endophenotypes have also been proposed, sometimes focusing on behavioral or neurological response to challenge and sometimes focused on broad but nonpathological characteristics such as shyness or perhaps anxiety sensitivity. To be optimal for etiological models, endophenotypes should appear early in a developmental process, perhaps reflecting the direct effect of genetic variation on brain circuitry or key brain systems. Variability in the serotonin transporter gene (5HTT), the most widely studied "psychiatric" gene, is associated with responsiveness of the amygdala to fear-related stimuli (Hariri et al., 2005), rendering reactivity of this system a potentially interesting endophenotype in a number of anxiety disorders. Likewise, variation in the serotonin transporter gene may also be related to the possible endophenotypes of neuroticism and shyness, suggesting that they may be particularly promising as intermediate steps between genotypes and symptomatic outcomes in the anxiety disorders (Sen, Burmeister, & Ghosh, 2004).

Because the serotonin transporter gene (5HTT) is likely to remain a key gene for researchers interested in anxiety and because it is useful to consider one example in greater detail to illustrate important structural features, we briefly review the structure of 5HTT. However, similar motifs will characterize other genes with variable number tandem repeats. The 5HTT consists of 14 exons (i.e., a sequence of DNA that codes information for protein synthesis that is transcribed to messenger RNA) and a single promoter (i.e., an area that does not code for a protein but influences the amount produced). Two structural elements of 5HTT are of potential relevance to the amount of gene transcription (and so the ultimate effect of the gene). The first is a variable number tandem repeat often referred to as the 5HTTLPR. The "short" variation at this locus results in lower level of gene transcription. The second structural element of interest is a region that surrounds Exon 1 (Philibert et al., 2007) and that appears to function as a promoter of gene activity. More highly methylated promoter regions tend to result in lower level of gene transcription. So, to oversimplify a bit, there are at least two ways to have less activity at the 5HTT: either have one or two copies of the short version of the 5HTTLPR or have a highly methylated promoter region. Given the presence of these genetic characteristics, it is of particular interest to discover how they may influence or transact with interpersonal processes in the anxiety disorders.

Interaction of Genes With the Social Environment

One way that genes and environments may influence one another is through a *Gene × Environment interaction*, which refers to a genetic susceptibility or sensitivity to environmental events. A variant of the familiar diathesis–stress models of psychopathology, this model proposes that people with a certain risk allele would be more likely to become anxious following a stressful life event than people without the risk allele. Of the recent demonstrations of Gene × Environment interactions, the most widely known is the work of Caspi et al. (2003). In this study, individuals with one or two copies of the short version of the 5HTTLPR showed greater sensitivity to the experience of severe childhood stress or an accumulation of stressors over time than did those with two copies of the long variant of the gene. In a subsequent study of abused children, Kaufman et al. (2004) found that variations in the 5HTTLPR interacted with both childhood stress and the presence of social support in the child's life. This pattern suggests the potential for genetic information to sharpen substantially the ability of researchers to identify links between the social environment and particular outcomes such as anxiety disorders. That is, when the effect of social environments is strongest in the context of a particular genetic diathesis, knowledge of this moderating variable will allow for better research designs and more robust statistical analyses. It seems possible that genetic variables could strengthen all the previously discussed interpersonal models either by accounting for previously unexplained variance or by allowing researchers to specify conditions under which interpersonal processes are most likely to have an impact on outcomes of interest (Beach, Brody, Kogan, Philibert, Chen, & Lei, 2009; Brody, Beacu, Philibert, Chen, Lei, Murry, & Brown, 2009). Similar effects are likely to be found for particular anxiety disorders. For example, to the extent that neuroticism interacts with the environment to predict anxiety, similar effects may be expected when examining genes that contribute to neuroticism (see, e.g., Fox, Hane, & Pine, 2005). The existing research on Gene × Environment interactions in anxiety disorders was summarized in the March 2008 special issue of the *European Archives of Psychiatry and Clinical Neuroscience* devoted to this topic (Poulton, Andrews, & Millichamp, 2008).

Epigenetic Regulation

In addition to the "hard-wired" variation in gene activity associated with variation in the 5HTTLPR, mechanisms by which Gene × Environment interactions confer long-term, and not merely immediate, risks for disorder are also beginning to be explored. Of particular interest in this regard are the promoter regions that regulate gene transcription. There are three different mechanisms that could potentially explain epigenetic effects: (a) methylation of promoter regions (CpG islands) controlling level of gene expression (e.g., Philibert et al., 2007), (b) production of posttranslation modifications that influence the activity of gene products (e.g., glycosolation processes), or (c) differential expression of partial transcripts that have a regulatory impact or that interfere with the activity of gene products. However, the pathway most likely to be examined in interpersonal models of anxiety in the near term is the mechanism of methylation of promoter regions. Indeed, it is likely that some environments change the functioning of genes by contributing to the methylation of the promoter region of the gene—typically resulting in reduced transcription at that locus—and perhaps setting the stage for increased vulnerability to an anxiety disorder. Currently, the best evidence of such effects is found in studies of nonhuman models. For example, poor maternal care by rat dams of their pups within the first 10 days of life has been shown to influence gene expression (Liu et al., 1997) by decreasing RNA expression in the hippocampus, resulting in increased sensitivity to stress that lasts over the entire lifetime of the maltreated pups (Liu et al., 1997). Conversely, good maternal care of infant monkeys at risk for anxiety symptoms moderates symptom expression (Suomi, 1999) and may transform genetic liabilities into genetic assets.

Models of Gene–Environment Transaction: A General Methodological Note

As theorists begin to develop genetically informed interpersonal models of anxiety, it will be important to remember that not all associations are interactions. Specifically, it will be important to consider alternative models of association in addition to the Gene × Environment interaction model exemplified by Caspi et al. (2003). These alternative ways that genes and environments come to be related may better account for the data in some cases. First, there is the potential for genes (or the endophenotypes they engender) to elicit particular environments or particular events. This relationship can produce *active gene–environment correlations* (rGEs). When genes have an active role in eliciting environments, the gene produces a phenotype that elicits differential response from the environment. It is possible for the environment to subsequently shape and intensify the endophenotype, but the resulting dynamic, developmental processes may still be best characterized as a gene–environment correlation rather than a Gene × Environment interaction. The resulting model will be different statistically and will result in different implications for intervention and prevention. For example, if a genetically influenced child behavior were found to elicit parental overprotection, which in turn was associated with child shyness, this would be better modeled as a gene–environment correlation (rGE) than as a Gene × Environment interaction. In this case, because the child's shyness elicits a particular parental response, the effect is an active rGE and suggests that a family-based intervention for this dynamic would need to overcome an elicited response rather than an unelicited propensity in the parent, creating the need for a somewhat different approach to intervention.

It is also possible for rGEs to emerge passively. For example, a family environment might prove to be correlated with an individual's genotype if the genotype is associated with a particular behavioral style—and the genotype is shared among family members. Using the preceding example, parental overprotection might be associated with childhood symptoms because it is reflective of the same genes that create risk of childhood symptoms of shyness, even though it has no direct effect on the etiology of the symptoms. A passive rGE may also be of interest for prevention and intervention but will once again carry different implications. For example, a passive rGE might suggest the need for familywide intervention so that family members can reinforce and support each other's change. Accordingly, it is important that each type of model be examined to the extent possible to see which best accounts for observed effects.

Although we are not aware of any research that has examined gene–environment correlations for interpersonal processes in the anxiety disorders, they have been studied with respect to mood disorders. For example, in a sample of female–female twin pairs, the genetic liability for major depression increases the risk of interpersonal stressful life events (Kendler & Karkowski-Shuman, 1997) and reduces the average level of relative and spouse support (Wade & Kendler, 2000). Similar research in the anxiety disorders would help to advance an understanding of the roles of genetic effects and interpersonal environments as risk factors for anxiety.

DIRECTIONS FOR FUTURE RESEARCH

Much of the research on interpersonal functioning and anxiety has been cross-sectional in design, in which interpersonal processes and anxiety have been shown to covary with one another at the same point in time. There are, however, two additional criteria that are required to establish that interpersonal processes are risk factors for anxiety disorder in addition to the criterion of covariation (Garber & Hollon, 1991). The second criterion for establishing that interpersonal processes are risk factors for anxiety disorders requires demonstrating that interpersonal processes precede the occurrence of anxiety disorders. Longitudinal research, therefore, is needed to demonstrate that interpersonal processes assessed at one point in time predict increases in anxiety or onset of anxiety disorders assessed at a subsequent point. Although prospective studies have been done for some interpersonal processes, this is clearly an important area of future research. The third criterion for establishing that interpersonal processes are risk factors for anxiety disorders is establishing that the association between interpersonal processes and anxiety disorders is not spurious (i.e., the association between interpersonal processes and anxiety disorders should not be better accounted for by a third variable). For example, it is possible that personality factors such as neuroticism or negative affect contribute both to interpersonal processes and to anxiety disorders; personality factors, therefore, represent a potential rival explanation for the association between interpersonal processes and anxiety. Conclusions regarding the potential causal role of interpersonal processes on anxiety will be strengthened to the extent that rival explanations are ruled out through methods such as equating groups of people with anxiety disorders and control groups on such variables or statistically controlling for the effects of rival variables. As an example of this kind of research, Whisman, Uebelacker, Tolejko, Chatav, and McKelvie (2006) reported that marital discord was associated with well-being in older adults and that this association remained significant when statistically controlling for Big Five personality traits. Depression should be a major consideration for future research evaluating the nonspurious nature of the association between interpersonal processes and anxiety, given that depression tends to co-occur with many anxiety disorders (Kessler et al., 2003) and that many of the interpersonal processes discussed in this chapter have also been studied as risk factors for depression (for a review, see Pettit & Joiner, 2006).

Our review of interpersonal processes and anxiety disorders has focused on general interpersonal models that were not specifically developed for anxiety. However, there may be interpersonal processes that are unique to anxiety disorders that are not captured by these general models. Consequently, theoretical development regarding interpersonal processes and anxiety disorders is important to guide future research. For example, Coyne (1976) proposed an interpersonal model of depression in which depression-prone individuals seek reassurance of approval and acceptance from others (because of their doubts that other people truly care about them) but that this excessive reassurance seeking in turn results in negative interpersonal reactions (e.g., frustration, feeling misunderstood) from significant others, which ultimately results in social rejection. This theory led to the development of measures of excessive reassurance seeking and a body of research evaluating excessive reassurance seeking and depression (Joiner, Metalsky, Katz, & Beach, 1999). A complete understanding of interpersonal processes associated with anxiety disorders, therefore, may require the development of novel interpersonal theories of anxiety, as well as the application of existing interpersonal theories of psychopathology. For example, consideration of interpersonal dynamics related to self-evaluation maintenance and response to criticism could point in new directions in understanding anxiety disorders.

CONCLUSION

In this chapter, we have reviewed several models for understanding interpersonal processes in anxiety disorders, and we have highlighted illustrative studies that have used that model to study anxiety disorders; detailed descriptions of the use of specific models to study specific disorders are provided in the remaining chapters of this volume.

The current focus on interpersonal functioning should not be interpreted as suggesting that interpersonal models should be viewed as being in competition with other well-established frameworks for understanding and treating anxiety disorders. Instead, we believe that interpersonal models are complementary to many other models. For example, we discussed how interpersonal processes may mediate the association between genes and anxiety and how genetic influences may moderate the impact of interpersonal processes on anxiety. Similarly, interpersonal experiences shape and are shaped by the beliefs that people have about themselves, other people, and the world around them, suggesting the potential for integrating interpersonal models with cognitive models of anxiety disorders. For some people, problematic interpersonal processes and relationships clearly contribute to the cause of anxiety; for other people, anxiety may be caused by other factors but, once present, contribute to problematic interpersonal processes and relationships that in turn complicate its course and treatment.

A comprehensive understanding of the onset, course, and treatment of anxiety disorders will likely require attention to biological, cognitive, behavioral, and social factors, a perspective that is emphasized in contemporary integrative biopsychosocial models of psychopathology. Promising support for interpersonal models of anxiety disorders suggests that problematic interpersonal processes and relationships represent important components that should be included in such integrative frameworks.

REFERENCES

Ainsworth, M. D. S., Blehar, M. C., Waters, E., & Wall, S. (1978). *Patterns of attachment: A psychological study of the Strange Situation*. Hillsdale, NJ: Erlbaum.

Alden, L. E., & Phillips, N. (1990). An interpersonal analysis of social anxiety and depression. *Cognitive Therapy and Research, 14*, 499–513.

Alden, L. E., & Taylor, C. T. (2004). Interpersonal processes in social phobia. *Clinical Psychology Review, 24*, 857–882.

Andrews, B., Brewin, C. R., Rose, S., & Kirk, M. (2000). Predicting PTSD symptoms in victims of violent crime: The role of shame, anger, and childhood abuse. *Journal of Abnormal Psychology, 109*, 69–73.

Antonucci, T. C., & Akiyama, H. (1987). An examination of sex differences in social support among older men and women. *Sex Roles, 17*, 737–749.

Bakan, D. (1966). *The duality of human existence: Isolation and communion in Western man*. Boston, MA: Beacon Press.

Baumeister, R. F., & Leary, M. R. (1995). The need to belong: Desire for interpersonal attachments as a fundamental human motivation. *Psychological Bulletin, 117*, 497–529.

Beach, S. R. H., Brody, G. H., Kogan, S. M., Philibert, R. A., Chen, Y., & Lei, M. (2009). Change in caregiver depression in response to parent training: Genetic moderation of intervention effects. *Journal of Family Psychology, 23*, 112–117.

Beach, S. R. H., Wamboldt, M. Z., Kaslow, N. J., Heyman, R. E., First, M. B., Underwood, L. G., & Reiss, D. (Eds.). (2006). *Relational processes and DSM–V: Neuroscience, assessment, prevention, and treatment*. Washington, DC: American Psychiatric Publishing.

Bokszczanin, A. (2008). Parental support, family conflict, and overprotectiveness: Predicting PTSD symptom levels of adolescents 28 months after a natural disaster. *Anxiety, Stress, and Coping, 21*, 325–335.

Bolton, F. G., Morris, L. A., & MacEachron, A. E. (1989). *Males at risk: The other side of child sexual abuse.* Newbury Park, CA: Sage.

Borkovec, T. D., Newman, M. G., Pincus, A. L., & Lytle, R. (2002). A component analysis of cognitive–behavioral therapy for generalized anxiety disorder and the role of interpersonal problems. *Journal of Consulting and Clinical Psychology, 70*, 288–298.

Bowlby, J. (1969). *Attachment and loss: Vol. 1. Attachment.* New York, NY: Basic Books.

Bradbury, T. N., Fincham, F. D., & Beach, S. R. H. (2000). Research on the nature and determinants of marital satisfaction: A decade in review. *Journal of Marriage and the Family, 62*, 964–980.

Brennan, K. A., Clark, C. L., & Shaver, P. R. (1998). Self-report measurement of adult attachment: An integrative overview. In J. A. Simpson & W. S. Rholes (Eds.), *Attachment theory and close relationships* (pp. 46–76). New York, NY: Guilford Press.

Brewin, C. R., Andrews, B., & Valentine, J. D. (2000). Meta-analysis of risk factors for posttraumatic stress disorder in trauma-exposed adults. *Journal of Consulting and Clinical Psychology, 68*, 748–766.

Brody, G. H., Beach, S. R. H., Philibert, R. A., Chen, Y., Lei, M.-K., Murry, V. M., & Brown, A. C. (2009). Parenting moderates a genetic vulnerability factor in longitudinal increases in youths' substance use. *Journal of Consulting and Clinical Psychology, 77*, 1–11.

Butzlaff, R. L., & Hooley, J. M. (1998). Expressed emotion and psychiatric relapse: A meta-analysis. *Archives of General Psychiatry, 55*, 547–552.

Caspi, A., Sugden, K., Moffitt, T. E., Taylor, A., Craig, I. W., Harrington, H., . . . Poulton, R. (2003, July 18). Influence of life stress on depression: Moderation by a polymorphism in the 5-HTT gene. *Science, 301*, 386–389.

Chambless, D. L., Fauerbach, J. A., Floyd, F. J., Wilson, K. A., Remen, A. L., & Renneberg, B. (2002). Marital interaction of agoraphobic women: A controlled, behavioral observation study. *Journal of Abnormal Psychology, 111*, 502–512.

Chambless, D. L., & Steketee, G. (1999). Expressed emotion and behavior therapy outcome: A prospective study with obsessive–compulsive and agoraphobic outpatients. *Journal of Consulting and Clinical Psychology, 67*, 658–665.

Chapman, D. P., Whitfield, C. L., Felitti, V. J., Dube, S. R., Edwards, V. J., & Anda, R. F. (2004). Adverse childhood experiences and the risk of depressive disorders in adulthood. *Journal of Affective Disorders, 82*, 217–225.

Charuvastra, A., & Cloitre, M. (2008). Social bonds and posttraumatic stress disorder. *Annual Review of Psychology, 59*, 301–328.

Cirulli, F., & Alleva, B. E. (2003). Early disruption of the mother–infant relationship: Effects on brain plasticity and implications for psychopathology. *Neuroscience and Biobehavioral Reviews, 27*, 73–82.

Coyne, J. C. (1976). Toward an interactional description of depression. *Psychiatry, 39*, 28–40.

Cunningham, M. R., & Barbee, A. P. (2000). Social support. In C. Hendrick & S. S. Hendrick (Eds.), *Close relationships: A sourcebook* (pp. 273–285). Thousand Oaks, CA: Sage.

Cutrona, C. E. (1996). *Social support in couples: Marriage as a resource in times of stress.* Thousand Oaks, CA: Sage.

Cutrona, C. E., Cohen, B., & Igram, S. (1990). Contextual determinants of the perceived supportiveness of helping behaviors. *Journal of Social and Personal Relationships, 7*, 553–562.

Cutrona, C. E., & Suhr, J. A. (1994). Social support communication in the context of marriage: An analysis of couples' supportive interactions. In B. R. Burleson, T. L. Albrecht, & I. G. Sarason (Eds.), *Communication of social support: Messages, interactions, relationships, and community* (pp. 113–135). Thousand Oaks, CA: Sage.

Finkelhor, D. (1990). Early and long-term effects of child sexual abuse: An update. *Professional Psychology: Research and Practice, 21*, 325–330.

Fox, N. A., Hane, A. A., & Pine, D. S. (2005). Plasticity for affective neurocircuitry: How the environment affects gene expression. *Current Directions in Psychological Science, 16*(1), 1–5.

Fraley, R. C., & Waller, N. G. (1998). Adult attachment patterns: A test of the typological model. In J. A. Simpson & W. S. Rholes (Eds.), *Attachment theory and close relationships* (pp. 77–114). New York, NY: Guilford Press.

Frans, O., Rimmo, P. A., Aberg, L., & Fredrikson, M. (2005). Trauma exposure and post-traumatic stress disorder in the general population. *Acta Psychiatrica Scandinavica, 111*, 291–299.

Friedmann, M. S., McDermut, W. H., Solomon, D. A., Ryan, C. E., Keitner, G. I., & Miller, I. W. (1997). Family functioning and mental illness: A comparison of psychiatric and nonclinical families. *Family Process, 36*, 357–367.

Garber, J., & Hollon, S. D. (1991). What can specificity designs say about causality in psychopathology research? *Psychological Bulletin, 110*, 129–136.

Gottesman, I. I., & Gould, T. D. (2003). The endophenotype concept in psychiatry: Etymology and strategic intentions. *American Journal of Psychiatry, 160*, 636–645.

Gunnar, M. R., & Donzella, B. (2002). Social regulation of the cortisol levels in early human development. *Psychoneuroendocrinology, 27*, 199–220.

Gunnar, M., & Quevedo, K. (2007). The neurobiology of stress and development. *Annual Review of Psychology, 58*, 145–173.

Gurtman, M. B. (1994). The circumplex as a tool for studying normal and abnormal personality: A methodological primer. In S. Strack & M. Lorr (Eds.), *Differentiating normal and abnormal personality* (pp. 243–263). New York: Springer.

Hammen, C. L. (1991). Generation of stress in the course of unipolar depression. *Journal of Abnormal Psychology, 100*, 555–561.

Hammen, C. (2006). Stress generation in depression: Reflections on origins, research, and future directions. *Journal of Clinical Psychology, 62*, 1065–1082.

Hankin, B. L., Kassel, J. D., & Abela, J. R. Z. (2005). Adult attachment dimensions and specificity of emotional distress symptoms: Prospective investigations of cognitive risk and interpersonal stress generation as mediating mechanisms. *Personality and Social Psychology Bulletin, 31*, 136–151.

Hariri, A. R., Drabant, E. M., Munoz, K. E., Kolachana, B. S., Mattay, V. S., Egan, M. F., . . . Weinberger, D. R. (2005). A susceptibility gene for affective disorders and the response of the human amygdala. *Archives of General Psychiatry, 62*, 146–152.

Hettema, J. M., Neale, M. C., & Kendler, K. S. (2001). A review and meta-analysis of the genetic epidemiology of anxiety disorders. *American Journal of Psychiatry, 158*, 1568–1578.

Hooley, J. M. (2007). Expressed emotion and relapse of psychopathology. *Annual Review of Clinical Psychology, 3*, 329–352.

Hooley, J. M., & Teasdale, J. D. (1989). Predictors of relapse in unipolar depressives: Expressed emotion, marital distress, and perceived criticism. *Journal of Abnormal Psychology, 98*, 229–235.

Huston-Hoburg, L., & Strange, C. (1986). Spouse support among male and female returning adult students. *Journal of College Student Personnel, 27*, 388–394.

Joiner, T. E., Jr., Metalsky, G. I., Katz, J., & Beach, S. R. H. (1999). Depression and excessive reassurance-seeking. *Psychological Inquiry, 10*, 269–278.

Julien, D., & Markman, H. J. (1991). Social support and social networks as determinants of individual and marital outcomes. *Journal of Social and Personal Relationships, 8*, 549–568.

Kachin, K. E., Newman, M. G., & Pincus, A. L. (2001). An interpersonal problem approach to the division of social phobia subtypes. *Behavior Therapy, 32*, 479–501.

Kaufman, J., Yang, B. Z., Douglas-Palumberi, H., Houshyar, S., Lipschitz, D., Krystal, J. H., & Gelernter, J. (2004). Social supports and serotonin transporter gene moderate depression in maltreated children. *Proceedings of the National Academy of Sciences, USA, 101*, 17316–17321.

Kelly, A. B., Fincham, F. D., & Beach, S. R. H. (2003). Communication skills in couples: A review and discussion of emerging perspectives. In J. O. Greene & B. R. Burleson (Eds.), *Handbook of communication and social interaction skills* (pp. 723–751). Mahwah, NJ: Erlbaum.

Kendler, K. S. (2001). Twin studies of psychiatric illness: An update. *Archives of General Psychiatry, 58*, 1005–1014.

Kendler, K. S., & Karkowski-Shuman, L. (1997). Stressful life events and genetic liability to major depression: Genetic control of exposure to the environment? *Psychological Medicine, 27*, 539–547.

Kessler, R. C., Berglund, P., Demler, O., Jin, R., Koretz, D., Merikangas, K. R., . . . Wang, P. S. (2003). The epidemiology of major depressive disorder: Results from the National Comorbidity Survey Replication (NCS-R). *JAMA, 289,* 3095–3105.

Kessler, R. C., Berglund, P., Demler, O., Jin, R., Merikangas, K. R., & Walters, E. E. (2005). Lifetime prevalence and age-of-onset distributions of DSM-IV disorders in the National Comorbidity Survey Replication. *Archives of General Psychiatry, 62,* 593–602.

Kiecolt-Glaser, J. K., Loving, T. J., Stowell, J. R., Malarkey, W. B., Lemeshow, S., Dickinson, S. L., & Glaser, R. (2005). Hostile marital interactions, proinflammatory cytokine production, and wound healing. *Archives of General Psychiatry, 62,* 1377–1384.

Kiecolt-Glaser, J. K., Malarkey, W. B., Chee, M., & Newton, T. (1993). Negative behavior during marital conflict is associated with immunological down-regulation. *Psychosomatic Medicine, 55,* 395–409.

Kiesler, D. J. (1983). The 1982 interpersonal circle: A taxonomy for complementarity in human transactions. *Psychological Review, 90,* 185–214.

Kreider, R. M., & Fields, J. M. (2001). *Number, timing, and duration of marriages and divorces: Fall 1996* (Current Population Reports, P70-80). Washington, DC: U.S. Census Bureau.

Leary, T. (1957). *Interpersonal diagnosis of personality: A functional theory and methodology for personality evaluation.* New York, NY: Ronald Press.

Liu, D., Diorio, J., Tannenbaum, B., Caldji, C., Francis, D., Freedman, A., . . . Meaney, M. J. (1997, September 12). Maternal care, hippocampal glucocorticoid receptors, and hypothalamic-pituitary-adrenal responses to stress. *Science, 277,* 1659–1662.

Meaney, M. J., & Szyf, M. (2005). Maternal care as a model for experience-dependent chromatic plasticity. *Trends in Neurosciences, 28,* 456–463.

Overbeek, G., Vollebergh, W., de Graaf, R., Scholte, R., de Kemp, R., & Engels, R. (2006). Longitudinal associations of marital quality and marital dissolution with the incidence of DSM–III–R disorders. *Journal of Family Psychology, 20,* 284–291.

Pettit, J. W., & Joiner, T. E. (2006). *Chronic depression: Interpersonal sources, therapeutic solutions.* Washington, DC: American Psychological Association.

Philibert, R. A., Madan, A., Anderson, A., Cadoret, R., Packer, H., & Sandhu, H. (2007). Serotonin transporter mRNA levels are associated with the methylation of an upstream CpG island. *American Journal of Medical Genetics Part B: Neuropsychiatric Genetics, 144B,* 101–105.

Poulton, R., Andrews, G., & Millichamp, J. (2008). Gene-environment interaction and the anxiety disorders [Special issue]. *European Archives of Psychiatry and Clinical Neuroscience, 258*(2), 65–68.

Reiss, H. T. (1990). The role of intimacy in interpersonal relations. *Journal of Social and Clinical Psychology, 9,* 15–30.

Renshaw, K. D., Chambless, D. L., & Steketee, G. (2001). Comorbidity fails to account for the relationship of expressed emotion and perceived criticism to treatment outcome in patients with anxiety disorders. *Journal of Behavior Therapy and Experimental Psychiatry, 32*, 145–158.

Renshaw, K. D., Chambless, D. L., & Steketee, G. (2003). Perceived criticism predicts severity of anxiety symptoms after behavioral treatment in patients with obsessive-compulsive disorder and panic disorder with agoraphobia. *Journal of Clinical Psychology, 59*, 411–421.

Sedlak, A. J., & Broadhurst, D. D. (1996). *Third national incidence study of child abuse and neglect.* Washington, DC: U.S. Department of Health and Human Services.

Seltzer, J. A. (2000). Families formed outside of marriage. *Journal of Marriage and the Family, 62*, 1247–1268.

Sen, S., Burmeister, M., & Ghosh, D. (2004). Meta-analysis of the association between a serotonin transporter promoter polymorphism (5-HTTLPR) and anxiety-related personality traits. *American Journal of Medical Genetics Part B: Neuropsychiatric Genetics, 127B*, 85–89.

Shumway, S. T., Wampler, R. S., Dersch, C., & Arredondo, R. (2004). A place for marriage and family services in employee assistance programs (EAPs): A survey of EAP client problems and needs. *Journal of Marital and Family Therapy, 30*, 71–79.

Spangler, G., & Schiecke, M. (1998). Emotional and adrenocortical responses of infants to the Strange Situation: The differential function of emotional expression. *International Journal of Behavioral Development, 22*, 681–706.

Spear, L. P. (2000). The adolescent brain and age-related behavioral manifestations. *Neuroscience and Biobehavioral Reviews, 24*, 417–463.

Suomi, S. J. (1999). Developmental trajectories, early experiences, and community consequences: Lessons from studies with rhesus monkeys. In D. P. H. Keating & Clyde Hertzman (Eds.), *Developmental health and the wealth of nations: Social, biological, and educational dynamics* (pp. 185–200). New York: Guilford Press.

Sullivan, H. S. (1953). *The interpersonal theory of psychiatry.* New York: W. W. Norton.

Thompson, M. P., Kingree, J. B., & Desai, S. (2004). Gender differences in long-term health consequences of physical abuse of children: Data from a nationally representative survey. *American Journal of Public Health, 94*, 599–604.

Ullman, S. E., & Filipas, H. H. (2005). Gender differences in social reactions to abuse disclosures, post-abuse coping, and PTSD of child sexual abuse survivors. *Child Abuse and Neglect, 29*, 767–782.

Vaughn, C., & Leff, J. (1976). The measurement of expressed emotion in families of psychiatric patients. *British Journal of Social and Clinical Psychology, 15*, 157–165.

Wade, T. D., & Kendler, K. S. (2000). The relationship between social support and major depression: Cross-sectional, longitudinal, and genetic perspectives. *Journal of Nervous and Mental Disease, 188*, 251–258.

Waller, N. G., & Meehl, P. E. (1998). *Multivariate taxometric procedures: Distinguishing types from continua.* Thousand Oaks, CA: Sage.

Wearden, A. J., Tarrier, N., Barrowclough, C., Zastowny, T. R., & Rahill, A. A. (2000). A review of expressed emotion research in health care. *Clinical Psychology Review, 20,* 633–666.

Weiss, R. S. (1974). The provisions of social relationships. In Z. Rubin (Ed.), *Support systems and mutual help* (pp. 17–26). Englewood Cliffs, NJ: Prentice-Hall.

Whisman, M. A. (1999). Marital dissatisfaction and psychiatric disorders: Results from the National Comorbidity Survey. *Journal of Abnormal Psychology, 108,* 701–706.

Whisman, M. A. (2007). Marital distress and DSM–IV psychiatric disorders in a population-based national survey. *Journal of Abnormal Psychology, 116,* 638–643.

Whisman, M. A., Dixon, A. E., & Johnson, B. (1997). Therapists' perspectives of couple problems and treatment issues in couple therapy. *Journal of Family Psychology, 11,* 361–366.

Whisman, M. A., Uebelacker, L. A., Tolejko, N., Chatav, Y., & McKelvie, M. (2006). Marital discord and well-being in older adults: Is the association confounded by personality? *Psychology and Aging, 21,* 626–631.

Wiggins, J. S. (1991). Agency and communion as conceptual coordinates for understanding and measurement of interpersonal behavior. In W. Grove & D. Cicchetti (Eds.), *Thinking clearly about psychology: Essays in honor of Paul E. Meehl* (Vol. 2, pp. 89–113). Minneapolis: University of Minnesota Press.

2

ASSESSING LINKAGES BETWEEN INTERPERSONAL PROCESSES AND ANXIETY DISORDERS

DOUGLAS K. SNYDER, RICHARD E. ZINBARG, RICHARD E. HEYMAN, STEPHEN N. HAYNES, MOLLY F. GASBARRINI, AND MANDY ULIASZEK

Growing evidence has affirmed the co-occurrence of interpersonal difficulties and anxiety disorders in both adults and youth. These linkages almost certainly reflect bidirectional and recursive influences. That is, evidence has suggested that relationship problems frequently contribute to, maintain, and exacerbate the subjective experience of both generalized and situational anxiety; similarly, both covert and behavioral expressions of anxiety frequently contribute to difficulties in developing and sustaining close relationships. Hence, for many individuals, intervention will be rendered less effective unless difficulties in both interpersonal and intrapersonal functioning are appropriately evaluated and addressed. Similarly, from a research perspective, theoretical developments and conceptual linkages between individual and relationship functioning will be constrained without valid assessment of both domains.

Whether from clinical or research perspectives, understanding and disentangling recursive influences of anxiety and interpersonal processes requires psychometrically sound assessment techniques for evaluating both. In this chapter, we begin with an overview of methodological issues relevant to clinical interview, self-report, and observational assessment strategies. We then consider these issues first as applied to assessment of interpersonal processes and then as relevant to assessing the spectrum of anxiety-related disorders. Within each domain, we consider specific techniques relevant to adults and then those germane to children and adolescents, as well as cross-generational measures where appropriate (e.g., when examining parent–child relationship processes).

Our review emphasizes principles and broad strategies of assessment rather than an exhaustive review of measurement techniques in this area. Specific assessment techniques are offered as exemplars within various domains and have been selected on the basis of evidence of psychometric soundness as well as their inclusion in research summarized in the subsequent chapters in this text.

PRINCIPLES AND STRATEGIES OF ASSESSMENT

Assessment approaches to both interpersonal processes and anxiety share common principles, namely: (a) the foci of assessment methods should be empirically linked to target problems and constructs; (b) selected assessment instruments and methods should demonstrate evidence of reliability, validity, and cost-effectiveness; (c) findings should be linked within a theoretical or conceptual framework of the presumed causes of target phenomena, as well as to clinical intervention or prevention as relevant; and (d) multimodal assessment including face-to-face interview, self- and other report using paper-and-pencil or computer-administered questionnaires, and behavioral measures (including observational and physiological techniques) is preferable to reliance on just one modality (Snyder, Heyman, & Haynes, 2009; Zinbarg, 1998). Assessment of interpersonal processes argues for further consideration of socioecological or systemic perspectives, particularly when considering disorders in a couple or family context.

Assessment Interview

The interview is perhaps the most versatile assessment method because it can provide information across multiple domains and response modes. For example, it can provide information on specific positive and negative exchanges with others, interpersonal sensitivity, decision-making skills, sources of conflict, cognitions related to both intrapersonal and interpersonal functioning, beliefs and attitudes toward oneself and others, and a wide range of emotions. It provides opportunity to explore bidirectional influences—for example, by asking about conflict during periods of high or low anxiety and about anxiety during times of high and low conflict. The assessment interview can also provide information on broader socioecological factors that may affect an individual's functioning or response to interventions.

Interviews vary in the extent to which they are flexible and open ended versus structured or semistructured. The latter are used more typically for diagnostic purposes (e.g., Structured Clinical Interview for *DSM–IV* Axis I Disorders [SCID-I]; First et al., 2002), whereas the former are better suited to case formulation and tailoring specific interventions to the individual. When conducting more flexible ("clinical") interviews, data should lead to initial hypotheses about ways in which an individual's behaviors, emotions, cognitions, and external stressors contribute to specific vulnerabilities. In this respect, the interview is one of the most useful methods of hypothesizing about the functional relations that account for someone's difficulties. The functional relations of greatest interest in clinical assessment are those that are strongly related to an individual's presenting problem and those that may be amenable to remediation. Identifying functional relations allows the assessor to hypothesize about why an individual experiences specific difficulties, what external factors contribute to or maintain the problems, and in what ways previous change efforts have been successful or not.

The interview should be sensitive to individual differences. Many studies have indicated that people's behavior problems, social interactions, beliefs, goals, and external stressors can differ as a function of ethnicity, age, education, religiosity, sexual orientation, intellectual abilities, and other individual differences (for an overview, see Tanaka-Matsumi, 2004).

Self- and Other-Report Measures

The rationale underlying self- and other-report measures is that they (a) are convenient and relatively easy to administer; (b) are capable of generating a wealth of information across a broad range of domains and levels of functioning germane to clinical assessment or research objectives; (c) lend themselves to data collection from large normative samples that can serve as a reference point; (d) allow disclosure about events and experiences that respondents may be reluctant to discuss with an interviewer or with another person present; and (e) can provide important data concerning internal phenomena opaque to observational approaches including thoughts and feelings, values and attitudes, expectations and attributions, and satisfaction and commitment.

The limitations of traditional self-report measures also bear noting. Specifically, data from self-report instruments (a) can reflect bias (or "sentiment override") in self- and other presentation in either a favorable or an unfavorable direction, (b) can be affected by differences in stimulus interpretation and errors in recollection of objective events, (c) can inadvertently influence respondents' nontest behavior in unintended ways (e.g., by sensitizing respondents and increasing their reactivity to specific issues), and (d) typically provide few fine-grained details concerning moment-to-moment interactions compared with behavioral observations. Because of their potential advantages and despite their limitations, self-report measures of both individual and relationship functioning have proliferated. However, many measures do not provide evidence regarding psychometric criteria of reliability or validity or clear evidence supporting their clinical utility.

Observational Measures

Observational assessment strives to obtain samples of target phenomena that, at least conceptually, should be less vulnerable to various response biases and more representative of behaviors of interest. Behavior observations may take place in natural settings (e.g., observing social anxiety in the classroom). Alternatively, an analog behavioral observation may be conducted in situations intended to elicit target behaviors (e.g., avoidance of feared objects or interpersonal exchanges) under more controlled conditions (e.g., an office, a laboratory).

Observational assessment has a rich tradition in the assessment of anxiety disorders and of couple and family distress. Concerns have been raised about the clinical utility of analog behavioral observations (e.g., Mash & Foster, 2001) because many coding systems—particularly those targeting interpersonal processes—require extensive training to reach adequate levels of interobserver agreement. Even if not striving to code behavioral observations in the manner required for scientific study, the empirically informed use of behavioral observations should be standard in clinicians' assessment repertoire. For example, when targeting relationship distress, collecting communication samples is essential because communication is the common pathway to relationship dysfunction and makes up a core mechanism of relationship change (Heyman, 2001).

Physiological Measures

Like analog behavioral observations, physiological measures are presumed to be less vulnerable to various response biases than interview or self-report measures. Moreover, various physiological indicators of autonomic arousal (e.g., heart rate acceleration, electrodermal activity, startle response) are theoretically and empirically linked to both covert experiences and overt expressions of anxiety and can be monitored during ambulation (Haynes & Yoshioka, 2007). Physiological assessment is not irrelevant to the study of interpersonal processes. For example, couple distress—particularly negative communication—has cardiovascular, endocrine, immune, neurosensory, and other physiological effects that, in turn, contribute to physical health problems (Kiecolt-Glaser & Newton, 2001). Whereas some physiological measures (e.g., heart rate) lend themselves to most clinical contexts, others (e.g., electrodermal or endocrine functioning) are more commonly restricted to research settings.

ASSESSING INTERPERSONAL PROCESSES

Although sharing fundamental principles, specific strategies for assessing interpersonal processes vary as a function of the age of participants (e.g., adults or youth) and the nature of their relationship (e.g., intimate partner, family member, friend).

General Considerations

Our discussion of assessment strategies for interpersonal processes begins with distressed relationships among adult intimate dyads for several reasons. First, the research linking interpersonal processes to anxiety disorders is stronger and more substantial in this domain than in any other. Second, the extensive research on couple distress has identified a diverse range of both individual and relationship characteristics essential to understanding interpersonal processes. Third, research in this area has contributed to the development of well-grounded assessment techniques potentially serving as templates for the extension of evaluation strategies to nondistressed adult dyads and to both distressed and nondistressed relationships at earlier developmental stages.

An important distinction involves distinguishing relationship distress from relationship functioning. The former is based on the subjective evaluation of dissatisfaction with the overall relationship quality by one or both partners, whereas the latter may be determined by external evaluations of partners' objective interactions. Such "insider" and "outsider" perspectives do not always converge (Olson, 1977). Moreover, partners may also disagree in their relationship accounts—either because of actual differences in subjective experiences of their relationship or because of differences in ability or willingness to convey these experiences via interview or self-report measures. Various methods for combining self-reports have been proposed, including *weak link* (using the score of the less satisfied partner), *strong link* (using the score of the more satisfied partner), and *averaged report* models. The last of these is likely the least justifiable approach because it obscures partner differences and provides no information about either resilience or vulnerability.

Fortunately, the increased reliance on multilevel modeling techniques in research permits individual differences within the dyad to be preserved.

Research examining behavioral components of relationship distress has emphasized two domains: the rates and reciprocity of positive and negative behaviors exchanged between partners and communication behaviors related to both emotional expression and decision making. Regarding the former, distressed dyads are distinguished from nondistressed dyads by (a) higher rates of negative verbal and nonverbal exchanges (e.g., disagreements, criticism, hostility); (b) higher levels of reciprocity in negative behavior (i.e., the tendency for negativity in Partner A to be followed by negativity in Partner B); (c) lengthier chains of negative behavior; (d) higher ratios of negative to positive behaviors, independent of their separate rates; and (e) lower rates of positive verbal and nonverbal behaviors (e.g., approval, empathy, smiling, positive touch; Weiss & Heyman, 1997). Findings have suggested a stronger linkage for negativity, compared with positivity, to overall couple distress.

Given the inevitability of disagreements arising in long-term relationships, numerous studies have focused on specific communication behaviors that exacerbate or impede the resolution of couple conflicts. Most notable among these are difficulties in articulating thoughts and feelings related to specific relationship concerns and deficits in decision-making strategies for containing, reducing, or eliminating conflict. Gottman (1994) observed that expression of criticism and contempt, along with defensiveness and withdrawal, predicted long-term distress and risk for relationship dissolution. Christensen and Heavey (1990) found that distressed couples were more likely than nondistressed couples to demonstrate a demand → withdraw pattern in which one person seeks or asks for change and the partner withdraws, with respective approach and retreat behaviors progressively intensifying. Given these findings, assessment of intimate dyads typically includes measures of the frequency, intensity, and specific content of conflicts as well as the effectiveness of the couple's conflict resolution strategies.

Social learning models of couple distress have emphasized the role of cognitive processes in moderating the impact of specific behaviors on relationship functioning (Baucom, Epstein, & LaTaillade, 2002). Research in this domain has focused on factors such as selective attention, attributions for positive and negative relationship events, and specific relationship assumptions, standards, and expectancies. For example, findings have indicated that distressed dyads often exhibit a bias toward selectively attending to negative partner behaviors and relationship events and ignoring or minimizing positive events (Sillars, Roberts, Leonard, & Dun, 2000). Compared with nondistressed dyads, distressed partners also tend to blame each other for problems and to attribute each other's negative behaviors to broad and stable traits

(Bradbury & Fincham, 1990). Distressed couples are also more likely to have unrealistic standards and assumptions about how relationships should work and lower expectancies regarding the other person's willingness or ability to change his or her behavior in some desired manner (Epstein & Baucom, 2002). Research on similar processes in other dyads (e.g., parent–adolescent, supervisor–employee) is scant or nonexistent. Hence, assessment of interpersonal processes from a cognitive perspective typically targets partners' ability to accurately observe and report both positive and negative relationship events, the interpretation or meaning they give to these events, and the beliefs or expectancies they hold regarding their own and the other's ability and willingness to change.

Research has also indicated that distressed dyads are distinguished from nondistressed dyads by higher overall rates, duration, and reciprocity of negative relationship affect and, to a lesser extent, by lower rates of positive relationship affect. Nondistressed couples show less reciprocity of positive affect, reflecting partners' willingness or ability to spontaneously express positive sentiment independent of their partner's affect (Gottman, 1999). By contrast, partners' influence on each other's negative affect has been reported for both proximal and distal outcomes. For example, Pasch, Bradbury, and Davila (1997) found that partners' negative mood before discussion of a personal issue predicted the lower levels of emotional support they provided to the other during their exchange. Such findings suggest that assessment of interpersonal processes in intimate dyads from an affective perspective should target the extent to which partners express and reciprocate negative and positive feelings about their relationship and toward each other, their ability to express strong feelings in a modulated manner, and the extent to which partners' negative affect generalizes across occasions.

Adult Intimate Relationships

A broad spectrum of approaches have been developed for assessing adult intimate relationships across interview, self- and partner report, and observational methods. In the sections that follow, we describe selected evidence-based exemplars of each.

Interviews

Heyman et al. (2001) developed a structured interview for couple distress (patterned after the SCID-I) based on 10 items, each rated on a 3-point scale. Overall, these items emphasize (a) relationship dissatisfaction as noted by reports of a sense of unhappiness, thoughts of divorce, or need for professional help for the relationship and (b) specific indicators of distress in behavioral, cognitive, or affective domains (e.g., escalating negativity during conflict or withdrawal, low expectations regarding potential for relationship change, persistent levels of anger and contempt or sadness).

An alternative approach to detecting relationship distress builds on taxometric analyses identifying a couple distress "taxon" reliably distinguishing clinic from community couples on the basis of partners' self-reports across five domains of relationship functioning assessed by the Marital Satisfaction Inventory—Revised (MSI–R; Snyder, 1997). Incorporating both taxometric findings and item-analytic procedures, Whisman, Snyder, and Beach (2009) constructed a 10-item interview with high sensitivity and specificity for detecting relationship distress; the same items can be administered in a self-report format (with different cutoffs for tailoring sensitivity and specificity to specific assessment purposes).

Self-Report Measures

The most frequently used global measure of relationship satisfaction is the Dyadic Adjustment Scale (Spanier, 1976), a 32-item instrument purporting to differentiate among four related subscales reflecting cohesion, satisfaction, consensus, and affectional expression. Factor analyses have failed to replicate the Dyadic Adjustment Scale subscales (Crane, Busby, & Larson, 1991), and typically the total composite score is reported. New global measures of relationship sentiment continue to be developed for both research and clinical purposes. These include the 10-item MSI–B screening measure, based on taxometric analyses described earlier (Whisman et al., 2009), and a new set of three Couple Satisfaction Index scales constructed using item response theory and consisting of 32, 16, and four items each (Funk & Rogge, 2007).

A variety of self-report measures have been developed to assess couples' behavioral exchanges, communication, and aggression. The Frequency and Acceptability of Partner Behavior Inventory (Doss & Christensen, 2006) assesses 20 positive and negative behaviors in four domains (affection, closeness, demands, and relationship violations). Among self-report measures specifically targeting partners' communication is the Communication Patterns Questionnaire (Christensen, 1987), designed to measure the temporal sequence of couples' interactions by soliciting partners' perceptions of their communication patterns before, during, and after conflict. The Communication Patterns Questionnaire can be used to assess characteristics of the demand → withdraw pattern frequently observed among distressed couples. Assessing relationship aggression by means of self-report measures assumes particular importance because of some individuals' reluctance to disclose the nature or extent of such aggression during an initial conjoint interview. By far the most widely used measure of couples' aggression is the Conflict Tactics Scale

(Straus, 1979; Straus, Hamby, Boney-McCoy, & Sugarman, 1996). The revised Conflict Tactics Scale uses 78 items to assess three modes of conflict resolution (reasoning, verbal aggression, and physical aggression) and includes items assessing sexual coercion and levels of physical injury.

Earlier we noted the importance of evaluating partners' attributions for relationship events. The Relationship Attribution Measure (Fincham & Bradbury, 1992) presents hypothetical situations and asks respondents to generate responsibility attributions indicating the extent to which the partner intentionally behaved negatively, was selfishly motivated, and was blameworthy for the event. For purposes of case conceptualization and treatment planning, well-constructed multidimensional measures of couple functioning—such as the MSI–R (Snyder, 1997)—are useful for discriminating among various sources of relationship strength, conflict, satisfaction, and goals. The MSI–R is a 150-item inventory designed to identify both the nature and the intensity of relationship distress in distinct areas of interaction including affective and problem-solving communication, aggression, leisure time together, finances, sexual relationship, role orientation, family of origin, and interactions regarding children. Studies have supported recent adaptations of the MSI–R for cross-cultural application with both clinic and community couples (Snyder et al., 2004) and use of the original English version with nontraditional (e.g., gay and lesbian) couples (Means-Christensen, Snyder, & Negy, 2003).

Observational Methods

A wide range of observational systems have been developed for coding couples' interactions. Detailed descriptions of representative coding systems with evidence of reliability and validity are offered elsewhere (Kerig & Baucom, 2004), as are briefer reviews and summaries (e.g., Heyman, 2001; Snyder et al., 2009). Although these systems vary widely, in general they target six major a priori classes of targeted behaviors: (a) affect (e.g., humor, affection, anger, criticism, contempt, sadness, anxiety), (b) behavioral engagement (e.g., demands, pressures for change, withdrawal, avoidance), (c) general communication skills (e.g., involvement, verbal and nonverbal negativity and positivity, information and problem description), (d) problem solving (e.g., self-disclosure, validation, facilitation, interruption), (e) power (e.g., verbal aggression, coercion, attempts to control), and (f) support–intimacy (e.g., emotional and tangible support, attentiveness). Among 15 couple coding systems summarized by Snyder et al. (2009), interrater reliability for nearly all was adequate or better after coder training. Although few studies have been conducted on the temporal stability of observed couple behaviors across tasks or settings, the limited evidence has suggested that couples' interactions likely vary across topic (e.g., high vs. low conflict), setting (e.g., home vs. clinic or research laboratory), and length of marriage (with longer-married couples exhibiting more enduring patterns).

One of the earliest and most widely used observational systems for coding couples' interactions is the Marital Interaction Coding System (MICS; Hops, Wills, Weiss, & Patterson, 1972). In its current version, the MICS–IV (Heyman, Weiss, & Eddy, 1995) codes partners' behaviors into nine categories: problem description, solution proposal, blame, facilitation, validation, invalidation, dysphoric affect, withdrawal, and irrelevant discourse. The MICS–IV is a microanalytic system that codes nearly 40 behaviors sequentially on an exchange-by-exchange basis, permitting analysis of behavior chains linked to couple distress. A more recent coding system, the Rapid Marital Interaction Coding System (RMICS; Heyman, 2004), codes interactions at the behavioral class level rather than a more granular level and affords high interrater agreement and greater ease of use. The RMICS includes five negative codes (psychological abuse, distress-maintaining attribution, hostility, dysphoric affect, withdrawal), four positive codes (acceptance, relationship-enhancing attribution, self-disclosure, humor), and one neutral code (constructive problem discussion–solution) derived from a factor analysis of more than 1,000 interactions coded by the MICS–IV. The RMICS codes have strong evidence of psychometric fitness and predict attrition and improvement in group treatment for partner aggression (Heyman, 2004).

Other Adult Relationships

Two theoretical perspectives have dominated the study of adult relationships in nonclinical settings: (a) interpersonal theory (Kiesler, 1983; T. Leary, 1957; Wiggins, 1991), exemplified in assessment methods derived from the Structural Analysis of Behavior (SASB; Benjamin, 2005); and (b) attachment theory, originally formulated in regard to children (Ainsworth, Blehar, Waters, & Wall, 1978; Bowlby, 1969) but subsequently extended to adult romantic relationships by Hazan and Shaver (1987).

The SASB is a comprehensive system for assessing intrapsychic and interpersonal components of social interaction along dimensions of affiliation and autonomy. It incorporates a circumplex model with three surfaces reflecting actions toward others (e.g., affirm, blame, ignore, protect), reactions to others (e.g., trust, recoil, sulk, disclose), and actions toward oneself (e.g., self-affirm, self-blame, self-neglect, self-protect). The SASB provides both a coding system for rating behavior and a set of self-report measures, the Intrex Questionnaires, varying in length (Benjamin & Cushing, 2000). The SASB coding system has been used to investigate interactions of families having a member diagnosed with a mental disorder, psychotherapy process and outcome, and interpersonal processes in representative community dyads. The

SASB Intrex Questionnaires have been used to examine individuals' representations of relation to self (e.g., self-concept) and of significant others (e.g., parents, romantic partners). The intermediate-length questionnaire has 16 items rating oneself at best and worst (e.g., "To become perfect, I force myself to do things correctly") and 64 items reflecting interactions with a significant other (Erickson & Pincus, 2005).

The Adult Attachment Interview (Main & Goldwyn, 1998) contains 20 questions that ask respondents about their experiences with parents and other attachment figures, significant losses and trauma, and, if relevant, experiences with their own children. The interview takes approximately 60 to 90 minutes to administer and is then transcribed and scored by a trained coder. Extensions of the Adult Attachment Interview have been developed for use with children and adolescents.

Given its complexity in scoring, the Adult Attachment Interview has been supplemented by self-report measures assessing individuals' levels of anxiety and avoidance in close relationships to classify them in four categories: secure (low on both dimensions), fearful (high on both dimensions), dismissive (low on anxiety but high on avoidance), and preoccupied (high on anxiety but low on avoidance). Among self-report measures of adult attachment, those more widely used include the 36-item Experiences in Close Relationships scale (Brennan, Clark, & Shaver, 1998) and the 30-item Relationship Scales Questionnaire (Griffin & Bartholomew, 1994). Items on the Experiences in Close Relationships scale are rated on a 7-point scale and generate scores on two dimensions of anxiety and avoidance. Items on the Relationship Scales Questionnaire are rated on a 5-point scale reflecting the extent to which each statement best describes the respondent's characteristic style in close relationships. Whereas the Experiences in Close Relationships scale deconstructs attachment in terms of anxiety and avoidance, the Relationship Scale Questionnaire deconstructs attachment in terms of working models of self and others (either positive or negative).

Family Relationships

Similar to approaches to assessing intimate adult relationships, methods for assessing family relationships have been developed across interview, self- and other report, and observational methods.

Interviews

The Camberwell Family Interview (CFI; Leff & Vaughn, 1985) was developed to study the influence of the family climate on the course of severe mental illnesses (e.g., schizophrenia, major affective disorders) as assessed by the construct of expressed emotion. *Expressed emotion* refers to the affective attitudes and behaviors (criticism, hostility, emotional overinvolvement) of a significant other toward a psychiatric patient. Considerable evidence has linked expressed emotion to relapse in psychiatric patients (Hooley, 2007). The CFI gathers factual and attitudinal information about the onset and development of the family member's illness, the patient's symptomatology, the quality of the relationship, and the amount of contact between the patient and his or her relative. The CFI takes about 90 minutes and is then coded on five dimensions: critical comments, hostility, positive remarks, warmth, and emotional overinvolvement.

Self-Report Measures

Numerous self-report measures of expressed emotion have been developed as supplements or replacements for the CFI. These include measures of varying length (from one to 90 items) completed by the patient or family members. Reviews of these measures (e.g., Hooley & Parker, 2006; Van Humbeeck, Van Audenhove, De Hert, Pieters, & Storms, 2002) have concluded that although some have strong concurrent validity with the CFI, most lack the same validity for predicting relapse. However, two measures of expressed emotion showing promise are the 30-item (5-point rating) Family Attitude Scale (Kavanagh et al., 1997) and the single-item (10-point rating) Perceived Criticism scale (Hooley & Teasdale, 1989).

Other widely used measures of family functioning have emerged separately from the expressed emotion literature. Three warranting mention are (a) the Family Environment Scale (Moos & Moos, 1994), consisting of 90 true–false statements scored on 10 scales falling in three domains: relationship (e.g., cohesion, conflict), personal growth (e.g., independence, achievement), and maintenance (e.g., organization, control); (b) the Family Adaptability and Cohesion Evaluation Scale (Olson, Gorall, & Tiesel, 2007), consisting of 42 items rated on a 6-point scale along dimensions of disengagement, enmeshment, rigidity, chaos, cohesion, and flexibility; and (c) the Family Assessment Device (Epstein, Baldwin, & Bishop, 1983), consisting of 60 items rated on a 4-point scale along six dimensions of problem solving, communication, roles, affective responsiveness, affective involvement, and behavior control. Similar to assessment of couple distress, several self-report measures have been developed to capture distress in parent–adolescent dyads, including the 44-item Issues Checklist (Robin & Foster, 1989), assessing the frequency, quantity, and anger intensity of conflicts.

Observational Methods

A variety of structured techniques have been developed for observing and analyzing family interactions—varying in activity type, amount of structure provided, family unit observed, and setting. Structured tasks designed for observations of parent–child interaction include structured play tasks, parent–child clean-up tasks, and teaching tasks. Interactions for parent–adolescent observation more typically include problem-solving tasks or discussions of daily events. Other tasks may be tailored to the specific setting or context, such as having individuals discuss feelings toward a family member with a psychiatric illness, as in the CFI described earlier. A wide range of family observational methods varying in theoretical underpinnings, levels of analysis (e.g., micro or macro level), interpersonal units of analysis (e.g., dyads, triads, whole families), and interaction tasks are described in a volume edited by Kerig and Lindahl (2000). A critical issue in family observational methods concerns their ecological validity; for example, interactions at home reliably elicit more negative behavior and negative reciprocity than do those in the laboratory (Kerig, 2000). Methodological issues in selecting one approach over another include level of analysis, reliability (e.g., across dyads within the family), relevance and construct validity of specific coding categories, live or videotaped coding, setting, and choice of tasks and participants (Lindahl, 2000).

From among the many family observational methods reported in the literature, we describe two here. The System for Coding Interactions and Family Functioning (Lindahl & Malik, 2000) was developed to assess functioning in each family subsystem: the family as a whole and each parent–child dyad. In addition to the assessment of the emotional climate of the family, the System for Coding Interactions and Family Functioning includes codes that relate to the overall structure and organization of the family, tapping into the flexibility–rigidity dimension of functioning, and the set of rules that govern family communication and decision making. The System for Coding Interactions and Family Functioning contains six family-level codes (e.g., negativity–conflict, cohesiveness), including one dyadic code (marital) and five individual parent codes (e.g., coerciveness, emotional support), and five individual child codes, including three assessing affect (e.g., anger–frustration) and two assessing behavior (e.g., withdrawal).

Fredman, Chambless, and Steketee (2004) developed an observational coding system for emotional overinvolvement (EOI) with three scales capturing intrusive, excessively self-sacrificing, or exaggerated emotional behavior displayed by the relative of a psychiatric patient. Noteworthy about this work was its application to 95 adult outpatients with obsessive–compulsive disorder or panic disorder with agoraphobia and their relatives. The three scales also showed good convergence with emotional overinvolvement ratings derived from the CFI.

Child and Adolescent Peer Relationships

Bierman (2004) provided a comprehensive model for assessing problematic peer relations targeting four domains: (a) peer context (e.g., peer responding, reputational biases), (b) peer relations (e.g., peer liking, disliking), (c) child social behaviors (e.g., aggressive–disruptive, anxious–avoidant), and (d) child self-esteem (e.g., social cognitions, emotion regulation). Various assessment strategies have been developed within each of these domains. These include (a) asking children themselves about elements of peer relations and friendships, (b) asking children about their perceptions of others within the peer group (sociometric ratings), (c) asking adults (e.g., parents and teachers) about the peer relations skills of children in their care, and (d) directly observing children during interactions with peers (Pepler & Craig, 1998).

Similar to self-reports in other domains, the primary advantage of self-ratings of peer relations is that they are relatively easy and inexpensive to gather. Their primary limitation is their potential for bias, including social cognition deficits and biases that hinder children's ability to appraise social contexts and evaluate their own responses. By contrast, peer sociometric ratings (e.g., evaluations of prosocial and aggressive behaviors, social support, friendship, peer acceptance, or social standing) tend to be highly stable and may be more accurate than adult ratings because peers are more likely to have opportunity to observe both prosocial and antisocial interactions across settings, tasks, and time. Parent and teacher perceptions of a child's social skills and peer relations may also be assessed by interview or various checklists—for example, the Teacher Rating of Social Skills (L. Clark, Gresham, & Elliott, 1985), a 52-item checklist eliciting ratings on a 3-point scale, with a parallel version for children.

Observations of children's interactions with peers overcome many of the biases and limitations of the strategies inherent in either self- or other report (Pepler & Craig, 1998) and may include either naturalistic or analog methods. Contrived (analog) settings have a potential limitation in ecological validity (generalization to naturalistic settings) but also have the advantage of eliciting problematic behaviors that otherwise have a low base rate (and hence are more difficult to capture naturalistically). Bierman (2004) reviewed several methods developed for observing and coding peer interactions and offered behavioral exemplars of six categories for assessing peer interactions, including physical aggression, verbal aggression, rough-and-tumble play, prosocial–agreeable behavior, neutral interaction, and solitary–unoccupied behavior. She noted that "the success of these observational procedures rests on identifying a combination of partners, setting, and task(s) that . . . will elicit social behavior reflecting the child's capacities for interpersonal interaction in natural social settings" (Bierman, 2004, p. 140).

ASSESSING ANXIETY-RELATED CONCERNS

An important consideration for the assessment of anxiety is evidence indicating a hierarchical structure of anxiety. For example, Zinbarg and Barlow (1996) found that narrow-band first-order factors (i.e., social anxiety, fear of fear, agoraphobia, obsessions and compulsions, and generalized dysphoric mood) differentiated among the anxiety disorders. However, these first-order factors were moderately intercorrelated, giving rise to a second-order, general factor that differentiated each of the anxiety disorders from a no-mental-disorder control group. Hence, researchers and clinicians should think carefully about which level of the hierarchy they are most interested in because anxiety measures vary in their level of specificity.

Adults

In the discussion that follows, we summarize information regarding some of the most widely used anxiety measures, including those representing the verbal–cognitive system (interviews, self-report), behavioral system (behavioral approach tests), and psychophysiological system (heart rate, electrodermal, and startle measures).

Interviews

The Anxiety Disorders Interview Schedule for *DSM–IV* (ADIS-IV; Di Nardo, Brown, & Barlow, 1994) is a semistructured interview that facilitates reliable diagnoses of *Diagnostic and Statistical Manual of Mental Disorders* (4th ed., or *DSM–IV*; American Psychiatric Association, 1994) anxiety disorders and mood disorders. As part of the ADIS-IV, a clinician severity rating is made for each diagnosis assigned and the Revised Hamilton Anxiety Rating Scale (Riskind, Beck, Brown, & Steer, 1987)—a clinical interview measure of the overall severity of somatic and psychic anxiety symptoms—is administered. The clinician severity rating reflects the severity of symptoms and distress and impairment associated with a given disorder and enables evaluation of treatment outcome.

The SCID-I (First et al., 2002) is another semistructured interview that facilitates reliable diagnoses of *DSM–IV* anxiety disorders and mood disorders. The SCID-I also includes optional modules for screening for psychotic symptoms or for making full differential diagnoses of psychotic disorders. Regarding a comparison between the SCID-I and the ADIS-IV, the ADIS-IV asks more detailed and extensive questions about the anxiety disorders, whereas the SCID-I is broader in the range of other disorders assessed.

There are also more focused interviews that assess one particular anxiety disorder only. For example, the Clinician-Administered Posttraumatic Stress Disorder Scale (Blake et al., 1995) and the PTSD Symptom Scale Interview

(Foa, Riggs, Dancu, & Rothbaum, 1993) are widely used interviews for assessing posttraumatic stress disorder (PTSD). Similarly, the Yale-Brown Obsessive Compulsive Scale Interview (Goodman et al., 1989) is widely used for assessing obsessive–compulsive disorders.

Self-Report Measures

We describe briefly here a variety of self-report questionnaires that assess the higher level general symptoms of anxiety and the more differentiated lower level dimensions corresponding to the specific anxiety disorders. We include most measures described in subsequent chapters and additional ones warranting inclusion because of their widespread use and psychometric fitness.

General Anxiety. Three widely used measures of general anxiety are the State–Trait Anxiety Inventory (Spielberger, Gorsuch, & Lushene, 1970), the Beck Anxiety Inventory (Beck, Epstein, Brown, & Steer, 1988), and the Mood and Anxiety Symptoms Questionnaire (Watson et al., 1995). The State–Trait Anxiety Inventory consists of two 20-item scales to assess state and trait anxiety. Although the State–Trait Anxiety Inventory demonstrates good convergent validity, its discriminant validity is suspect given its high correlations with depression measures and content analyses suggesting that some items tap depression (Endler, Cox, Parker, & Bagby, 1992). The Beck Anxiety Inventory is a widely used 21-item measure of general anxiety that demonstrates good convergent and discriminant validity (e.g., Osman et al., 2002). The 90-item Mood and Anxiety Symptoms Questionnaire was designed to assess constructs described in a tripartite model of anxiety and depression (L. A. Clark & Watson, 1991). Three subscales assess nonspecific levels of anxiety, depression, and mixed features of both; two additional scales assess constructs thought to be specific to anxiety (Anxious Arousal) and depression (Anhedonic Depression).

Panic Disorder and Agoraphobia. A number of measures have been developed to assess the symptoms of panic attacks and subjective reactions to these symptoms, as well as behaviors and cognitions associated more specifically with agoraphobia. Exemplars of the former include the Panic Attack Questionnaire (Norton, Zvolensky, Bonn-Miller, Cox, & Norton, 2008), the Anxiety Sensitivity Index (Peterson & Reiss, 1992), the Body Sensations Questionnaire (Chambless, Caputo, Bright, & Gallagher, 1984), and the Agoraphobic Cognitions Questionnaire (Chambless et al., 1984). The Panic Attack Questionnaire is designed to identify people with a history of panic attacks; it assesses the number and symptoms of panic attacks within the past year and month and the extent of agoraphobic avoidance. The 16-item Anxiety Sensitivity Index is a measure of anxiety sensitivity, or the fear of experiencing anxiety-related sensations. The Anxiety Sensitivity Index has been shown to prospectively predict panic attacks and to distinguish people with panic disorder from those with other anxiety disorders (Zinbarg, Barlow, & Brown, 1997). Similarly, the 17-item Body Sensations Questionnaire lists physical sensations associated with anxiety that people can find disturbing. The 14-item Agoraphobic Cognitions Questionnaire was developed as a companion measure to the Body Sensations Questionnaire and assesses catastrophic thoughts associated with feeling nervous or frightened.

A measure more specific to agoraphobia is the Mobility Inventory for Agoraphobia (Chambless, Caputo, Jasin, Gracely, & Williams, 1985). The Mobility Inventory for Agoraphobia lists 26 situations commonly avoided by agoraphobic individuals and is scored as to the degree to which the person avoids them while alone and while accompanied. The Mobility Inventory for Agoraphobia is sensitive to changes in clinical status and shows good specificity and sensitivity.

Social Phobia. Among measures targeting social phobia are the Social Phobia Scale and Social Interaction Anxiety Scale developed by Mattick and Clarke (1998). The Social Phobia Scale consists of 20 items measuring social anxiety in situations in which the individual may be observed by others, whereas the Social Interaction Anxiety Scale contains 19 items assessing reactions to typical situations requiring social interaction in dyads or groups. Both measures reliably distinguish people with social phobia from those with other anxiety disorders and those with no mental disorders (Brown et al., 1997). Other measures of social phobia include a 45-item Social Phobia and Anxiety Inventory (Turner, Beidel, Dancu, & Stanley, 1989) assessing cognitive, somatic, and behavioral dimensions of social anxiety; a 24-item Social Anxiety Scale (Liebowitz, 1987) distinguishing between levels of anxiety and avoidance in common social situations; and a more recent 10-item Social Phobia Diagnostic Questionnaire (Newman, Kachin, Zuellig, Constantino, & Cashman, 2003) assessing social phobia on the basis of *DSM–IV* criteria. Two related Fear of Negative Evaluation Scales (a 30-item Fear of Negative Evaluation scale [Watson & Friend, 1969] and a 12-item brief Fear of Negative Evaluation scale [M. R. Leary, 1983]) assess apprehension of being negatively evaluated.

Posttraumatic Stress Disorder. The Posttraumatic Diagnostic Scale (Foa, Cashman, Jaycox, & Perry, 1997) is a 17-item measure of PTSD based on the *Diagnostic and Statistical Manual of Mental Disorders* (3rd ed.; American Psychiatric Association, 1980) and *DSM–IV* criteria. The Posttraumatic Diagnostic Scale has shown an 82% agreement with the SCID-I, with sensitivity of .89 and specificity of .75. An alternative measure, the PTSD Checklist (Weathers, Litz, Herman, Huska, & Keane, 1993), offers parallel versions tailored to civilian, military, or other specific contexts. The Impact of Events Scale (Horowitz, Wilner, & Alverez, 1979) is designed to assess the psychological impact of traumatic events. The respondent indicates how often each of 15 reactions was experienced during the past week, with two subscales targeting avoidance and intrusion. The Impact of Events Scale should not be used as a diagnostic tool because it does not assess the hyperarousal symptoms of PTSD as defined by the *DSM–IV*.

Specific Phobia. The Fear Survey Schedule—III (Wolpe & Lang, 1964) is a 76-item measure assessing specific feared objects or situations. Factor analyses have revealed four reliable and valid factors: Social, Blood–Injury–Death, Undesirable Animals and Insects, and Agoraphobic–Environmental Fears.

Generalized Anxiety Disorder. Several measures have been developed to assess symptoms of a generalized anxiety disorder. The Generalized Anxiety Disorder Questionnaire (Newman et al., 2002) contains 14 items specifically targeting *DSM–IV* criteria for generalized anxiety disorder. The Penn State Worry Questionnaire (Meyer, Miller, Metzger, & Borkovec, 1990) consists of 16 items assessing the generality, excessiveness, and uncontrollability of worry. The Worry Domains Questionnaire (Tallis, Eysenck, & Mathews, 1992) uses 25 items to measure nonpathological worry in nonclinical samples, covering five domains of everyday worries: relationships, lack of confidence, aimless future, work incompetence, and finances.

Obsessive–Compulsive Disorder. A variety of self-report measures have been developed to assess recurrent intrusive thoughts and behaviors characteristic of obsessive–compulsive disorder. The Obsessive Compulsive Inventory—Revised (Foa et al., 2002) is an 18-item questionnaire assessing obsessive–compulsive disorder symptoms in six domains: washing, checking–doubting, obsessing, neutralizing, ordering, and hoarding. An alternative measure, the 30-item Maudsley Obsessional Compulsive Inventory (Hodgson & Rachman, 1977), has been used extensively in clinical trials because of its sensitivity to treatment effects (e.g., Frost, Steketee, Krause, & Trepanier, 1995). Finally, the Padua Inventory (Sanavio, 1988) is a 60-item questionnaire targeting common obsessions and compulsions, including exaggerated doubts and ruminations, contamination, checking, and violent–antisocial urges. The Padua Inventory distinguishes between people with obsessive–compulsive disorder and those with other anxiety disorders (e.g., Kyrios, Bhar, & Wade, 1996; MacDonald & de Silva, 1999).

Observational Measures

A prevalent method for assessing anxiety involves behavioral approach tests, or BATs (sometimes referred to alternatively as *behavioral avoidance tests*), in which the individual is asked to approach a feared situation or object in a series of steps. In addition to observing how closely the individual approaches the feared situation or object, the assessor will also typically ask the person for anxiety ratings. Psychophysiological responses (see the next section) may also be recorded during a BAT. A variable found to influence the construct validity of a BAT is the level of demand placed on the individual (Miller & Bernstein, 1972). In a high-demand condition in which participants were instructed to remain in the fearful situation for the duration of the BAT, a measure of avoidance behavior was uncorrelated with self-reported anxiety and psychophysiological arousal. Hence, low-demand BATs appear to have greater construct validity than high-demand ones.

Physiological Measures

Heart rate acceleration has sometimes been touted as the psychophysiological response that is most strongly related to anxiety (e.g., Holden & Barlow, 1986). However, heart rate acceleration has also been shown to be associated with motor activity, active coping sets, and appetitive motivational states (e.g., Fowles, 1988). Hence, someone whose heart rate is accelerated while approaching a potential danger may be experiencing a sense of mastery or readiness to actively cope, not anxiety. Measures of electrodermal activity, including skin conductance level and skin conductance responses, have also been commonly used to assess anxiety. Skin conductance level indexes the basal level of sweat gland activity, whereas skin conductance response indexes fluctuations in sweat gland activity. There is some evidence suggesting that the number of skin conductance responses is specific to anxiety, whereas the magnitude of skin conductance responses is a nonspecific measure of arousal (Fowles, 1988; Lang, Bradley, & Cuthbert, 1990).

Startle response has emerged over the past 20 years as an important tool for the study of emotion and psychopathology (e.g., Cook, 1999; Lang et al., 1990). Especially relevant for the assessment of anxiety disorders is the phenomenon of fear-potentiated startle. Numerous studies have documented that the magnitude of a startle response is potentiated when the individual is fearful or anxious (e.g., Bradley, Cuthbert, & Lang, 1999; Cook, 1999). Although results for individual differences in trait anxiety and neuroticism are less consistent than those for fearfulness (e.g., Grillon, Ameli, Foot, & Davis, 1993), a number of studies have indicated that these individual differences also modulate the fear-potentiated startle response in a similar way.

Children and Adolescents

Assessment of anxiety in children and adolescents presents both conceptual and methodological issues distinct from those for adults (Silverman & Ollendick, 2008). From a conceptual perspective, the construct constancy of anxiety disorders across development is only moderate, at best. That is, there are anxiety disorders of childhood (e.g., separation anxiety, reactive attachment disorder) not relevant to adults, just as some disorders of adulthood (e.g., agoraphobia) have less relevance to children. Similarly, even when diagnostic categories transcend developmental periods, the situational precipitants, subjective experience, and behavioral expression of those disorders may vary.

For example, young children may be more likely than adults to express subjective anxiety through externalizing behaviors (e.g., Mireault, Rooney, Kouwenhoven, & Hannan, 2008). From a methodological perspective, both children and adolescents may be unable to provide accurate accounts of their anxiety either verbally (limitations in expressive language) or in response to written or orally administered questionnaires (limitations in reading or comprehension). Children may also be less able to recognize emotional states or the situational contexts in which they arise, independent of limitations in language. Hence, assessment of both children and adolescents (particularly the former) often relies on an informant (e.g., parent, teacher, other caregiver). Evidence is mixed regarding the extent to which informant reports can be biased by characteristics of the informant beyond limited access to samples of relevant anxiety-related phenomena in the target child or adolescent (Richters, 1992). Instructions for some measures encourage reading the items to young children, but the effects of this administration format on responses remains unknown.

Our brief review here emphasizes assessment strategies specific to anxiety in children and adolescents. Several of the techniques noted here reflect downward extensions of measures initially developed for adults. In most cases, such extensions reflect modifications in content to capture differences in the phenomenon across development, alterations in language to facilitate comprehension at a lower reading level, and simplification of response format.

Interviews

Two widely used diagnostic interviews for anxiety disorders in children and adolescents parallel their counterparts developed for adults. The downward extension of the ADIS-IV provides child and parent versions designed to assess anxiety in the child or adolescent; the parent version contains items targeting additional concerns (e.g., conduct and oppositional defiant disorders). The National Institute of Mental Health Diagnostic Interview Schedule for Children, originally developed in 1983, has undergone several revisions culminating in its most recent iteration tailored to *DSM–IV* (DISC-IV; Shaffer, Fisher, Lucas, Dulcan, & Schwab-Stone, 2000). The Diagnostic Interview Schedule for Children is a structured interview for assessing anxiety disorders, mood disorders, disruptive disorders, substance use disorders, schizophrenia, and miscellaneous disorders, with parallel parent, teacher, and child versions. Similar to comparisons between the ADIS and SCID-I for adults, the ADIS for children asks more detailed and extensive questions about the anxiety disorders, whereas the Diagnostic Interview Schedule for Children is broader in the range of other disorders assessed.

Other diagnostic interviews for assessing anxiety-related concerns in children and adolescents include the Diagnostic Interview for Children and Adolescents (Herjanic & Reich, 1982) and the Child and Adolescent Psychiatric Assessment (Angold & Costello, 2000). The latter is distinguished by inclusion of items assessing life events, family functioning, peer relationships, and school functioning. A downward extension of the Yale-Brown Obsessive Compulsive Scale has been developed (Scahill et al., 1997) for interviewing children and adolescents regarding 10 common obsessions and compulsions.

Self-Report Measures

Among measures of general anxiety are downward extensions of measures originally developed for adult use (e.g., the State–Trait Anxiety Inventory for Children; Spielberger, Edwards, Lushene, Montuori, & Platzek, 1973). Measures of general anxiety in children tend to be heterogeneous in content, typically addressing multiple domains. Among the better known are the 66-item Screen for Child Anxiety-Related Emotional Disorders (Muris & Steerneman, 2001), the 39-item Multidimensional Anxiety Scale for Children (March, Parker, Sullivan, Stallings, & Conners, 1997), the 38-item Children's Anxiety Scale (Spence, 1998), and the 49-item Revised Children's Manifest Anxiety Scale (Reynolds & Richmond, 1978).

A variety of measures have been developed for assessing social anxiety and phobias. Domains targeted in these measures parallel those of their adult counterparts, for example, anxiety in common social situations, avoidance of new situations, and fear of negative evaluation. These include the 26-item Social Phobia and Anxiety Inventory for Children (Beidel, Turner, & Morris, 1995) and two parallel Social Anxiety Scales for children (La Greca & Stone, 1993) and adolescents (La Greca & Lopez, 1998).

Additional measures specific to panic disorder, phobias, and generalized anxiety in children and adolescents reflect downward extensions of adult measures in these domains. These include the 18-item Child Anxiety Sensitivity Index (Silverman, Fleisig, Rabian, & Peterson, 1991) assessing fear of anxiety-related sensations, the 80-item Fear Survey Schedule for Children— Revised (Ollendick, 1983) targeting common fear responses to objects and situations, and the Penn State Worry Questionnaire for Children (Chorpita, Tracey, Brown, Collica, & Barlow, 1997) assessing the generality, excessiveness, and uncontrollability of worry.

Observational and Physiological Measures

Behavioral observations of children's approach–avoidance behaviors in specific feared situations provide critical incremental information beyond self- or informant report, particularly in developing more detailed functional analytic assessments of situational variables contributing to, maintaining, or ameliorating the anxious behavior. Similarly, physiological measures (e.g., heart rate, skin conductance, startle response) may provide particularly useful information about young respondents less able to provide reliable or valid descriptions of their subjective phenomenology. A caveat concerns the level of intrusiveness associated with physiological recording that may produce reactive anxiety linked to the measure itself rather than to the target situation.

CONCLUSIONS

Given empirical evidence linking relationship processes and anxiety, studies targeting either domain may profit from assessment methods including the other. Similarly, the co-occurrence of interpersonal difficulties and anxiety disorders in both adults and youth suggests the need to routinely screen for both when either one is the focus of intervention. In clinical settings, assessment foci should progress from broad to narrow—first identifying relationship concerns or general anxiety at the broader construct level and then examining more specific facets of each as indicated using a finer grained analysis. As a general rule, assessment should begin with nomothetic approaches but then progress to idiographic methods facilitating functional analysis of factors related to target concerns.

Assessment of both interpersonal processes and anxiety should integrate findings across multiple assessment methods. Self- and other report measures may complement findings from interview or behavioral observation in generating data across diverse domains both central or conceptually related to an individual's difficulties or across those domains potentially more challenging to assess because of their sensitive nature or their not being amenable to direct observation. At the same time, assessment will be most efficient when choosing evaluation strategies and modalities that complement each other and by following a sequential approach that uses increasingly narrow-band measures to target problem areas that have been identified by other assessment techniques. As linkages between interpersonal processes and anxiety become clarified in further research, both assessment strategies and selected measurement techniques will profit from tailoring these to the specific target constructs and populations of interest.

REFERENCES

Ainsworth, M. D. S., Blehar, M. C., Waters, E., & Wall, S. (1978). *Patterns of attachment: A psychological study of the strange situation*. Hillsdale, NJ: Erlbaum.

American Psychiatric Association. (1980). *Diagnostic and statistical manual of mental disorders* (3rd ed.). Washington, DC: Author.

American Psychiatric Association. (1994). *Diagnostic and statistical manual of mental disorders* (4th ed.). Washington, DC: Author.

Angold, A., & Costello, E. J. (2000). The Child and Adolescent Psychiatric Assessment (CAPA). *Journal of the American Academy of Child & Adolescent Psychiatry, 39,* 39–48.

Baucom, D. H., Epstein, N., & LaTaillade, J. J. (2002). Cognitive-behavioral couple therapy. In A. S. Gurman & N. S. Jacobson (Eds.), *Clinical handbook of couple therapy* (3rd ed., pp. 26–58). New York, NY: Guilford Press.

Beck, A. T., Epstein, N., Brown, G., & Steer, R. A. (1988). An inventory measuring clinical anxiety: Psychometric properties. *Journal of Consulting and Clinical Psychology, 56,* 893–897.

Beidel, D. C., Turner, S. M., & Morris, T. L. (1995). A new inventory to assess social anxiety and phobia: The Social Phobia and Anxiety Inventory for Children. *Psychological Assessment, 7,* 73–79.

Benjamin, L. S. (2005). Interpersonal theory of personality disorders: The structural analysis of social behavior and interpersonal reconstructive therapy. In M. F. Lenzenweger & J. F. Clarkin (Eds.), *Major theories of personality* (2nd ed., pp. 157–230). New York, NY: Guilford Press.

Benjamin, L. S., & Cushing, G. (2000). *Manual for coding social interactions in terms of structural analysis of social behavior.* Salt Lake City, UT: University of Utah.

Bierman, K. L. (2004). *Peer rejection: Developmental processes and intervention strategies.* New York, NY: Guilford Press.

Blake, D. D., Weathers, F. W., Nagy, L. M., Kaloupek, D. G., Gusman, F. D., Charney, D. S., & Keane, T. M. (1995). The development of a clinician-administered PTSD scale. *Journal of Traumatic Stress, 8,* 75–90.

Bowlby, J. (1969). *Attachment and loss: Vol. 1. Attachment.* New York, NY: Basic Books.

Bradbury, T. N., & Fincham, F. D. (1990). Attributions in marriage: Review and critique. *Psychological Bulletin, 107,* 3–33.

Bradley, M. M., Cuthbert, B. N., & Lang, P. J. (1999). Affect and the startle reflex. In M. E. Dawson, A. M. Schell, & A. H. Böhmelt (Eds.), *Startle modification: Implications for neuroscience, cognitive science, and clinical science* (pp. 157–183). New York, NY: Cambridge University Press.

Brennan, K. A., Clark, C. L., & Shaver, P. (1998). Self-report measures of adult romantic attachment. In J. A. Simpson & W. S. Rholes (Eds.), *Attachment theory and close relationships* (pp. 46–76). New York, NY: Guilford Press.

Brown, E. J., Turovsky, J., Heimberg, R. G., Juster, H. R., Brown, T. A., & Barlow, D. H. (1997). Validation of the Social Interaction Anxiety Scale and the Social Phobia Scale across the anxiety disorders. *Psychological Assessment, 9,* 21–27.

Chambless, D. L., Caputo, G. C., Bright, P., & Gallagher, R. (1984). Assessment of fear in agoraphobics: The Body Sensations Questionnaire and the Agoraphobic Cognitions Questionnaire. *Journal of Consulting and Clinical Psychology, 52,* 1090–1097.

Chambless, D. L., Caputo, G. C., Jasin, S. E., Gracely, E. J., & Williams, C. (1985). The Mobility Inventory for Agoraphobia. *Behaviour Research and Therapy, 23*, 35–44.

Chorpita, B. F., Tracey, S. A., Brown, T. A., Collica, T. J., & Barlow, D. H. (1997). Assessment of worry in children and adolescents: An adaptation of the Penn State Worry Questionnaire. *Behaviour Research and Therapy, 35*, 569–581.

Christensen, A. (1987). Detection of conflict patterns in couples. In K. Hahlweg & M. J. Goldstein (Eds.), *Understanding major mental disorder: The contribution of family interaction research* (pp. 250–265). New York, NY: Family Process Press.

Christensen, A., & Heavey, C. L. (1990). Gender and social structure in the demand/withdraw pattern of marital conflict. *Journal of Personality and Social Psychology, 59*, 73–81.

Clark, L., Gresham, F. M., & Elliott, S. N. (1985). Development and validation of a social skills assessment measure: The TROSS-C. *Journal of Psychoeducational Assessment, 3*, 347–356.

Clark, L. A., & Watson, D. (1991). Tripartite model of anxiety and depression: Psychometric evidence and taxonomic implications. *Journal of Abnormal Psychology, 100*, 316–336.

Cook, E. W. (1999). Affective individual differences, psychopathology, and startle reflex modification. In M. E. Dawson, A. M. Schell, & A. H. Böhmelt (Eds.), *Startle modification: Implications for neuroscience, cognitive science, and clinical science* (pp. 187–208). New York, NY: Cambridge University Press.

Crane, D. R., Busby, D. M., & Larson, J. H. (1991). A factor analysis of the Dyadic Adjustment Scale with distressed and nondistressed couples. *American Journal of Family Therapy, 19*, 60–66.

Di Nardo, P. A., Brown, T. A., & Barlow, D. H. (1994). *Anxiety Disorders Interview Schedule for DSM–IV: Lifetime version (ADIS-IV-L)*. San Antonio, TX: Psychological Corporation.

Doss, B. D., & Christensen, A. (2006). Acceptance in romantic relationships: The Frequency and Acceptability of Partner Behavior Inventory. *Psychological Assessment, 18*, 289–302.

Endler, N. S., Cox, B. J., Parker, J. D. A., & Bagby, R. M. (1992). Self-reports of depression and state–trait anxiety: Evidence for differential assessment. *Journal of Personality and Social Psychology, 63*, 832–838.

Epstein, N. B., Baldwin, L. M., & Bishop, D. S. (1983). The McMaster Family Assessment Device. *Journal of Marital and Family Therapy, 9*, 171–180.

Epstein, N. B., & Baucom, D. H. (2002). *Enhanced cognitive–behavioral therapy for couples: A contextual approach*. Washington, DC: American Psychological Association.

Erickson, T. M., & Pincus, A. L. (2005). Using structural analysis of social behavior (SASB) measures of self- and social perception to give interpersonal meaning to symptoms: Anxiety as an exemplar. *Assessment, 12*, 243–254.

Fincham, F. D., & Bradbury, T. N. (1992). Assessing attributions in marriage: The Relationship Attribution Measure. *Journal of Personality and Social Psychology, 62,* 457–468.

First, M. B., Bell, C. C., Cuthbert, B., Krystal, J. H., Malison, R., Offord, D. R., . . . Wisner, K. L. (2002). Personality disorders and relational disorders: A research agenda for addressing crucial gaps in DSM. In D. J. Kupfer, M. B. First, & D. A. Regier (Eds.), *A research agenda for DSM–V* (pp. 123–199). Washington, DC: American Psychiatric Association.

Foa, E. B., Cashman, L., Jaycox, L., & Perry, K. (1997). The validation of a self-report measure of posttraumatic stress disorder: The Posttraumatic Diagnostic Scale. *Psychological Assessment, 9,* 445–451.

Foa, E. B., Huppert, J. D., Leiberg, S., Langner, R., Kichic, R., Hajcak, G., & Salkovskis, P. M. (2002). The Obsessive–Compulsive Inventory: Development and validation of a short version. *Psychological Assessment, 14,* 485–496.

Foa, E. B., Riggs, D. S., Dancu, C. V., & Rothbaum, B. O. (1993). Reliability and validity of a brief instrument for assessing post-traumatic stress disorder. *Journal of Traumatic Stress, 6,* 459–473.

Fowles, D. C. (1988). Psychophysiology and psychopathology: A motivational approach. *Psychophysiology, 25,* 373–391.

Fredman, S. J., Chambless, D. L., & Steketee, G. (2004). Development and validation of an observational coding system for emotional overinvolvement. *Journal of Family Psychology, 18,* 339–347.

Frost, R. O., Steketee, G., Krause, M. S., & Trepanier, K. L. (1995). The relationship of the Yale-Brown Obsessive Compulsive Scale (YBOCS) to other measures of obsessive compulsive symptoms in a nonclinical population. *Journal of Personality Assessment, 65,* 158–168.

Funk, J., & Rogge, R. (2007). Testing the ruler with item response theory: Increasing precision of measurement for relationship satisfaction with the Couples Satisfaction Index. *Journal of Family Psychology, 21,* 572–583.

Goodman, W. K., Price, L. H., Rasmussen, S. A., Mazure, C., Fleischmann, R. L., Hill, C. L., . . . Charney, D. S. (1989). The Yale-Brown Obsessive Compulsive Scale: I. Development, use, and reliability. *Archives of General Psychiatry, 46,* 1006–1011.

Gottman, J. M. (1994). *What predicts divorce? The relationship between marital processes and marital outcomes.* Hillsdale, NJ: Erlbaum.

Gottman, J. M. (1999). *The marriage clinic: A scientifically-based marital therapy.* New York, NY: Norton.

Griffin, D., & Bartholomew, K. (1994). Models of the self and other: Fundamental dimensions underlying measures of adult attachment. *Journal of Personality and Social Psychology, 67,* 430–445.

Grillon, C., Ameli, R., Foot, M., & Davis, M. (1993). Fear-potentiated startle: Relationship to the level of state/trait anxiety in healthy subjects. *Biological Psychiatry, 33,* 566–574.

Haynes, S. N., & Yoshioka, D. (2007). Clinical assessment applications of ambulatory biosensors. *Psychological Assessment, 19,* 44–57.

Hazan, C., & Shaver, P. R. (1987). Romantic love conceptualized as an attachment process. *Journal of Personality and Social Psychology, 59,* 511–524.

Herjanic, B., & Reich, W. (1982). Development of a structured psychiatric interview for children: Agreement between child and parent on individual symptoms. *Journal of Abnormal Child Psychology, 10,* 307–324.

Heyman, R. E. (2001). Observation of couple conflicts: Clinical assessment applications, stubborn truths, and shaky foundations. *Psychological Assessment, 13,* 5–35.

Heyman, R. E. (2004). Rapid Marital Interaction Coding System (RMICS). In P. K. Kerig & D. H. Baucom (Eds.), *Couple observational coding systems* (pp. 67–94). Mahwah, NJ: Erlbaum.

Heyman, R. E., Feldbau-Kohn, S. R., Ehrensaft, M. K., Langhinrichsen-Rohling, J., & O'Leary, K. D. (2001). Can questionnaire reports correctly classify relationship distress and partner physical abuse? *Journal of Family Psychology, 15,* 334–346.

Heyman, R. E., Weiss, R. L., & Eddy, J. M. (1995). Marital Interaction Coding System: Revision and empirical evaluation. *Behavioural Research and Therapy, 33,* 737–746.

Hodgson, R. J., & Rachman, S. (1977). Obsessional compulsive complaints. *Behaviour Research and Therapy, 15,* 389–395.

Holden, A. E., & Barlow, D. H. (1986). Heart rate and heart rate variability recorded in vivo in agoraphobics and nonphobics. *Behavior Therapy, 17,* 26–42.

Hooley, J. M. (2007). Expressed emotion and relapse of psychopathology. *Annual Review of Clinical Psychology, 3,* 329–352.

Hooley, J. M., & Parker, H. A. (2006). Measuring expressed emotion: An evaluation of the shortcuts. *Journal of Family Psychology, 20,* 386–396.

Hooley, J. M., & Teasdale, J. D. (1989). Predictors of relapse in unipolar depressives: Expressed emotion, marital distress, and perceived criticism. *Journal of Abnormal Psychology, 98,* 229–235.

Hops, H., Wills, T. A., Weiss, R. L., & Patterson, G. R. (1972). *Marital Interaction Coding System* (National Auxiliary Publication Service No. 02077). Eugene, OR: University of Oregon and Oregon Research Institute.

Horowitz, M., Wilner, N. J., & Alverez, W. (1979). Impact of Events Scale: A measure of subjective stress. *Psychosomatic Medicine, 41,* 209–218.

Kavanagh, D. J., O'Halloran, P., Manicavasagar, V., Clark, D., Piatkowska, O., Tennant, C., & Rosen, A. (1997). The Family Attitude Scale: Reliability and validity of a new scale for measuring the emotional climate of families. *Psychiatry Research, 70,* 185–195.

Kerig, P. K. (2000). Introduction and overview: Conceptual issues in family observational research. In P. K. Kerig & K. M. Lindahl (Eds.), *Family observational coding systems: Resources for systemic research* (pp. 1–22). Mahwah, NJ: Erlbaum.

Kerig, P. K., & Baucom, D. H. (Eds.). (2004). *Couple observational coding systems.* Mahwah, NJ: Erlbaum.

Kerig, P. K., & Lindahl, K. M. (2000). *Family observational coding systems: Resources for systemic research*. Mahwah, NJ: Erlbaum.

Kiecolt-Glaser, J. K., & Newton, T. L. (2001). Marriage and health: His and hers. *Psychological Bulletin, 12,* 472–503.

Kiesler, D. J. (1983). The 1982 interpersonal circle: A taxonomy for complementarity in human transactions. *Psychological Review, 90,* 185–214.

Kyrios, M., Bhar, S., & Wade, D. (1996). The assessment of obsessive-compulsive phenomenon: Psychometric and normative data on the Padua Inventory from an Australian non-clinical student sample. *Behaviour Research and Therapy, 34,* 85–95.

La Greca, A. M., & Lopez, N. (1998). Social anxiety among adolescents: Linkages with peer relations and friendships. *Journal of Abnormal Child Psychology, 26,* 83–94.

La Greca, A. M., & Stone, W.L. (1993). The Social Anxiety Scale for Children—Revised: Factor structure and concurrent validity. *Journal of Clinical Child Psychology, 22,* 17–27.

Lang, P. J., Bradley, M. M., & Cuthbert, B. N. (1990). Emotion, attention, and the startle reflex. *Psychological Review, 97,* 377–395.

Leary, M. R. (1983). A brief version of the Fear of Negative Evaluation Scale. *Personality and Social Psychology Bulletin, 9,* 371–375.

Leary, T. (1957). *Interpersonal diagnosis of personality: A functional theory and methodology for personality evaluation.* New York: Ronald Press.

Leff, J. P., & Vaughn, C. E. (1985). *Expressed emotion in families.* New York: Guilford Press.

Liebowitz, M. R. (1987). Social phobia. *Modern Problems in Psychopharmacology, 22,* 141–173.

Lindahl, K. M. (2000). Methodological issues in family observational research. In P. K. Kerig & K. M. Lindahl (Eds.), *Family observational coding systems: Resources for systemic research* (pp. 23–32). Mahwah, NJ: Erlbaum.

Lindahl, K. M., & Malik, N. M. (2000). The System for Coding Interactions and Family Functioning. In P. K. Kerig & K. M. Lindahl (Eds.), *Family observational coding systems: Resources for systemic research* (pp. 77–91). Mahwah, NJ: Erlbaum.

MacDonald, A. M., & de Silva, P. (1999). The assessment of obsessionality using the Padua Inventory: Its validity in a British non-clinical sample. *Personality and Individual Differences, 27,* 1027–1046.

Main, M., & Goldwyn, R. (1998). *Adult attachment classification system.* Unpublished manuscript, University of California, Berkeley.

March, J. S., Parker, J. D. A., Sullivan, K., Stallings, P., & Conners, C. K. (1997). The Multidimensional Anxiety Scale for Children (MACS): Factor structure, reliability, and validity. *Journal of the American Academy of Child & Adolescent Psychiatry, 36,* 554–565.

Mash, E. J., & Foster, S. L. (2001). Exporting analogue behavioral observation from research to clinical practice: Useful or cost-defective? *Psychological Assessment, 13*, 86–98.

Mattick, R. P., & Clarke, J. C. (1998). Development and validation of measures of social phobia scrutiny fear and social interaction anxiety. *Behaviour Research and Therapy, 36*, 455–470.

Means-Christensen, A. J., Snyder, D. K., & Negy, C. (2003). Assessing nontraditional couples: Validity of the Marital Satisfaction Inventory—Revised (MSI–R) with gay, lesbian, and cohabiting heterosexual couples. *Journal of Marital and Family Therapy, 29*, 69–83.

Meyer, T. J., Miller, M. L., Metzger, R. L., & Borkovec, T. D. (1990). Development and validation of the Penn State Worry Questionnaire. *Behaviour Research and Therapy, 28*, 487–495.

Miller, B. V., & Bernstein, D. A. (1972). Instructional demand in a behavioral avoidance test for claustrophobic fears. *Journal of Abnormal Psychology, 80*, 206–210.

Mireault, G., Rooney, S., Kouwenhoven, K., & Hannan, C. (2008). Oppositional behavior and anxiety in boys and girls: A cross-sectional study in two community samples. *Child Psychiatry and Human Development, 39*, 519–527.

Moos, R. H., & Moos, B. S. (1994). *Family Environment Scale manual.* Palo Alto, CA: Consulting Psychologists Press.

Muris, P., & Steerneman, P. (2001) The revised version of the Screen for Child Anxiety Related Emotional Disorders (SCARED-R): First evidence for its reliability and validity in a clinical sample. *British Journal of Clinical Psychology, 40*, 35–44.

Newman, M. G., Kachin, K. E., Zuellig, A. R., Constantino, M. J. & Cashman, L. (2003). The Social Phobia Diagnostic Questionnaire: Preliminary validation of a new self-report diagnostic measure of social phobia. *Psychological Medicine, 33*, 623–635.

Newman, M. G., Zuellig, A. R., Kachin, K. E., Constantino, M. J., Przeworski, A., Erickson, T., & Cashman-McGrath, L. (2002). Preliminary reliability and validity of the Generalized Anxiety Disorder Questionnaire-IV: A revised self-report diagnostic measure of generalized anxiety disorder. *Behavior Therapy, 33*, 215–233.

Norton, P. J., Zvolensky, M. J., Bonn-Miller, M. O., Cox, B. J., & Norton, G. R. (2008). Use of the Panic Attack Questionnaire-IV to assess nonclinical panic attacks and limited symptom panic attacks in student and community samples. *Journal of Anxiety Disorders, 22*, 1159–1171.

Ollendick, T. H. (1983). Reliability and validity of the Revised Fear Survey Schedule for Children (FSSC-R). *Behaviour Research and Therapy, 21*, 685–692.

Olson, D. H. (1977). Insiders' and outsiders' view of relationships: Research and strategies. In G. Levinger & H. Raush (Eds.), *Close relationships* (pp. 115–135). Amherst, MA: University of Massachusetts Press.

Olson, D. H., Gorall, D. M., & Tiesel, J. W. (2007). *FACES IV manual*. Minneapolis, MN: Life Innovations.

Osman, A., Hoffman, J., Barrios, F. X., Kopper, B. A., Breitenstein, J. L., & Hahn, S. K. (2002). Factor structure, reliability, and validity of the Beck Anxiety Inventory in adolescent psychiatric inpatients. *Journal of Clinical Psychology, 58*, 443–456.

Pasch, L. A., Bradbury, T. N., & Davila, J. (1997). Gender, negative affectivity, and observed social support behavior in marital interaction. *Personal Relationships, 4*, 361–378.

Pepler, D. J., & Craig, W. M. (1998). Assessing children's peer relationships. *Child Psychology and Psychiatry Review, 3*, 176–182.

Peterson, R. A., & Reiss, S. (1992). *Anxiety Sensitivity Index revised manual*. Worthington, OH: IDS.

Reynolds, C. R., & Richmond, B. O. (1978). What I think and feel: A revised measure of children's manifest anxiety. *Journal of Abnormal Child Psychology, 6*, 271–280.

Richters, J. E. (1992). Depressed mothers as informants about their children: A critical review of the evidence for distortion. *Psychological Bulletin, 112*, 485–499.

Riskind, J. H., Beck, A. T., Brown, G., & Steer, R. A. (1987). Taking the measure of anxiety and depression: Validity of the reconstructed Hamilton scales. *Journal of Nervous and Mental Disease, 175*, 474–479.

Robin, A. L., & Foster, S. L. (1989). *Negotiating parent-adolescent conflict: A behavioral-family systems approach*. New York: Guilford Press.

Sanavio, E. (1988). Obsessions and compulsions: The Padua Inventory. *Behaviour Research and Therapy, 26*, 169–177.

Scahill, L., Riddle, M. A., McSwiggin-Hardin, M., Ort, S. I., King, R. A., Goodman, W. K., . . . Leckman, J. F. (1997). Children's Yale-Brown Obsessive Compulsive Scale: Reliability and validity. *Journal of the American Academy of Child & Adolescent Psychiatry, 36*, 844–852.

Shaffer, D., Fisher, P., Lucas, C. P., Dulcan, M. K., & Schwab-Stone, M. E. (2000). NIMH Diagnostic Interview Schedule for Children Version IV (NIMH DISC-IV): Description, differences from previous versions, and reliability of some common diagnoses. *Journal of the American Academy of Child & Adolescent Psychiatry, 39*, 28–38.

Sillars, A., Roberts, L. J., Leonard, K. E., & Dun, T. (2000). Cognition during marital conflict: The relationship of thought and talk. *Journal of Social and Personal Relationships, 17*, 479–502.

Silverman, W. K., Fleisig, W., Rabian, B., & Peterson, R. A. (1991). Child Anxiety Sensitivity Index. *Journal of Clinical Child Psychology, 20*, 162–168.

Silverman, W. K., & Ollendick, T. H. (2008). Child and adolescent anxiety disorders. In J. Hunsley & E. J. Mash (Eds.), *A guide to assessments that work* (pp. 181–206). New York: Oxford University Press.

Snyder, D. K. (1997). *Manual for the Marital Satisfaction Inventory—Revised*. Los Angeles: Western Psychological Services.

Snyder, D. K., Cepeda-Benito, A., Abbott, B. V., Gleaves, D. H., Negy, C., Hahlweg, K., & Laurenceau, J. P. (2004). Cross-cultural applications of the Marital Satisfaction Inventory—Revised (MSI–R). In M. E. Maruish (Ed.), *Use of psychological testing for treatment planning and outcomes assessment* (3rd ed., pp. 603–623). Mahwah, NJ: Erlbaum.

Snyder, D. K., Heyman, R. E., & Haynes, S. N. (2009). Assessing couples. In J. N. Butcher (Ed.), *Oxford handbook of personality assessment* (pp. 457–484). New York, NY: Oxford University Press.

Spanier, G. B. (1976). Measuring dyadic adjustment: New scales for assessing the quality of marriage and similar dyads. *Journal of Marriage and the Family, 38,* 15–28.

Spence, S. H. (1998). A measure of anxiety symptoms among children. *Behaviour Research and Therapy, 36,* 545–566.

Spielberger, C. D., Edwards, C. D., Lushene, R. E., Montuori, J., & Platzek, D. (1973). *Preliminary manual for the State-Trait Anxiety Inventory for Children*. Palo Alto, CA: Consulting Psychologists Press.

Spielberger, C. D., Gorsuch, R. C., & Lushene, R. E. (1970). *Manual for the State-Trait Anxiety Inventory*. Palo Alto, CA: Consulting Psychologists Press.

Straus, M. A. (1979). Measuring intrafamily conflict and violence: The Conflict Tactics (CT) Scales. *Journal of Marriage and the Family, 41,* 75–88.

Straus, M. A., Hamby, S. L., Boney-McCoy, S., & Sugarman, D. B. (1996). The revised Conflict Tactics Scales (CTS2): Development and preliminary psychometric data. *Journal of Family Issues, 17,* 283–316.

Tallis, F., Eysenck, M. W., & Mathews, A. (1992). A questionnaire for the measurement of nonpathological worry. *Personality and Individual Differences, 13,* 161–168.

Tanaka-Matsumi, J. (2004). Individual differences and behavioral assessment. In S. N. Haynes & E. M. Heiby (Eds.), *Comprehensive handbook of psychological assessment: Vol. 3. Behavioral assessment* (pp. 128–139). Hoboken, NJ: Wiley.

Turner, S. M., Beidel, D. C., Dancu, C. V., & Stanley, M. A. (1989). An empirically derived inventory to measure social fears and anxiety: The Social Phobia and Anxiety Inventory. *Psychological Assessment, 1,* 35–40.

Van Humbeeck, G., Van Audenhove, C., De Hert, M., Pieters, G., & Storms, G. (2002). Expressed emotion: A review of assessment instruments. *Clinical Psychology Review, 22,* 321–341.

Watson, D., & Friend, R. (1969). Measurement of social-evaluative anxiety. *Journal of Consulting and Clinical Psychology, 33,* 448–457.

Watson, D., Weber, K., Assenheimer, J. M., Clark, L., Strauss, M. E., & McCormick, R. A. (1995). Testing a tripartite model: I. Evaluating the convergent and discriminant validity of anxiety and depression symptom scales. *Journal of Abnormal Psychology, 104,* 3–14.

Weathers, F., Litz, B., Herman, D., Huska, J., & Keane, T. (1993, October). *The PTSD Checklist (PCL): Reliability, validity, and diagnostic utility*. Paper presented at the meeting of the International Society for Traumatic Stress Studies, San Antonio, TX.

Weiss, R. L., & Heyman, R. E. (1997). A clinical-research overview of couples interactions. In W. K. Halford & H. J. Markman (Eds.), *Clinical handbook of marriage and couples intervention* (pp. 13–41). New York, NY: Wiley.

Whisman, M. A., Snyder, D. K., & Beach, S. R. H. (2009). Screening for marital and relationship discord. *Journal of Family Psychology, 23*, 247–254.

Wiggins, J. S. (1991). Agency and communion as conceptual coordinates for understanding and measurement of interpersonal behavior. In W. Grove & D. Cicchetti (Eds.), *Thinking clearly about psychology: Essays in honor of Paul E. Meehl* (Vol. 2, pp. 89–113). Minneapolis, MN: University of Minnesota Press.

Wolpe, J., & Lang, P. J. (1964). A fear survey schedule for use in behavior therapy. *Behaviour Research and Therapy, 2*, 27–30.

Zinbarg, R. E. (1998). Concordance and synchrony in measures of anxiety and panic reconsidered: A hierarchical model of anxiety and panic. *Behavior Therapy, 29*, 301–323.

Zinbarg, R. E., & Barlow, D. H. (1996). The structure of anxiety and the anxiety disorders: A hierarchical model. *Journal of Abnormal Psychology, 105*, 181–193.

Zinbarg, R. E., Barlow, D. H., & Brown, T. A. (1997). Hierarchical structure and general factor saturation of the Anxiety Sensitivity Index: Evidence and implications. *Psychological Assessment, 9*, 277–284.

II

INTERPERSONAL PROCESSES IN SPECIFIC ANXIETY DISORDERS

3

INTERPERSONAL PROCESSES AND THE ANXIETY DISORDERS OF CHILDHOOD

THOMAS H. OLLENDICK, NATALIE M. COSTA, AND KRISTY E. BENOIT

The anxiety disorders constitute a broad array of syndromes ranging from very circumscribed fears and phobias to pervasive anxiety or worry. According to the most recent editions of the *Diagnostic and Statistical Manual of Mental Disorders* (4th ed., or *DSM–IV*; APA, 1994) and the *International Statistical Classification of Diseases and Related Health Problems* (10th rev., or *ICD-10*; World Health Organization, 1992), children can be categorized by eight major diagnostic syndromes associated with anxiety: panic disorder with agoraphobia, panic disorder without agoraphobia, agoraphobia without history of panic, specific phobia, social phobia, obsessive–compulsive disorder, posttraumatic stress disorder, and generalized anxiety disorder. In addition, the *DSM–IV* and *ICD-10* specify one anxiety disorder unique to childhood—separation anxiety disorder. Earlier versions of the *DSM* included two additional anxiety diagnoses specific to childhood, namely, avoidant disorder and overanxious disorder. In the most recent revision, avoidant disorder and overanxious disorder have been subsumed under the diagnoses of social phobia and generalized anxiety disorder, respectively.

In the past 2 decades, epidemiological studies have estimated the prevalence of anxiety disorders (including specific phobias) in general community samples of children to range from 5.7% to 17.7% (e.g., Kessler et al., 2008; Kessler & Wang, 2008). Anxiety disorders tend to be more prevalent in girls than in boys and in older than in younger children. Some children may have only one anxiety disorder as per *DSM–IV* or *ICD-10* criteria. However, most children who have one anxiety disorder tend to be comorbid with other anxiety or phobic disorders; as such, it is not uncommon for children to present in epidemiological studies with multiple anxiety disorders (Ollendick & Seligman, 2006). Children in clinic samples exhibit even higher levels of comorbidity than those observed in general community samples (see Ollendick, King, & Muris, 2002). It is not uncommon for clinic-referred children with anxiety disorders to present with not only additional anxiety disorders but also other internalizing disorders, including major depressive disorder and dysthymia and externalizing disorders such as oppositional defiant disorder and attention-deficit/hyperactivity disorder. Thus, the clinical picture can be quite complex because of the presence of overlapping disorders. Comorbidity appears to be the rule, not the exception.

Moreover, anxiety disorders have a complex etiology, with genetic factors, temperament characteristics (especially behavioral inhibition), parenting practices (attachment histories, socialization of emotions), parental psychopathology (anxiety and depression, in particular), specific social learning histories (including traumatic and vicarious experiences), information-processing and emotion regulation deficits, and impaired peer relationships all being implicated. Consistent with a developmental psychopathology framework, there may be multiple pathways to any one anxiety disorder or any combination of anxiety disorders. In addition, any combination of protective factors (e.g., secure attachment or good peer relationships) can serve to prevent anxiety disorders or, in cases in which clinical anxiety is present, mitigate the severity of the disorder (for a review, see Ollendick et al., 2002).

Unfortunately, *DSM–IV* and *ICD-10* are relatively silent as to the role of interpersonal processes in the development and expression of the anxiety disorders in childhood, with the notable exception of social phobia and separation anxiety disorder. In social phobia, there must be the capacity for age-appropriate social relationships, and the anxiety must be present in peer settings, not just in interactions with adults. Typically, young children with social phobia appear excessively shy, shrink from contact with others, refuse to participate in group play, and stay on the periphery of social activities. Thus, social phobia is fundamentally an interpersonal disorder. In separation anxiety disorder, the cardinal symptom is the presence of developmentally inappropriate and excessive anxiety concerning separation from those to whom the child is attached. When separated from attachment figures, these children frequently need to know their whereabouts and need to stay in contact with them (e.g., through frequent phone calls). Moreover, they often display clinging behavior, that is, staying close to and shadowing the parent. Overall, they display an insecure attachment. As such, separation anxiety disorder—like social phobia—is fundamentally an interpersonal disorder. For the other anxiety disorders, however, there is little to no mention in the major diagnostic systems of interpersonal processes or interpersonal situations that might serve to occasion the disorders or to qualify their expressions.

In this chapter, we have three primary goals: (a) to review normative interpersonal development, (b) to explicate interpersonal processes that might lead to the development and expression of anxiety disorders in childhood, and (c) to explore the implications of interpersonal processes for the treatment of these disorders in children.

NORMATIVE INTERPERSONAL DEVELOPMENT

Normative interpersonal development involves four primary processes. The first process is the ability to form an attachment within the parent–child relationship. The second process is the ability to regulate emotions through the development of skills such as responding appropriately, being flexible, and resolving conflicts in social situations. The third process involves the socialization of emotion through parental practices and behaviors. The last process is the ability to form peer relationships, which play a powerful role in the socialization of emotion because interactions with peers constitute an important developmental context for children (Rubin, Bukowski, & Parker, 1998). We discuss each of these processes briefly.

The first process is the ability to form a close, emotional bond or relationship with a caregiver, otherwise known as *attachment*. Parent–child attachment is considered to be one of the most influential and important relationships in development. The type of attachment children have is characterized by the quality of the parent–child relationship in terms of the security and trust that children have in their caregiver (Bowlby, 1973). More specifically, whether a child is securely or insecurely attached to his or her caregiver is directly related to how safe the child feels when interacting with her or his environment. Securely attached children tend to explore their environment more willingly and confidently and feel like their caregiver is caring, loving, accessible, communicative, trustworthy, and responsive to their needs (Bowlby, 1973). A young child, for example, who is securely attached is able to separate from his or her caregiver and play with other children in the park (with his or her caregiver nearby). Securely attached children are more self-confident, trusting, and competent in their attachments to other people in their life, and they have higher self-regulatory abilities, which can allow even fearful or inhibited children to confront perceived threat because their caregiver is available to assist them if need be (Thompson, 2001). The feelings that securely attached children have about their own abilities to handle stress or interact with their environment are not thought to be solely "in" the child but rather embedded in the parent–child context. Given this, secure attachment is considered to be an interpersonal factor that protects the child against the development of anxiety and related disorders.

Attachment in middle childhood (approximately ages 5–10) marks the beginning of children starting to use other adults and peers as a secure base from which to explore their environment. This is mainly because of the introduction of different school environments and structured social and athletic activities in which there are increasingly longer periods of separation from caregivers. Whereas physical proximity is the central theme of attachment in the early years, Bowlby (1987) proposed that availability of the attachment figure becomes more important during middle childhood. Although children in this age group are developing more cognitive, emotional, and physical skills to begin taking responsibility for their own protection, they are still not making decisions solely on their own. Knowing and having the security that an attachment figure is available to help if need be may be critical to the progression of normative interpersonal development during middle childhood, not only because of the direct effects that a secure attachment has on the parent–child relationship but also because of the indirect effects it has on children's interactions and experiences with other people throughout life.

The next process in interpersonal development, the ability to regulate emotions, has been a central focus of developmental psychology for many years. Research in this area has produced a bounty of work on the specific mechanisms through which children are thought to regulate their emotions and behavior. Although various operational definitions have been put forth for this concept (Eisenberg, 2002), most researchers have agreed that it encompasses physiological, cognitive, and behavioral processes that allow individuals to modulate how they experience and express positive and negative emotions.

The main mechanism through which emotion regulation is thought to occur is effortful control or "the ability to inhibit a dominant response to perform a subdominant response" (Rothbart & Bates, 1998, p. 137). This includes two processes, the first of which is attentional control, or the ability to shift and focus attention as need be. Research has shown that children exhibit less distress when they are able to shift their focus away from distressing stimuli and toward nondistressing stimuli (Rothbart, Posner, & Boylan, 1990). Attentional processes can also be used to redirect attention internally by thinking positive thoughts or distracting oneself when faced with a distressing situation, such as when a child focuses on his or her caregiver when approached by a frightening costumed character or when meeting someone new. The second process of effortful control is inhibitory control, or the ability to suppress inappropriate responses. This includes the ability to inhibit aggressive responses when in anger-provoking situations or inhibit avoidant responses when in anxiety-arousing situations, such as when a child answers the question asked of him by the teacher, even though he is anxious that the other children in the class might laugh at him.

In addition to these inhibitory functions, Thompson (1994) emphasized that emotion regulation also involves the ability to enhance and maintain emotion when needed, such as when children increase their anger to confront bullies or to become courageous in fear-producing situations. This also occurs with positive emotions, such as when children recall pleasant experiences to feel increased levels of positive arousal. When children successfully master these processes, they are better able to keep their emotions in check and respond appropriately in interpersonal contexts, demonstrate flexibility in these situations, and resolve conflicts. Such interpersonal skills then lead to more successful interpersonal relationships.

The third process by which children develop interpersonally occurs through the socialization of emotion. Emotion socialization occurs via parental practices and behaviors that influence how a child experiences, expresses, and regulates emotion and emotion-related behaviors (Eisenberg, Losoya, et al., 2001). This process is closely linked to the second process of emotion regulation discussed earlier inasmuch as children often regulate their emotions, at least early in life, via external influences, most often through the efforts of their parents. The interpersonal relationship between parent and child is important in this regard because children learn from their parents how to behave competently in social contexts (Thompson, 1994). Emotion socialization has been shown to occur primarily as a result of processes engaged in by others, such as selective reinforcement and modeling of emotional expressions. Other indirect processes of socialization include social referencing and creating an overall "safe" affective environment, and direct processes include coaching and teaching, discussing emotions, and establishing contingencies for emotional behavior (Klimes-Dougan & Zeman, 2007). These indirect and direct approaches can be thought of in terms of a tripartite model in which children's socialization of emotions are affected by parents as interactive partners, direct instructors, and providers of opportunity (Parke, Orstein, Rieser, & Zahn-Waxler, 1994).

The emotional competence skills that emerge in children via emotion regulation and socialization have been linked to social competence with peers. Some examples of this include research showing that when parents comfort their children during times of negative emotion, children tend to exhibit more constructive anger reactions with their peers (Eisenberg & Fabes, 1994). Children are also more aware and understanding of the emotions of others when their parents willingly discuss emotions with them. Moreover, when fathers comfort and accept emotional distress in their children, the children tend to have more positive peer relationships (Roberts, 1994).

In regard to the fourth process, peer relationships, middle childhood represents a dramatic change in children's social context because interactions with peers increase and take on greater significance. Peer relationships in middle childhood are characterized by particular behaviors, thoughts, and emotions. For example, Eisenberg and Fabes (1998) reported that positive social behaviors such as generosity, helpfulness, or cooperation increase during this time period. Children's understanding of friendships also changes during middle childhood. Children begin to develop a sense of continuity and reciprocity in their choice of friends. Perspective-taking abilities become salient in that children begin to appreciate the thoughts and feelings of others (Selman & Schultz, 1990).

From a developmental perspective, one of the most important tasks of middle childhood is to learn acceptable ways of interacting with one's peers. Although interpersonal abilities and skills accrued from a secure attachment relationship and healthy parental socialization of emotions affect this learning, the majority of this learning occurs within the context of peer groups. As such, interactions with peers are thought to play an important role in children's interpersonal, social, and cognitive development. Certain social skills are necessary for children to form successful peer relationships (Rubin et al., 1998). These social skills include, but are not limited to, the ability to (a) understand the thoughts and feelings of others; (b) begin, maintain, and end interactions in a positive way; (c) appropriately express emotions and behaviors; and (d) inhibit behaviors that might be construed as negative by others. Peer acceptance is thought to be, in part, a function of these social skills. Concerns about peer acceptance take on a significant role during this time period. More important, peer acceptance is a significant predictor of short- and long-term adjustment. Hence, normative interpersonal development consists of children possessing the social skills that enable them to form peer relationships and subsequently be accepted by their peers.

INTERPERSONAL PROCESSES LEADING TO THE DEVELOPMENT OF CHILDHOOD ANXIETY DISORDERS

Thus far, we have focused on normative interpersonal development. This discourse begs the question of what then constitutes nonnormative interpersonal development. In other words, what happens when these developmental processes go awry? One possible answer is that the risk of developing psychopathology is heightened in children who do not evidence normative interpersonal functioning. Support for this contention has been shown in the area of childhood depression. Interpersonal characteristics such as insecure attachment, increased impulsivity and submissiveness, poor emotion regulation, decreased assertiveness, negative self-perceptions, and lower rates of peer acceptance have all emerged as salient components of the depressive experience in children (e.g., Hammen & Goodman-Brown, 1990). Given the demonstrated link between interpersonal development and childhood depression, our purpose in this part of the chapter is to extend this thinking to childhood anxiety. Specifically, we now examine the applicability of these concepts to childhood anxiety from an interpersonal development perspective. We first review temperament, specifically behavioral inhibition, because this is postulated to be an innate biological characteristic that affects all later interpersonal relationships. Second, we discuss the proposed interpersonal processes of attachment, emotion regulation and parental socialization of emotions, and peer relationships; in doing so, we emphasize the role they play in the onset of childhood anxiety. Last, we discuss the role of parenting behaviors and operant conditioning because these processes influence the development of childhood anxiety disorders not only directly but also indirectly via interactions with aspects of normative interpersonal development to increase risk for these disorders.

Temperament

Temperament has been defined as "constitutionally based individual differences in reactivity and self-regulation, influenced over time by heredity, maturation, and experience" (Rothbart & Ahadi, 1994, p. 55). The most widely researched temperamental characteristic linked to anxiety problems is behavioral inhibition. *Behavioral inhibition* is defined as an overt representation of a psychological and physiological state of uncertainty that results from exposure to unfamiliar objects, people, and stressful situations (Kagan, 1994). It is often described as the tendency to restrict exploration and avoid novelty and is characterized by withdrawal, clinging or dependence on parents, fearfulness, timidity, shyness, and emotional restraint behaviors when exposed to unfamiliar stimuli (Kagan, Reznick, & Gibbons, 1989). Behavioral inhibition is also characterized by several physiological reactions, such as increases in heart rate, blood pressure, muscle tension, and levels of secreted cortisol (Kagan et al., 1989). The combination of behavioral responses characterized by withdrawal and avoidance and physiological responses characterized by increased sympathetic arousal is similar to what is seen in the anxiety disorders (Ollendick et al., 2002).

Empirical research has highlighted the importance of behavioral inhibition as a risk factor in the emergence of anxiety disorders. For example,

Biederman et al. (1990) examined inhibited and uninhibited infants from two studies by Kagan, Reznick, and Snidman (1987, 1988) when the infants were 7 to 8 years of age. Results indicated that inhibited children were higher in rates of specific anxiety disorders than were uninhibited children (i.e., separation anxiety disorder, 9.1% vs. 5.3%; social phobia, 31.8% vs. 5.3%). Similarly, Hirshfeld et al. (1992) reported that children with behavioral inhibition had significantly higher rates of other anxiety disorders than uninhibited children, including the tendency to have more than one anxiety disorder. In these studies, behaviorally inhibited children tended to display fears related primarily to interpersonal situations, including speaking in front of the class, being around strangers, and going into crowded situations or places. Inasmuch as behavioral inhibition is characterized by withdrawal, dependence on parents, fearfulness, and shyness when exposed to unfamiliar people, the tendency to exhibit these interpersonal reactions may be a risk factor for other childhood anxiety disorders as well. Consistent with this speculation, the presence of behavioral inhibition during childhood has been found to predict adolescent anxiety disorders more broadly as well (Dumas, LaFreniere, & Serketich, 1995).

Attachment

As noted earlier, Bowlby (1987) theorized that early interpersonal experiences within the parent–child attachment relationship play an important role in interpersonal experiences in adolescence and adulthood. Furthermore, others have demonstrated that attachment style predicts later psychopathology (Mason, Platts, & Tyson, 2005). Given this, attachment theory provides a framework for conceptualizing the influence of interpersonal relationships on the development and course of childhood anxiety (Manassis & Bradley, 1994). The model by Manassis and Bradley (1994), for example, posits that insecure attachments provide an environmental context that influences, promotes, and reinforces the development and maintenance of trait anxiety over time. Consistent with this model, child insecure attachment has been found to be a risk factor for the development of anxiety disorders in children (Manassis, Bradley, Goldberg, Hood, & Swinson, 1994; Warren, Huston, Egeland, & Sroufe, 1997).

Attachment theory posits that insecure attachments convey the message to children that caregivers are unreliable, unavailable, untrustworthy, and largely uncommunicative. Children who receive these types of messages can develop a maladaptive approach to future interpersonal situations or relationships on the basis of the expectation that their needs will not be met by others, causing either low interpersonal contact and avoidance behaviors or high interpersonal contact and demanding behaviors. These behaviors elicit negative reactions from others, which serve to strengthen the distorted beliefs that these insecure children have. This distorted view can be expressed in maladaptive forms of coping and avoidance behaviors creating a chronic and persistent state of anxiety within children, thus placing them at higher risk of the development of anxiety disorders (Manassis & Bradley, 1994).

Research has supported insecure attachment as a risk factor in the development of anxiety. For example, Warren et al. (1997) examined 172 insecurely attached children at age 12 months and found that they were more likely than securely attached children to have an anxiety disorder at age 17 years. Manassis et al. (1994) examined attachment patterns in clinically anxious mothers and their children and found that infants of anxious mothers not only displayed insecure attachments but also evidenced higher rates of subsequent anxiety disorders. In yet another study, Manassis, Bradley, Goldberg, Hood, and Swinson (1995) found that insecurely attached children experienced higher levels of anxiety than securely attached children. In addition, Muris and Meesters (2002) demonstrated that insecure attachment independently and uniquely predicted child anxiety as reported by parents and children.

Emotion Regulation and Parental Socialization of Emotions

Children's ability to learn how to modulate, maintain, and enhance emotion increases the chances of successful social interactions. Recent work has suggested that children with anxiety disorders have inherent difficulty with this important developmental process, most notably in the areas of interpreting emotionally arousing events and regulating attentional processes (Thompson, 2001). Typically developing children can ordinarily manage their emotional arousal by reinterpreting or reframing situations that evoke emotion. Examples of this include recasting frightening accounts in more calming terms, such as "it's just a story" and "there is nothing to be really afraid of" when watching a scary movie. Parents play an important role in this arena as well, such as when they calm a child before a dental visit by saying it will simply be "tooth tickling" or by giving support and encouragement when a shy child meets a new neighbor (Miller & Green, 1985). However, children with anxiety disorders are different in that their interpretations of the world tend to be biased toward threat and impending doom, even when situations are benign and relatively innocuous. They see a world that is more threatening than do nonanxious children, such as when children with separation anxiety disorder fear being kidnapped or worry excessively that their parents are going to be harmed. This persistent focus on negative outcomes makes it difficult for these children to reinterpret events in less threatening ways. This is especially true if parents are overprotective or overcontrolling and do not encourage alternative and more healthy interpretations in their children. The more they and their children avoid the feared situations, the less likely they are to come to see them in more realistic and "safe" ways.

In the area of attentional processes, attentional control may reduce internalizing problems by facilitating children's ability to shift attention away from distressing thoughts, events, and objects and thus modulate the level of negative emotional arousal (Hannesdottir & Ollendick, 2007). For example, if children can tolerate delayed rewards by directing their attention away from the desired object and distracting themselves with another activity, less anxiety will likely occur. Parents again act as socialization agents in this regard by distracting children during upsetting events, limiting their child's awareness of distressing information, or focusing their child's attention on the positive aspects of difficult situations. When children are not properly socialized to these modulating processes of emotional control, they appear to be at an increased risk of developing anxiety disorders. As shown by Lemery, Essex, and Smider (2002), low attention focusing is linked to higher levels of anxiety and fearfulness in children. Furthermore, children who develop internalizing behavior problems may grant attention to many minor stressors at one time and have difficulty shifting attention away from these arousing stimuli. As such, children's inability to shift attention away from minor stressors and distress in general may increase emotional arousal. Persistently high levels of fearful or sad emotional arousal may then lead to childhood internalizing problems. Examples of this include clinically anxious children who selectively shift their attention toward threat-relevant cues and test-anxious children who engage in negative self-talk and are overly concerned with their performance, resulting in increased arousal and interference with test performance (Vasey, Daleiden, Williams, & Brown, 1995). Because of the tendency of these children to have difficulty disengaging from threatening stimuli, it is more difficult for them to regulate their emotions, which can then have a negative impact on their interpersonal relationships.

Peer Relationships

The ability to form peer relationships is also viewed as an important interpersonal process associated with the anxiety disorders. Two characteristics apply. The first characteristic is the outlook children have about future interpersonal relationships, which is based largely on the parent–child attachment relationship (McDowell & Parke, 2009). The second characteristic is the child's temperament and how it elicits or occasions certain behaviors from others. Both the parent–child attachment relationship and the child's temperament, especially behavioral inhibition, directly and indirectly affect the formation of peer relationships (Ollendick & Hirshfeld-Becker, 2002) and subsequent anxiety disorders (Ollendick, 1998).

The optimal outcome in forming good peer relationships is for children to feel that they are accepted and valued by their peers. However, the opposite of being accepted and valued by one's peers is being rejected by them. When children are rejected by their peers, anxiety may develop. Rubin et al. (1998) described this pathway well. Beginning with behavioral inhibition, the pathway to social wariness, withdrawal, and rejection unfolds. Parents dealing with behaviorally inhibited children may have the tendency to become insensitive and unresponsive because of the high frequency of these behaviors and because their attempts to soothe or comfort their child have failed (Rubin, Both, Zahn-Waxler, Cummings, & Wilkinson, 1991). Subsequently, the interaction of the child's behaviors and the parent's behaviors toward the child result in the solidification of an insecure parent–child attachment. It is thought to be this sequence of events that hinders a child's ability to form subsequent good peer relationships.

How does not being able to form peer relationships result in the development of an anxiety disorder? Insecurely attached children are thought to be afraid of rejection; therefore, these children withdraw from their peers in anticipation of avoiding rejection. This social withdrawal, in turn, results in children not being able to establish normal social relationships, thereby decreasing their chances of being exposed to normative social behaviors (Rubin et al., 1998). This results in children having increased anxiety when placed in settings with peers, which then results in higher levels of withdrawal in these settings. As children progress through middle childhood, their withdrawal behaviors become increasingly recognized by peer groups (Younger & Boyko, 1987), which then serves to increase anxiety in the already anxious and withdrawn child (Verduin & Kendall, 2008). Thus, the ability to form good peer relationships can have a dramatic effect on the development of anxiety in middle childhood.

Parental Behaviors

Certain parenting behaviors provide an environmental context that contributes to the development of anxiety disorders in children over time (see Wood, McLeod, Sigman, Hwang, & Chu, 2003). In a meta-analysis of the anxiety and parenting literature, Wood et al. (2003) identified four main parenting behaviors associated with the development of anxiety: (a) psychological control, (b) overprotectiveness, (c) rejection–criticism, and (d) modeling or reinforcing anxious or avoidant behaviors. Interestingly, research has shown that both anxious mothers and mothers with anxious children (although these mothers might not be anxious themselves) display these parenting characteristics during interactions with their children, whereas nonanxious mothers or mothers with nonanxious children do not display these characteristics (Whaley, Pinto, & Sigman, 1999).

First, *psychological control* is defined as intrusive behaviors that inhibit psychological autonomy granting, induce guilt, instill anxiety, and withdraw love (Barber & Harmon, 2001). Dumas et al. (1995) found that psychological control was associated with higher levels of anxiety in children, and Siqueland, Kendall, and Steinberg (1996) demonstrated that mothers of children with anxiety disorders were more psychologically controlling than mothers of nonanxious children. Other studies examining children's reports of psychological control have found significant associations between perceived parental psychological control and anxiety in both children and adolescents (Costa & Weems, 2005). Finally, Whaley et al. (1999) showed that anxious mothers were more psychologically controlling and that anxious mothers with anxious children were the most psychologically controlling of all.

Second, parental overprotection consists of parental behaviors that are overly restrictive and protective of a child's behaviors and activities, resulting in the child developing less autonomy. In two separate studies, Dadds and Barrett (1996) and Hudson and Rapee (2002) found that mothers with anxious children demonstrated higher levels of domineering and overprotective parenting behaviors. Perceived ratings of behavioral control by children and adolescents have also been shown to be related to high levels of anxiety (Costa & Weems, 2006; Ollendick & Horsch, 2007). Both Whaley et al. (1999) and Moore, Whaley, and Sigman (2004) demonstrated that anxious mothers with anxious children displayed the highest level of maternal behavioral control as compared with anxious mothers with nonanxious children or control mothers and children.

Third, rejection–criticism is characterized by disapproving, judgmental, and dismissive parenting behaviors. It has been hypothesized that parents who criticize and minimize their children's feelings do not promote children's emotion regulation (Wood et al., 2003). Specifically, rejection and criticism do not afford children the opportunity to learn, through trial and error, how to deal with and tolerate negative affect, thereby increasing children's sensitivity to anxiety. Overall, research has shown that higher rates of rejection and criticism are related to higher levels of anxiety in children (Dumas et al. 1995; Silverman & Ginsburg, 1998). Furthermore, research on anxious mothers has demonstrated that they exhibit less warmth and positivity than control mothers with nonanxious children (Whaley et al., 1999).

These parenting behaviors are thought to enhance children's anxiety by (a) increasing the likelihood that children will cognitively interpret these behaviors as a signal that a particular situation is threatening or dangerous, (b) preventing children from facing fear-provoking events and seeing that their fear is either ultimately unfounded or that their fear does not result in the catastrophic consequence they expect, and (c) hindering children's ability to develop effective solutions to face fear (Rapee, 1997).

The last way that parenting behaviors can increase the risk of children developing anxiety disorders is through the modeling and reinforcement of anxious or avoidant behaviors. The modeling of anxiety by parents occurs when parents actively exhibit avoidance and anxious behaviors in front of their child, who is then seemingly reinforced by these behaviors (Barrett, Rapee, Dadds, & Ryan, 1996). Furthermore, one of the main reasons why children's fears persist in these circumstances is that they have limited opportunity to habituate to feared stimuli because their parents frequently fear the same stimuli and shield their children from them (Menzies & Harris, 2001). The reinforcement of anxiety is thought to occur by parents paying attention to, agreeing with, tolerating, and reciprocating avoidant behaviors exhibited by their children (Barrett, Rapee, et al., 1996). When parents continually allow and encourage their child to avoid and escape from the situations he or she fears, that fear gets reinforced. It is the reduction in anxiety that occurs on escape from the situation that powerfully reinforces the avoidance behavior. The opposite approach of having the child face what he or she fears introduces anxiety in the short term, but it also is likely to reduce anxiety in the long term by allowing the child to be exposed to the situation. This reduction in anxiety resulting from exposure is thought to be a result of realizing that the fear or the cognitive error associated with that fear is unwarranted.

Last, a pathway to the maintenance of anxiety occurs when avoidance prevents mastery of normal developmental processes (Ollendick, Vasey, & King, 2001). Because anxious children tend to avoid a number of social and interpersonal contexts, they tend to show less competence in these areas. Accordingly, research has shown that anxiety is associated with deficits in social behavior (Vernberg, Abwender, Ewell, & Beery, 1992). One such demonstrated pathway to this social incompetence can be seen in the case of anxious withdrawal. Rubin (1993), for example, showed that by middle to late childhood, social anxiety and withdrawal led to peer rejection and unpopularity. The rejection and social failure experienced by these children was hypothesized to at least partially be accounted for by their lack of practice in social situations because of their anxiety and withdrawal, resulting in social skills deficits.

ROLE OF INTERPERSONAL PROCESSES IN THE TREATMENT OF ANXIETY DISORDERS IN CHILDREN

Thus far, we have focused on delineating the processes of normative interpersonal development and demonstrating how these interpersonal factors may be related to the onset and maintenance of anxiety disorders in children. We now turn our attention to the role that interpersonal processes play in the treatment of childhood anxiety disorders. We should note from the outset, however, that most interventions have not attended to these interpersonal processes and that treatments have largely conceptualized and treated the anxiety disorders as intrapersonal and not interpersonal in scope (Woody & Ollendick, 2006). That is, most interventions have viewed the anxiety disorder as being "in" the child, with little attention paid to the interpersonal context in which the anxiety is embedded.

Although various interventions have been used to treat childhood anxiety disorders, only cognitive–behavioral therapy (CBT) has been recognized as an efficacious treatment (Ollendick, King, & Chorpita, 2006; Silverman, Pina, & Viswesvaran, 2008; Walkup et al., 2008). CBT is a psychosocial intervention that variably includes relaxation and anxiety management strategies, in vivo exposure, participant modeling, reinforcement, cognitive restructuring, social skills and problem-solving training, and homework. Recently, In-Albon and Schneider (2006) identified 24 randomized clinical trials (RCTs) examining the treatment of anxious children, and all used a variant of CBT (e.g., individual–group, child–family). The vast majority of these trials examined the effects of CBT delivered individually to children between 7 and 14 years of age; both boys and girls were treated, and the average age across studies was approximately 10 years of age. The children treated in these interventions presented with various anxiety disorders (e.g., social anxiety disorder, overanxious disorder–generalized anxiety disorder, social phobia–avoidant disorder). Parents and peers were minimally involved in these studies. Overall, about 67% of the treated children were diagnosis free at posttreatment, compared with fewer than 10% of those in wait-list control conditions. Maintenance of treatment gains was evidenced at 1-, 3-, and 7-year follow-ups (Kendall, 1994; Kendall et al., 1997; Kendall, Safford, Flannery-Schroeder, & Webb, 2004; Kendall & Southam-Gerow, 1996).

Group CBT has also been found to be highly effective in treating anxious children (Barrett, 1998; Flannery-Schroeder & Kendall, 2000; Manassis et al., 2002; Silverman, Kurtines, Ginsburg, Weems, Lumpkin, & Carmichael, 1999), with improvement rates comparable with those found with individual CBT at posttreatment (e.g., 64%–69% vs. 6%–25% for those in wait-list control conditions) and follow-up at 3 to 12 months. In general, no differences have been found between individual and group CBT treatments for anxious children (Flannery-Schroeder & Kendall, 2000; Manassis et al., 2002). These findings are somewhat surprising given the potential utility of peers as socialization agents for children and the opportunity for the treated children to acquire and use appropriate social and emotion regulation skills in the group context.

In addition to these studies, a number of other studies have shown that individual or group CBT supplemented with family or parent anxiety management strategies, or both, also produces greater outcomes than those observed in wait-list control conditions. Silverman, Kurtines, Ginsburg, Weems, Rabian, and Serafini (1999), for example, showed that group CBT supplemented with parent–child contingency management procedures produced outcomes superior to wait-list control conditions for 6- to 16-year-old children (mean age = 9. 8) with an anxiety disorder. Moreover, other studies have shown that family-enhanced CBT might produce even greater outcomes than those obtained with individual or group CBT alone (Barrett, Dadds, & Rapee, 1996; Cobham, Dadds, & Spence, 1998; Shortt, Barrett, & Fox, 2001), at least with younger children and children whose parents also have an anxiety disorder. To illustrate, Barrett, Dadds, and Rapee (1996) showed that a parent-augmented treatment produced greater outcomes at posttreatment (84%) and 1-year follow-up (95%) than did individual CBT (57% at post-treatment and 70% at 1-year follow-up). Notably, the enhanced effects of this treatment were observed only for children between 7 and 11 years of age and not for early adolescents between 12 and 14 years of age. For the young adolescents, no differences between individual and parent-augmented interventions were observed.

Similarly, Cobham et al. (1998) compared individual CBT with parent-enhanced CBT with anxious children between 7 and 14 years of age (mean age = 9.6 years) whose parents were either high or low in trait anxiety. They reported differences at both posttreatment (77% vs. 39%) and at 6-month follow-up (88% vs. 44%) in favor of the parent-enhanced intervention. However, these effects were observed only for children whose parents were high in trait anxiety; for those whose parents were low in trait anxiety, no differences were detected. Finally, in a more recent study, Wood, Piacentini, Southam-Gerow, Chu, and Sigman (2006) showed that family-focused CBT produced outcomes superior to individual CBT with 6- to 13-year-old children (mean age = 9.8 years) who had an anxiety disorder. In this study, in contrast to earlier studies that focused on training parents to help their anxious child deal with anxiety in a more adaptive manner, individual CBT was supplemented with an intervention focused on parenting practices found to be directly related to the development and maintenance of childhood anxiety disorders; namely, parental intrusiveness and failure to grant autonomy to their children. In the enhanced group, 79% were diagnosis free at posttreatment compared with 53% in the individual CBT group.

However, other studies have found no differences between parent- or family-enhanced treatments. Spence, Donovan, and Brechman-Toussaint (2000), for example, assigned 7- to 14-year-old children (mean age = 10.6 years) with social phobia to individual CBT, individual CBT supplemented with parent involvement, or a wait-list control condition. In this study, parents were taught specific coping skills to assist their children with exposure exercises and constructive ways to reinforce and encourage social behavior in their children. Although both active treatments were superior to the wait-list control condition, no differences were observed between the two treatment groups. More recently, Nauta, Scholing, Emmelkamp, and Minderaa (2003) reported similar findings with children who were diagnosed primarily with generalized anxiety disorder and separation anxiety disorder, as did Kendall, Hudson, Gosch, Flannery-Schroeder, and Suveg (2008). We should note, however, that these latter studies did not use the procedures recommended by Wood et al. (2006), which targeted parental intrusiveness and failure to grant autonomy to their children.

Taken together, this emerging body of literature suggests that parents and families may have an impact on treatment outcome for children as we would expect on the basis of an interpersonal perspective of childhood anxiety disorders. This is not surprising inasmuch as research has supported the role of parents and families as interpersonal agents and contexts in which childhood anxiety disorders develop and flourish. Although some studies did not support the inclusion of parents and families, it may be the case that the parent-enhanced and family-enhanced strategies used in these studies were simply not the "right" ones and were not powerful enough to produce the anticipated effects. Still, as Barmish and Kendall (2005) asserted, "Alluring as it might be to include parents as co-clients for multiple theoretical reasons, the belief cannot be mistaken as evidence" (p. 578). They went on to recommend that "additional comparative research is needed and that the acceptance of either approach as superior is not yet justified" (p. 579). Although we agree, we maintain that if the programs involve the parents and families as facilitators of emotion regulation and emotion socialization, beneficial effects might more likely be obtained.

In addition to parent or family involvement, two RCTs have directly examined the role of peer involvement in the treatment of children with an anxiety disorder. From an interpersonal perspective, we might expect that treatments involving peers would be particularly effective. The first study examined the effects of peer involvement (along with parent involvement) in the treatment of children with a variety of anxiety disorders (generalized anxiety disorder, separation anxiety disorder, social phobia), whereas the second explored the use of peers in the treatment of socially phobic children, without parental involvement. Shortt et al. (2001) evaluated the efficacy of the FRIENDS program, a family and peer-group CBT intervention for anxious children. In addition to the standard individual CBT elements of intervention, the FRIENDS program instructs parents to reward children for coping with their fears and worries and encourages children to be their own friend and reward themselves when they try hard; to make friends so that they can build their social support network; and to talk to their friends when they are

in difficult or worrying situations. The group format encourages the development of parent support groups and provides considerable peer interchanges
to practice what has been learned in treatment. In addition, systematic homework assignments with peers in the community are designed to reinforce
social interaction skills acquired in the groups. In this study, 6- to 10-year-old
children and their parents were randomly assigned to the FRIENDS condition
or a waiting-list control condition. At posttreatment, 69% of children in the
FRIENDS condition were diagnosis free compared with 6% in the wait-list
control condition. Quite obviously, this program shows considerable promise;
however, at this time, it is unclear what components of the program are critical ones inasmuch as similar diagnostic outcomes have been achieved with
individual CBT, group CBT, and individual or group CBT when augmented
with parent or family involvement. The unique feature of this intervention—
the role of peers and the training and reinforcement of friendship skills—
needs to be evaluated systematically. Moreover, the effects of the program in
improving interpersonal skills and in producing changes in sociometric networks and friendship patterns have yet to be demonstrated.

In the second major RCT involving peers, Beidel and her colleagues
evaluated the efficacy of social effectiveness therapy for children (SET-C)
with 8- to 12-year-old children with social phobia (Beidel, Turner, & Morris,
2000). On the basis of considerable evidence that children with social phobia tend to have few friends, have limited involvement in outside activities,
and lack important interpersonal and social skills (Beidel, Turner, & Morris,
1999; Ollendick & Hirshfeld-Becker, 2002), this 12-week intervention consists primarily of group social skills intervention (90 minutes), peer generalization activities (90 minutes), and individualized in vivo exposure exercises
(60 to 90 minutes). As is evident, each weekly session lasts about 3 hours,
considerably longer than the other interventions described earlier (all consisting of 8 to 16 one-hour therapy sessions). Of importance, the intervention
was designed to address the children's interpersonal and social skill deficits
and their anxiety about social engagement. SET-C was compared with an
active intervention designed to address test anxiety (Testbusters), a phenomenon frequently observed in socially phobic children. At posttreatment, children in the SET-C condition demonstrated enhanced social skills, reduced
social anxiety, and increased overall social functioning; moreover, 67% no
longer met diagnostic criteria for social phobia compared with 5% of children
in the Testbusters control condition. At 3-year follow-up, 72% continued to
be free of a social phobia diagnosis (Beidel, Turner, Young, & Paulson, 2005),
and at a 5-year follow-up, 81% were diagnosis free (Beidel, Turner, & Young,
2006). Of additional importance, at the time of this 5-year follow-up, the children were mid-adolescents (13- to 17-year-olds), the most common age of onset
for social phobia and, because of the increased focus on peer relationships

during this developmental period, an age at which relapse might likely occur. However, only one adolescent who was diagnosis free at follow-up relapsed at the 5-year follow-up. Inasmuch as social phobia tends not to remit without intervention, especially when onset is before age 11, these findings are particularly encouraging.

In contrast to CBT interventions (whether delivered in an individual or a group format, and with or without parent–family or peer components), other interventions have fared less well or not been investigated at all. For example, given the salutatory effects of attachment-based and interpersonal psychotherapies with depressed children and adolescents (Diamond, Reiss, Diamond, Siqueland, & Isaacs, 2002; Mufson, Moreau, Weissman, & Klerman, 1993), and the proposed role that attachment and interpersonal processes have in the development and expression of the anxiety disorders, it is surprising that these interventions have not been investigated to date. Moreover, although uncontrolled clinical trials (cf. Muratori, Picchi, Bruni, Patarnello, & Romagnoli, 2003) and retrospective chart reviews (cf. Target & Fonagy, 1994) illustrate the potential efficacy of psychodynamic-based psychotherapy, firm support is lacking for it, and no RCT trials have been reported. In its most recent statement on practice parameters for the childhood anxiety disorders, the American Academy of Child and Adolescent Psychiatry (2007) indicated that "there is limited research on efficacy and effectiveness of psychodynamic psychotherapy alone, or in combined treatments, or compared with other modalities" (p. 274). Similarly, there is little to no support for other commonly practiced interventions such as play therapy or family therapy (Ollendick et al., 2006). In its practice parameters statement, the American Academy of Child and Adolescent Psychiatry did not include play therapy, attachment-based psychotherapy, or interpersonal psychotherapy in its recommendation of potentially useful interventions and commented on family therapy only as an adjunctive aid to CBT. Thus, considerably more research is needed before interventions other than CBT can be recommended.

CONCLUSIONS

The study of interpersonal relationships and the childhood anxiety disorders is clearly in its own stage of infancy. Although important interpersonal factors such as attachment, temperament, emotion regulation, parental socialization of emotion, and peer relationships have been identified and associated with the development and expression of anxiety disorders in childhood, they have been largely ignored in the development of treatment interventions with few notable exceptions (for the effects of parenting, see Wood & McLeod, 2008; for the effects of emotion regulation, see Hannesdottir & Ollendick,

2007; for the effects of peers, see Beidel et al., 2000). Moreover, even when such factors are included, it is not at all clear that they alone result in significant change or that they enhance treatment outcomes above and beyond those found in standard CBT trials. Still, it is evident that anxiety does not exist solely in the child and that interpersonal factors need to be examined in RCT trials. In addition, systematic dismantling trials that isolate the individual and synergistic effects of these components are needed. Thus, much work remains to be done, both in the conceptualization of meaningful interpersonal processes and in the elucidation of their role in the treatment of children with anxiety disorders. Nonetheless, they show considerable promise and represent the next generation of studies that might well eventuate in even more successful outcomes for children with anxiety disorders and their families.

REFERENCES

American Academy of Child and Adolescent Psychiatry. (2007). Practice parameter of the assessment and treatment of children and adolescents with anxiety disorders. *Journal of the American Academy of Child and Adolescent Psychiatry, 46,* 267–282.

American Psychiatric Association. (1994). *Diagnostic and statistical manual of mental disorders* (4th ed.). Washington, DC: Author.

Barber, B. K., & Harmon, E. L. (2001). Violating the self: Parental psychological control of children and adolescents. In B. K. Barber (Ed.), *Intrusive parenting: How psychological control affects children and adolescents* (pp. 125–159). Washington, DC: American Psychological Association.

Barmish, A. J., & Kendall, P. C. (2005). Should parents be co-clients in cognitive behavior therapy for anxious youth? *Journal of Clinical Child and Adolescent Psychology, 34,* 569–581.

Barrett, P. M. (1998). Evaluation of cognitive-behavioral group treatments for childhood anxiety disorders. *Journal of Clinical Child Psychology, 27,* 459–468.

Barrett, P. M., Dadds, M. R., & Rapee, R. M. (1996). Family treatment of childhood anxiety: A controlled trial. *Journal of Consulting and Clinical Psychology, 64,* 333–342.

Barrett, P. M., Rapee, R. M., Dadds, M. M., & Ryan, S. M. (1996). Family enhancement of cognitive style in anxious and aggressive children: Threat bias and the FEAR effect. *Journal of Abnormal Child Psychology, 24,* 187–203.

Beidel, D. C., Turner, S. M., & Morris, T. L. (1999). Psychopathology of childhood social phobia. *Journal of the American Academy of Child & Adolescent Psychiatry, 38,* 643–650.

Beidel, D. C., Turner, S. M., & Morris, T. L. (2000). Behavioral treatment of childhood social phobia. *Journal of Consulting and Clinical Psychology, 68,* 1072–1080.

Beidel, D. C., Turner, S. M., & Young, B. J. (2006). Social effectiveness therapy for children: Five years later. *Behavior Therapy, 37,* 416–425.

Beidel, D. C., Turner, S. M., Young, B. J., & Paulson, A. (2005). Social effectiveness therapy for children: Three-year follow-up. *Journal of Consulting and Clinical Psychology, 73,* 721–725.

Biederman, J., Rosenbaum, J. E., Hirshfeld, D. N., Faraone, S. V., Bolduc, G., Gersten, M., . . . Reznick, J. S. (1990). Psychiatric correlates of behavioral inhibition in young children of parents with and without psychiatric disorders. *Archives of General Psychiatry, 47,* 21–26.

Bowlby, J. (1973). *Attachment and loss: Volume 2. Separation anxiety and anger.* New York, NY: Basic Books.

Bowlby, J. (1987). *Attachment and the therapeutic process.* Madison, CT: International Universities Press.

Cobham, V. E., Dadds, M. R., & Spence, S. H. (1998). The role of parental anxiety in the treatment of childhood anxiety. *Journal of Consulting and Clinical Psychology, 66,* 893–905.

Costa, N. M., & Weems, C. F. (2005). Maternal and child anxiety: Do attachment beliefs or children's perceptions of maternal control mediate their association? *Social Development, 14,* 574–590.

Dadds, M. R., & Barrett, P. M. (1996). Family processes in child and adolescent anxiety and depression. *Behaviour Change, 13,* 231–239.

Diamond, G. S., Reiss, B., Diamond, G. M., Siqueland, L., & Isaacs, L. (2002). Attachment-based family therapy for depressed adolescents: A treatment development study. *Journal of the American Academy of Child & Adolescent Psychiatry, 41,* 1190–1196.

Dumas, J. E., LaFreniere, P. J., & Serketich, W. J. (1995). "Balance of power": A transactional analysis of control in mother–child dyads involving socially competent, aggressive, and anxious children. *Journal of Abnormal Psychology, 104,* 104–113.

Eisenberg, N. (2002). Emotion-related regulation and its relation to quality of social functioning. In W. W. Hartup & R. A. Weinberg (Eds.), *Minnesota Symposia on Child Psychology: Vol. 32. Child psychology in retrospect and prospect: In celebration of the 75th anniversary of the Institute of Child Development* (pp. 133–171). Mahwah, NJ: Erlbaum.

Eisenberg, N., & Fabes, R. A. (1994). Emotion regulation and the development of social competence. In M. Clark (Ed.), *Review of personality and social psychology* (pp. 119–150). Newbury Park, CA: Sage.

Eisenberg, N., & Fabes, R. A. (1998). Prosocial development. In W. Damon & N. Eisenberg (Eds.), *Handbook of child psychology: Social, emotional, and personality development* (5th ed., Vol. 3, pp. 701–778). New York, NY: Wiley.

Eisenberg, N., Losoya, S., Fabes, R., Guthrie, I., Reiser, M., Murphy, B., . . . Padgett, S. J. (2001). Parental socialization of children's dysregulated expression of emotion and externalizing problems. *Journal of Family Psychology, 15,* 183–205.

Flannery-Schroeder, E. C., & Kendall, P. C. (2000). Group and individual cognitive-behavioral treatments for youth with anxiety disorders: A randomized clinical trial. *Cognitive Therapy and Research, 24,* 251–278.

Hammen, C., & Goodman-Brown, T. (1990). Self-schemas and vulnerability to specific life stress in children at risk for depression. *Cognitive Therapy and Research, 14,* 215–227.

Hannesdottir, D. K., & Ollendick, T. H. (2007). The role of emotion regulation in the treatment of child anxiety disorders. *Clinical Child and Family Psychology Review, 10,* 275–293.

Hirshfeld, D. R., Rosenbaum, J. F., Biederman, J., Bolduc, E. A., Faraone, S. V., Snidman, N., . . . Kagan, J. (1992). Stable behavioral inhibition and its association with anxiety disorder. *Journal of the American Academy of Child & Adolescent Psychiatry, 31,* 103–111.

Hudson, J., & Rapee, R. (2002). Parent-child interactions in clinically anxious children and their siblings. *Journal of Clinical Child and Adolescent Psychology, 31,* 548–555.

In-Albon, T., & Schneider, S. (2006). Psychotherapy of childhood anxiety disorders: A meta-analysis. *Psychotherapy and Psychosomatics, 14,* 1–10.

Kagan, J. (1994). Inhibited and uninhibited temperaments. In W. B. Carey & S. C. McDevitt (Eds.), *Prevention and early intervention: Individual differences and risk factors for the mental health of children* (pp. 35–41). New York, NY: Brunner/Mazel.

Kagan, J., Reznick, J. S., & Gibbons, J. (1989). Inhibited and uninhibited types of children. *Child Development, 60,* 838–845.

Kagan, J., Reznick, J. S., & Snidman, N. (1987). The physiology and psychology of behavioral inhibition. *Child Development, 58,* 1459–1473.

Kagan, J., Reznick, J. S., & Snidman, N. (1988, April 8). Biological bases of childhood shyness. *Science, 240,* 167–171.

Kendall, P. C. (1994). Treating anxiety disorders in children: Results of a randomized clinical trial. *Journal of Consulting and Clinical Psychology, 62,* 100–110.

Kendall, P. C., Flannery-Schroeder, E., Panichelli-Mindel, S. M., Southam-Gerow, M., Henin, A., & Warman, M. (1997). Therapy for youths with anxiety disorders: A second randomized clinical trial. *Journal of Consulting and Clinical Psychology, 65,* 366–380.

Kendall, P. C., Hudson, J. L., Gosch, E., Flannery-Schroeder, E., & Suveg, C. (2008). Cognitive–behavioral therapy for anxiety disordered youth: A randomized clinical trial evaluating child and family modalities. *Journal of Consulting and Clinical Psychology, 76,* 282–297.

Kendall, P. C., Safford, S., Flannery-Schroeder, E., & Webb, A. (2004). Child anxiety treatment: Outcomes in adolescence and impact on substance use and depression at 7.4-year follow-up. *Journal of Consulting and Clinical Psychology, 72,* 276–287.

Kendall, P. C., & Southam-Gerow, M. A. (1996). Long-term follow-up of a cognitive–behavioral therapy for anxiety-disordered youth. *Journal of Consulting and Clinical Psychology, 64,* 724–730.

Kessler, R. C., Gruber, M., Hettema, J. M., Hwang, I., Sampson, N., & Yonkers, K. A. (2008). Co-morbid major depression and generalized anxiety disorders in the National Comorbidity Survey follow-up. *Psychological Medicine, 38*, 365–374.

Kessler, R.C., & Wang, P. S. (2008). The descriptive epidemiology of commonly occurring mental disorders in the United States. *Annual Review of Public Health, 29*, 115–129.

Klimes-Dougan, B., & Zeman, J. (2007). Introduction to the special issue of *Social Development:* Emotion socialization in childhood and adolescence. *Social Development, 16*, 203–209.

Lemery, K. S., Essex, M., & Smider, N. (2002). Revealing the relationship between temperament and behavior problem symptoms by eliminating measurement confounding: Expert ratings and factor analyses. *Child Development, 73*, 867–882.

Manassis, K., & Bradley, S. (1994). The development of childhood anxiety disorders: Toward an integrated model. *Journal of Applied Developmental Psychology, 15*, 345–366.

Manassis, K., Bradley, S., Goldberg, S., Hood, J., & Swinson, L. (1994). Attachment in mothers with anxiety disorders and their children. *Journal of the American Academy of Child & Adolescent Psychiatry, 33*, 1106–1113.

Manassis, K., Bradley, S., Goldberg, S., Hood, J., & Swinson, R. P. (1995). Behavioural inhibition, attachment and anxiety in children of mothers with anxiety disorders. *Canadian Journal of Psychiatry, 40*, 87–92.

Manassis, K., Mendlowitz, S. L., Scapillato, D., Avery, D., Fiksenbaum, L., Freire, M., . . . Owens, M. (2002). Group and individual cognitive–behavioral therapy for childhood anxiety disorders. A randomized trial. *Journal of the American Academy of Child & Adolescent Psychiatry, 41*, 1423–1430.

Mason, O., Platts, H., & Tyson, M. (2005). Early maladaptive schemas and adult attachment in a UK clinical population. *Psychology and Psychotherapy: Theory, Research, and Practice, 78*, 549–564.

McDowell, D. J., & Parke, R. (2009). Parental correlates of children's peer relations: An empirical test of the tripartite model. *Developmental Psychology, 45*, 224–235.

Menzies, R., & Harris, L. (2001). Nonassociative factors in the development of phobias. In M. Vasey & M. Dadds (Eds.), *The developmental psychopathology of anxiety* (pp. 183–204). New York, NY: Oxford University Press.

Miller, S. M., & Green, M. L. (1985). Coping with stress and frustration: Origins, nature, and development. In M. Lewis & C. Saarni (Eds.), *The socialization of emotions* (pp. 263–314). New York, NY: Plenum.

Moore, P. S., Whaley, S. E., & Sigman, M. (2004). Interactions between mothers and children: Impact of maternal and child anxiety. *Journal of Abnormal Psychology, 113*, 471–476.

Mufson, L., Moreau, D., Weissman, M. M., & Klerman, G. L. (1993). *Interpersonal psychotherapy for depressed adolescents.* New York, NY: Guilford Press.

Muratori, F., Picchi, L., Bruni, G., Patarnello, M., & Romagnoli, G. (2003). A two-year follow-up of psychodynamic psychotherapy for internalizing disorders in children. *Journal of the American Academy of Child & Adolescent Psychiatry, 42,* 331–339.

Muris, P., & Meesters, C. (2002). Attachment, behavioral inhibition, and anxiety disorders: Symptoms in normal adolescents. *Journal of Psychopathology and Behavioral Assessment, 24,* 97–106.

Nauta, M. H., Scholing, A., Emmelkamp, P. M. G., & Minderaa, R. B. (2003). Cognitive-behavioral therapy for children with anxiety disorders in a clinical setting: No additional effect of a cognitive parent training. *Journal of the American Academy of Child & Adolescent Psychiatry, 42,* 1270–1278.

Ollendick, T. H. (1998). Panic disorder in children and adolescents: New developments, new directions. *Journal of Clinical Child Psychology, 27,* 234–245.

Ollendick, T., & Hirshfeld-Becker, D. (2002). The developmental psychopathology of social anxiety disorder. *Biological Psychiatry, 51,* 44–58.

Ollendick, T., & Horsch, L. (2007). Fears in clinic-referred children: Relations with child anxiety sensitivity, maternal overcontrol, and maternal phobic anxiety. *Behavior Therapy, 38,* 402–411.

Ollendick, T. H., King, N. J., & Chorpita, B. F. (2006). Empirically supported treatments for children and adolescents. In P. C. Kendall (Ed.), *Child and adolescent therapy: Cognitive-behavioral procedures* (3rd ed., pp. 492–520). New York, NY: Guilford Press.

Ollendick, T. H., King, N. J., & Muris, P. (2002). Fears and phobias in children: Phenomenology, epidemiology, and aetiology. *Child and Adolescent Mental Health, 7,* 98–106.

Ollendick, T. H., & Seligman, L. D. (2006). Anxiety disorders in children and adolescents. In C. Gillberg, R. Harrington, & H. Steinhausen (Eds.), *Clinician's desk book of child and adolescent psychiatry* (pp. 144–187). Cambridge, England: Cambridge University Press.

Ollendick, T. H., Vasey, M. W., & King, N. J. (2001). Operant conditioning influences in childhood anxiety. In M. Vasey & M. Dadds (Eds.), *The developmental psychopathology of anxiety* (pp. 231–252). New York, NY: Oxford University Press.

Parke, R. D., Orstein, P. A., Rieser, J. J., & Zahn-Waxler, C. (1994). The past as prologue: An overview of a century of developmental psychology. In R. D. Parke, P. A. Orstein, J. J. Rieser, & C. Zahn-Waxler (Eds.), *A century of developmental psychology* (pp. 1–75). Washington, DC: American Psychological Association.

Rapee, R. M. (1997). Potential role of childrearing practices in the development of anxiety and depression. *Clinical Psychology Review, 17,* 47–67.

Roberts, W. (1994, June). *The socialization of emotional expression: Relation with competence in preschool.* Paper presented at the meetings of the Canadian Psychological Association, Penticton, British Columbia, Canada.

Rothbart, M. K., & Ahadi, S. A. (1994). Temperament and the development of personality. *Journal of Abnormal Psychology, 130,* 55–66.

Rothbart, M. K., & Bates, J. E. (1998). Temperament. In W. Damon (Series Ed.) & N. Eisenberg (Vol. Ed.), *Handbook of child psychology: Social, emotional, and personality development* (Vol. 3, pp. 105–176). New York, NY: Wiley.

Rothbart, M. K., Posner, M. I., & Boylan, A. (1990). Regulatory mechanisms in infant development. In J. Enns (Ed.), *The development of attention: Research and theory*. Dordrecht, the Netherlands: Elsevier North-Holland.

Rubin, K. H. (1993). The Waterloo longitudinal project: Correlates and consequences of social withdrawal from childhood to adolescence. In K. H. Rubin & J. B. Asendorpf (Eds.), *Social withdrawal, inhibition, and shyness* (pp. 291–314). Hillsdale, NJ: Erlbaum.

Rubin, K., Both, L., Zahn-Waxler, C., Cummings, M., & Wilkinson, M. (1991). The dyadic play behaviors of children of well and depressed mothers. *Development and Psychopathology, 3*, 243–251.

Rubin, K. H., Bukowski, W., & Parker, J. G. (1998). Peer interactions, relationships, and groups. In N. Eisenberg (Ed.), *Handbook of child psychology: Social, emotional, and personality development* (5th ed., Vol. 3, pp. 619–700). New York, NY: Wiley.

Selman, R., & Schultz, L. (1990). *Making a friend in youth: Developmental theory and pair therapy*. Chicago, IL: University of Chicago Press.

Shortt, A. L., Barrett, P. M., & Fox, T. L. (2001). Evaluating the FRIENDS Program: A cognitive-behavioral group treatment for anxious children and their parents. *Journal of Clinical Child Psychology, 30*, 525–535.

Silverman, W. K., & Ginsburg, G. S. (1998). Anxiety disorders. In T. Ollendick & M. Hersen (Eds.), *Handbook of child psychopathology* (3rd ed., pp. 239–268). New York, NY: Plenum Press.

Silverman, W. K., Kurtines, W. M., Ginsburg, G. S., Weems, C. F., Lumpkin, P. W., & Carmichael, D. H. (1999). Treating anxiety disorders in children with group cognitive–behavioral therapy: A randomized clinical trial. *Journal of Consulting and Clinical Psychology, 67*, 995–1003.

Silverman, W. K., Kurtines, W. M., Ginsburg, G. S., Weems, C. F., Rabian, B., & Serafini, L. T. (1999). Contingency management, self-control, and education support in the treatment of childhood phobic disorders: A randomized clinical trial. *Journal of Consulting and Clinical Psychology, 67*, 675–687.

Silverman, W. K., Pina, A., & Viswesvaran, C. (2008). Evidence-based psychosocial treatments for phobic and anxiety disorders in children and adolescents. *Journal of Clinical Child and Adolescent Psychology, 37*, 105–130.

Siqueland, L., Kendall, P. C., & Steinberg, L. (1996). Anxiety in children: Perceived family environments and observed family interaction. *Journal of Clinical Child Psychology, 25*, 225–237.

Spence, S. H., Donovan, C., & Brechman-Toussaint, M. (2000). The treatment of childhood social phobia: The effectiveness of a social skills training-based, cognitive–behavioural intervention, with and without parental involvement. *Journal of Child Psychology and Psychiatry, 41*, 713–726.

Target, M., & Fonagy, P. (1994). Efficacy of psychoanalysis for children with emotional disorders. *Journal of the American Academy of Child & Adolescent Psychiatry, 33*, 361–371.

Thompson, R. A. (1994). Emotion regulation: A theme in search of definition. *Monographs of the Society for Research in Child Development, 59*(2–3, Serial No. 240), 25–52.

Thompson, R. A. (2001). Childhood anxiety disorders from the perspective of emotion regulation and attachment. In M. Vasey & M. Dadds (Eds.), *The developmental psychopathology of anxiety* (pp. 160–182). New York, NY: Oxford University Press.

Vasey, M. W., Daleiden, E. L., Williams, L. L., & Brown, L. (1995). Biased attention in childhood anxiety disorders: A preliminary study. *Journal of Abnormal Child Psychology, 23*, 267–279.

Verduin, T. L., & Kendall, P. C. (2008). Peer perceptions and liking of children with anxiety disorders. *Journal of Abnormal Child Psychology, 36*, 459–469.

Vernberg, E. M., Abwender, D. A., Ewell, K. K., & Beery, S. H. (1992). Social anxiety and peer relationships in early adolescence: A prospective analysis. *Journal of Clinical Child Psychology, 21*, 189–196.

Walkup, J. T., Albano, A. M., Piacentini, J., Birmaher, B., Scompton, S., Sherrill, J. T., . . . Kendall, P. C. (2008). Cognitive behavioral therapy, sertraline, or a combination in child anxiety. *New England Journal of Medicine, 359*, 2753–2766.

Warren, S. L., Huston, L., Egeland, B., & Sroufe, L. A. (1997). Child and adolescent anxiety disorders and early attachment. *Journal of the American Academy of Child & Adolescent Psychiatry, 30*, 637–644.

Whaley, S. E., Pinto, A., & Sigman, M. (1999). Characterizing interactions between anxious mothers and their children. *Journal of Consulting and Clinical Psychology, 67*, 826–836.

Wood, J. J., & McLeod, B. D. (2008). *Child anxiety disorders: A family-based treatment manual for practitioners.* New York, NY: W. W. Norton.

Wood, J. J., McLeod, B. D., Sigman, M., Hwang, W., & Chu, B. C. (2003). Parenting and childhood anxiety: Theory, empirical findings, and future directions. *Journal of Child Psychology and Psychiatry, 44*, 134–151.

Wood, J. J., Piacentini, J. C., Southam-Gerow, M., Chu, B. C., & Sigman, M. (2006). Family cognitive behavioral therapy for child anxiety disorders. *Journal of the American Academy of Child & Adolescent Psychiatry, 45*, 314–321.

Woody, S. R., & Ollendick, T. H. (2006). Technique factors in treating anxiety disorders. In L. Castonguay & L. E. Beutler (Eds.), *Principles of therapeutic change that work* (pp. 167–186). New York, NY: Oxford University Press.

World Health Organization. (1992). *International classification of diseases, 10th revision.* Geneva: Author.

Younger, A., & Boyko, K. (1987). Aggression and withdrawal as social schemas underlying children's peer perceptions. *Child Development, 58*, 1094–1100. 27

4

ANXIETY DISORDERS IN ADOLESCENCE

JOANNE DAVILA, ANNETTE M. LA GRECA, LISA R. STARR, AND RYAN R. LANDOLL

Adolescence is a time of significant change and identity development, particularly interpersonally. Although some activities do not directly predict future functioning, much that happens in adolescence can have significant implications for subsequent adjustment. That adolescents experience high rates of anxiety during this formative time suggests that anxiety may have consequences for relational functioning and that interpersonal experiences may have consequences for the course of anxiety. In this chapter, we focus on interpersonal processes relevant to anxiety disorders and treatment in adolescence. As demonstrated, there is relatively little theory and research, and some of it is not well distinguished from the larger literature on childhood anxiety. As such, aspects of this chapter reflect commonalities across the child and adolescent literature. We feel it is important to review literature on youth, including childhood, to facilitate theoretical and empirical development. However, we make sure to highlight processes unique to adolescence and to present our discussion within a developmental context. To that end, we begin with a brief review of the epidemiology of adolescent anxiety disorders, followed by a section on developmental considerations. Throughout the chapter we use the term *youth* when referring to processes general to children and adolescents, *adolescence* when referring to the entire developmental period (approximately ages 12–18), and *early adolescence* when referring to ages 12 to 14.

EPIDEMIOLOGY

Anxiety disorders are a common mental health concern throughout adolescence. During adolescence, the most common anxiety disorders are specific phobia, social phobia, and generalized anxiety disorder (Lewinsohn, Hops, Roberts, Seeley, & Andrews, 1993). The prevalence of separation anxiety declines from childhood to adolescence and is uncommon among older adolescents referred for treatment (see Wicks-Nelson & Israel, 2009). In contrast, panic disorder is considered an adolescent-onset disorder, with a mean age of onset of 13.9 years (Costello, Foley, & Angold, 2006). Additionally, social phobia and panic disorder typically present for the first time in adolescence along with a cluster of other psychological disorders (i.e., depression) as compared with other types of anxiety disorders (i.e., separation anxiety, specific phobia; Costello et al., 2006).

Community estimates of the prevalence of anxiety disorders among adolescents are difficult to gauge and have been drawn primarily from the Oregon Adolescent Depression Project, a large-scale epidemiological study of high school students (Lewinsohn et al., 1993) and, more recently, the Great Smoky Mountains Study, a longitudinal community-based study that followed children from ages 9 to 16 (e.g., Costello, Mustillo, Erkanli, Keeler, & Angold, 2003). For anxiety disorders in general, aggregated point-prevalence estimates are between 1.6% and 4.7% and vary by gender (girls are higher than boys) and age (15-year-olds were higher than other adolescents in the Great Smoky Mountains Study; Costello et al., 2003; Lewinsohn et al., 1993). Substantially higher estimates of 7.7% for boys and 12.1% for girls were observed in studies examining cumulative prevalence rates by age 16 (Costello et al., 2003). In addition, lifetime prevalence rates of 5.6% for boys and 11.7% for girls were reported in the Oregon Adolescent Depression Project (Lewinsohn et al., 1993). For specific anxiety disorders, point-prevalence estimates among adolescents are as follows: for boys, 0.73% for simple phobia, 0.24% for social phobia, 0.24% for overanxious (generalized anxiety) disorder, and 0.24% for panic disorder; for girls, 2.02% for simple phobia, 1.57 % for social phobia, 0.67% for overanxious (generalized anxiety) disorder, and 0.45% for panic disorder (Lewinsohn et al., 1993). Prior estimates of lifetime prevalence for these four disorders ranged from a low of 0.49% for boys (for social phobia and panic disorder) to a high of 2.81% for girls (for simple phobia; Lewinsohn et al., 1993). However, a more recent review of several large-scale epidemiological studies has indicated a wide range of lifetime prevalence rates in adolescents for social phobia (from 1.6% to 13.1%), simple phobia (from 2.3% to 12.2%), generalized anxiety disorder (from 0.6% to 0.8%), and panic disorder (from 0.5% to 3.1%; Costello, Egger, & Angold, 2005). This range can be attributed in part to different assessment tools, different diagnostic criteria (i.e., the third revised and fourth editions of the *Diagnostic and Statistical Manual of Mental Disorders;* American Psychiatric Association, 1987, 1994), and different samples. Additionally, community based-samples of adolescents have found high levels of posttraumatic stress disorder (PTSD), ranging from 0.7% to 6.3% (Costello et al., 2005). Taken together, it is clear that anxiety disorders represent a significant mental health problem for many adolescents.

DEVELOPMENTAL CONSIDERATIONS

Adolescence is a critical period for relationships. Although parents typically remain the primary attachment figures, youth begin to develop increased autonomy. Young people also begin to develop more relationships with peers and romantic partners, including relationships of greater significance and intensity that involve reciprocity (Kuttler & La Greca, 2004). Also, adolescents' accumulated experiences begin to coalesce into more generalized expectations that underpin consistent individual personality and relationship styles (e.g., Furman & Simon, 2004).

Family Relations

Perhaps the primary change in family relationships involves adolescents' striving for greater autonomy (e.g., Grotevant & Cooper, 1985). Adolescents spend more time with peers than with parents (Larson, 1983) and experience more conflict with parents (Laursen, Coy, & Collins, 1998). To facilitate healthy autonomy development, adolescents may need different things from parents than they did in childhood. For instance, parents may need to support adolescents' emotional and cognitive independence and their developing sense of self, whereas support of physical and behavioral independence is more relevant for children (see Allen et al., 2003). Negotiating these changes can be challenging. Thus, one of the key tasks of adolescence is to achieve autonomy while maintaining a positive relationship with parents (e.g., Grotevant & Cooper, 1985). Indeed, failure to do so is associated with a variety of negative outcomes, including internalizing and externalizing symptoms (e.g., Allen, Hauser, Eickholt, Bell, & O'Connor, 1994). It is not hard to imagine that anxiety might interfere with the development of autonomy, that autonomy struggles might contribute to anxiety, or that parenting style during the negotiation of this key task might affect risk for anxiety. These ideas are discussed further in the following sections.

Peer Relations

Adolescence is marked by an expansion of peer networks and increased importance of close friendships. Two specific aspects of peer relations that are especially critical for emotional development are acceptance from peers and close friendships (Hartup, 1996; La Greca & Prinstein, 1999). Acceptance from peers generally provides youth with a sense of belonging–acceptance, whereas close friends provide a sense of intimacy, companionship, and emotional support (Berndt, 1982). Also during adolescence, romantic attachments introduce a new dimension to social functioning: the desire to be accepted as a romantic partner (Harter, 1988).

Most adolescents have a peer network that includes peer crowds, friendship groups or cliques, best friends and other close friends, and romantic relationships (La Greca & Prinstein, 1999). Because adolescents interact with a large number of peers, they need to establish their identity and find where they fit in the larger social system. In this context, adolescent peer crowds reflect adolescents' peer acceptance and reputation, as well as the primary attitudes and behaviors by which adolescents are known to their peers (Brown, 1990; La Greca, Prinstein, & Fetter, 2001). Peer crowds are much larger than friendship cliques, and crowd members may not necessarily know one another (Brown, 1990). Peer crowds provide adolescents with a sense of belonging, acceptance, and identity and opportunities for social activities. The importance of peer crowds peaks in mid- to late adolescence, as youth focus greater attention on close friends and romantic relationships (Brown, 1990; Brown, Eicher, & Petrie, 1986). In contrast, adolescents' peer interactions occur primarily in the context of dyadic interactions with friends or romantic partners or in cliques. Cliques are friendship-based groupings that vary in size (usually five to eight members), density (degree to which members regard each other as friends), and tightness (degree to which they are closed to outsiders; Brown, 1989; Urberg, Degirmencioglu, & Tolson, 1995). Cliques are the primary basis for adolescents' peer interactions (Brown, 1989), and best friends are likely to participate in the same clique (Urberg et al., 1995). Also, as adolescents begin to date, same-sex cliques may transition to mixed-sex groups (Kuttler & La Greca, 2004). Over time, cliques are replaced by adolescents' interactions with close friends, romantic partners, or smaller friendship-based groups (La Greca & Prinstein, 1999).

During adolescence, close friends take on increasing importance as they surpass parents as adolescents' primary source of social support and contribute to adolescents' adjustment and well-being (La Greca & Prinstein, 1999).

Adolescents' close friendships have many of the same qualities that are observed in children's friendships (companionship, trust, affiliation) but are increasingly characterized by intimacy (i.e., sharing of private thoughts and feelings; knowledge of intimate details about each other; Berndt, 1982). Girls report more close friends than boys and more intimacy in these relationships (Berndt, 1982; Urberg et al., 1995). However, boys have more open friendship groups than girls and are more willing to let others join ongoing interactions (Urberg et al., 1995). During adolescence, having close other-sex friends also becomes common (Kuttler, La Greca, & Prinstein, 1999) and sets the stage for romantic relationships.

Romantic Relationships

In addition to a growing peer network, adolescents also become more attuned to and interested in romantic relationships. With puberty typically comes romantic attraction and sexual desire, which prompt interest and engagement in romantic and sexual activity (e.g., Bellis, Downing, & Ashton, 2006). Estimates have indicated that by age 16, most adolescents report having had a romantic relationship (Carver, Joyner, & Udry, 2003). Beginning in early adolescence, there is a normative trajectory to romantic engagement and a developmental progression in the function of relationships (Connolly & Goldberg, 1999; Shulman & Scharf, 2000). For example, in early adolescence romantic interactions typically occur in mixed-gender groups, and romantic relationships tend to be marked by affiliation and companionship. During late adolescence, intimate and committed relationships are often formed and evolve into couple dating. In line with this, caretaking, greater levels of intimacy and closeness, deeper mutual feelings, and often more extensive sexual activity occur. Thus, during adolescence youth face interpersonal tasks that may be increasingly demanding and central to the development of adaptive functioning in dyadic relationships. Anxiety has the potential to interfere in a variety of ways.

Pubertal and Gender Issues

As mentioned earlier, puberty may prompt romantic interest and involvement. That it does so is worth highlighting because there is some evidence that puberty, particularly early pubertal development, is linked with internalizing disorders (e.g., Ge, Brody, Conger, & Simons, 2006). Moreover, a number of scholars have suggested that the link between pubertal development and internalizing symptoms may be best understood in the context of romantic activities that emerge with the onset of puberty (e.g., Natsuaki, Biehl, & Ge, 2009; Stroud & Davila, 2008). Although these researchers have focused on depression, a similar case can be made for anxiety. Therefore, research should continue to examine the role of pubertal development in adolescent anxiety, particularly in the interpersonal context.

It is also important to consider gender differences in interpersonal models of anxiety disorders in adolescence. Females are at greater risk for internalizing symptoms, including anxiety (e.g., Lewinsohn et al. 1993). Females also are more relationally attuned and more sensitive to interpersonal stressors (Compton et al., 2000; Rose & Rudolph, 2006; Rudolph, 2002). This suggests that there may be unique associations for girls compared with boys. However, there is little theory or research that addresses this issue.

ETIOLOGICAL FORMULATIONS AND THEORETICAL MODELS

We now turn to interpersonal processes that may help explain the onset, maintenance, and course of adolescent anxiety.

Family Processes That Contribute to Anxiety, Maintain Anxiety, or Both

Offspring of individuals with anxiety disorders are at risk of developing these disorders. Research supporting this claim has largely come from studies of risk in children. For instance, Beidel and Turner (1997) found that the 7- to 12-year-old children of parents with an anxiety disorder were more likely to be diagnosed with an anxiety disorder than those of parents without an anxiety disorder. Maternal phobic anxiety may be particularly related to separation anxiety in children (e.g., Bernstein, Layne, & Egan, 2005; Kearney, Sims, Pursell, & Tillotson, 2003). Although a component of this increased risk may reflect genetic transmission, family and parenting factors likely also account for increased risk.

Evidence has suggested that aspects of the parent–child relationship and parenting style are associated with risk of anxiety disorders (see Bögels & Brechman-Toussaint, 2006; McLeod, Wood, & Weisz, 2007). With respect to parent–child relationships, scholars have long speculated on the role of attachment insecurity in the development of anxiety. Bowlby (1973) theorized that children's anxiety is related to their pattern of attachment with their primary caregiver and that anxiety disorders are related to concerns about the availability of the attachment figure. Mattis and Ollendick (1997) elaborated on this, reasoning that because insecurely attached (particularly anxious–ambivalent) youth tend to be highly reactive to distress, have poor self-regulation, and lack caregiver support to regulate distress, they have difficulty escaping from anxiety and are more prone to experience panic. Data have supported these ideas. In addition to an association between infant insecure attachment and subsequent anxiety in childhood (e.g., Bar Haim, Dan, & Eshel, 2007), there is evidence of an association well into adolescence. Not only do insecurely attached adolescents report greater anxiety and anxiety sensitivity (e.g., Muris, Mayer, & Meesters, 2000; Rosenstein & Horowitz, 1996; Weems, Berman, & Silverman, 2002), but infant attachment insecurity predicts anxiety disorders in adolescence (e.g., Warren, Huston, Egeland, & Sroufe, 1997), and these associations hold when factors such as temperament and maternal anxiety are controlled (e.g., Muris et al., 2000; Warren et al., 1997). Thus, early relationships that reflect a basic lack of safety and security may underlie the experience of later anxiety, perhaps because of the individual's inability to regulate and escape from anxiety. This is important in the context of adolescence where attachment security is associated with mothers' ability to support adolescents' autonomy strivings (Allen et al., 2003). Insecure youth may experience increases in anxiety during adolescence in relation to the challenge of developing autonomy. Similarly, parents who cannot effectively support autonomy may reinforce anxiety in their adolescents.

Parenting styles, such as overprotection and control, also play a role in risk of anxiety disorders among children and adolescents. In a recent meta-analysis (McLeod et al., 2007; see also van der Bruggen, Stams, & Bögels, 2008), overcontrol and low autonomy-granting accounted for the most variance in youth anxiety (including anxiety disorders, especially social anxiety, as well as continuous measures of trait anxiety) compared with parental rejection and lack of warmth. This finding was not moderated by age, indicating that it is true for children and adolescents. However, the amount of variance was low (18%), suggesting that other factors also affect risk (McLeod et al., 2007). That age did not moderate the McLeod et al. (2007) findings is important and suggests that parental control variables retain their association with anxiety across childhood and adolescence. This makes sense from a developmental perspective. Parental overcontrol may be problematic in adolescence during the struggle for autonomy, particularly in the face of an expanding peer world. It would be important to consider whether and how overcontrolling parenting during adolescence may interact with functioning in peer relationships to increase risk of anxiety.

It is interesting that Ollendick and Horsch (2007) recently failed to find an association between maternal-reported overcontrol and anxiety among older youth but did find the association among younger girls. Perhaps by the time youth with anxiety problems reach adolescence, overcontrolling parenting has already taken its toll. This raises important directions for research with regard to the timing of the effects of different aspects of parenting and their interaction with age of onset of youth anxiety. Findings may also differ on the basis of the informant; primarily, "youth-perceived" maternal overprotection, psychological pressure, alienation, and rejection have been associated with adolescent anxiety (Bögels, van Oosten, & Muris, 2001; Hale, Engels, & Meeus, 2006; van Brakel, Muris, & Bögels, 2006; Wolfradt, Hempel, & Miles, 2003). McLeod et al. (2007) found weaker associations between parenting and youth anxiety when parents were the informants, compared with youth or observers.

Several other parenting–family variables have been proposed as risk factors for youth anxiety, although research has largely been based on children. For example, the attributions parents make for children's withdrawal can affect parenting, resulting in either overcontrolling or nonresponsive styles (Mills & Rubin, 1993; Rubin, Nelson, Hastings, & Asendorpf, 1999). In addition, elevated rates of expressed emotion in families have been observed among youth with obsessive–compulsive disorder, which then predicts poorer subsequent functioning (Leonard et al., 1993). Finally, Spence, Najman, and Bor (2002) found that maternal marital distress and divorce were associated with anxiety at age 14, although the underlying mechanisms are unknown.

Although parenting styles may contribute to anxiety in youth, it is important to recognize that parenting variables may also result from parental anxiety. For example, mothers high on trait anxiety are less responsive to their infants (Nicol-Harper, Harvey, & Stein, 2007), which may form the basis for the development of an insecure attachment. Anxious mothers' own attachment-related fears of rejection and dependency needs are associated with youth's anxiety symptoms, suggesting that these fears and needs may be transmitted to children (Costa & Weems, 2005). Anxious mothers also catastrophize during challenging discussions with their child (e.g., talking about a conflict; Moore, Whaley, & Sigman, 2004), which may transmit anxiety through social learning. There is also evidence that anxious parents and youth influence one another's anxiety. For instance, Greenbaum, Cook, Melamed, Abeles, and Bush (1988) found that distress in children increased after mothers' display of anxious agitation and that children's expression of anxiety increased mothers' anxious agitation (consequently increasing children's distress). As such, parent–child interactions may reinforce anxiety in children (and parents), which could affect the successful negotiation of key adolescent tasks (autonomy, identity development). Because this research focused on children, its application to adolescence is speculative.

An additional way in which parent–child interactions could reinforce anxiety in youth is via family accommodation of symptoms, which has been studied in pediatric obsessive–compulsive disorder (Waters & Barrett, 2000). Family accommodation (e.g., participation in symptoms or rituals, modification of personal and family routines) is a common occurrence among parents of adolescents with obsessive–compulsive disorder (Allsopp & Verduyn, 1990; Storch, Geffen, & Merlo, 2007) and is associated with greater symptom severity, parent-rated functional impairment, and greater internalizing and externalizing behavior problems (Storch et al., 2007).

In sum, parenting styles and aspects of the parent–child relationship may play a role in the development and maintenance of anxiety in adolescence. This may occur through insecure parent–child attachments and through parental overcontrol and overprotection, although some of the key factors may interact with the task of developing autonomy from parents. However, it is important to note that much of the research supporting these associations does not come from studies that uniquely focused on adolescents. Future research should focus more explicitly on adolescents and on how risk for and maintenance of anxiety is affected by parent–adolescent relationship factors in the context of autonomy development.

Peer Processes That Contribute to Anxiety, Maintain Anxiety, or Both

Youngsters' peer relationships and close friendships also play an important role in their emotional development. Problematic peer relations consistently predict negative outcomes during adolescence (Hartup, 1996; La Greca & Prinstein, 1999). For example, adolescents who are disliked by peers display high rates of internalizing difficulties, such as depression, anxiety, and loneliness (Asher & Wheeler, 1985; La Greca & Lopez, 1998; La Greca & Stone, 1993). Most of the relevant literature has focused on linkages between peer relations and either social anxiety or general anxiety levels in youth. Conceptualizations of social anxiety (e.g., Leary, 1983; Watson & Friend, 1969) underscore the importance of both the subjective experience of anxiety in social situations and the behavioral consequences of anxiety. This distinction is important because some individuals who experience social anxiety function adequately in social settings, whereas others experience subjective distress and are socially avoidant. Research with adolescents has conceptualized social anxiety and also dating anxiety as containing elements of both negative social evaluation and behavioral inhibition (Glickman & La Greca, 2004; La Greca & Lopez, 1998).

Theory and research have supported the notion that social anxiety may result from problematic peer relations (e.g., aversive or exclusionary experiences with peers). In turn, feelings of social anxiety may inhibit positive social interactions that are necessary for satisfactory emotional development. Thus, social anxiety plays a role in the development of socially withdrawn or avoidant behavior, leading to missed opportunities for social experiences and thus to further problems with interpersonal relations. Subsequent problems in interpersonal relations may further exacerbate feelings of anxiety.

Peer Rejection, Peer Victimization, and Aversive–Exclusionary Peer Experiences

Adolescents place considerable importance on acceptance from peers and on companionship, intimacy, and emotional support from close friends (La Greca & Prinstein, 1999). Consequently, exclusion, rejection, or victimization from peers, close friends, or romantic partners represent significant stressors that may contribute to the development of anxiety. Community studies have revealed that adolescents who are actively rejected by peers report significantly higher levels of social anxiety than those who are more accepted (Inderbitzen, Walters, & Bukowsky, 1997; La Greca & Lopez, 1998). Rejected adolescents report both social evaluative concerns and high levels of social avoidance and distress, and in addition, "submissive rejected" adolescents report significantly more social anxiety than "aggressive rejected" teens (Interbitzen et al., 1997). These latter findings suggest that adolescents who may already be somewhat anxious or inhibited are more affected by peer rejection experiences than more aggressive teens.

Studies have also examined the relation between peer crowd identification and adolescents' reports of social anxiety. La Greca and Harrison (2005) found that adolescents who identified with high-status peer crowds reported lower levels of social anxiety than other adolescents, although adolescents identifying with low-status peer crowds also reported lower levels of social anxiety than others. This suggests that the low peer status associated with certain crowds may have been offset by the benefits of affiliating with a crowd.

More recently, a growing body of research has examined peer victimization (PV) as an interpersonal stressor that may have adverse effects on adolescent adjustment (De Los Reyes & Prinstein, 2004; Hawker & Boulton, 2000; La Greca & Harrison, 2005). Three types of PV have been identified: *overt* (e.g., physical violence and threats), *relational* (e.g., friendship withdrawal and social exclusion), and *reputational* (e.g., spreading rumors; e.g., De Los Reyes & Prinstein, 2004). Acquaintances and other peers may be the aggressors for reputational and overt victimization, but close friends are likely to be the perpetrators of relational victimization. All three types of PV have been associated with adolescents' reports of social anxiety (e.g., La Greca & Harrison, 2005; Siegel, La Greca, & Harrison, 2009), although these studies have also suggested that relational victimization is the aspect of PV most strongly related to social anxiety. Moreover, Vernberg, Abwender, Ewell, and Beery (1992) found that rejecting and exclusionary peer experiences predicted increases in adolescents' social evaluative anxiety over a 2-month period; over the course of the school year, peer exclusion contributed to significant increases in generalized social avoidance and distress. Recent prospective work has also pointed to relational victimization as leading to increases in adolescents' social anxiety over time (Siegel et al., 2009) and to increases in levels of social phobia (Storch, Masia-Warner, Crisp, & Klein, 2005).

In contrast, evidence is mixed regarding the potential impact of social anxiety on adolescents' subsequent PV. Studies of middle school students did not find that high levels of social anxiety predicted increases in PV over the course of a year (Storch et al., 2005; Vernberg et al., 1992), but among older adolescents, those with high levels of social anxiety did display increases in relational victimization over a 2-month period (Siegel & La Greca, 2008). Although the reason for these discrepant findings is not clear, it is possible that the shorter, 2-month time period of the latter study was more conducive to observing increases in PV. Over time, socially anxious youth may learn to avoid social situations, thus limiting opportunities for further PV. Studies that examine the potential bidirectional influences of PV and social anxiety, as well as mediating variables, are needed.

Close Friendships

Close friendships are a critical aspect of adolescents' interpersonal functioning. Problems in close friendships represent an interpersonal stressor that could contribute to social anxiety and lead to avoidance or inhibition in close relationships, thereby interfering with the development of close, supportive ties (La Greca & Lopez, 1998). In fact, community studies have found that adolescent girls who reported high levels of social anxiety had fewer best friends, felt less competent in friendships, and perceived friendships as less supportive, less intimate, and lower in companionship (La Greca & Lopez, 1998). Social avoidance was the aspect of social anxiety most strongly associated with the friendship variables. More recently, La Greca and Harrison (2005) examined multiple aspects of adolescents' peer relations as predictors of concurrent social anxiety. Even after controlling for peer crowd affiliations and PV, adolescents who reported fewer positive and more negative interactions in best friendships had significantly higher levels of social anxiety.

Longitudinal work by Vernberg et al. (1992) has provided some support for bidirectional influences between social anxiety and close friendships. Specifically, among seventh and eighth graders, high levels of social anxiety at the beginning of the school year predicted less intimacy and companionship in adolescents' close friendships months later, especially for girls. Moreover, as social anxiety increased over the school year, concomitant decreases in adolescents' levels of intimacy and companionship in their close friendships were observed.

Together, these findings implicate problems in close friendships as contributing to social anxiety, especially for adolescent girls. Because girls emphasize intimacy and emotional support in their close friendships to a greater extent than boys (Buhrmester & Furman, 1987), girls may be more vulnerable than boys to being adversely affected by problems in their close friendships.

Romantic Relationships

Although important to consider, little research has addressed the contributions of romantic relationships to anxiety in adolescents. One complication is that adolescents who are socially anxious are significantly less likely to date or be involved in romantic relationships than their less socially anxious peers (Glickman & La Greca, 2004; La Greca & Harrison, 2005). Among adolescents who are involved in romantic relationships (and who thus may be less socially anxious), La Greca and Harrison (2005) found that low levels of positive interactions (e.g., support, intimacy) in adolescents' romantic relationships were associated with high levels of social anxiety. A subsequent study (La Greca & Mackey, 2007) revealed that adolescents with fewer other-sex friends and those with fewer positive and more negative interactions with their best friends reported high levels of dating anxiety. In addition, adolescents who reported never having a romantic relationship, who did not have a current romantic partner, and who had less positive and more negative interactions with their romantic partners reported higher levels of dating anxiety. It is noteworthy that adolescents' interactions with their romantic partners uniquely contributed to feelings of dating anxiety.

It is not surprising that negative interactions with a romantic partner were associated with high levels of dating anxiety. A critical aspect of romantic relationships is to make one feel accepted and loved, and adolescents, in particular, have a heightened sensitivity to rejection from romantic partners (Downey, Bonica, & Rincon, 1999). Thus, when conflict, exclusion, or other negative interactions emerge in a romantic relationship, they may lead to considerable anxiety and distress.

In addition, low levels of positive interactions with a romantic partner were related to high levels of dating anxiety. Adolescents who feel anxious in dating situations might be more inhibited and thus display fewer positive interactions with their partner or perceive their partner as displaying fewer positive behaviors. Alternatively, low levels of positive interactions with a partner might elicit concern about the relationship and thus contribute to feelings of anxiety.

Understanding the psychological impact of romantic relationships is important because troubled romantic relationships in adolescence may foreshadow future difficulties in adult romantic relationships (Downey et al., 1999). Continued research, and especially prospective studies on the interplay of romantic relationships and anxiety over time, will be important.

Other Potentially Relevant Interpersonal Variables

A number of additional factors, such as stressful life events, may be relevant for understanding interpersonal processes that contribute to adolescent anxiety. The literature on PTSD has indicated that among other traumatic events, family violence is associated with risk for PTSD among adolescents, as is physical and sexual assault perpetrated, in particular, by a family member or nonstranger (e.g., Lawyer, Ruggiero, & Resnick, 2006; Margolin & Vickerman, 2007). Furthermore, maternal PTSD, in addition to perhaps conveying genetic risk to offspring (Koenen, 2003), may serve as a stressor that could increase PTSD risk in adolescents, resulting in intergenerational transmission of the disorder (Linares & Cloitre, 2004). Moreover, social support may be important for understanding adolescents' risk because higher levels of social support can protect against risk for PTSD (e.g., Haden, Scarpa, & Jones, 2007; Ozer & Weinstein, 2004).

The broader life-event literature has also documented an association between stressful life events and youth anxiety (e.g., Gothelf, Aharonovsky, & Horesh, 2004; Ollendick, Langley, Jones, & Kephart, 2001), although relatively little research has been conducted with adolescents. In addition, this literature has typically not examined whether specific types of events are differentially related to anxiety. However, Grover, Ginsburg, and Ialongo (2005) found that adolescents who experienced more losses and deaths in childhood experienced greater anxiety. In addition, Eley and Stevenson (2000) found that threat-related events, including events that threatened the loss of an attachment figure, were uniquely associated with youth anxiety compared with depression. However, chronic interpersonal difficulties were uniquely associated with depression compared with anxiety. These findings point to the importance of understanding the role of comorbid symptoms, particularly depression, in the association between anxiety and interpersonal processes, as we discuss further.

Evidence for the salience of interpersonal experiences can also be seen in the literature on social skills and social anxiety. For example, adolescents who rate themselves high on social anxiety are treated more negatively by classmates when giving a speech, even when controlling for observer ratings of how anxious the person was during the speech (Blöte, Kint, & Westenberg, 2007). This suggests that it was not simply the anxious behavior during the speech that contributed to the negative ratings.

Summary

Theoretical conceptualizations of the manner in which interpersonal processes contribute to the development or maintenance of anxiety in adolescents are lacking. Nevertheless, research has linked family variables, peer processes, and other interpersonal factors with anxiety in adolescence. It is possible that certain interpersonal processes are more salient for some types of anxiety-related problems than others. For instance, parenting styles and aspects of the parent–child relationship might play a relatively greater role in the development of phobias, panic disorder, or generalized anxiety disorder in youth than do peer processes, whereas peer variables may make a larger contribution to the development of social anxiety and social phobia than family variables. Future research might begin to elucidate the specific pathways by which family and peer influences contribute to different types of anxiety disorders in adolescence and how they do so in the context of important developmental processes (e.g., autonomy striving, pubertal development, romantic interests). Prospective and longitudinal studies that examine bidirectional influences between anxiety and interpersonal processes are needed, as are studies that examine moderating variables (e.g., gender, ethnicity, genetic vulnerability).

INTERPERSONAL PROCESSES AND COMORBIDITY

Anxiety disorders rarely occur in isolation. In the Oregon Adolescent Depression Project, 70% of adolescents with an anxiety disorder also had another mental disorder, and conversely 16% of adolescents with any non–anxiety disorder were diagnosed with an anxiety disorder (Lewinsohn, Zinbarg, Seeley, Lewinsohn, & Sack, 1997). Essau (2003) found that 51% of adolescents with an anxiety disorder also had an additional non–anxiety disorder, and 15% had two or more non–anxiety disorders. The ubiquity of comorbidity has important implications for research on interpersonal aspects of anxiety disorders in adolescence. First, interpersonal aspects of anxiety may play a role in the development of comorbidity. Second, comorbidity may distort how anxiety relates to interpersonal variables because co-occurring disorders may confound analyses. Third, comorbidity may have consequences for interpersonal outcomes. Research on how these considerations are relevant for adolescent anxiety disorders is limited. Next, we review the existing literature, focusing mainly on anxiety–depression comorbidity, which has received the most attention.

Depression

In the Oregon Adolescent Depression Project, 54% of anxiety cases also met lifetime criteria for major depressive disorder, more than any other disorder. A number of anxiety disorders tend to have their onset in early childhood (Kessler, Berglund, Demler, Jin, & Walters, 2005), whereas depression rates are low in childhood but spike in adolescence (Lewinsohn et al., 1993).

Thus, adolescence may often be the period in which anxiety–depression comorbidity first develops. Little research has considered whether interpersonal factors contribute to anxiety–depression comorbidity. It seems logical, however, that they play a role. As we have covered elsewhere, anxiety has negative consequences for relationships. Depression, in turn, is affected by interpersonal distress (for a review, see Davila, Stroud, & Starr, 2008). Thus, anxiety may affect one's social environment, which in turn produces depression. Grant, Beck, Farrow, and Davila (2007) found that among college students, dysfunctional interpersonal styles mediated the longitudinal relation between social anxiety and depression over 1 year. This hypothesis has yet to be replicated in samples of younger adolescents.

Evidence has suggested that co-occurring depression confounds the relation between anxiety and interpersonal variables. Starr and Davila (2008) found that social anxiety and depressive symptoms showed positive correlations with family- and peer-related interpersonal variables in a sample of early adolescent girls. However, when controlling for depressive symptoms, the relation between social anxiety and most family variables disappeared, and the relation between social anxiety and peer variables (e.g., lower interpersonal competence, fewer close friends) became stronger. Conversely, when controlling for social anxiety, depressive symptoms were more strongly related to family variables. Starr and Davila (2009) also examined the effect of comorbidity on the relation between social anxiety and co-rumination (i.e., excessive negative discussion of problems within friendships). Co-rumination correlates with generalized anxiety and depressive symptoms (Rose, 2002; Rose & Rudolph, 2006). However, when controlling for depressive symptoms, Starr and Davila (2009) found that social anxiety was negatively correlated with co-rumination. Evidence has also suggested that comorbid depression affects the interpersonal outcomes of anxiety. Starr and Davila (2008) found that adolescents with both social anxiety and depression reported greater alienation from friends and family and fewer same-sex friends than those with either "pure" (i.e., noncomorbid) social anxiety or "pure" depressive symptoms. Comorbidity is also associated with greater conflict with parents and worse overall quality of life (Lewinsohn, Rohde, & Seeley, 1995; Rush et al., 2005). Finally, interpersonal therapy has poorer outcomes for depressed teens with comorbid anxiety (Young, Mufson, & Davies, 2006).

Body Image Concerns and Eating Disorders

Body image concerns and disordered eating are often salient in adolescence and may co-occur with anxiety disorders (Keel, Klump, Miller, McGue, & Iacono, 2005). Little research has examined the role of interpersonal factors in this comorbidity, although it is quite likely. Disordered eating is often a means of achieving social acceptance. Negative body image is related to several social variables, including negative friendship qualities (Compian, Gowen, & Hayward, 2004; Schutz & Paxton, 2007). Given anxiety's transactional relation to peer relationships, it makes sense that anxiety would generate interpersonal stress that may in turn lead to disordered eating. However, no existing research has explicitly addressed this issue.

Substance Use and Abuse

Substance disorders are second only to depression in their comorbidity with anxiety disorders in adolescence (Lewinsohn et al., 1997). Many researchers have suggested that this is a reflection of the tendency of anxious individuals to self-medicate to reduce anxiety (Carrigan & Randall, 2003). In many cases, the stimulus for self-medication may be interpersonal; this is likely to be the case with social phobia (which strongly predicts the development of substance abuse disorders; Bakken, Landheim, & Vaglum, 2005; Zimmermann et al., 2003). Socially anxious individuals may rely on substances to control their anxiety in social situations (although evidence is mixed as to whether substances are effective in doing so; Carrigan & Randall, 2003). Furthermore, individuals with social phobia may be more apt to use substances as a result of social pressures (Sonntag, Wittchen, Hofler, Kessler, & Stein, 2000).

INTERPERSONAL PROCESSES AND IMPLICATIONS FOR TREATMENT

Existing treatments for anxiety reflect the fact that interpersonal processes are involved in adolescent anxiety. Most treatments are based on cognitive–behavioral therapy (CBT), with interpersonal components added, and include parents and peers as coaches or supporters of the interventions. Some treatments were designed to specifically target interpersonal functioning, and they also actively include parents, peers, or both. All of the treatments attempt to target relational issues (e.g., parent–child communication, peer acceptance) that reflect important developmental processes.

Family-Based CBT

Family-based CBT for youth (typically ages 7–16) builds on individual CBT by including parents in session with the goals of teaching them CBT skills, modifying maladaptive beliefs and expectations, teaching them how to respond to their child's anxious distress, encouraging support of their child's mastery, teaching effective parent–child communication skills, and, when relevant, encouraging them to apply the skills to cope with their own anxiety. Studies have shown that family-based CBT is as effective as individual CBT in treating a variety of anxiety disorders in youth (Kendall, Hudson, & Gosch, 2008; Wood, Piacentini, & Southam-Gerow, 2006), most often general anxiety disorder, social phobia, and separation anxiety disorder. Indeed, a recent meta-analysis found comparable effect sizes for individual versus family- or parent-based CBT (Ishikawa, Okajima, & Matsuoka, 2007), and Silverman, Pina, and Viswesvaran (2008) considered family-based CBT to be a possibly efficacious treatment using standard criteria for classifying evidence-based psychosocial treatments. Furthermore, family-based CBT was more effective than individual CBT when both parents had an anxiety disorder (Kendall et al., 2008). There is also promising evidence that parent-only group CBT, which teaches parents skills to manage their child's anxiety, results in reductions in child anxiety and changes in parental attitudes (Thienemann, Moore, & Tompkins, 2006). This intervention appears to work well for parents who have anxiety disorders. As such, these treatments may reduce the reciprocal reinforcement of anxiety that can occur between parents and youth.

Attachment-Based Family Therapy

Attachment-based family therapy for anxiety (Diamond, 2005) focuses on attachment-related family interactional issues. The goal is to promote adolescent autonomy by helping parents become less overprotective and controlling. The treatment involves individual and joint meetings for adolescents and parents in which the emphasis is on changing family dynamics to encourage adolescent independence, intimacy, and healthy attachment. A small-sample randomized clinical trial comparing attachment-based family therapy with CBT indicated that adolescents (with generalized anxiety disorder, separation anxiety disorder, or social phobia) in the two treatment groups did not differ at posttest (67% symptom free in the CBT group and 40% symptom free in attachment-based family therapy) or at the 6-month follow-up (100% in CBT and 80% in attachment-based family therapy no longer meeting diagnostic criteria; Siqueland, Rynn, & Diamond, 2005).

Adolescent Intensive Panic Control Treatment With Situational Exposure

Adolescent intensive panic control treatment with situational exposure (see Ollendick & Pincus, 2008) was modeled on panic control treatment for adolescents (Hoffman & Mattis, 2000; Ollendick, 1995) and was designed to be conducted over a shorter period of time in longer sessions. It also includes more intensive parental involvement than panic control treatment for adolescents. Parents join each session for at least 30 minutes to learn the same CBT skills as the adolescents and are encouraged to be coaches at home to encourage therapeutic exposure. An open clinical trial of 18 adolescents yielded decreases in anxiety to nonclinical levels in all but 1 participant at 1-month follow-up, and parents reported improved family interactions (Ollendick & Pincus, 2008). A randomized controlled trial is underway.

Social Effectiveness Therapy

Social effectiveness therapy (Beidel, Turner, & Morris, 2000) was designed to treat youth with social phobia. Social effectiveness therapy focuses on exposure and social skills training. Youth attend two sessions per week (one individual exposure session and one group social skills session) as well as social activities with unfamiliar peers for skill practice. A randomized controlled trial of children ages 8 through 12 indicated that social effectiveness therapy was efficacious at posttreatment and 3 and 5 years later, with more than 80% of adolescents no longer meeting criteria for social phobia at the 5-year follow-up (Beidel, Turner, & Young, 2005, 2006). Social effectiveness therapy has also recently been demonstrated to perform as well as medication and to have somewhat longer lasting effects in a sample of 7- to 17-year-olds (Beidel et al., 2007). In addition, social effectiveness therapy is considered by Silverman et al. (2008) to be a probably efficacious treatment. Although promising, no randomized clinical trials with adolescents alone have been conducted as yet.

Skills for Social and Academic Success

Skills for Social and Academic Success (Fisher, Masia-Warner, & Klein, 2004) is a CBT, school-based intervention for adolescents with social anxiety disorder that emphasizes social skills as well as in vivo exposure in group and individual sessions. Key interpersonally relevant components of the program include weekend social events with peers from participants' schools who serve as peer assistants to help with exposures and skills and psychoeducation with both parents and teachers to improve their ability to help youth conduct exposures and manage anxiety. In a randomized controlled trial of adolescents with social anxiety disorder, Masia-Warner et al. (2005) found that, compared with waiting-list controls, adolescents in Skills for Social and Academic Success demonstrated decreased anxiety and avoidance and increased overall functioning, with more than two thirds no longer meeting diagnostic criteria at a 9-month follow-up.

CBT–Interpersonal Therapy

Scapillato and Manassis (2002) described a group CBT–interpersonal treatment for anxious adolescents. In addition to CBT components (e.g., psychoeducation, exposure, cognitive restructuring), the program emphasizes relevant developmental and interpersonal contexts. The group is seen as a "transitional social environment" in which adolescents can reduce feelings of social isolation, garner peer acceptance and support, increase social competence, and become more independent. Such a focus is consistent with the literature reviewed earlier, indicating that poor peer relationships and low levels of autonomy in the family are associated with greater anxiety in youth. Although this treatment has not been rigorously tested, its foci are well grounded in the interpersonal and developmental literature.

CONCLUSIONS

As demonstrated in this chapter, there is ample evidence that interpersonal processes play an important role in adolescent anxiety. This is true for both family and peer relationships and in the etiology, course, and treatment of anxiety. Healthy parent–adolescent relationships characterized by security, appropriate control and autonomy granting, low levels of criticism, and behaviors that do not reinforce anxiety are associated with less anxiety among adolescents. Negative peer relationships, particularly in the form of rejection, victimization, and exclusion, are associated with greater anxiety, particularly social anxiety. Not surprisingly then, inclusion of parents and peers in treatment for adolescent anxiety, especially treatment that promotes more adaptive relationships and helps parents and peers learn new skills, is effective in reducing adolescent anxiety. However, as we have noted, specific, theory-driven interpersonal models of adolescent anxiety are lacking, particularly with regard to mechanisms of the association between interpersonal processes and anxiety, as well as with regard to how different interpersonal processes might be uniquely relevant for different anxiety disorders and how the particular challenges of adolescence, compared with those of childhood and adulthood, might confer unique risks or interact with interpersonal factors differently. As such, there is great opportunity for continued research in this area.

REFERENCES

Allen, J. P., Hauser, S. T., Eickholt, C., Bell, K. L., & O'Connor, T. G. (1994). Autonomy and relatedness in family interactions as predictors of expressions of negative adolescent affect. *Journal of Research on Adolescence, 4,* 535–552.

Allen, J. P., McElhaney, K. B, Land, D. J., Kuperminc, G. P, Moore, C. W., O'Beirne-Kelly, H., & Kilmer, S. L. (2003). A secure base in adolescence: Markers of attachment security in the mother–adolescent relationship. *Child Development, 74,* 292–307.

Allsopp, M., & Verduyn, C. (1990). Adolescents with obsessive–compulsive disorder: A case note review of consecutive patients referred to a provincial regional adolescent psychiatry unit. *Journal of Adolescence, 13,* 157–169.

American Psychiatric Association. (1987). *Diagnostic and statistical manual of mental disorders* (3rd ed., rev.). Washington, DC: Author.

American Psychiatric Association. (1994). *Diagnostic and statistical manual of mental disorders* (4th ed.). Washington, DC: Author.

Asher, S. R., & Wheeler, V. A. (1985). Children's loneliness: A comparison of rejected and neglected peer status. *Journal of Consulting and Clinical Psychology, 53,* 500–505.

Bakken, K., Landheim, A. S., & Vaglum, P. (2005). Substance-dependent patients with and without social anxiety disorder: Occurrence and clinical differences: A study of a consecutive sample of alcohol-dependent and poly-substance-dependent patients treated in two counties in Norway. *Drug and Alcohol Dependence, 80,* 321–328.

Bar-Haim, Y., Dan, O., & Eshel, Y. (2007). Predicting children's anxiety from early attachment relationships. *Journal of Anxiety Disorders, 21,* 1061–1068.

Beidel, D. C., & Turner, S. M. (1997). At risk for anxiety: I. Psychopathology in the offspring of anxious parents. *Journal of the American Academy of Child & Adolescent Psychiatry, 36,* 918–924.

Beidel, D. C., Turner, S. M., & Morris, T. L. (2000). Behavioral treatment of childhood social phobia. *Journal of Consulting and Clinical Psychology, 68,* 1072–1080.

Beidel, D. C., Turner, S. M., Sallee, F. R., Ammerman, R. T., Crosby, L. A., & Pathak, S. (2007). SET-C versus fluoxetine in the treatment of childhood social phobia. *Journal of the American Academy of Child & Adolescent Psychiatry, 46,* 1622–1632.

Beidel, D. C., Turner, S. M., & Young, B. J. (2005). Social effectiveness therapy for children: Three-year follow-up. *Journal of Consulting and Clinical Psychology, 73,* 721–725.

Beidel, D. C., Turner, S. M., & Young, B. J. (2006). Social effectiveness therapy for children: Five years later. *Behavior Therapy, 37,* 416–425.

Bellis, M. A., Downing, J., & Ashton, J. R. (2006). Adults at 12? Trends in puberty and their public health consequences. *Journal of Epidemiology and Community Health, 60,* 910–911.

Berndt, T. J. (1982). The features and effects of friendship in early adolescence. *Child Development, 53,* 1447–1460.

Bernstein, G. A., Layne, A. E., & Egan, E. A. (2005). Maternal phobic anxiety and child anxiety. *Journal of Anxiety Disorders, 19,* 658–672.

Blöte, A. W., Kint, M. J. W., & Westenberg, P. M. (2007). Peer behavior toward socially anxious adolescents: Classroom observations. *Behaviour Research and Therapy, 45*, 2773–2779.

Bögels, S. M., & Brechman-Toussaint, M. L. (2006). Family issues in child anxiety: Attachment, family functioning, parental rearing and beliefs. *Clinical Psychology Review, 26*, 834–856.

Bögels, S. M., van Oosten, A., & Muris, P. (2001). Familial correlates of social anxiety in children and adolescents. *Behaviour Research and Therapy, 39*, 273–287.

Bowlby, J. (1973). *Attachment and loss: Vol. 2. Separation, anxiety, and anger.* New York, NY: Basic Books.

Brown, B. B. (1989). The role of peer groups in adolescents' adjustment to secondary school. In T. J. Berndt & G. W. Ladd (Eds.), *Peer relationships in child development* (pp. 188–215). Oxford, England: Wiley.

Brown, B. B. (1990). Peer groups and peer cultures. In S. S. Feldman & G. R. Elliot (Eds.), *At the threshold: The developing adolescent* (pp. 171–196). Cambridge, MA: Harvard University Press.

Brown, B. B., Eicher, S. A., & Petrie, S. (1986). The importance of peer group ("crowd") affiliation in adolescence. *Journal of Adolescence, 9*, 73–96.

Buhrmester, D., & Furman, W. (1987). The development of companionship and intimacy. *Child Development, 58*, 1101–1113.

Carrigan, M. H., & Randall, C. L. (2003). Self-medication in social phobia: A review of the alcohol literature. *Addictive Behaviors, 28*, 269–284.

Carver, K., Joyner, K., & Udry, J. R. (2003). National estimates of adolescent romantic relationships. In P. Florsheim (Ed.), *Adolescent romantic relationships and sexual behavior: Theory, research, and practical implications* (pp. 291–329). New York, NY: Cambridge University Press.

Compian, L., Gowen, L. K., & Hayward, C. (2004). Peripubertal girls' romantic and platonic involvement with boys: Associations with body image and depression symptoms. *Journal of Research on Adolescence, 14*, 23–47.

Compton, S. N., Nelson, A. H., & March, J. S. (2000). Social phobia and separation anxiety symptoms in community and clinical samples of children and adolescents. *Journal of the American Academy of Child & Adolescent Psychiatry, 39*, 1040–1046.

Connolly, J. A., & Goldberg, A. (1999). Romantic relationships in adolescence: The role of friends and peers in their emergence and development. In W. Furman, B. B. Brown, & C. Feiring (Eds.), *The development of romantic relationships in adolescence* (pp. 266–290). New York, NY: Cambridge University Press.

Costa, N. M., & Weems, C. F. (2005). Maternal and child anxiety: Do attachment beliefs or children's perceptions of maternal control mediate their association? *Social Development, 14*, 574–590.

Costello, E. J., Egger, H. L., & Angold, A. (2005). The development epidemiology of anxiety disorders: Phenomenology, prevalence, and comorbidity. *Child and Adolescent Psychiatric Clinics of North America, 14*, 631–648.

Costello, E. J., Foley, D. L., & Angold, A. (2006). 10-year research update review: The epidemiology of child and adolescent psychiatric disorders: II. Developmental epidemiology. *Journal of the American Academy of Child & Adolescent Psychiatry, 45*, 8–25.

Costello, E. J., Mustillo, S., Erkanli, A., Keeler, G. & Angold, A. (2003). Prevalence and development of psychiatric disorders in childhood and adolescence. *Archives of General Psychiatry, 60*, 837–844.

Davila, J., Stroud, C. B., & Starr, L. R. (2008). Depression in couples and families. In I. H. Gotlib & C. Hammen (Eds.), *Handbook of depression* (2nd ed., pp. 467–491). New York, NY: Guilford Press.

De Los Reyes, A., & Prinstein, M. J. (2004). Applying depression-distortion hypotheses to the assessment of peer victimization in adolescents. *Journal of Clinical Child and Adolescent Psychology, 33*, 325–335.

Diamond, G. S. (2005). Attachment-based family therapy for depressed and anxious adolescents. In J. L. Lebow (Ed.), *Handbook of clinical family therapy* (pp. 17–41). Hoboken, NJ: Wiley.

Downey, G., Bonica, C., & Rincon, C. (1999). Rejection sensitivity and adolescent romantic relationships. In W. Furman, B. B. Brown, & C. Feiring (Eds.), *The development of romantic relationships in adolescence* (pp. 148–174). Cambridge, England: Cambridge University Press.

Eley, T. C., & Stevenson, J. (2000). Specific life events and chronic experiences differentially associated with depression and anxiety in young twins. *Journal of Abnormal Child Psychology, 28*, 383–394.

Essau, C. A. (2003). Comorbidity of anxiety disorders in adolescents. *Depression and Anxiety, 18*, 1–6.

Fisher, P. H., Masia-Warner, C., & Klein, R. G. (2004). Skills for social and academic success: A school-based intervention for social anxiety disorder in adolescents. *Clinical Child and Family Psychology Review, 7*, 241–249.

Furman, W., & Simon, V. A. (2004). Concordance in attachment states of mind and styles with respect to fathers and mothers. *Developmental Psychology, 40*, 1239–1247.

Ge, X., Brody, G. H., Conger, R. D., & Simons, R. L. (2006). Pubertal maturation and African American children's internalizing and externalizing symptoms. *Journal of Youth and Adolescence, 35*, 531–540.

Glickman, A. R., & La Greca, A. M. (2004). The Dating Anxiety Scale for Adolescents: Scale development and associations with adolescent functioning. *Journal of Clinical Child and Adolescent Psychology, 33*, 566–578.

Gothelf, D., Aharonovsky, O., & Horesh, N. (2004). Life events and personality factors in children and adolescents with obsessive-compulsive disorder and other anxiety disorders. *Comprehensive Psychiatry, 45*, 192–198.

Grant, D. M., Beck, J. G., Farrow, S. M., & Davila, J. (2007). Do interpersonal features of social anxiety influence the development of depressive symptoms? *Cognition and Emotion, 21*, 646–663.

Greenbaum, P. E., Cook, E. W., Melamed, B. G., Abeles, L. A., & Bush, J. P. (1988). Sequential patterns of medical stress: Maternal agitation and child distress. *Child & Family Behavior Therapy, 10,* 9–18.

Grotevant, H. D., & Cooper, C. R. (1985). Patterns of interaction in family relationships and the development of identity exploration in adolescence. *Child Development, 56,* 415–428.

Grover, R. L., Ginsburg, G. S., & Ialongo, N. (2005). Childhood predictors of anxiety symptoms: A longitudinal study. *Child Psychiatry & Human Development, 36,* 133–153.

Haden, S. C., Scarpa, A., & Jones, R. T. (2007). Posttraumatic stress disorder symptoms and injury: The moderating role of perceived social support and coping for young adults. *Personality and Individual Differences, 42,* 1187–1198.

Hale, W.W., III, Engels, R., & Meeus, W. (2006). Adolescent's perceptions of parenting behaviours and its relationship to adolescent generalized anxiety disorder symptoms. *Journal of Adolescence, 29,* 407–417.

Harter, S. (1988). *Manual for the Self-Perception Profile for Children and Adolescents.* Denver, CO: Author.

Hartup, W. W. (1996). The company they keep: Friendships and their developmental significance. *Child Development, 67,* 1–13.

Hawker, D. S. J, & Boulton, M. J. (2000). Twenty years' research on peer victimization and psychosocial maladjustment: A meta-analytic review of cross-sectional studies. *Journal of Psychology and Psychiatry, 41,* 441–455.

Hoffman, E. C., & Mattis, S. G. (2000). A developmental adaptation of panic control treatment for panic disorder in adolescence. *Cognitive and Behavioral Practice, 7,* 253–261.

Inderbitzen, H. M., Walters, K. S., & Bukowsky, A. L. (1997). The role of social anxiety in adolescent peer relations: Differences among sociometric status groups and rejected subgroups. *Journal of Clinical Child Psychology, 26,* 338–348.

Ishikawa, S., Okajima, I., & Matsuoka, H. (2007). Cognitive behavioural therapy for anxiety disorders in children and adolescents: A meta-analysis. *Child and Adolescent Mental Health, 12,* 164–172.

Kearney, C. A., Sims, K. E., Pursell, C. R., & Tillotson, C. A. (2003). Separation anxiety disorder in young children: A longitudinal and family analysis. *Journal of Clinical Child and Adolescent Psychology, 32,* 593–598.

Keel, P. K., Klump, K. L., Miller, K. B., McGue, M., & Iacono, W. G. (2005). Shared transmission of eating disorders and anxiety disorders. *International Journal of Eating Disorders, 38,* 99–105.

Kendall, P. C., Hudson, J. L., & Gosch, E. (2008). Cognitive–behavioral therapy for anxiety disordered youth: A randomized clinical trial evaluating child and family modalities. *Journal of Consulting and Clinical Psychology, 76,* 282–297.

Kessler, R. C., Berglund, P., Demler, O., Jin, R., & Walters, E. E. (2005). Lifetime prevalence and age-of-onset distributions of *DSM–IV* disorders in the National Comorbidity Survey Replication. *Archives of General Psychiatry, 62,* 593–602.

Koenen, K. C. (2003). A brief introduction to genetics research in PTSD. *PTSD Research Quarterly, 14*, 1–3.

Kuttler, A. F., & La Greca, A. M. (2004). Adolescents' romantic relationships: Do they help or hinder close friendships? *Journal of Adolescence, 27*, 395–414.

Kuttler, A. F., La Greca, A. M., & Prinstein, M. J. (1999). Adolescents' close friendships: Same- versus cross-sex friends. *Journal of Research in Adolescence, 9*, 339–366.

La Greca, A. M., & Harrison, H. W. (2005). Adolescent peer relations, friendships and romantic relationships: Do they predict social anxiety and depression? *Journal of Clinical Child and Adolescent Psychology, 34*, 49–61.

La Greca, A. M., & Lopez, N. (1998). Social anxiety among adolescents: Linkages with peer relations and friendships. *Journal of Abnormal Child Psychology, 26*, 83–94.

La Greca, A. M., & Mackey, E. R. (2007). Adolescents' anxiety in dating situations: Do friends and romantic partners contribute? *Journal of Clinical Child and Adolescent Psychology, 34*, 522–533.

La Greca, A. M., & Prinstein, M. J. (1999). Peer group. In W. K. Silverman & T. H. Ollendick (Eds.), *Developmental issues in the clinical treatment of children* (pp. 171–198). Needham Heights, MA: Allyn & Bacon.

La Greca, A. M., Prinstein, M. J., & Fetter, M. (2001). Adolescent peer crowd affiliation: Linkages with health-risk behaviors and close friendships. *Journal of Pediatric Psychology, 26*, 131–143.

La Greca, A. M., & Stone, W. L. (1993). The Social Anxiety Scale for Children—Revised: Factor structure and concurrent validity. *Journal of Clinical Child Psychology, 22*, 17–27.

Larson, R. W. (1983). Adolescents' daily experience with family and friends: Contrasting opportunity systems. *Journal of Marriage and the Family, 45*, 739–750.

Laursen, B., Coy, K. C., & Collins, W. A. (1998). Reconsidering changes in parent-child conflict across adolescence: A meta-analysis. *Child Development, 69*, 817–832.

Lawyer, S. R., Ruggiero, K. J., & Resnick, H. S. (2006). Mental health correlates of the victim-perpetrator relationship among interpersonally victimized adolescents. *Journal of Interpersonal Violence, 21*, 1333–1353.

Leary, M. R. (1983). Social anxiousness: The construct and its measurement. *Journal of Personality Assessment, 47*, 66–75.

Leonard, H., Swedo, S. E., Lenane, M. C., Rettew, D. C., Hamburger, S. D., Bartko, J. J., & Rapoport, J. L. (1993). A 2- to 7-year follow-up study of 54 obsessive-compulsive children and adolescents. *Archives of General Psychiatry, 50*, 429–439.

Lewinsohn, P. M., Hops, H., Roberts, R. E., Seeley, J. R., & Andrews, J. A. (1993). Adolescent psychopathology: I. Prevalence and incidence of depression and other DSM–III–R disorders in high school students. *Journal of Abnormal Psychology, 102*, 133–144.

Lewinsohn, P. M., Rohde, P., & Seeley, J. R. (1995). Adolescent psychopathology: III. The clinical consequences of comorbidity. *Journal of the American Academy of Child & Adolescent Psychiatry, 34*, 510–519.

Lewinsohn, P. M., Zinbarg, R., Seeley, J. R., Lewinsohn, M., & Sack, W. H. (1997). Lifetime comorbidity among anxiety disorders and between anxiety disorders and other mental disorders in adolescents. *Journal of Anxiety Disorders, 11*, 377–394.

Linares, L. O., & Cloitre, M. (2004). Intergenerational links between mothers and children with PTSD spectrum illnesses. In R. R. Silva (Ed.), *Handbook of posttraumatic stress disorders in children and adolescents* (pp. 177–201). New York, NY: Norton.

Margolin, G., & Vickerman, K. A. (2007). Posttraumatic stress in children and adolescents exposed to family violence: I. Overview and issues. *Professional Psychology: Research and Practice, 38*, 613–619.

Masia-Warner, C., Klein, R. G., Dent, H. C., Fisher, P. H., Alvir, J., Albano, A. M., & Guardino, M. (2005). School-based intervention for adolescents with social anxiety disorder: Results of a controlled study. *Journal of Abnormal Child Psychology, 33*, 707–722.

Mattis, S. G., & Ollendick, T. H. (1997). Panic in children and adolescents: A developmental analysis. *Advances in Clinical Child Psychology, 19*, 27–74.

McLeod, B. D., Wood, J. J., & Weisz, J. R. (2007). Examining the association between parenting and childhood anxiety: A meta-analysis. *Clinical Psychology Review, 27*, 155–172.

Mills, R. S. L., & Rubin, K. H. (1993). Socialization factors in the development of social withdrawal. In K. H. Rubin & J. B. Asendorpf (Eds.), *Social withdrawal, inhibition, and shyness in childhood* (pp. 117–148). Hillsdale, NJ: Erlbaum.

Moore, P. S., Whaley, S. E., & Sigman, M. (2004). Interactions between mothers and children: Impacts of maternal and child anxiety. *Journal of Abnormal Psychology, 11*, 471–476.

Muris, P., Mayer, B., & Meesters, C. (2000). Self-reported attachment style, anxiety, and depression in children. *Social Behavior and Personality, 28*, 157–162.

Natsuaki, M. N., Biehl, M. C., & Ge, X. (2009). Trajectories of depressed mood from early adolescence to young adulthood: The effects of pubertal timing and adolescent dating. *Journal of Research on Adolescence, 19*, 47–74.

Nicol-Harper, R., Harvey, A. G., & Stein, A. (2007). Interactions between mothers and infants: Impact of maternal anxiety. *Infant Behavior and Development, 30*, 161–167.

Ollendick, T. H. (1995). Cognitive behavioral treatment of panic disorder with agoraphobia in adolescents: A multiple baseline design analysis. *Behavior Therapy, 26*, 517–531.

Ollendick, T. H., & Horsch, L. M. (2007). Fears in clinic-referred children: Relations with child anxiety sensitivity, maternal overcontrol, and maternal phobic anxiety. *Behavior Therapy, 38*, 402–411.

Ollendick, T. H., Langley, A. K., Jones, R. T., & Kephart, C. (2001). Fear in children and adolescents: Relations with negative life events, attributional style, and avoidant coping. *Journal of Child Psychology and Psychiatry, 42*, 1029–1034.

Ollendick, T. H., & Pincus, D. (2008). Panic disorder in adolescents. In R. G. Steele, T. D. Elkin, & M. C. Roberts (Eds.), *Handbook of evidence-based therapies for children and adolescents: Bridging science and practice* (pp. 83–102). New York, NY: Springer.

Ozer, E. J., & Weinstein, R. S. (2004). Urban adolescents' exposure to community violence: The role of support, school safety, and social constraints in a school–based sample of boys and girls. *Journal of Clinical Child and Adolescent Psychology, 33,* 463–476.

Rose, A. J. (2002). Co-rumination in the friendships of girls and boys. *Child Development, 73,* 1830–1843.

Rose, A. J., & Rudolph, K. D. (2006). A review of sex differences in peer relationship processes: Potential trade-offs for the emotional and behavioral development of girls and boys. *Psychological Bulletin, 132,* 98–131.

Rosenstein, D. S., & Horowitz, H. A. (1996). Adolescent attachment and psychopathology. *Journal of Consulting and Clinical Psychology, 64,* 244–253.

Rubin, K. H., Nelson, L. J., Hastings, P., & Asendorpf, J. (1999). The transaction between parents' perceptions of their children's shyness and their parenting styles. *International Journal of Behavioral Development, 23,* 937–958.

Rudolph, K. D. (2002). Gender differences in emotional responses to interpersonal stress during adolescence. *Journal of Adolescent Health, 30,* 3–13.

Rush, A. J., Zimmerman, M., Wisniewski, S. R., Fava, M., Hollon, S. D., Warden, D., . . . Trivedi, M. H. (2005). Comorbid psychiatric disorders in depressed outpatients: Demographic and clinical features. *Journal of Affective Disorders, 87,* 43–55.

Scapillato, D., & Manassis, K. (2002). Cognitive–behavioral/interpersonal group treatment for anxious adolescents. *Journal of the American Academy of Child & Adolescent Psychiatry, 41,* 739–741.

Schutz, H. K., & Paxton, S. J. (2007). Friendship quality, body dissatisfaction, dieting and disordered eating in adolescent girls. *British Journal of Clinical Psychology, 46,* 67–83.

Shulman, S., & Scharf, M. (2000). Adolescent romantic behaviors and perceptions: Age- and gender-related differences, and links with family and peer relationships. *Journal of Research on Adolescence, 10,* 99–118.

Siegel, R., La Greca, A. M., & Harrison, H. M. (2009). Peer victimization and social anxiety in adolescents: Prospective and reciprocal findings. *Journal of Youth and Adolescence, 38,* 1096–1109.

Silverman, W., Pina, A., & Viswesvaran, C. (2008). Evidence-based psychosocial treatments for phobic and anxiety disorders in children and adolescents. *Journal of Clinical Child and Adolescent Psychology, 37,* 105–130.

Siqueland, L., Rynn, M., & Diamond, G. S. (2005). Cognitive behavioral and attachment based family therapy for anxious adolescents: Phase I and II studies. *Journal of Anxiety Disorders, 19,* 361–381.

Sonntag, H., Wittchen, H. U., Hofler, M., Kessler, R. C., & Stein, M. B. (2000). Are social fears and DSM–IV social anxiety disorder associated with smoking and nicotine dependence in adolescents and young adults? *European Psychiatry, 15,* 67–74.

Spence, S. H., Najman, J. M., & Bor, W. (2002). Maternal anxiety and depression, poverty and marital relationship factors during early childhood as predictors of anxiety and depressive symptoms in adolescence. *Journal of Child Psychology and Psychiatry, 43,* 457–470.

Starr, L. R., & Davila, J. (2008). Differentiating interpersonal correlates of depressive symptoms and social anxiety in adolescence: Implications for models of comorbidity. *Journal of Clinical Child and Adolescent Psychology, 37,* 337–349.

Starr, L. R., & Davila, J. (2009). Clarifying co-rumination: Association with internalizing symptoms and romantic involvement among adolescent girls. *Journal of Adolescence, 32,* 19–37.

Storch, E. A., Geffken, G. R., & Merlo, L. J. (2007). Family accommodation in pediatric obsessive–compulsive disorder. *Journal of Clinical Child and Adolescent Psychology, 36,* 207–216.

Storch, E. A., Masia-Warner, C., Crisp, H., & Klein, R. G. (2005). Peer victimization and social anxiety in adolescence: A prospective study. *Aggressive Behavior, 31,* 437–452.

Stroud, C. B., & Davila, J. (2008). Pubertal timing and depressive symptoms in early adolescents: The roles of romantic competence and romantic experiences. *Journal of Youth and Adolescence, 37,* 953–966.

Thienemann, M., Moore, P., & Tompkins, K. (2006). A parent-only group intervention for children with anxiety disorders: Pilot study. *Journal of the American Academy of Child & Adolescent Psychiatry, 45,* 37–46.

Urberg, K. A., Degirmencioglu, S. M., & Tolson, J. M. (1995). The structure of adolescent peer networks. *Developmental Psychology, 31,* 540–547.

van Brakel, A. M. L., Muris, P., & Bögels, S. M. (2006). A multifactorial model for the etiology of anxiety in non-clinical adolescents: Main and interactive effects of behavioral inhibition, attachment and parental rearing. *Journal of Child and Family Studies, 15,* 569–579.

van der Bruggen, C. O., Stams, G. J. J. M., & Bögels, S. M. (2008). The relation between child and parent anxiety and parental control: A meta-analytic review. *Journal of Child Psychology and Psychiatry, 49,* 1257–1269.

Vernberg, E. M., Abwender, D. A., Ewell, K. K., & Beery, S. H. (1992). Social anxiety and peer relationships in early adolescence: A prospective analysis. *Journal of Clinical Child Psychology, 21,* 189–196.

Warren, S. L., Huston, L., Egeland, B., & Sroufe, L. A. (1997). Child and adolescent anxiety disorders and early attachment. *Journal of the American Academy of Child & Adolescent Psychiatry, 36,* 637–644.

Waters, T. L., & Barrett, P. M. (2000). The role of the family in childhood obsessive–compulsive disorder. *Clinical Child and Family Psychology Review, 3,* 173–184.

Watson, D., & Friend, R. (1969). Measurement of social–evaluative anxiety. *Journal of Consulting and Clinical Psychology, 33,* 448–457.

Weems, C. F., Berman, S. L., & Silverman, W. K. (2002). The relation between anxiety sensitivity and attachment style in adolescence and early adulthood. *Journal of Psychopathology and Behavioral Assessment, 24,* 159–168.

Wicks-Nelson, R., & Israel, A. C. (2009). *Abnormal child and adolescent psychology* (7th ed.). Upper Saddle River, NJ: Pearson Prentice Hall.

Wolfradt, U., Hempel, S., & Miles, J. N.V. (2003). Perceived parenting styles, depersonalisation, anxiety and coping behavior in adolescents. *Personality and Individual Differences, 34,* 521–532.

Wood, J. J., Piacentini, J. C., & Southam-Gerow, M. (2006). Family cognitive behavioral therapy for child anxiety disorders. *Journal of the American Academy of Child & Adolescent Psychiatry, 45,* 314–321.

Young, J. F., Mufson, L., & Davies, M. (2006). Impact of comorbid anxiety in an effectiveness study of interpersonal psychotherapy for depressed adolescents. *Journal of the American Academy of Child & Adolescent Psychiatry, 45,* 904–912.

Zimmermann, P., Wittchen, H. U., Hofler, M., Pfister, H., Kessler, R. C., & Lieb, R. (2003). Primary anxiety disorders and the development of subsequent alcohol use disorders: A 4-year community study of adolescents and young adults. *Psychological Medicine, 33,* 1211–1222.

5

INTERPERSONAL PROCESSES IN SOCIAL ANXIETY DISORDER

LYNN E. ALDEN AND CHARLES T. TAYLOR

Social anxiety disorder (SAD), or social phobia, is unique among the anxiety disorders in that interpersonal dysfunction is a core feature of the condition. In this chapter, we analyze SAD from the perspective of interpersonal and relational models of human behavior. Our overarching goal is identify the interpersonal processes associated with social anxiety and present an interpersonal model of SAD on the basis of those findings. Our central thesis is that the interpersonal perspective is useful in drawing together findings from diverse areas and provides a framework within which to consider such topics as comorbidity between SAD and other disorders. We end the chapter by describing how strategies based on interpersonal principles are readily integrated with established CBT regimens. In keeping with the theme of this volume, we focus on interpersonal processes alone. It is important to recognize, however, that innate biological factors often set those processes in motion and that comprehensive models must include biological vulnerabilities.

CLINICAL DESCRIPTION

SAD is characterized by a marked and persistent fear of one or more social or performance situations in which the person is exposed to unfamiliar people or to possible scrutiny by others (American Psychiatric Association, 1994). People with SAD fear that they will act in such a way or show anxiety symptoms that will be embarrassing or humiliating or that may result in negative evaluation by others. Consequently, the feared situations are avoided, or else endured with intense distress. SAD is described as *generalized* if the person experiences fear in most social situations and as *nongeneralized* or *circumscribed* if the person experiences fear in only a few situations. SAD occurs at a lifetime prevalence of approximately 8% in the general population, making it the fourth most prevalent psychiatric disorder (Kessler, Berglund, Demler, Jin, & Walters, 2005). SAD typically has an early age of onset, surfacing in either childhood or adolescence, and it often persists well into adulthood following a chronic, unremitting course that causes significant functional impairment and diminished quality of life (e.g., Eng, Coles, Heimberg, & Safren, 2005).

SAD AND CLOSE OTHERS

People with SAD have fewer social relationships than members of the general population or patients with other anxiety disorders (e.g., Hart, Turk, Heimberg, & Liebowitz, 1999; Mendlowicz & Stein, 2000). People with generalized SAD have particular difficulty. They are less likely to date or marry, they have fewer friends, have lower levels of perceived social support, and are more likely to be socially isolated than people with nongeneralized SAD (e.g., Mendlowicz & Stein, 2000). When they do develop friendships or romantic relationships, those relationships tend to have problems (e.g., Davila & Beck, 2002; Wenzel, Graff-Dolezal, Macho, & Brendle, 2005). These same difficulties are found in socially anxious children (e.g., Beidel, Turner, & Morris, 1999; Spence, Donovan, & Brechman-Toussaint, 1999) and nonclinical populations (e.g., Dodge, Heimberg, Nyman, & O'Brien, 1987).

ETIOLOGICAL FORMULATIONS/THEORETICAL MODELS

Contemporary models emphasize the role of cognitive processes in the development and maintenance of SAD. The cognitive–behavioral model of Rapee and Heimberg (1997) and the cognitive model of Clark and Wells (1995) are influential examples. These theorists proposed that people with

SAD have negative beliefs that lead to overly negative predictions and anticipatory anxiety before social events. As a result, these individuals closely monitor their behavior and selectively attend to negative internal sensations and external cues. Selective attention leads to negative interpretations of events, which are further consolidated in memory by postevent rumination. Interpersonal processes per se enter into these models in two ways. These writers recognized that negative social learning experiences often contribute to the development of dysfunctional social beliefs (e.g., Bruch & Heimberg, 1994) and noted that negative cognitive processes result in subtle avoidance behaviors (safety behaviors) that can disrupt interpersonal interactions and produce negative social outcomes.

Interpersonal Theories

Our central thesis is that interpersonal constructs and empirical findings can be used to enrich our understanding of SAD (Alden, 2001; Alden & Taylor, 2004). A painful aspect of this condition is that social anxiety impairs the person's ability to develop close relationships, and thus these individuals often find themselves socially isolated. The interpersonal perspective provides leads as to how individuals with SAD short circuit the natural process of relating to others and how this might be changed.

Several theories are of particular relevance: parenting (attachment) models from developmental theorists (Bowlby, 1971; Rubin, Nelson, Hastings, & Asendorpf, 1999), interpersonal circumplex theories (e.g., Kiesler, 1996; T. F. Leary, 1957), and relational theories of friendship formation (Reis & Shaver, 1988).

Interpersonal theories share several underlying tenets. First, these writers have adopted a developmental perspective that emphasizes the way in which early social processes shape biological tendencies to form enduring interpersonal patterns. Second, these theorists have proposed that people's sense of self (self-schema) develops in large part from others' reactions to them (e.g., M. R. Leary, 2007). Regularities in transactions with significant others are hypothesized to be stored in memory in organized knowledge structures, variously labeled *working models* (Bowlby, 1971) or *relational schema* (Baldwin, 1992), which depict oneself in relation to others. These schema function as cognitive maps that shape people's social perceptions and lead them to select behavioral strategies to negotiate their social worlds as they see them (Baldwin & Ferguson, 2001).

Third, formative developmental situations and relational schema set in motion interpersonal cycles that perpetuate the person's views of self and others. Interpersonal writers have noted that any act emitted in a social situation sends an interpersonal message that invites (or "pulls") certain types of reactions, which tend to reaffirm the actor's original beliefs and behaviors (Horowitz, 2004; Kiesler, 1996; T. F. Leary, 1957). Social transactions are said to follow principles of complementarity—that is, specific behavioral patterns tend to elicit particular types of interpersonal responses. One robust finding is that social behavior evokes corresponding responses in terms of affiliation (e.g., friendliness elicits friendliness; coldness elicits coldness; e.g., Sadler & Woody, 2003). In line with that principle, relational theorists underscore the role of open, genuine expression of one's feelings and opinions in the development of close relationships. Reciprocal self-disclosure fosters the mutual trust, perceived similarity, and liking that motivate people to develop the friendships and romantic relationships that help them to value themselves (e.g., Laurenceau, Barrett, & Pietromonaco, 1998; Reis & Shaver, 1988). Although self-disclosure is generally studied in the context of willingness to talk about personal matters, on a broader level it involves the willingness to be oneself around others.

Finally, whereas existing SAD models tend to emphasize the desire to avoid negative outcomes, interpersonal writers have noted that social behavior is guided by two motivational systems, approach and avoidance. The dual motivational model raises the possibility that reducing social avoidance does not necessarily facilitate social approach behavior. This distinction has important implications for theories and treatment of SAD.

In summary, interpersonal theorists have proposed that there are interpersonal themes that run through a person's life, linking past and present. Developmental experiences shape people's sense of who they are. The interpersonal patterns learned from those experiences are perpetuated across the life span and if dysfunctional, contribute to psychopathology. We turn now to a review of the research literature that addresses each tenet of the interpersonal framework.

SOCIAL DEVELOPMENTAL EXPERIENCES

Although innate, biological influences contribute to the development of social anxiety (e.g., Kagan, Reznick, Snidman, Gibbons, & Johnson, 1988), interpersonal theorists are interested in the way in which the social environment shapes the expression of these tendencies. Retrospective reports of adults with SAD have pointed to three types of early family environments associated with shyness and social anxiety, namely, (a) parental intrusiveness and control; (b) parental hostility, abuse, and neglect; and (c) limited family socializing (for reviews, see Alden & Taylor, 2004; Rapee & Spence, 2004; and Chapter 3 of this volume). Those reports are confirmed in observational studies of parent–child interactions. Relative to mothers of other children, the mothers of anxious–withdrawn children displayed more controlling or intrusive involvement, used nonresponsiveness or criticism, and encouraged social avoidance (e.g., Dadds, Barrett, & Rapee, 1996; Dumas, LaFreniere, & Serketich, 1995). The most compelling evidence for the causal role of specific parenting behaviors comes from a recent study by de Wilde and Rapee (2008), who randomly assigned mothers of nonanxious children to use either overly or minimally controlling behavior while their child prepared a speech. During a subsequent speech that children prepared alone, the children of the overly controlling mothers displayed greater anxiety relative to children whose mothers had exhibited minimal control.

Longitudinal studies have revealed that the relationship between socially anxious children and their parents is bidirectional. Child wariness and behavioral inhibition were found to elicit restrictive, controlling parental behavior (e.g., Rubin et al., 1999). In return, overprotection, intrusiveness, and derisive maternal behavior have all been shown to maintain child social reticence (e.g., Rubin, Burgess, & Hastings, 2002). Moreover, anxious children displayed the highest degree of noncompliance when their mothers were highly controlling (Dumas et al., 1995), a pattern of behavior that may perpetuate dysfunctional transactions. Existing evidence has increasingly supported the interpersonal concept of cyclical interaction patterns between parents and socially anxious children that perpetuate the child's social reticence. However, specific parenting styles explain only a modest amount of variance in symptoms of child anxiety (see McLeod, Wood, & Weisz, 2007). Social experiences outside of the family can influence the expression of social anxiety as well. For example, behavioral inhibition tends to decrease over time when children are placed in nonparental child care environments (e.g., Fox, Henderson, Rubin, Calkins, & Schmidt, 2001).

Negative peer experiences also play a role. Social anxiety is associated with a variety of adverse peer behaviors, including overt displays of bullying, harassment, and rejection, as well as more subtle forms of exclusion and neglect (see Chap. 4, this volume). As with parent interactions, the relationship between socially anxious children and their peers is bidirectional. For example, social withdrawal was increasingly associated with negative peer perceptions and peer-related difficulties from early to late elementary school (Hymel, Rubin, Rowden, & LeMare, 1990). In return, negative social environments exacerbate social anxiety. Anxious solitary children displayed stable or increasing levels of social avoidance and depression in the context of high peer exclusion (Gazelle & Rudolph, 2004). More important, low peer exclusion was associated with more social approach behaviors and lower levels of depression in these children.

Less research has been devoted to understanding children's close friendships. Interestingly, despite peer exclusion and rejection, shy and/or withdrawn children are as likely as nonshy children to have stable best friendships

(Rubin, Wojslawowicz, Rose-Krasnor, Booth-LaForce, & Burgess, 2006). Unfortunately, withdrawn children and their friends reported lower friendship quality than did their control counterparts. Moreover, friendship instability predicted increasing levels of social withdrawal over the course of middle school (Oh et al., 2008). Poor relationship quality (i.e., high negativity) within girls' (but not boys') best friendships was associated with increased risk of low peer acceptance (Greco & Morris, 2005). Considered together, these findings suggest that friendship quality is an equally, if not more, important determinant of social anxiety than friendship quantity.

To summarize, the literature has suggested that the interpersonal patterns developed in childhood continue in interactions with peers. Socially anxious youth elicit negative peer responses that intensify their self-doubts and evaluative fears. Although positive social environments can ameliorate these negative consequences, anxiety-driven behaviors appear to choke off the development of the positive peer relationships that might accomplish this.

THE RELATIONAL SELF

Relational theorists have proposed that these developmental experiences lead to relational schema in which the self is viewed as deficient or inadequate and others are viewed as critical or ignoring (e.g., Baldwin & Ferguson, 2001; M. R. Leary, 2007). Social events are inherently complex and ambiguous. Schema are believed to direct attention to relevant aspects of this complex environment and result in selective processing of that information. Many of the well-known characteristics of schematic processing have been documented in the social anxiety literature. For example, Veljaca and Rapee (1998) reported that socially anxious people selectively attend to negative and ignore positive audience behaviors, even when both are present in equal numbers. In addition, people with SAD more rapidly identified angry compared with happy faces immersed in pictures of neutral crowds (Gilboa-Schectman, Foa, & Amir, 1999), assigned more negative evaluations to those crowds, and made those negative evaluations more rapidly than did people with depression or nonclinical controls (Gilboa-Schectman, Presburger, Marom, & Hermesh, 2005). Socially anxious people were also shown to selectively process negative facial clues (e.g., Winton, Clark, & Edelmann, 1995). All of these studies support the idea that people with SAD process complex nonverbal cues in light of negative relational schema.

There is also evidence that cognitive representations of others are closely linked to self-representations and that judgments about the self are influenced by the activation of this other-related information. Higgins and his colleagues (e.g., Strauman & Higgins, 1987) proposed that the self-structure consists of multiple elements, including the *actual self*, *ideal self*, and *ought-other self*, that is, the self people believe that others think they ought to be. They hypothesized that social anxiety occurs when people become aware of discrepancies between the actual and ought-other self-structures. In support of this reasoning, people with SAD were found to display larger discrepancies between the actual and ought-other self-structures than did depressed patients or controls (e.g., Strauman, 1989). In a similar vein, people with SAD were shown to evaluate themselves in light of their perceptions of other people's standards rather than their own standards (Alden & Wallace, 1995; Wallace & Alden, 1997).

Research by Baldwin has also provided support for the idea that cognitive structures representing the self are tightly linked to structures representing other people. Baldwin used a variety of experimental manipulations to prime a positive or negative other, including pictures of frowning versus smiling authority figures or thinking about a supportive or critical person. Even when the priming stimulus was presented surreptitiously as pictures hanging in the background, people displayed negative biases in their interpretations of social vignettes, greater anxiety, and lower state self-esteem when a disapproving as opposed to supportive other was primed (Baldwin & Ferguson, 2001). Thus, priming internalized representations of disapproving others resulted in cognitive and emotional responses similar to those found in socially anxious people. To summarize, people with SAD appear to have well-developed negative relationship schema, and their chronic interpersonal patterns can be understood in terms of the ease with which these schema are brought to mind by contemporary social situations.

Several studies have addressed the link between social developmental experiences and interpretation of social events. Taylor and Alden (2005) found that patients with SAD who reported histories of parental hostility displayed negative interpretations of ambiguous partner behavior, a pattern not observed for patients with other backgrounds. In contrast, patients who reported parental overprotection failed to discriminate between neutral and positive conversational partners, which led to negative reactions from the positive partners (Taylor & Alden, 2006). These studies support the notion that social learning experiences result in relational schema that influence interpretations of contemporary social events.

MALADAPTIVE TRANSACTION PATTERNS

A large body of research has attested to the fact that people with social anxiety and SAD are rated by objective observers as lacking social skill and displaying anxious mannerisms (e.g., Glass & Arnkoff, 1989). Of greater interest from an interpersonal perspective is how others respond to the behaviors displayed by socially anxious people. The research literature has confirmed that others often have negative perceptions of socially anxious people. Shy individuals were viewed as less warm, less competent, and less likable by objective interviewers and, even more significantly, by their best friends (e.g., Gough & Thorne, 1986). Several studies have indicated that shy individuals are seen as less intelligent than nonshy people by peers, even though there is no actual association between social anxiety and intelligence (Gough & Thorne, 1986; Paulhus & Morgan, 1997). Thus, other people's perceptions of socially anxious individuals seem to be colored by a global negative halo.

Creed and Funder (1998) found that college friends viewed socially anxious students as sensitive to demands, having brittle ego defenses, moody, and self-pitying. Moreover, during interactions between unacquainted people, partners of socially anxious individuals attempted to dominate the interaction, talked at rather than with them, and expressed irritability. Thus, not only did socially anxious students evoke negative reactions in friends, they also irritated and alienated strangers very rapidly. In a similar vein, Heerey and Kring (2007) found that socially anxious students were less likely to reciprocate the types of smiles displayed by their nonanxious partners and asked fewer questions during a laboratory conversation. Their partners, in turn, viewed the interaction more negatively and failed to experience the increase in positive affect reported by students interacting with nonanxious individuals.

Consistent with theories of relationship development, the interpersonal behavior of socially anxious people appears to short circuit the development of close relationships. For example, after getting-acquainted conversations, the partners of socially anxious students were less likely to desire future interaction with them than with nonanxious individuals (e.g., Meleshko & Alden, 1993). Moreover, failure to be open with others (i.e., low self-disclosure) played a key role in those partners' negative reactions (Alden & Bieling, 1998; Mesleshko & Alden, 1993). The same pattern was found in clinical populations. Alden and Wallace (1995) found that patients with SAD who participated in open-ended discussions were rated by observers and by their partners as conveying less warmth and interest and emitting fewer positive verbal behaviors than nonclinical controls. More important, both partners and observers were less likely to desire subsequent interaction with the SAD participants. Finally, in the most comprehensive study to date, Vöncken, Alden, Bögels, and Roelofs (2008) used structural equation modeling to examine potential mediators of the relationship between social anxiety and social rejection in patients with SAD. The results revealed a chain of events in which social anxiety symptoms were associated with social behaviors that evoked negative emotions in other people. Negative emotional reactions were associated with lower judgments of similarity between themselves and SAD patients. Others' judgments of (dis)similarity, in turn, directly predicted social rejection. Thus, the extant literature has supported relational models of friendship formation (e.g., Reis & Shaver, 1988).

Only a few studies have examined the effect of social anxiety on close relationships in adults. Davila and Beck (2002) found that social anxiety was associated with avoidance of expressing emotions, conflict avoidance, and nonassertiveness in students' relationships with their friends, acquaintances, family, and romantic partners. Interestingly, socially anxious individuals also reported overreliance on others, which suggests that they felt overly dependent on the few relationships they had (Davila & Beck, 2002). A second study found that avoidance of expressing emotions to friends, family, and romantic partners predicted an increase in depressive symptoms over the subsequent year (Grant, Beck, Farrow, & Davila, 2007). Those findings are notable given that emotional suppression was found to elicit negative cardiovascular responses (i.e., increased blood pressure), interfere with the development of rapport, and inhibit relationship formation between unacquainted conversation partners (Butler et al., 2003). In addition to eliciting negative responses in their partners, emotion suppressors themselves reported significantly less positive and more negative emotions about their interaction partner relative to controls. Together these findings suggest that avoidance of expressing emotions may be toxic to the formation and maintenance of close relationships.

Wenzel (2002) found that patients with SAD reported lower levels of emotional and social intimacy in their close relationships and were more likely to display fearful or preoccupied adult attachment styles. Interestingly, they were also more likely to attribute the cause of negative relationship events to some stable characteristic of their spouse, which suggested they were more blaming toward their partners (Wenzel, 2002). In a second study, socially anxious and nonanxious students and their romantic partners were observed as they discussed various topics. Relative to nonanxious people, socially anxious students displayed more extremely negative behaviors, particularly when discussing relationship problems, and engaged in fewer positive behaviors across all types of conversations (Wenzel et al., 2005). Wenzel et al. (2005) concluded that social anxiety is associated with deficits in the interpersonal strategies needed to maintain and enhance close relationships. All in all, studies of close relationships paint a picture consistent with the patterns found in transactions with unfamiliar people, namely, that socially anxious people have difficulty being open and engage in less positive behavior and their relationships are characterized by lower levels of intimacy.

To summarize, across all types of relationships—unfamiliar people, friends, and close others—people with SAD conceal themselves and fail to reciprocate openness on the part of others. Lack of openness reduces other people's willingness to engage in future interactions, which maintains the person's social and emotional isolation (e.g., Alden & Bieling, 1998). Thus, socially anxious people are caught in a maladaptive cycle in which their social behavior, rather than inviting others to affiliate with them, sends a disaffiliative message that evokes negative reactions and disengagement by others, thereby impeding the development of closer relationships and maintaining social isolation.

BIVARIATE SOCIAL MOTIVATION

Research has confirmed that human behavior is governed by two partially independent motivational systems, often labeled the *approach* and *avoidance* systems (e.g., Davidson, Jackson, & Kalin, 2000; Gable, Reis, & Elliot, 2003). These systems arise from different central nervous system circuits and appear to regulate behavior through different processes (Davidson et al., 2000; Fredrickson, 2001). The approach system is involved in a variety of beneficial processes, including social interest and behavior, and some types of positive affect (Gable & Reis, 2001). Positive affect, in turn, helps to facilitate recovery from the physiological and behavioral effects of negative emotions (e.g., Fredrickson, 2001; Tugade & Fredrickson, 2004), broadens and expands the individual's thought–action repertoire, and facilitates social approach behaviors (e.g., Folkman & Moskowitz, 2000; Gable, Reis, & Elliot, 2000).

Social anxiety and SAD have been shown to be associated with low positive affect (e.g., Brown, Chorpita, & Barlow, 1998; Hughes et al., 2006), which may indicate that socially anxious people suffer from dysregulation of the approach system in addition to overactivation of the avoidance system. Signs of hedonic dysregulation also occur in cognitive judgments. Hirsch and Mathews (2000) found that SAD was associated with an absence of the positive inferential bias that maintains self-esteem in nonanxious people.

Studies that measured social motivation have also supported this idea. Whereas nonanxious participants reported that they were predominantly driven to attain positive social outcomes (e.g., closeness to partners), socially anxious participants displayed equal amounts of approach and avoidance motivation (Meleshko & Alden, 1993; Wallace & Alden, 1997). On an encouraging note, the relative balance of the two motives responded to changes in social cues. Patients with SAD displayed increases in approach goals when conversational partners were friendly than when they were not (e.g., Wallace & Alden, 1997). More important, recent work in our laboratory has found that experimental manipulations that helped patients with SAD reduce self-protective behaviors led these individuals to make less negative judgments about the interaction and to engage in more prosocial behavior, which then elicited more positive partner reactions (Taylor & Alden, 2008).

Several studies have suggested that approach motives may be suppressed by negative social judgments. For example, SAD patients expect positive social outcomes to come at some cost (Gilboa-Schectman, Franklin, & Foa, 2000). In addition, people with SAD fail to savor positive social experiences because they interpret those events in ways that maintain rather than reduce anxiety (Alden, Taylor, Mellings, & Laposa, 2008). Whereas nonsocially anxious people interpret positive social events as meaning that all is well, people with social anxiety and SAD remain on guard, cautioning themselves that positive events might lead to more social demands and future disappointment.

Surprisingly little work has addressed whether reducing concern with negative outcomes and social avoidance in SAD patients leads to increases in social approach behavior. Eng et al. (2005) found that SAD patients' satisfaction with social functioning improved after cognitive–behavioral group therapy. It is notable, however, that their satisfaction remained significantly lower than that of nonanxious individuals (Eng et al., 2005). Together, these studies point to the need for future research that considers social approach motives and behavior in SAD.

AN INTERPERSONAL MODEL OF SAD

The literature discussed earlier underscores the important role of interpersonal processes in SAD and provides considerable evidence for the four key tenets of the interpersonal perspective in the context of social anxiety. These tenets can be combined to form an interpersonal model of SAD, which can be summarized as follows (see Figure 5.1). Children who are high in behavioral inhibition or social timidity are vulnerable to aversive social experiences with parents or peers. In addition, their behavior shapes the behavior of significant others toward them, establishing fear-maintaining interactive cycles. Over time, episodic memories of negative interactions become linked together to produce a generic relational schema (e.g., "I am inadequate and others will disapprove of me"). Thus, negative social experiences not only create or maintain behavioral inhibition and social anxiety, they also affect the timid child's developing sense of self. Socially anxious people come to view themselves as different and unacceptable to others. As a result, they become exquisitely sensitive to others' reactions. Their negative relational schema leads to negative expectations for, and biased perceptions of, social events, and their behavior is driven by avoidance rather than approach motives.

Our experience has suggested that another aspect of relational schema is a sense of what one has to do to make oneself acceptable to others. For example, a man who believed others saw him as boring would push himself to be witty, which would unfortunately increase his anxiety during social

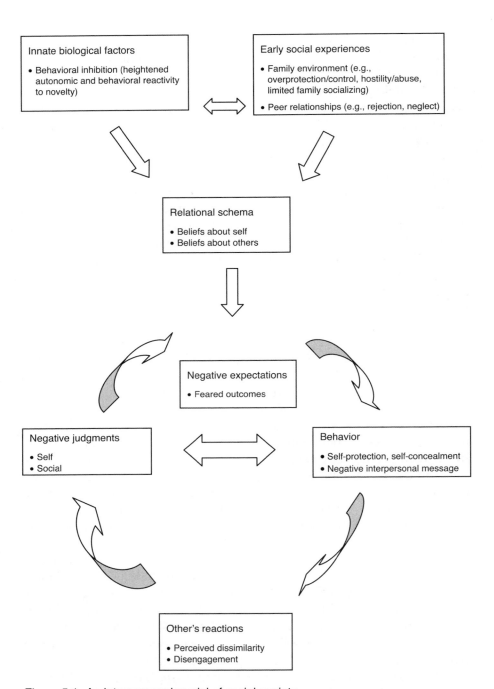

Figure 5.1. An interpersonal model of social anxiety.

events. Overall, people with SAD develop interpersonal strategies designed to protect and conceal the vulnerable self from others rather than to genuinely engage them. Such strategies take a variety of forms, including avoidance, feigned disdain, and excessive agreeableness. With all these strategies, however, the person avoids revealing his or her true self; spontaneity, expressing personal opinions, and sharing emotions and significant experiences are inhibited. Once learned, those self-protective strategies are applied to new social situations and people and choke off the mutual openness necessary to develop friends and romantic relationships. Others perceive people with SAD as dissimilar and less likable and fail to pursue the ongoing contact that would eventually lead to friendship. By late adolescence, socially anxious people tend to have a history of social isolation or failure that perpetuates their negative self-views and self-concealment. Finally, the bivariate model of social goals underscores the fact that treatment may need to address approach deficiencies and impaired relationship development in individuals with SAD.

INTERPERSONAL PROCESSES AND COMORBIDITY

SAD is a heavily comorbid condition, with as many as 80% of these individuals meeting diagnostic criteria for at least one comorbid disorder (e.g., Merikangas & Angst, 1995). The interpersonal model described earlier offers one way to examine the nature of the relationships between SAD and these other conditions. We focus here on the most prevalent comorbid disorders, major depressive disorder (MDD), generalized anxiety disorder (GAD), and alcohol use disorders (AUD). Interestingly, the onset of SAD typically precedes all three conditions. Although temporal precedence raises the possibility that social anxiety plays a causal relationship in their development, it is important to note that co-occurrence can also arise from shared etiological factors, such as genetically mediated neurochemical processes (e.g., Hettema, An, et al., 2006), personality features (e.g., Hettema, Neale, Myers, Prescott, & Kendler, 2006), and childhood adversity (e.g., Kessler, Davis, & Kendler, 1997).

Depression

MDD has one of the highest comorbidity rates with SAD, and SAD precedes MDD in between 70% and 91% of cases (e.g., Regier, Rae, Narrow, Kaelberg, & Schatzberg, 1998). Although it is easy to envision how the social isolation produced by SAD might contribute to the onset of depression, co-occurrence is known to be influenced by a variety of other factors. The two disorders share some common genetic vulnerabilities (e.g., Kendler, Neale, Kessler, & Heath, 1993). For example, both disorders (and GAD) were found to be associated with genetically mediated neurochemical abnormalities in the gamma aminobutyric acid (GABA) system, which may explain the emotional reactivity found in these conditions (Hettema, An, et al., 2006). On an interpersonal level, SAD and MDD share certain social developmental experiences, for example, childhood emotional abuse (Gibb, Chelminski, & Zimmerman, 2007). In addition, maternal depression, even of a subclinical level, predicts the presence of behavioral inhibition in children (Moehler et al., 2007), a known risk factor for SAD. Finally, in one of the few studies to examine etiological links, Beck and her colleagues found that failure to express emotions resulted in an increase in depressive symptoms in socially anxious people (Grant et al., 2007), which suggests that the interpersonal behaviors of socially anxious people may indeed play a causal role in dysphoric mood. Thus, the relationship between SAD and MDD is complex and multifactorial, with the two disorders woven together via a combination of biological and social developmental vulnerabilities and sequential interpersonal effects.

Depression is often triggered by social loss events. Interpersonal theorists, such as Coyne (1976) and Hammen (for an overview, see Hammen, 2006) have demonstrated that the interpersonal behavior of depressed people plays a significant role in generating the social events that trigger or perpetuate their mood disorders. Coyne (1976) proposed that hostile–dependent behavior alienates spouses, as well as other people. Hammen's (2006) intergenerational transmission model depicts how parental depression leads to dysfunctional parenting styles, which result in maladaptive interpersonal functioning and mate selection in vulnerable offspring. Those factors, in turn, generate interpersonal conflict and negative social events that trigger depressive episodes (Hammen, 2006).

There are similarities between interpersonal models of depression and of SAD; both propose that social developmental experiences result in interpersonal behaviors that perpetuate emotional problems. In addition, empirical studies have revealed that people with SAD and MDD display some similarities in social functioning. Both disorders are associated with social withdrawal and avoidance. Both groups display self-critical cognitions before and after social interactions, attribute negative social outcomes to personal failings, and believe that other people have negative reactions to them (see reviews by Alden, Bieling, & Meleshko, 1995; Ingram, Ramel, Chavira, & Scher, 2001).

Those factors notwithstanding, MDD and SAD, and their subclinical counterparts, are more characterized by interpersonal distinctions than by similarities. The two groups self-identify different core interpersonal problems (Stangier, Esser, Leber, Risch, & Heidenreich, 2006) and show evidence of having developed different relational schema. For example, whereas people with SAD are hypervigilant to and selectively process angry faces, people with depression are quicker to process sad facial cues and slower to process happy facial cues (Gilboa-Schechtman et al., 2005; Joormann & Gotlib, 2006).

The two disorders are also associated with distinct patterns of behavior. In social situations, SAD is marked by arousal-linked behaviors (e.g., fidgeting, blushing), whereas depressed individuals without comorbid SAD typically do not exhibit arousal (Ingram et al., 2001). SAD is associated with lower rates of talking and failure to express emotions and opinions. In contrast, depressed people express more negative emotions, engage in more overt self-criticism, emit a lower proportion of positive comments, and express more anger toward or blaming of others compared with clinical and nonclinical controls (e.g., Biglan et al., 1985; Blumberg & Hokanson, 1983; Gotlib & Robinson, 1982; Jacobson & Anderson, 1982). Finally, although other people are reluctant to seek ongoing contact with either socially anxious or depressed people relative to controls, the behavioral mechanism underlying social rejection appears to differ. People with SAD are hesitant about revealing themselves, even when others talk openly. Therefore, others perceive them to be different than themselves and are less willing to seek ongoing contact with them. In contrast, depression is associated with negatively toned, overly revealing personal comments (e.g., Jacobson & Anderson, 1982) and excessive reassurance seeking (e.g., Haeffel, Voelz, & Joiner, 2007), which become burdensome to others and lead them to disengage from the depressed person (Coyne, 1976).

Consistent with interpersonal theories, laboratory studies of marital interactions reveal that women with MDD are more likely to express negativity in comments toward their partners (e.g., Hautziner, Linden, & Hoffman, 1982; Nelson & Beach, 1990), which may contribute to marital discord and subsequent depressogenic events. Individuals with SAD more typically have difficulty developing intimacy, and their marital problems primarily arise from lack of assertion and avoidance of emotion expression and conflict (Darcy, Davila, & Beck, 2005; Davila & Beck, 2002; Grant et al., 2007), not from complaining or excessive reassurance seeking, as is more characteristic of people with MDD. Thus, one puzzle to be resolved is how people with SAD and MDD, who share significant genetic, neurochemical, and childhood vulnerabilities, come to develop these distinct interpersonal patterns.

Generalized Anxiety Disorder

The defining features of GAD are believed to be pathological worry and intolerance of uncertainty that in tandem result in a general state of heightened anxiety (Dugas & Robichaud, 2007). Various studies have revealed comorbidity rates of 33% to 59% between the two conditions (e.g., Sanderson, Di Nardo,

Rapee, & Barlow, 1990). SAD precedes GAD in about two thirds of cases (e.g., Lampe, Slade, Issakidis, & Andrews, 2003).

In terms of interpersonal profile, research has increasingly suggested that many of the feared outcomes of worriers involve social evaluation (e.g., Ladouceur, Freeston, Fournier, Dugas, & Doucet, 2002). Moreover, worry is correlated with public self-consciousness (e.g., Pruzinski & Borkovec, 1990). Because evaluation concerns and self-consciousness are key features of SAD, it seems likely that social anxiety might increase a person's tendency to develop pathological worry about criticism and embarrassment. Despite the logic of that speculation, research has yet to examine psychological factors that may contribute to etiological links. As noted earlier, SAD and GAD also share genetically mediated neurochemical processes that likely contribute to their co-occurrence. Finally, people with GAD display a broad range of interpersonal problems (Salzer et al., 2008), which raises the possibility that various types of interpersonal dysfunction, not just social anxiety and avoidance, increase vulnerability to GAD in people predisposed toward dysfunctional repetitive thinking.

Alcohol Use Disorders

Epidemiological surveys of community samples have revealed significant lifetime comorbidity rates between alcohol abuse and SAD (e.g., Regier et al., 1998). The large National Epidemiological Survey on Alcohol and Related Conditions revealed that SAD preceded alcohol dependence in 83% of cases and alcohol abuse in 81% of cases (Falk, Yi, & Hilton, 2008). Additionally, twin studies have suggested that the association between SAD and AUD does not derive from shared genetic vulnerabilities but from a nonfamilial causal relationship (Merikangas & Angst, 1995).

In light of those findings, researchers have attempted to identify the link between AUD and SAD. The predominant theory, a version of the self-medication (tension reduction) hypothesis, is that people with SAD drink to reduce anxiety symptoms (see the review by Carrigan & Randall, 2003). Interestingly, research evaluating whether alcohol's pharmacological effects actually do reduce social anxiety has yielded inconsistent results (e.g., Abrams, Kushner, Medina, & Voight, 2001, 2002; Himle et al., 1999). What is clear is that people with SAD and social anxiety believe that alcohol will reduce their social anxiety (Abrams et al., 2001, 2002; Himle et al., 1999; Stewart, Morris, Mellings, & Komar, 2006; Tran & Haaga, 2002). Moreover, research has indicated that alcohol expectancies distinguish people with comorbid SAD and AUD from those without AUD (e.g., Tran & Haaga, 2002) and may mediate the link between social anxiety and alcohol problems (Stewart et al., 2006). It is notable that the combination of alcohol's pharmacological and psychological effects led to increases in positive thoughts and decreases in negative thoughts in a speech task (Abrams, Kushner, & Reinertsen, 2002), which suggests that changes in anxiety-relevant cognitions mediated the relationship between alcohol use and subsequent anxiety reduction. Together these findings point to a self-perpetuating cycle in which socially anxious people drink because they expect alcohol to reduce anxiety symptoms. Alcohol use, in turn, results in a more positive cognitive state that actually does reduce anxiety, thereby fueling further consumption and subsequent alcohol problems. Finally, Stewart et al. (2006) found that conformity motives, that is, drinking to avoid peer disapproval, also mediated the link between social anxiety and alcohol problems in university students.

TREATMENT FOR SAD

Any treatment for SAD must address social dysfunction to some extent because this is the core feature of the condition. The most widely used treatments are cognitive–behavioral group therapy (CBGT; Heimberg & Becker, 2002) and cognitive therapy (CT; Clark & Wells, 1995). Both regimens focus on the way in which socially anxious people think about social situations, especially their beliefs about and expectations (predictions) for social events with the goal of correcting these negative cognitive processes. Patients are encouraged to conduct behavioral experiments to examine the accuracy of their social predictions and beliefs. The effectiveness of both CBGT and CT are well supported by randomized controlled clinical trials. The seminal studies conducted by Heimberg, Liebowitz, and their colleagues demonstrated that CBGT was generally as effective in reducing SAD symptoms as a pharmacological regimen, although changes occurred more slowly (Heimberg et al., 1998). Moreover, follow-up studies indicated that treatment gains were maintained and that CBGT may offer some benefits in terms of greater relapse prevention (Liebowitz et al., 1999). Clark et al. (2003, 2006) conducted two well-controlled randomized clinical trials to evaluate CT, delivered in an individual format. Individualized CT was shown to produce much larger treatment effects than applied relaxation or a pharmacotherapy regimen (Clark et al., 2006).

INTERPERSONAL COGNITIVE–BEHAVIORAL THERAPY

Although all treatments for SAD inevitably address interpersonal dysfunction, existing regimens do not take full advantage of interpersonal theoretical perspectives and empirical findings. The primary target of those treatments is reducing anxiety-related symptoms and behaviors, whereas less attention is explicitly directed toward relationship development and satisfaction. Our recent efforts have been directed toward evaluating the feasibility of integrating empirically established interpersonal concepts with cognitive–behavioral therapy (CBT) regimens (Alden & Taylor, 2008). The resulting interpersonal CBT (ICBT) regimen includes standard CBT strategies of self-monitoring and behavioral experiments. In addition, key interpersonal principles are presented and accompanied by between-session exercises designed to apply those principles in participants' daily interactions following the behavioral experiment format. Exercises include asking patients to identify the interpersonal impact of their behavior and the likely response evoked in others, to conduct behavioral experiments with different patterns of social behavior to increase interpersonal flexibility and control, and to experiment with self-expression and disclosure to increase and decrease the emotional closeness of social transactions. Patients also learn to identify the social developmental origins of their social beliefs and strategies and to map the transaction cycles established by those beliefs and strategies. Each of these exercises follows the standard structured CBT format: Principles are presented didactically; patients complete homework exercises on the basis of those principles; and the results of those exercises are reviewed in subsequent sessions. Treatment begins with strategies focused on reducing avoidance and safety behaviors and then moves to enhancing social approach and relationship development behaviors.

As a first step toward validating the feasibility of ICBT, 55 patients with generalized SAD were randomly assigned to either the ICBT regimen or a wait-list control condition. ICBT participants received 12 weekly group treatment sessions, and wait-list participants completed pre- and postassessments at a 12-week interval. Results indicated that ICBT produced significant change relative to the wait-list condition, as measured by both patient self-report and interviewer ratings of social fear, avoidance, and overall SAD severity. Across the patient- and clinician-rated symptom measures, the average effect size for the ICBT group was 1.4 compared with 0.2 for the wait-list group (Alden & Taylor, 2009). In addition to evaluating symptom change, we also included measures of interpersonal outcomes, including frequency of engaging in various prosocial behaviors (e.g., initiating social interactions) and satisfaction with various types of relationships. The ICBT regimen also produced significant increases in prosocial behaviors and relationship satisfaction, although the changes in these domains were generally smaller than changes on SAD symptoms.

All in all, these findings indicated that CBT treatment strategies based on interpersonal models and principles are readily incorporated with extant CBT procedures, that people with generalized SAD respond positively to these ICBT strategies, and that the regimen produced improvements in social affiliation behaviors and relationship satisfaction in addition to reductions in social avoidance. Continued research is needed to refine the existing protocol, conduct treatment comparison studies, and enhance the relationship development component of treatment.

INTERPERSONAL FACTORS AND TREATMENT PROCESS

In light of the difficulties people with SAD have establishing relationships with others, it is surprising that only a handful of studies have examined how interpersonal factors might affect treatment process and outcome. This work reveals that response to group CBT was not related to the patient–therapist working alliance (Woody & Adessky, 2002) but was related to group cohesion (Taube-Schiff, Suvak, Antony, Bieling, & McCabe, 2007). Interpersonal differences among people with SAD and avoidant personality disorder also affected treatment response. Specifically, interpersonal behavior marked by anger (Erwin, Heimberg, Schneier, & Liebowitz, 2003) or emotional detachment (Alden & Capreol, 1993) boded poorly for treatment outcome and may require particular attention from therapists. Finally, SAD patients who reported childhood abuse developed weaker therapeutic alliances and displayed a trend toward less symptom improvement (Alden, Taylor, Laposa, & Mellings, 2006). Clearly, more work is needed to determine how the interpersonal processes described in this chapter play out in treatment.

CONCLUSIONS

Our goals in this chapter were to examine SAD within the framework of interpersonal theory and to demonstrate that this framework offers heuristic advantages in terms of integrating the diverse bodies of research found in the developmental, personality, social cognition, and clinical literatures. In addition, the interpersonal model points to new directions. Questions for future research include studying how to facilitate relationship development in people with SAD and how to help these individuals function better in the close relationships they are able to establish. Our review has tended to emphasize how avoidance of positive social behavior (e.g., lack of openness and other social approach behaviors) chokes off the development of close relationships. However, the literature has also hinted at the existence of other types of negative interpersonal patterns in socially anxious people, such as overdependency (Davila & Beck, 2002), reassurance seeking (e.g., Heerey & Kring, 2007), and anger (e.g., Erwin et al., 2003). It may be that different types of interpersonal dysfunction surface in various types of social situations (e.g., close relationships, treatment). Conversely, some of these patterns may arise from comorbid conditions such as depression (e.g., Moscovitch, McCabe, Antony, Rocca, & Swinson, 2008). This issue remains to be resolved. We close this chapter by saying that we believe understanding and treatment of SAD can be enhanced by considering interpersonal processes and relationship development.

REFERENCES

Abrams, K., Kushner, M., Medina, K., & Voight, A. (2001). The pharmacologic and expectancy effects of alcohol on social anxiety in individuals with social phobia. *Drug and Alcohol Dependence, 64*, 219–231.

Abrams, K., Kushner, M., Medina, K., & Voight, A. (2002). Self-administration of alcohol before and after a public speaking challenge by individuals with social phobia. *Psychology of Addictive Behaviors, 16*, 121–128.

Abrams, K., Kushner, M., & Reinertsen, K. (2002). Effects of alcohol on anxiety-relevant cognitions in individuals with social phobia. *Cognitive Behaviour Therapy, 31*, 97–110.

Alden, L. E. (2001). Interpersonal perspectives on social phobia. In R. Crozier & L. E. Alden (Eds.), *International handbook of social anxiety* (pp. 381–404). Chichester, England: Wiley.

Alden, L. E., & Bieling, P. M. (1998). Interpersonal consequences of the pursuit of safety. *Behaviour Research and Therapy, 36*, 1–9.

Alden, L. E., Bieling, P. J., & Meleshko, K. G. A. (1995). An interpersonal comparison of depression and social anxiety. In K. D. Craig & D. S. Dobson (Eds.), *Anxiety and depression in adults and children*. Thousand Oaks, CA: Sage.

Alden, L. E., & Capreol, M. (1993). Interpersonal problem patterns in avoidant personality disordered outpatients: Prediction of treatment response. *Behavior Therapy, 24*, 356–376.

Alden, L. E., & Taylor, C. T. (2004). Interpersonal perspectives on social phobia. *Clinical Psychology Review, 24*, 857–882.

Alden, L. E., & Taylor, C. T. (2009). *Evaluation of a cognitive–behavioral version of interpersonal therapy for generalized social anxiety disorder.* Manuscript submitted for publication.

Alden, L. E., Taylor, C. T., Laposa, J. M., & Mellings, T. M. B. (2006). Social developmental experiences and response to cognitive-behavioral therapy for generalized social phobia. *Journal of Cognitive Psychotherapy, 20*, 407–416.

Alden, L. E., Taylor, C. T., Mellings, T. M. B., & Laposa, J. M. (2008). Social anxiety and the interpretation of positive events. *Journal of Anxiety Disorders, 22*, 577–590.

Alden, L. E., & Wallace, S. T. (1995). Social phobia and social appraisal in successful and unsuccessful interactions. *Behaviour Research and Therapy, 33*, 497–506.

American Psychiatric Association. (1994). *Diagnostic and statistical manual of mental disorders* (4th ed.). Washington, DC: Author.

Baldwin, M. W. (1992). Relational schemas and the processing of social information. *Psychological Bulletin, 112*, 461–484.

Baldwin, M. W., & Ferguson, P. (2001). Relational schemas: The activation of interpersonal knowledge structures in social anxiety. In R. Crozier & L. E. Alden (Eds.), *International handbook of social anxiety: Concepts, research and interventions relating the self and shyness* (pp. 137–158). Chichester, England: Wiley.

Beidel, D. C., Turner, S. M., & Morris, T. L. (1999). Psychopathology of childhood social phobia. *Journal of the American Academy of Child & Adolescent Psychiatry, 38*, 643–650.

Biglan, A., Hops, H., Sherman, L., Friedman, L. S., Arthur, J., & Osteen, V. (1985). Problem-solving interactions of depressed women and their husbands. *Behavior Therapy, 16*, 431–451.

Blumberg, S. R., & Hokanson, J. E. (1983). The effects of another person's response style on interpersonal behavior in depression. *Journal of Abnormal Psychology, 92*, 196–209.

Bowlby, J. (1971). *Attachment,* New York, NY: Penguin.

Brown, T. A., Chorpita, B. F., & Barlow, D. H. (1998). Structural relationships among dimensions of DSM–IV anxiety and mood disorders and dimensions of negative affect, positive affect, and autonomic arousal. *Journal of Abnormal Psychology, 107*, 179–192.

Bruch, M. A., & Heimberg, R. G. (1994). Differences in perceptions of parental and personal characteristics between generalized and nongeneralized social phobics. *Journal of Anxiety Disorders, 8*, 155–168.

Butler, E. A., Egloff, B., Wilhelm, F. H., Smith, N. C., Erickson, E. A., & Gross, J. J. (2003). The social consequences of expressive suppression. *Emotion, 3*, 48–67.

Carrigan, M. H., & Randall, C. L. (2003). Self-medication in social phobia: A review of the alcohol literature. *Addictive Behaviors, 28*, 269–284.

Clark, D. M., Ehlers, A., Hackmann, A., McManus, F., Fennell, M., Grey, N., . . . Wild, J. (2006). Cognitive therapy versus exposure and applied relaxation in social phobia: A randomized controlled trial. *Journal of Consulting and Clinical Psychology, 74*, 568–578.

Clark, D. M., Ehlers, A., McManus, R., Hackman, A., Fennell, M. J. V., Campbell, H., . . . Louis, B. (2003). Cognitive therapy versus fluoxetine in generalized social phobia: A randomized placebo-controlled trial. *Journal of Consulting and Clinical Psychology, 71*, 1058–1067.

Clark, D. M., & Wells, A. (1995). A cognitive model of social phobia. In R. G. Heimberg, M. Liebowitz, D. Hope, & F. Schneier (Eds.), *Social phobia: Diagnosis, assessment, and treatment* (pp. 69–93). New York, NY: Guilford Press.

Coyne, J. D. (1976). Depression and the response of others. *Journal of Abnormal Psychology, 85*, 186–193.

Creed, A. T., & Funder, D. C. (1998). Social anxiety: From the inside and outside. *Personality and Individual Differences, 25*, 19–33.

Dadds, M. R., Barrett, P. M., & Rapee, R. M. (1996). Family process and child anxiety and aggression: An observational analysis. *Journal of Abnormal Child Psychology, 24*, 715–734.

Darcy, K., Davila, J., & Beck, J. G. (2005). Is social anxiety associated with both interpersonal avoidance and interpersonal dependence? *Cognitive Therapy and Research, 29*, 171–186.

Davidson, R. J., Jackson, D. C., & Kalin, N. H. (2000). Emotion, plasticity, context, and regulation: Perspectives from affective neuroscience. *Psychological Bulletin, 126*, 890–909.

Davila, J., & Beck, J. G. (2002). Is social anxiety associated with impairment in close relationships? A preliminary investigation. *Behavior Therapy, 33*, 427–444.

de Wilde, A., & Rapee, R. M. (2008). Do controlling maternal behaviours increase state anxiety in children's response to a social threat? A pilot study. *Journal of Behavior Therapy and Experimental Psychiatry, 39*, 526–537.

Dodge, C. S., Heimberg, R. G., Nyman, D., & O'Brian, G. T. (1987). Daily interactions of high and low socially anxious college students: A diary study. *Behavior Therapy, 18*, 90–96.

Dugas, M. J., & Robichaud, M. (2007). *Cognitive–behavioral treatment for generalized anxiety disorder*. New York: Routledge.

Dumas, J. E., LaFreniere, P. J., & Serketich, W. J. (1995). "Balance of power": A transactional analysis of control in mother–child dyads involving socially competent, aggressive, and anxious children. *Journal of Abnormal Psychology, 104*, 104–113.

Eng, W., Coles, M. E., Heimberg, R. G., & Safren, S. A. (2005). Domains of life satisfaction in social anxiety disorder: Relation to symptoms and response to cognitive–behavioral therapy. *Journal of Anxiety Disorders, 19*, 143–156.

Erwin, B. A., Heimberg, R. G., Schneier, F. R., & Liebowitz, M. R. (2003). Anger experience and expression in social anxiety disorder: Pretreatment profile and predictors of attrition and response to cognitive-behavioral treatment. *Behavior Therapy, 34*, 331–350.

Falk, D. E., Yi, H.-Y., & Hilton, M. E. (2008). Age of onset and temporal sequencing of lifetime *DSM-IV* alcohol use disorders relative to comorbid mood and anxiety disorders. *Drug and Alcohol Dependence, 94*, 234–245.

Folkman, S., & Moskowitz, J. T. (2000). Positive affect and the other side of coping. *American Psychologist, 55*, 647–654.

Fox, N. A., Henderson, H. A., Rubin, K. H., Calkins, S. D., & Schmidt, L. A. (2001). Continuity and discontinuity of behavioral inhibition and exuberance. *Child Development, 72*, 1–21.

Fredrickson, B. L. (2001). The role of positive emotions in positive psychology: The broaden-and-build theory of positive emotions. *American Psychologist, 56,* 218–226.

Gable, S. L., & Reis, H. T. (2001). Appetitive and aversive social interaction. In J. H. Harvey & A. E. Wenzel (Eds.), *Close romantic relationship maintenance and enhancement* (pp. 169–194). Mahwah, NJ: Erlbaum.

Gable, S. L., Reis, H. T., & Elliot, A. J. (2000). Behavioral activation and inhibition in everyday life. *Journal of Personality and Social Psychology, 78,* 1135–1149.

Gable, S. L., Reis, H. T., & Elliot, A. J. (2003). Evidence for bivariate systems: An empirical test of appetition and aversion across domains. *Journal of Research in Personality, 37,* 349–372.

Gazelle, H., & Rudolph, K. D. (2004). Moving toward and away from the world: Social approach and avoidance trajectories in anxious solitary youth. *Child Development, 75,* 829–849.

Gibb, B. E., Chelminski, I., & Zimmerman, M. (2007). Childhood emotional, physical, and sexual abuse, and diagnoses of depressive and anxiety disorders in adult psychiatric outpatients. *Depression and Anxiety, 24,* 256–263.

Gilboa-Schectman, E., Foa, E. B., & Amir, N. (1999). Attentional biases for facial expression in social phobia: The effects of target and distractor in the "face-in-the-crowd" task. *Cognition & Emotion, 13,* 305–318.

Gilboa-Schechtman, E., Franklin, M. E., & Foa, E. B. (2000). Anticipated reactions to social events: Differences among individuals with generalized social phobia, obsessive–compulsive disorder, and nonanxious controls. *Cognitive Therapy and Research, 24,* 731–746.

Gilboa-Schechtman, E., Presburger, G., Marom, S., & Hermesh, H. (2005). The effects of social anxiety and depression on the evaluation of facial crowds. *Behaviour Research and Therapy, 43,* 467–474.

Glass, C. R., & Arnkoff, D. B. (1989). Behavioral assessment of social anxiety and social phobia. *Clinical Psychology Review, 9,* 75–90.

Gotlib, I. H., & Robinson, L. A. (1982). Responses to depressed individuals: Discrepancies between self-report and observer rated behavior. *Journal of Abnormal Psychology, 9,* 231–240.

Gough, H., & Thorne, A. (1986). Positive, negative and balanced shyness: Self-definitions and the reactions of others. In W. H. Jones, J. M. Cheek, & S. R. Briggs (Eds.), *Shyness: Perspectives on research and treatment* (pp. 205–225). New York, NY: Plenum Press.

Grant, D. M., Beck, J. G., Farrow, S. M., & Davila, J. (2007). Do interpersonal features of social anxiety influence the development of depressive symptoms? *Cognition & Emotion, 21,* 646–663.

Greco, L. A., & Morris, T. L. (2005). Factors influencing the link between social anxiety and peer acceptance: Contributions of social skills and close friendships during middle childhood. *Behavior Therapy, 36,* 197–205.

Haeffel, G. J., Voelz, Z. R., & Joiner, T. E. (2007). Vulnerability to depressive symptoms: Clarifying the role of excessive reassurance-seeking and perceived social support in an interpersonal model of depression. *Cognition & Emotion, 21*, 681–688.

Hammen, C. (2006). Stress generation in depression: Reflections on origins, research, and future directions. *Journal of Clinical Psychology, 62*, 1065–1082.

Hart, T. A., Turk, C. L., Heimberg, R. G., & Liebowitz, M. R. (1999). Relation of marital status to social phobia severity. *Depression and Anxiety, 10*, 28–32.

Hautziner, M., Linden, M., & Hoffman, N. (1982). Distressed couples with and without a depressed partner: An analysis of their verbal interaction. *Journal of Behaviour Therapy and Experimental Psychiatry, 13*, 307–314.

Heerey, E. A., & Kring, A. M. (2007). Interpersonal consequences of social anxiety. *Journal of Abnormal Psychology, 116*, 125–134.

Heimberg, R. G., & Becker, R. E. (2002). *Cognitive-behavioral group therapy for social phobia*. New York, NY: Guilford Press.

Heimberg, R. G., Liebowitz, M. R., Hope, D. A., Schneier, R. F., Holt, C. S., Welkowitz, L. A., . . . Klein, D. F. (1998). Cognitive-behavioral group therapy versus phenelzine therapy in social phobia: 12-week outcome. *Archives of General Psychiatry, 55*, 1133–1141.

Hettema, J. M., An, S. S., Neale, M. C., Bukszar, J., van den Oord, E. J., Kendler, K. S., & Chen, X. (2006). Association between glutamic acid decarboxylase genes and anxiety disorders, major depression, and neuroticism. *Molecular Psychiatry, 11*, 752–762.

Hettema, J. M., Neale, M. C., Myers, J. M., Prescott, C. A., & Kendler, K. S. (2006). Population-based twin study of the relationship between neuroticism and internalizing disorders. *American Journal of Psychiatry, 163*, 857–864.

Himle, J. A., Abelson, J. L., Haghightgou, H., Hill, E., Nesse, R., & Curtis, G. (1999). Effects of alcohol on social phobic anxiety. *American Journal of Psychiatry, 156*, 1237–1243.

Hirsch, C. R., & Mathews, A. (2000). Impaired positive inferential bias in social phobia. *Journal of Abnormal Psychology, 109*, 705–712.

Horowitz, L. M. (2004). *Interpersonal foundations of psychopathology*. Washington, DC: American Psychological Association.

Hughes, A. A., Heimberg, R. G., Coles, M. E., Gibb, B. E., Liebowitz, M. R., & Schneier, F. R. (2006). Relation of factors of the tripartite model of anxiety and depression to types of social anxiety. *Behaviour Research and Therapy, 44*, 1629–1641.

Hymel, S., Rubin, K. H., Rowden, L., & LeMare, L. (1990). Children's peer relationships: Longitudinal prediction of internalizing and externalizing problems from middle to late childhood. *Child Development, 61*, 2004–2021.

Ingram, R. E, Ramel, W., Chavira, D., & Scher, C. (2001). Social anxiety and depression. In W. R. Crozier & L. E. Alden (Eds.), *International handbook of social anxiety: Concepts, research and interventions relating to the self and shyness* (pp. 357–380). London, England: Wiley.

Jacobson, N. S., & Anderson, E. A. (1982). Interpersonal skill and depression in college students: An analysis of the timing of self-disclosures. *Behavior Therapy, 13,* 271–282.

Joormann, J., & Gotlib, I. H. (2006). Is this happiness I see? Biases in the identification of emotional facial expressions in depression and social phobia. *Journal of Abnormal Psychology, 115,* 705–714.

Kagan, J., Reznick, J. S., Snidman, N., Gibbons, J., & Johnson, M. O. (1988). Childhood derivatives of inhibition and lack of inhibition to the unfamiliar. *Child Development, 59,* 1580–1589.

Kendler, K. S., Neale, M. C., Kessler, R. C., & Heath, A. C. (1993). Major depression and phobias: The genetic and environmental sources of comorbidity. *Psychological Medicine, 23,* 361–371.

Kessler, R. C., Berglund, P., Demler, O., Jin, R., & Walters, E. E. (2005). Lifetime prevalence and age-of-onset disturbances of DSM-IV disorders in the National Comorbidity Survey replication. *Archives of General Psychiatry, 62,* 593–602.

Kessler, R. C., Davis, C. G., & Kendler, K. S. (1997). Childhood adversity and adult psychiatric disorder in the US National Comorbidity Survey. *Psychological Medicine, 27,* 1101–1119.

Kiesler, D. J. (1996). *Contemporary interpersonal theory and research: Personality, psychopathology and psychotherapy.* New York, NY: Wiley.

Ladouceur, R., Freeston, J. H., Fournier, S., Dugas, M. J., & Doucet, C. (2002). The social basis of worry in three samples: High school students, university students, and older adults. *Behavioural and Cognitive Psychotherapy, 30,* 427–438.

Lampe, L., Slade, T., Issakidis, C., & Andrews, G. (2003). Social phobia in the Australian National Survey of Mental Health and Well-Being (NSMHWB). *Psychological Medicine, 33,* 637–646.

Laurenceau, J.-P., Barrett, L. F., & Pietromonaco, P. R. (1998). Intimacy as an interpersonal process: The importance of self-disclosure, partner disclosure, and perceived partner responsiveness in interpersonal exchanges. *Journal of Personality and Social Psychology, 74,* 1238–1251.

Leary, M. R. (2007). Motivational and emotional aspects of the self. *Annual Review of Psychology, 58,* 317–344.

Leary, T. F. (1957). *Interpersonal diagnosis of personality.* New York, NY: Ronald.

Liebowitz, M. R., Heimberg, R. G., Schneier, F. R., Hope, D. A., Devies, S., Holt, C. S., . . . Klein, D. F. (1999). Cognitive-behavioral group therapy versus phenelzine in social phobia: Long-term outcome. *Depression and Anxiety, 10,* 89–98.

Mannuzza, S., Schneier, F. R., Chapman, T. F., Liebowitz, M. R., Klein, D. F., & Fyer, A. J. (1995). Generalized social phobia: Reliability and validity. *Archives of General Psychiatry, 52,* 230–237.

McLeod, B. D., Wood, J. J., & Weisz, J. R. (2007). Examining the association between parenting and childhood anxiety: A meta-analysis. *Clinical Psychology Review, 27,* 155–172.

Meleshko, K. A., & Alden, L. E. (1993). Anxiety and self-disclosure: Toward a motivational model. *Journal of Personality and Social Psychology, 64*, 1000–1009.

Mendlowicz, M. V. & Stein, M. B. (2000). Quality of life in individuals with anxiety disorders. *American Journal of Psychiatry, 157*, 669–682

Merikangas, K. R., & Angst, J. (1995). Comorbidity and social phobia: Evidence from clinical, epidemiologic, and genetic studies. *European Archives of Psychiatry and Clinical Neuroscience, 244*, 297–303.

Moehler, E., Kagan, J., Parzer, P., Brunner, R., Reck, C., Wiebel, A., . . . Resch, R. (2007). Childhood behavioral inhibition and maternal symptoms of depression. *Psychopathology, 40*, 446–452.

Moscovitch, E. A., McCabe, R. E., Antony, M. M., Rocca, L., & Swinson, R. P. (2008). Anger experience and expression across the anxiety disorders. *Depression and Anxiety, 25*, 107–113.

Nelson, G. M., & Beach, S. R. (1990). Sequential interaction in depression: Effects of depressive behavior on spousal aggression. *Behavior Therapy, 21*, 167–182.

Oh, W., Rubin, K. H., Bowker, J. C., Booth-LaForce, C., Rose-Krasnor, L., & Laursen, B. (2008). Trajectories of social withdrawal from middle childhood to early adolescence. *Journal of Abnormal Child Psychology, 36*, 553–566.

Paulhus, D. L., & Morgan, K. L. (1997). Perceptions of intelligence in leaderless groups: The dynamic effects of shyness and acquaintance. *Journal of Personality and Social Psychology, 72*, 581–591.

Pruzinski, T., & Borkovec, T. D. (1990). Cognitive and personality characteristics of worriers. *Behaviour Research and Therapy, 28*, 507–512.

Rapee, R. M., & Heimberg, R. G. (1997). A cognitive–behavioral model of anxiety in social phobia. *Behaviour Research and Therapy, 35*, 741–756.

Rapee, R. M., & Spence, S. H. (2004). The etiology of social phobia: Empirical evidence and an initial model. *Clinical Psychology Review, 24*, 737–767.

Regier, D. A., Rae, D. S., Narrow, W. E., Kaelber, C. T., & Schatzberg, A. F. (1998). Prevalence of anxiety disorders and their comorbidity with mood and addictive disorders. *British Journal of Psychiatry, 173*, 24–28.

Reis, H. T., & Shaver, P. (1988). Intimacy as an interpersonal process. In S. Duck, D. F. Hay, S. E. Hobfoll, W. Ickes, & B. M. Montgomery (Eds.), *Handbook of personal relationships: Theory, research and interventions* (pp. 367–389). Oxford, England: Wiley.

Rubin, K. H., Burgess, K. B., & Hastings, P. D. (2002). Stability and social-behavioral consequences of toddlers' inhibited temperament and parenting behavior. *Child Development, 73*, 483–495.

Rubin, K. H., Nelson, L. J., Hastings, P., & Asendorpf, J. B. (1999). Transaction between parents' perceptions of their children's shyness and their parenting styles. *International Journal of Behavioral Development, 23*, 937–957.

Rubin, K. H., Wojslawowicz, J., Rose-Krasnor, L., Booth-LaForce, C., & Burgess, K. (2006). The best friendships of shy/withdrawn children: prevalence, stability, and relationship quality. *Journal of Abnormal Child Psychology, 34*, 143–157.

Sadler, P., & Woody, E. (2003). Is who you are who you're talking to? Interpersonal style and complementarity in mixed-sex interaction. *Journal of Personality and Social Psychology, 84,* 80–96.

Salzer, S., Pincus, A. L., Hoyer, J., Kreische, R., Leichsenring, F., & Liebing, E. (2008). Interpersonal subtypes within generalized anxiety disorder. *Journal of Personality Assessment, 90,* 292–299.

Sanderson, W. C., DiNardo, P. A., Rapee, R. M., & Barlow, D. H. (1990). Syndrome comorbidity in patients diagnosed with a *DSM–III–R* anxiety disorder. *Journal of Abnormal Psychology, 99,* 308–312.

Spence, S. H., Donovan, C., & Brechman-Toussaint, M. (1999). Social skills, social outcomes, and cognitive features of childhood social phobia. *Journal of Abnormal Psychology, 108,* 211–221.

Stangier, U., Esser, F., Leber, S. M., Risch, A. K., & Heidenreich, T. (2006). Interpersonal problems in social phobia versus unipolar depression. *Depression and Anxiety, 23,* 418–421.

Stewart, S. H., Morris, E., Mellings, T., & Komar, J. (2006). Relations of social anxiety variables to drinking motives, drinking quantity and frequency, and alcohol-related problems in undergraduates. *Journal of Mental Health, 15,* 671–682.

Strauman, T. J. (1989). Self-discrepancies in clinical depression and social phobia: Cognitive structures that underlie emotional disorders? *Journal of Abnormal Psychology, 98,* 14–22.

Strauman, T. J., & Higgins, E. T. (1987). Automatic activation of self-discrepancies and emotional syndromes: When cognitive structures influence affect. *Journal of Personality and Social Psychology, 53,* 1004–1014.

Taube-Schiff, M., Suvak, M. K., Antony, M. M., Bieling, P. J., & McCabe, R. E. (2007). Group cohesion in cognitive-behavioral group therapy for social phobia. *Behaviour Research and Therapy, 45,* 687–698.

Taylor, C. T., & Alden, L. E. (2005). Social developmental experiences and social interpretation in generalized social phobia. *Behaviour Research and Therapy, 43,* 759–777.

Taylor, C. T., & Alden, L. E. (2006). Parental overprotection and interpersonal behavior in generalized social phobia. *Behavior Therapy, 47,* 11–22.

Taylor, C. T., & Alden, L. E. (2008). *Safety behavior reduction and judgment biases in social interactions.* Manuscript submitted for publication.

Tran, G. Q., & Haaga, D. A. (2002). Coping responses and alcohol outcome expectancies in alcohol abusing and nonabusing social phobics. *Cognitive Therapy and Research, 26,* 1–17.

Tugade, M. M., & Fredrickson, B. L. (2004). Resilient individuals use positive emotions to bounce back from negative emotional experiences. *Journal of Personality and Social Psychology, 86,* 320–333.

Veljaca, K. A., & Rapee, R. M. (1998). Detection of negative and positive audience behaviours by socially anxious subjects. *Behaviour Research and Therapy, 36,* 311–321.

Vöncken, M., Alden, L. E., Bögels, S. M., & Roelofs, J. (2008). Social rejection in social anxiety disorder: The role of performance deficits. *British Journal of Clinical Psychology, 47*, 439–450.

Wallace, S. T., & Alden, L. E. (1997). Social phobia and positive social events: The price of success. *Journal of Abnormal Psychology, 106*, 1–10.

Wenzel, A. (2002). Characteristics of close relationships in individuals with social phobia: A preliminary comparison with nonanxious individuals. In J. H. Harvey & A. Wenzel (Eds.), *Maintaining and enhancing close relationships: A clinician's guide* (pp. 199–213). Mahwah, NJ: Erlbaum.

Wenzel, A., Graff-Dolezal, J., Macho, M., & Brendle, J. R. (2005). Communication and social skills in socially anxious and nonanxious individuals in the context of romantic relationships. *Behaviour Research and Therapy, 43*, 505–519.

Winton, E. C., Clark, D., & Edelmann, R. J. (1995). Social anxiety, fear of negative evaluation, and the detection of negative emotion in others. *Behaviour Research and Therapy, 33*, 193–196.

Woody, S. R., & Adessky, R. S. (2002). Therapeutic alliance, group cohesion, and homework compliance during cognitive-behavioral group treatment of social phobia. *Behavior Therapy, 33*, 5–27.

6

OBSESSIVE–COMPULSIVE DISORDER

KEITH D. RENSHAW, GAIL STEKETEE, CAMILA S. RODRIGUES,
AND CATHERINE M. CASKA

Obsessive–compulsive disorder (OCD) has a lifetime prevalence rate of 2.5% in adults, with an equal risk of occurrence across sexes (American Psychiatric Association, 2000). The key features of this disorder are recurrent obsessions or compulsions that cause significant impairment or distress. The *Diagnostic and Statistical Manual of Mental Disorders* (4th ed., text rev., or *DSM–IV–TR*; American Psychiatric Association, 2000) describes *obsessions* as persistent and intrusive thoughts, images, or impulses that an individual recognizes as inappropriate and a product of his or her own mind but feels unable to control. Obsessions are more than recurrent worries about real-life problems, and the individual must attempt to suppress them with some action or thought. Common obsessions include thoughts about contamination, requiring specific order, violent impulses, and sexual imagery.

Compulsions are described as repetitive behaviors or mental acts that an individual feels an urge to perform in an attempt to reduce or prevent anxiety usually associated with an obsession. Common compulsions include hand washing, checking, and repeating specific behaviors. *DSM–IV–TR* criteria require that at some point the individual recognize that his or her obsessions or compulsions are unreasonable. However, if the person does not currently recognize this, a specifier of "with poor insight" can be included. In addition to causing marked distress or impairment, obsessions or compulsions must last more than 1 hour per day or create significant interference in the person's daily routine, occupational or academic functioning, and social relationships (American Psychiatric Association, 2000; Clark, 2004).

Several subtypes exist that are intended to highlight the primary obsession or compulsion that the individual is experiencing. The most common obsession subtypes and their compulsive counterparts include fear of contamination (washing and cleaning) and pathological doubt (checking; Clark, 2004; Rasmussen & Eisen, 1992; Steketee, Grayson, & Foa, 1985). Other common subtypes include intrusive sexual or aggressive thoughts and images, a compulsive need to ask or confess, somatic obsessions, need for symmetry and precision, compulsive hoarding, and religious or blasphemy obsessions (Clark, 2004; Rasmussen & Eisen, 1992). The use of symptom subtypes is a topic of debate among leading professionals, in part because of the belief that the diagnosis implies the individual has only one constant and primary obsessive or compulsive symptom, which is often not the case. However, others have argued that the use of subtypes may be helpful for treatment development and for determining specific etiological factors (Clark, 2004).

ETIOLOGICAL FORMULATIONS

There is a wide array of theoretical conceptualizations of OCD and its associated behaviors, ranging from psychoanalytic to cognitive–behavioral to biological. Although Freud was one of the first individuals to recognize and write about OCD, Esman (2001) noted that since Anna Freud's (1966) review of the subject, "virtually nothing has appeared in the psychoanalytic literature that has added to our understanding of the disorder or enhanced the very limited therapeutic influence of psychoanalysis in such cases" (p. 145). In contrast, the literature regarding biological, neuropsychological, cognitive, and behavioral underpinnings of OCD has burgeoned over the past few decades. A broad review of the biological and neuropsychological underpinnings of OCD is beyond the scope of this chapter (see reviews by Fontenelle, Mendlowicz, Mattos, & Versiani, 2006; Friedlander & Desrocher, 2006; Menzies et al., 2008), but a brief overview of cognitive and behavioral factors will help elucidate some of the interpersonal aspects of this disorder.

The *DSM–IV–TR* (American Psychiatric Association, 2000) notes that "in most cases, the person feels driven to perform the compulsion to reduce the distress that accompanies an obsession" (p. 457). Thus, from a behavioral perspective, compulsions are negatively reinforced when the intense anxiety associated with obsessions is reduced. Moreover, achieving anxiety reduction via compulsions prevents the individual from learning that the anxiety will eventually subside on its own. This conceptualization has strong empirical support, including the considerable success of exposure and response prevention (ERP), which has as its explicit focus breaking of the association between compulsions and anxiety reduction (Abramowitz, Taylor, & McKay, 2007).

The cognitive perspective of OCD is based on the well-supported notion that intrusive thoughts, images, and impulses are actually normative (e.g., Rachman & de Silva, 1978). These intrusive phenomena can become problematic when an individual attaches particular meaning to them. Along these lines, the Obsessive Compulsive Cognitions Working Group (2005) identified three primary cognitive tendencies that are often observed in those with OCD: (a) importance and need to control thoughts, (b) perfectionism and intolerance of uncertainty, and (c) overestimation of threat and responsibility. If a person demonstrates one or more of these tendencies, he or she is hypothesized to become much more distressed by certain types of intrusive thoughts and, thus, more likely to attempt to neutralize them in some way. This progression is hypothesized to lead to compulsions.

These three belief domains in OCD have some interpersonal relevance. Thought content may seem at first blush to be a private affair, known only to the OCD patient unless reported to others. However, overconcern about the content and control of thoughts is partly a result of expectations of the (critical) evaluation of others. It is hardly surprising that a thought like "I might throw my infant in front of the oncoming train" or "What if just thinking about it could cause my loved one to have an accident?" could engender obsessive concern on the part of a vulnerable parent or family member who might fear that others would consider him or her a horrible person if they knew of such thoughts. Often, it is this image of themselves through someone else's eyes that frightens individuals with OCD. Likewise, perfectionism and the need for certainty reflect excessive striving to meet an unrealistic internal standard or avoid a mistake that is often theorized to have roots in excessive parental expectations. Finally, anecdotal clinical evidence has suggested that OCD patients' inflated responsibility often centers on the possibility of preventing harm to others rather than to oneself. For instance, a mother with contamination fears may be more likely to worry about the possibility of passing an illness on to her children than simply of contracting the illness herself. At the same time, it is clear that a number of individuals with OCD are concerned with preventing harm to themselves. We are unaware of any studies to date that have compared the effects of perceived responsibility for preventing harm to others versus self. Such studies could help clarify the potential role of interpersonally oriented versus individually oriented responsibility in OCD.

Despite these potential interpersonal influences, the overwhelming empirical support for the importance of cognitive, behavioral, biological, neuropsychological, and neurobiological factors in OCD, and the high success of concomitant treatments for OCD (see review by Franklin & Foa, 2002), may seem to leave little room for consideration of interpersonal influences in this disorder. However, it is important to recognize that as many as 25% of OCD patients fail to respond to existing treatments, and an even larger percentage of patients experience relapse after making treatment gains, particularly after stopping medications (Franklin & Foa, 2002). Thus, there is a need to better understand a wider variety of influences on this disorder. Indeed, one area that has gained much attention over the past 2 decades is the interpersonal context of the maintenance and treatment of a variety of mental health conditions, including OCD. In the next section, we review the research in this area from the perspective of an interpersonal model of the maintenance of OCD, and we discuss the treatment implications of this model.

INTERPERSONAL ASPECTS OF OCD

In this section, we review general data regarding the interpersonal functioning of individuals with OCD, after which we posit an overarching interpersonal model of the maintenance of OCD. We then review the existing evidence regarding the interpersonal nature of OCD in the context of this model.

Interpersonal Relationships

Adults with OCD who seek treatment are less likely to be married than those in the general population (e.g., Koran, 2000; Lensi, Cassano, Correddu, Ravagli, & Kunovac, 1996; Steketee, 1993); nearly 25% may still live with their parents (e.g., Steketee & Pruyn, 1998). However, nearly 80% of those meeting criteria for OCD in epidemiological research were married (Steketee, 1997). This may reflect a tendency for those who are not married to be more likely to seek treatment; alternatively, it may be that those who are more severely affected are both more likely to seek treatment and less likely to be married. Regardless, when considering interpersonal aspects of OCD, one needs to recognize the wide variety of individuals who might be involved.

Interpersonal Model of OCD

Data are emerging to support a transactional model of the effects of OCD symptoms on interpersonal variables. This model was first posited by Van Noppen and colleagues (Livingston-Van Noppen, Rasmussen, Eisen, & McCartney, 1990; Van Noppen, Rasmussen, Eisen, & McCartney, 1991), who focused on a spectrum of family response to OCD that ranged from antagonistic and hostile at one end to overly accommodating at the other. On the basis of growing research over the past 2 decades, we proposed adaptations to this model (Renshaw, Steketee, & Chambless, 2005), and we expand on these here. The evidence regarding the model is reviewed in detail in the following sections.

The symptoms of OCD, particularly the overt compulsive behaviors, often lead to high levels of both accommodation and criticism or hostility in family members. Relatives might accommodate a person's rituals for any number of reasons, such as a desire to reduce the person's immediate suffering, a desire to stop the person from engaging in embarrassing behavior in front of others, or a perceived need to enable themselves or the person to meet an obligation (e.g., leave the house for an appointment). Accommodation can encompass a range of behaviors, such as arranging extra time for a person to complete rituals, providing needed materials (e.g., cleaning products), and actually participating in rituals (e.g., helping a person clean). In turn, such behavior can lead to a worsening of OCD symptoms because having one's rituals accommodated can inadvertently perpetuate compulsions by reinforcing beliefs that rituals are necessary for relief of anxiety. Such accommodation can also interfere with the potential benefits of ERP by blocking successful completion of exposure assignments.

Criticism and hostility can also arise for a number of reasons, such as embarrassment about the person's need to ritualize, frustration or irritation regarding OCD behaviors and their consequences, or a belief that people should be able to recognize the irrationality of their obsessions. These types of responses can range from mild criticisms or expressions of displeasure to highly antagonistic responses, such as screaming at the person, threatening to end the relationship, or other physical or emotional attacks. Overtly hostile attitudes can create environments of greater stress for people with OCD, which can lead to symptom exacerbation because of the tendency for symptoms to worsen around times of extreme stress (e.g., Horowitz, 1975). However, growing evidence (see the Effects of Others on the Course of OCD section) has suggested that the best family scenario with regard to OCD may not simply be one that is devoid of any critical responding, but one in which relatives display some level of critical (but not attacking) behavior with people with OCD. Relatives who act in this manner may be most likely to encourage people with OCD to confront feared situations, without being harsh or hostile. This type of interpersonal environment is consistent with the aims of ERP, and as Chambless and Steketee (1999, p. 663) noted, firm criticism that is not rejecting of the person as a whole "may have motivational properties" that help people fully engage in the extremely difficult exposure aspects of this treatment. Also, for individuals with mild to moderate OCD symptoms, relatives might even facilitate the person's recognition of the natural reduction in anxiety that can occur without ritualizing outside of the context of treatment. The overview of these reciprocal effects is summarized in Figure 6.1.

Two points of clarification are important with regard to this model. First, family accommodation and antagonism are independent dimensions, not opposite ends of the same unitary dimension. The account from the husband of a woman with OCD given later in the chapter demonstrates how a relative can engage in accommodating behavior while simultaneously expressing anger about the very accommodating behavior he or she feels compelled to perform. Also, empirical data derived from research in expressed emotion (EE; Leff & Vaughn, 1985) support the notion that these are independent responses. EE consists of three primary components: criticism, hostility, and emotional overinvolvement. Emotional overinvolvement is conceptually similar to accommodation, and although it is typically lumped together with criticism and hostility into an overall rating of either high or low EE, it is actually typically uncorrelated with either criticism or hostility (e.g., Chambless & Steketee, 1999).

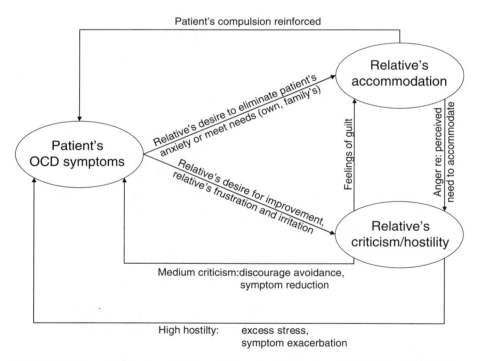

Figure 6.1. Transactional model of patient s obsessive–compulsive disorder (OCD) symptoms and relatives' accommodating and critical responses.

Second, this model is transactional in nature. There is no assumption about how these behaviors originate; neither the patient nor the relative is presumed to be primarily at fault. Rather, the behaviors are presumed to be interdependent, varying across individuals and family systems, and related to multiple intraindividual and interpersonal variables. It is nearly impossible to determine whether a patient's behavior preceded a relative's or vice versa; more important, such a distinction is irrelevant. Interventions can be made at multiple points in this cycle, all of which can help break the cycle.

Evidence regarding this model is reviewed in the following sections. We first review evidence supporting the notion that family members of individuals with OCD display higher levels of both accommodating and antagonistic responding. Afterward, we discuss data regarding the effects of family members' behaviors and attitudes on symptom course and treatment response. We conclude with treatment recommendations based on this interpersonal model of OCD.

Effects of Symptoms on Others

Adults with OCD and their relatives describe significant impairment in family functioning and family relationships. For example, in a study of 19 OCD patients and their spouses, Black, Gaffney, Schlosser, and Gabel (1998) found that 47% of patients reported unhealthy functioning on the Family Assessment Device (Epstein, Baldwin, & Bishop, 1983). In addition, 87% of the spouses reported disruptions in family and social life in response to a questionnaire developed by these investigators. Similarly, Livingston-Van Noppen et al. (1990) found that compared with control families, relatives of 50 OCD patients had a significantly higher percentage of unhealthy scores on all dimensions of the Family Assessment Device except communication. In a study of 54 OCD patients, Riggs, Hiss, and Foa (1992) found that not only did 47% report marital distress before ERP, but 42% of those patients no longer reported marital distress after a posttreatment reduction in OCD symptoms. Finally, Simmons, Gordon, and Chambless (2005) also found that 50% of patients with OCD or panic and 40% of their spouses were classified as maritally dissatisfied on the Dyadic Adjustment Scale (Spanier, 1976).

It is unclear, however, whether the distress reported by relatives of those with OCD is greater than that reported by relatives of individuals with other mental disorders. Lochner et al. (2003) did find that dysfunction was higher in families of people with OCD compared with families of those with panic or social phobia. However, Erol, Yazici, and Toprak (2007) found no differences in family functioning of those with OCD compared with those with eating disorders. There is also no clear evidence to suggest that these relatives' perceptions of burden are higher than those reported by relatives of individuals with other disorders (Magliano, Tosini, Guarneri, Marasco, & Catapano, 1996; Renshaw et al., 2000). Similarly, relatives of adults and children with OCD have reported greater impairments in physical health, psychological and emotional well-being, and social functioning in comparison to normal populations, but their levels of impairment in these areas do not appear to exceed those of relatives whose family members have other mental disorders (Albert, Salvi, & Saracco, 2007; Derisley, Libby, Clark, & Reynolds, 2005; Renshaw et al., 2000; but see Magliano et al., 1996). Thus, it appears that OCD is associated with similar levels of general psychological and functional impairments in relatives as are other mental health problems.

OCD does, however, exhibit specific effects on others in the form of accommodation behaviors and in the cognitive and emotional reactions to actual or perceived requests or demands for such behaviors. As presented in the model earlier, accommodation involves altering one's own behaviors in response to a person's ritualizing. For example, Calvocoressi et al. (1995) reported on the wife of an individual with OCD who could not cook or clean in her house because of the amount of newspapers her husband hoarded and the mother of a child with OCD who had to use a neighbor's bathroom because her son used theirs so frequently. Between 75% and 89% of families of adults with OCD endorse some level of accommodation on self-report questionnaires and in interviews (Calvocoressi et al., 1995, 1999; Ferrão, Shavitt, & Nádia 2006; Shafran, Ralph, & Tallis, 1995), and it is difficult to envision a family of someone with OCD in which such behavior never occurs. Moreover, some relatives go beyond simple accommodation to active participation in rituals, for instance, personally engaging in washing rituals to alleviate the anxiety of a family member with contamination fears. Although slightly lower than the rates of accommodation, the rates of family members who report such active participation are between 39% and 67% (Black et al., 1998; Calvocoressi et al., 1995, 1999; Cooper, 1996; Shafran et al., 1995). In addition, Shafran et al. (1995) reported that when questioned more specifically, only 2% of families in their sample denied ever having participated in rituals at some point. Not surprisingly, accommodation and participation are also seen frequently among parents whose children have OCD (e.g., Bolton, Collins, & Steinberg, 1983; Cooper, 1996; Storch, Geffken, & Merlo, 2007).

Accommodation of and participation in rituals are associated with significantly greater psychological distress and family dysfunction, as reported by relatives (e.g., Calvocoressi et al., 1995, 1999). Higher percentages of relatives (70%–90%) endorse significant distress specifically because of OCD-related behaviors (Black et al., 1998; Cooper, 1996; Hollander et al., 1996, 1998; Piacentini, Bergman, Keller, & McCracken, 2003; Shafran et al., 1995; Toro, Cervera, & Osejo, 1992), as compared with general levels of family distress. For example, in a survey of 181 family members of OCD patients,

Cooper (1996) found that 69% of relatives reported marital discord as a result of OCD in the family, 90% reported experiencing depression, 75% reported disruption of family and social life, and 58% were greatly disturbed by their accommodation of patients' ritualizing behaviors. Similarly, Shafran et al. (1995) found that 90% of relatives of individuals with OCD reported distress from the interference of OCD-related behaviors in their lives. Moreover, 60% of relatives reported participating in rituals with patients, and 40% of these relatives reported complying with requests to perform rituals themselves. Likewise, Black et al. (1998) found that 67% of relatives of adults with OCD reported participating in rituals. Other researchers (e.g., Hollander et al., 1998; Piacentini et al., 2003; Toro et al., 1992) have also found that more than two thirds of relatives of patients with OCD report significant distress as a result of OCD-related behaviors.

Relatives can also experience a wide variety of emotional reactions to implicit and explicit requests (or demands) by people with OCD for accommodation, participation, or both, including worry, guilt, empathy, frustration, and anger. In addition, relatives of individuals with OCD commonly report elevated perceptions of burden related to living with people with OCD (e.g., Magliano et al., 1996; Renshaw et al., 2000; Stengler-Wenzke, Trosbach, & Dietrich, 2004). Overall, then, behavioral, cognitive, and emotional distress commonly accompanies accommodation and participation, and such distress can be equally (or even more) intense when relatives resist such behavior because people with OCD often become quite upset.

In addition to accommodation, the interpersonal model of OCD described earlier posits the existence of elevated criticism, anger, and hostility in relatives. Although such responses garner less attention in the literature, there is empirical support for the presence of such antagonism in relatives. Several case studies and investigations with small samples have documented the presence of harsh criticism in relatives (e.g., Hafner, 1982; Hafner, Gilchrist, Bowling, & Kahicy, 1981; Tynes, Salins, & Winstead, 1990), and Allsopp and Verduyn (1990) reported that 20% of parents in their sample responded to OCD symptoms with "open anger" (p. 163). Also, in a sample of relatives of individuals with OCD and panic disorder, Chambless and Steketee (1999) found that 40% of relatives demonstrated high levels of criticism, with 33% of those expressing overt hostility (no differences between relatives of those with different diagnoses were detected). Finally, Hibbs et al. (1991) reported that 82% of a sample of 49 children with OCD had at least one parent rated high in EE, which is typically dependent on ratings of high criticism or hostility (see meta-analysis by Butzlaff & Hooley, 1998).

It is interesting that relatives often report that when they criticize the person with OCD, they do so with the belief that they are trying to help the person change his or her behavior (e.g., Chambless, Bryan, Aiken, Steketee,

& Hooley, 1999; Tynes et al., 1990). Thus, such criticism may not necessarily reflect malicious intent. Moreover, individual relatives often experience both accommodating and antagonistic responses, sometimes even on the same occasion (Renshaw et al., 2005). Consider the following excerpts from a personal account of the 38-year-old husband of a slightly younger wife who has severe OCD contamination and doubting fears, accompanied by washing and checking rituals. Her biggest fear is that something will happen to her husband or two small children, and she tries to prevent this by repeating her immediately preceding actions whenever she has such thoughts.

> She can't put [dirty] clothes in the [laundry] machine, so I do. If I don't, the pile gets so big it takes two days to wash it all. . . . My wife will hang everything out on the line and bring it all in. I think she feels guilty that people will see her doing her touching when she is outside, so she behaves herself. Unfortunately, as soon as she does bring the clothes inside, she dumps them on the living room floor. Putting them away is too much to hope for. We just dig for the day's outfit. GOOD LUCK!
>
> Cleaning the kitchen is done about every three weeks and that is usually by me. . . . The mess is unbelievable! I will come in from work at about 9:00 at night and will clean until about 12:00. . . .
>
> When we first met, she used to hide her OCD symptoms. Every now and then, I would catch her doing something unusual, but it wasn't too bad; in fact, some things were cute. . . . Our sex life was imaginative, creative, and fun. Now, I "contaminate" her. I don't even feel like asking her anymore. . . .
>
> We have been [seen] for medication treatment for three months, but so far nothing has helped. Somebody help her? Help me! (Steketee & White, 1990, pp. 15–16)

This account from Steketee and White (1990) reveals the frustration, anger, and accommodation commonly seen in family members of those with OCD. The husband accommodates his wife's symptoms out of perceived necessity but simultaneously expresses great frustration and anger with her. In our clinical experience, such a mixture is typical of the family members of those who struggle with this debilitating disorder, and this type of frustration and anger are in no way limited to relatives who are generally more aggressive or hostile as individuals. As our model indicates, these behaviors in relatives can, in turn, affect OCD symptoms in their family members. We turn now to a review of the evidence in regard to such effects.

Effects of Others on the Course of OCD

Research on the effects that family members' responses have on patients' course of OCD symptoms has centered primarily on the prediction of treatment outcome by family variables. Findings are generally consistent with the model presented earlier and support the importance of considering these specific types of responses in family members rather than more general constructs of relationship satisfaction or overall family functioning. General family functioning and relationship satisfaction have been found to be unrelated to treatment response in OCD (Riggs et al., 1992; Steketee, 1993; Wever & Rey, 1997), but multiple studies have detected negative relationships between the specific behaviors of accommodation or hostility and worse symptom course. For instance, Steketee (1993) found that although pretreatment ratings of perceived support did not predict OCD symptom severity after completion of ERP, patients' perceptions of their romantic partners as critical or angry did predict worse outcome and higher rates of relapse over the 9 months after treatment. Also, decreases in active participation in rituals by spouses or partners were associated with better outcome at 9 months. Similarly, Amir, Freshman, and Foa (2000) found a strong, significant relationship between higher pretreatment accommodation in family members and less improvement after ERP. Although family members' participation in rituals was not significantly related to patients' treatment response, this was likely the result of low power because the relationship was reflective of a medium effect size ($r = .33$). Thus, these studies provide support for negative effects of specifically antagonistic and accommodating responses, with a lack of association between treatment outcome and more general measures of interpersonal support and relationship satisfaction.

Further evidence for this model has been obtained in studies of OCD that use the construct of EE. As mentioned earlier, given the conceptual overlap of EE-related hostility with antagonistic responses and of emotional overinvolvement with accommodating responses, high EE might be viewed as a proxy for either of these types of responses. Emmelkamp, Kloek, and Blaauw (1992) found that patients who perceived high EE from their relatives had higher rates of relapse than those who perceived low EE over 1 to 3 years after receiving ERP. Moreover, in a larger study of 101 patients with OCD or panic disorder, Chambless and Steketee (1999) investigated each of the three components of EE separately in the prediction of response to exposure-based treatment. In this study, relatives' hostility and EOI both predicted negative outcomes, such as higher rates of dropout and poorer social functioning, after exposure therapy. However, when the effects of hostility were statistically controlled, relatives' criticism was actually associated with better response to exposure therapy (for both OCD and panic disorder), as measured by behavioral avoidance tests before and after treatment. This finding is consistent with earlier research on agoraphobic patients (Peter & Hand, 1988) and more recent research on patients with generalized anxiety disorder (Zinbarg, Lee, & Yoon, 2007), which found similar benefits of nonhostile criticism.

In evaluating these results, it is important to fully understand the difference between criticism and hostility in the context of EE. Hostility is coded when family members express global rejections of the patient in an interview (e.g., "He is just lazy, and he'll never work hard enough to get better"). In contrast, criticism consists of the total number of circumscribed critical comments made by the family member (e.g., "I think he could work harder in treatment") during that same interview. Therefore, EE-related hostility represents a high level of antagonistic responding, whereas EE-related criticism would fall more toward the middle of the proposed continuum of response. In this context, Chambless and Steketee's (1999) findings are consistent with the notion that a moderate level of firm but nonattacking criticism is beneficial for such patients. A similar effect was also observed anecdotally in Mehta's (1990) study of 30 patients with OCD who received either family-based ERP or standard individual ERP. In addition to significantly greater treatment response in those who received family-based ERP, Mehta noted that "nonanxious, firm relatives were more successful than anxious and inconsistent family members" in family-based ERP (Mehta, 1990, p. 135).

Additional results consistent with this model come from research investigating the underlying beliefs of family members of patients with OCD. For instance, Steketee (1993) found higher rates of relapse 9 months after ERP in patients whose spouses or partners believed that patients could control the symptoms of their OCD. Such attributions are generally associated with antagonism in family members in the form of higher EE-related hostility (Barrowclough & Hooley, 2003; Renshaw, Chambless, & Steketee, 2006). On the other end of the spectrum, Renshaw et al. (2006) reported that patients whose relatives attributed negative events and problems in patients' lives to the patients' disorder (OCD or panic) were less likely to improve after exposure therapy. Such relatives would seem to be more likely to engage in accommodating behaviors because they see the patient's disorder as a disabling condition. Furthermore, in recent follow-up analyses, it appears that relatives' attributions of problems to a patient's OCD (or panic disorder) are only associated with poorer outcome when the problem being discussed is judged by objective coders to be unrelated to the disorder (Thorgusen, Renshaw, & Chambless, 2008). In other words, only when relatives misattribute problems to a person's disorder is there any negative effect on treatment outcome; appropriate attributions of disorder-related problems to the disorder do not predict outcome. Again, it seems likely that relatives who overattribute problems to the person's OCD would be particularly vulnerable to engaging in accommodating or participation behaviors. These findings begin to offer an understanding not only of how family members might develop accommodating or antagonistic styles of responding but also of potential targets for interventions aimed at reducing such types of responding (see Implications for Treatment section).

In sum, empirical findings have supported the notion that both behaviors and cognitions of people with OCD's relatives and significant others can play a large role in the treatment response of people with OCD. These actions and beliefs can be conceptualized within the model presented earlier. Emerging evidence has suggested that low levels of accommodation and a moderate level of nonhostile but firm criticism, together with a clear understanding of behaviors that are and are not related to OCD, may be the optimal interpersonal environment for people with OCD. It is important to note that nearly all of the results in support of this model have been obtained in the context of response to ERP. To date, there have been no studies of the associations of these types of interpersonal processes with the longitudinal course of OCD in adults who are receiving other forms of treatment or no treatment. Such research would help elucidate whether these interpersonal behaviors and cognitions are broadly associated with better prognosis, or whether their potential benefits are limited to behavioral treatment outcomes.

Interpersonal Processes and Comorbidity

Little research has been conducted in the area of how interpersonal processes may be associated with comorbid conditions in people with OCD. It is conceivable, however, that the high rates of family dysfunction and distress in relatives could contribute to increased rates of depression in those with OCD. A large body of literature has indicated that relationship dissatisfaction and depression are highly related (see review by Whisman, 2001), and depressive disorders are highly comorbid with OCD, with some estimating that nearly half of people with OCD also suffer from depression (e.g., Crino & Andrews, 1996; Nestadt et al., 2001). Thus, it is plausible that OCD, relationship problems, and depression have transactional relationships within those with OCD.

IMPLICATIONS FOR TREATMENT OF OCD

On the basis of the model of interpersonal processes presented earlier, we make the following recommendations for involving family members in the treatment of OCD. These recommendations are meant to take place in the context of ERP-based treatment, not to replace such treatment.

Whom to Involve

To date, there is no empirical evidence regarding which types of relatives are advantageous to include in family-based treatment for adults with OCD. However, anyone with whom adults with OCD spend significant amounts of time, particularly those with whom they live, is likely to be influential in their functioning; thus, we recommend that therapists be flexible with regard to involving spouses, romantic partners, parents, children, siblings, other relatives, or even close friends. A primary determining factor should be whether the person with OCD desires the individual or individuals to participate. Although the specifics of how the following recommendations are implemented might take different forms with different types of relatives (e.g., spouses vs. parents), the principles are generally applicable to any individual the person with OCD feels is influential in his or her life.

Format of Treatment Delivery for Relatives

What is more difficult to decide is how to involve relatives who fall toward the extremes of accommodation and criticism. Family members who are extremely accommodating may exhibit overly controlling, sometimes infantilizing attitudes and behaviors toward people with OCD, and highly critical individuals may be hostile and rejecting toward these people and possibly more likely to be generally noncompliant with treatment. Notwithstanding these potential challenges, relatives at the extremes of these dimensions are potentially the most important ones to engage in family-based treatment because successful reductions in accommodating and hostile behaviors are the changes most likely to have positive impacts on the treatment response of people with OCD.

Individuals who display more extreme accommodating and hostile behaviors may be best integrated into treatment via an adjunctive group for family members only, while people with OCD receive individual (or group) ERP. Although they did not report on the levels of accommodation or hostile responding in relatives, Grunes, Neziroglu, and McKay (2001) found that a relatives-only group, administered once weekly over 8 weeks, was associated with better patient outcomes compared with standard individual ERP only. These gains were also maintained at 1-month follow-up. A separate relatives-only group of this nature can allow family members more latitude to voice their frustrations and anger without directly harming people with OCD or adding stress that could compromise their treatment response. Grunes et al. included a specific portion of one session devoted to such discussion, but in the current context, family members who are at the extremes of these dimensions may require more than a single session for such complaints. In a group of relatives only (without individuals with OCD present), time can be devoted to empathizing with relatives' views and frustrations while gradually helping them understand and accept the roots of the behaviors of people with OCD and learn how they might be able to adapt their own responses to enhance these individuals' improvement (see the next section for more detail on this aspect of family-based treatment).

For relatives and friends who exhibit less severe accommodation or hostility, it might be feasible to integrate them directly into a family-based ERP approach that treats the person with OCD and relative together as a dyad. Such involvement should be made only with the explicit agreement of the person with OCD to ensure that therapy remains a safe place for that person to address his or her symptoms.

A final consideration is that regardless of the treatment format, relatives and significant others who are invited to participate in assessment or treatment often experience some fear that they will be blamed for the person's symptoms. This fear may influence their attitude during treatment or prevent them from coming at all. In fact, Grunes et al. (2001) reported that nearly 25% of family members randomized to their relatives-only group never attended a single group. Although no information was given comparing these individuals to family members who completed the group, this level of nonattendance suggests that a significant proportion of family members may be resistant to involvement in a patient's therapy. Thus, finding ways to make therapy appealing to family members should be paramount. To do this, therapists can highlight the multitude of reasons for such participation (e.g., the effects that OCD can have on the family as a whole, the potential benefits of relatives' involvement in therapy), taking care to alleviate relatives' potential fears that family treatment will be aimed at "fixing" them. Thus, clinicians may want to incorporate some of the recommendations in the following sections when presenting even the possibility of family involvement in treatment, to help enhance the likelihood of relatives' attendance.

Psychoeducation

An overview of the known influences on OCD, including biological, neuropsychological, and cognitive components, can help relatives develop an informed understanding of the patients' disorder. It is probably less important to provide the nuances of each perspective (e.g., the potential involvement of the orbitofrontal circuit; Saxena, Brody, Schwartz, & Baxter, 1998) than it is to help the relative achieve a balanced understanding of the many factors that can contribute to OCD. In this context, linking physiology, cognitions, behaviors, and emotions can help relatives understand both the array of influences at play in OCD and the fact that intervening in any one of these areas can affect the others. In this way, psychoeducation can help relatives understand why behavioral interventions might work, without implying that people with OCD are in full control of their symptoms and are suffering because they have failed to exert appropriate effort in the past.

Another primary focus of psychoeducation should be the physiological, cognitive, and behavioral components of anxiety responses, including the natural progression of anxiety (i.e., declining naturally over time). In this context, the therapist can make behavioral connections between obsessions and compulsions, thus providing a rationale for ERP. Incorporating analogies (e.g., a simple phobia that the relative may have) can assist in this task; however, a strong emphasis should be placed on the extreme distress that obsessions usually generate in people with OCD seeking treatment and the very difficult nature of the exposure assignments that are part of ERP. This emphasis can help underscore the need for a therapist's assistance and prevent the relative from minimizing the person's distress.

Finally, emerging research has suggested that relatives' interpretation of the behaviors of people with OCD can have an impact both on relatives' own behavior and on people with OCD's treatment response to ERP (Renshaw et al., 2006; Thorgusen et al., 2008). It appears that appropriate, reasonable expectations for a person with OCD can help relatives avoid demanding too much of the person while simultaneously recognizing how helping people with OCD can bleed into accommodation or participation behavior (see the next section for further discussion). Overall, the goal of psychoeducation is to help ensure a balanced view of the etiology, maintenance, functioning, and potential intervention points for OCD.

Psychoeducation containing elements similar to those recommended here has been included in two separate studies of family-based ERP. Grunes et al. (2001) included elements of psychoeducation in their successful adjunctive group for family members, described earlier. In addition, Van Noppen, Steketee, McCorkle, and Pato (1997) included psychoeducation in multifamily groups that included both patients and family members. Although they did not detect significant differences in overall posttreatment symptom severity between those in multifamily groups and those in patient-only groups, they did find that more patients in the multifamily groups met criteria for reliable change and clinically significant improvement at both posttreatment and 1-year follow-up. Thus, these studies suggested that family-based treatments that incorporate psychoeducation might enhance treatment response to ERP in those with OCD. However, the research in this area has not progressed to the point of testing the independent contribution of family psychoeducation to patient improvement. In both of these studies, the family interventions contained multiple elements. Therefore, further research is needed to determine the independent contributions of this and all recommended elements of family-based treatment.

Addressing Relatives' Reactions to OCD Behaviors

When working with relatives of individuals with OCD, the primary OCD-related behaviors to address are accommodation, participation, and hostile behaviors. It is important to remember that any of these behaviors may be present even in well-meaning, caring relatives. When accommodation, hostile responses, or both are present, the therapist should work to help family members develop appropriate, balanced ways of responding to OCD behaviors. This is best accomplished in the context of open communication between people with OCD and their relatives about the best way for relatives to respond as the person with OCD progresses through ERP tasks. For example, if an upcoming ERP assignment involves prevention of a person's reassurance-seeking behavior, the person with OCD and his or her relative can discuss this in session to develop a standard response to requests for reassurance that will not be anxiety reducing but will also not create added hostility or resentment. Similarly, standard responses that relatives can use when the person with OCD becomes frustrated or anxious about ERP tasks may also prove helpful.

Both of the studies of successful family-based ERP discussed earlier (Grunes et al., 2001; Van Noppen et al., 1997) incorporated accommodation and antagonistic behaviors as targets of their family-based interventions. In addition, in a study of family-based ERP delivered to individual patients and family members, Mehta (1990) incorporated specific instructions for relatives to avoid accommodation and participation and to provide support for patients. At posttreatment and 1-month follow-up, the 15 patients who received this family-based ERP exhibited significantly greater improvements in levels of anxiety, obsessive–compulsive symptomatology, depression, and social interaction among family members and in occupational settings than did the 15 individuals who received standard ERP. Thus, although no component analyses have yet been conducted, this type of family instruction is also associated with enhanced treatment outcome for people with OCD.

It is important to note that when a relative reduces or stops accommodating or hostile behavior, other shifts may be needed. For example, the relative may feel a need to express his or her frustration regarding OCD symptoms to someone. Similarly, a relative who has accommodated the rituals of a person with OCD by completing all of the household cleaning tasks may find that despite an overwhelming desire for change, he or she is in some ways reluctant to give up those tasks. Such issues should be addressed in a straightforward problem-solving manner by identifying the potential problem, clarifying its importance to both the person with OCD and the relative, brainstorming possible solutions, deciding on a solution, implementing that solution for a specified trial period, and evaluating the outcome. If the proposed strategy is unsuccessful, another potential solution can be tried.

Involving Relatives as Coaches

If the person with OCD agrees, the therapist can review some ways in which the relative can coach him or her during ERP tasks or even assist in the selection and implementation of such tasks. This should always involve active participation on the part of the person with OCD to reinforce his or her feeling of control. If the person agrees to this strategy, the focus should be on teaching the relative how to best engage in such coaching. Such teaching should involve a combination of knowledge regarding appropriate therapeutic methods of coaching (e.g., never forcibly preventing a person from engaging in rituals, encouraging a person to return to an exposure situation as soon as possible after any ritualizing) and the person's desires for how the relative should be involved. Again, open communication between people with OCD and relatives can clearly facilitate the success of this type of intervention and guide the relative regarding the tone and style of comments. This approach was also included in all three of the family-based ERP studies discussed earlier (Grunes et al., 2001; Mehta, 1990; Van Noppen et al., 1997).

Addressing Relationship Issues

Individuals with OCD and their relatives often present with a variety of relationship problems, some of which are related to OCD behaviors and some of which are not. A careful assessment should be conducted to determine the overall quality of the relationship, its strengths and weaknesses, the investment of both (or all, if more than one family member) individuals in the relationship, and the investment of all individuals in addressing the person's OCD. Even in nonromantic relationships, standard marital assessment practices (e.g., observations of communication during a problem-solving task) can be used to guide this assessment (e.g., Epstein & Baucom, 2002).

The presence of relationship difficulties does not inherently prohibit the integration of a family member into treatment of OCD. From the perspective of a family-based approach to ERP, relationship difficulties should be conceptualized in regard to potential interference with person with OCD's and family members' intentions and capacity to work together toward common treatment goals of reducing OCD symptoms. Such difficulties should be addressed before focusing on actual exposure tasks. Again, standard marital and family therapy practices are wholly appropriate for this portion of treatment (e.g., Epstein & Baucom, 2002). For example, when poor communication could inhibit a person with OCD and his or her relative from discussing how the relative can respond to the person's desire to engage in rituals (see earlier section, Addressing Relatives Reactions to OCD Behavior), communication skills can be taught before the exposure portion of treatment.

To be clear, it is not the goal of family-based ERP to provide full marital or family counseling. In cases in which relationship distress is very high or in which relatives are not committed to the approach and goals of ERP or their appropriate role within that context, a referral for separate relationship-focused therapy should be considered, and the family member should probably be excluded from tasks like setting exposure assignments or helping to monitor exposures and rituals. In general, from the perspective of family-based ERP, the therapist should consider how the quality and characteristics of the relationship could affect the relative's participation in the specific ERP-related tasks discussed earlier and make modifications when needed.

Addressing Relatives' Distress

It is important to note that for family-based ERP to be optimally successful, attention should be paid to family members' distress related to the individual's OCD. An overly heavy focus on how family members can best aid in the treatment of the person with the identified disorder to the exclusion of addressing family members' own distress can alienate relatives and potentially reinforce their fear that the clinician sees them as partially responsible for causing the person's problems. Thus, careful attention should be paid to the distress of the relatives in family-based ERP.

When relatives exhibit severe distress that could interfere with their ability to encourage and assist the person with ERP, therapists might consider referring the relative for individual therapy. In many cases, however, distress will be manageable and largely related to the effect of the person's OCD on relatives' lives. This type of distress can be addressed in the family-based ERP setting. As mentioned earlier, relatives with more extreme reactions (e.g., severe accommodation or hostility) may best be treated in the context of a relatives-only group so that their frustration and distress with OCD-related problems can be fully aired without fear of harm to the person with OCD. If the distress is more contained, and if the person with OCD and the relative are able to discuss such problems in a constructive manner, then such work can be incorporated into a family-based ERP setting focused on the patient–relative dyad. This can take the form of teaching communication skills (e.g., Epstein & Baucom, 2002) and encouraging the person with OCD and his or her relative to use these skills to communicate about OCD and its effects on their lives. Effective communication in this regard can help relatives feel more understood and committed to treatment, and it may also serve to enhance the motivation of the person with OCD for treatment, as noted by Chambless and Steketee (1999).

Finally, therapists might consider holding one or more individual sessions with the relative alone in the context of family-based ERP, presuming the person with OCD gives permission. Such an approach has potential drawbacks, however, including disruption in the therapeutic alliance with the patient, discomfort in patients who are wondering what has been discussed, and problems with confidentiality if the relative raises treatment-relevant issues he or she does not want discussed with the patient. Thus, therapists should consider all relevant issues carefully before engaging in individual work with the relative only.

CONCLUSION

OCD is perhaps one of the most heavily researched mental illnesses, with substantial evidence of successful treatment with behavioral, cognitive–behavioral, and psychopharmacological interventions. However, it is increasingly clear that interpersonal influences play a large role in this disorder as well. An understanding of these influences and how to improve patient and relative relationships as they pertain to OCD symptoms may help enhance treatment response in this debilitating disorder. Future research focused on the proposed model of family response, and more specifically on treatments that target accommodation and hostility in family members, can help clarify our understanding of these interpersonal influences. Such knowledge can then be used to guide clinicians in working with family members in ways that may improve treatment response in patients struggling with OCD.

REFERENCES

Abramowitz, J. S., Taylor, S., & McKay, D. (2007). Psychological theories of obsessive-compulsive disorder. In E. A. Storch, G. R. Geffken, & T. K. Murphy (Eds.), *Handbook of child and adolescent obsessive-compulsive disorder* (pp. 109–129). Mahwah, NJ: Erlbaum.

Albert, U., Salvi, V., & Saracco, P. (2007). Health-related quality of life among first degree relatives of patients with obsessive–compulsive disorder in Italy. *Psychiatric Services, 58*, 970–976.

Allsopp, M., & Verduyn, C. (1990). Adolescents with obsessive compulsive disorder: A case note review of consecutive patients referred to a provincial regional adolescent psychiatry unit. *Journal of Adolescence, 13*, 157–169.

American Psychiatric Association. (2000). *Diagnostic and statistical manual of mental disorders* (4th ed., text revision). Washington, DC: Author.

Amir, N., Freshman, M., & Foa, E. B. (2000). Family distress and involvement in relatives of obsessive-compulsive disorder patients. *Journal of Anxiety Disorders, 14*, 209–217.

Barrowclough, C., & Hooley, J. M. (2003). Attributions and expressed emotion: A review. *Clinical Psychology Review, 23*, 849–880.

Black, D. W., Gaffney, G., Schlosser, S., & Gabel, J. (1998). The impact of obsessive-compulsive disorder on the family: Preliminary findings. *Journal of Nervous and Mental Disease, 186*, 440–442.

Bolton, D., Collins, S., & Steinberg, D. (1983). The treatment of obsessive–compulsive disorder in adolescence—A report of 15 cases. *British Journal of Psychiatry, 142*, 456–464.

Butzlaff, R. L., & Hooley, J. M. (1998). Expressed emotion and psychiatric relapse: A meta-analysis. *Archives of General Psychiatry, 55*, 547–552.

Calvocoressi, L., Lewis, B., Harris, M., Trufan, S. J., Goodman, W. K., McDougle, C. J., & Price, L. H. (1995). Family accommodation in obsessive–compulsive disorder. *American Journal of Psychiatry, 152*, 441–443.

Calvocoressi, L., Mazure, C., Stanislav, K., Skolnick, J., Fisk, D., Vegso, S., . . . Price, L. (1999). Reliability and validity of the Family Accommodation Scale for obsessive-compulsive disorder. *Journal of Nervous and Mental Disease, 187*, 636–642.

Chambless, D. L., Bryan, A. D., Aiken, L. S., Steketee, G., & Hooley, J. (1999). The structure of expressed emotion: A three-construct representation. *Psychological Assessment, 11*, 67–76.

Chambless, D. L., & Steketee, G. (1999). Expressed emotion and behavior therapy outcome: A prospective study with obsessive–compulsive and agoraphobic out-patients. *Journal of Consulting and Clinical Psychology, 67*, 658–665.

Clark, D. A. (2004). *Cognitive-behavioral therapy for OCD.* New York: Guilford Press.

Cooper, M. (1996). Obsessive–compulsive disorder: Effects on family members. *American Journal of Orthopsychiatry, 66*, 296–304.

Crino, R., & Andrews, G. (1996). Obsessive–compulsive disorder and Axis I comorbidity. *Journal of Anxiety Disorders, 19*, 37–46.

Derisley, J., Libby, S., Clark, S., & Reynolds, S. (2005). Mental health, coping and family-functioning in parents of young people with obsessive–compulsive disorder and with anxiety disorders. *British Journal of Clinical Psychology, 44*, 439–444.

Emmelkamp, P. M. G., Kloek, J., & Blaauw, E. (1992). Obsessive–compulsive disorders. In P. H. Wilson (Ed.), *Principles and practice of relapse prevention* (pp. 213–234). New York, NY: Guilford Press.

Epstein, N. B., Baldwin, L., & Bishop, D. S. (1983). The McMaster Family Assessment Device. *Journal of Marital and Family Therapy, 9*, 171–180.

Epstein, N. B., & Baucom, D. H. (2002). *Enhanced cognitive–behavioral therapy for couples: A contextual approach.* Washington, DC: American Psychological Association.

Erol, A., Yazici, F., & Toprak, G. (2007). Family functioning of patients with an eating disorder compared with that of patients with obsessive compulsive disorder. *Comprehensive Psychiatry, 48*, 47–50.

Esman, A. H. (2001). Obsessive-compulsive disorder: Current views. *Psychoanalytic Inquiry, 21*, 145–156.

Ferrão, Y. A., Shavitt, R. G., & Nádia, R. (2006). Clinical features associated to refractory obsessive-compulsive disorder. *Journal of Affective Disorders, 94*, 199–209.

Fontenelle, L. F., Mendlowicz, M. V., Mattos, P., & Versiani, M. (2006). Neuropsychological findings in obsessive-compulsive disorder and its potential implications for treatment. *Current Psychiatry Reviews, 2,* 11–26.

Franklin, M. E., & Foa, E. B. (2002). Cognitive behavioral treatments for obsessive compulsive disorder. In P. E. Nathan & J. M. Gorman (Eds.), *A guide to treatments that work* (2nd ed., pp. 367–386). New York, NY: Oxford University Press.

Freud, A. (1966). Obsessional neurosis: A summary of psychoanalytic views as presented at the Congress. *International Journal of Psychoanalysis, 47,* 116–122.

Friedlander, L., & Desrocher, M. (2006). Neuroimaging studies of obsessive-compulsive disorder in adults and children. *Clinical Psychology Review, 26,* 32–49.

Grunes, M. S., Neziroglu, F., & McKay, D. (2001). Family involvement in the behavioral treatment of obsessive-compulsive disorder: A preliminary investigation. *Behavior Therapy, 32,* 803–820.

Hafner, R. J. (1982). Marital interaction in persisting obsessive-compulsive disorders. *Australian and New Zealand Journal of Psychiatry, 16,* 171–178.

Hafner, R. J., Gilchrist, P., Bowling, J., & Kahicy, R. (1981). The treatment of obsessional neurosis in a family setting. *Australian and New Zealand Journal of Psychiatry, 15,* 145–151.

Hibbs, E. D., Hamburger, S. D., Lenane, M., Rapoport, J. L., Kruesi, M. J. P., Keysor, C. S., & Goldstein, M. J. (1991). Determinants of expressed emotion in families of disturbed and normal children. *Journal of Child Psychology and Psychiatry, 32,* 757–770.

Hollander, E., Kwon, J. H., Stein, D. J., Broatch, J., Rowland, C. T., & Himelein, C. A. (1996). Obsessive-compulsive and spectrum disorders: Overview and quality of life issues. *Journal of Clinical Psychiatry, 57*(Suppl. 8), 3–6.

Hollander, E., Stein, D., Kwon, J., Rowland, C., Wong, C., Broatch, J., & Himelein, C. A. (1998). Psychosocial function and economic costs of obsessive-compulsive disorder. *CNS Spectrum, 5*(Suppl. 1), 48–58.

Horowitz, M. (1975). Intrusive and repetitive thoughts after experimental stress. *Archives of General Psychiatry, 32,* 1457–1463.

Koran, L. M. (2000). Quality of life in obsessive–compulsive disorder. *Psychiatric Clinics of North America, 23,* 509–517.

Leff, J., & Vaughn, C. (1985). *Expressed emotion in families.* New York, NY: Guilford Press.

Lensi, P., Cassano, G. B., Correddu, G., Ravagli, S., & Kunovac, J. J. (1996). Obsessive–compulsive disorder: Familial–developmental history, symptomatology, comorbidity and course with special reference to gender-related differences. *British Journal of Psychiatry, 169,* 101–107.

Livingston-Van Noppen, B., Rasmussen, S. A., Eisen, J., & McCartney, L. (1990). Family function and treatment in obsessive-compulsive disorder. In M. Jenike, L. Baer, & W. E. Minichiello (Eds.), *Obsessive compulsive disorder: Theory and management* (2nd ed., pp. 325–340). Chicago, IL: Year Book.

Lochner, C., Mogotsi, M., du-Toit, P. L., Kaminer, D., Niehaus, D. J., & Stein, D. J. (2003). Quality of life in anxiety disorders: A comparison of obsessive–compulsive disorder, social anxiety disorder, and panic disorder. *Psychopathology, 36,* 255–262.

Magliano, L., Tosini, P., Guarneri, M., Marasco, C., & Catapano, F. (1996). Burden on the families of patients with obsessive–compulsive disorder: A pilot study. *European Psychiatry, 11,* 192–197.

Mehta, M. (1990). A comparative study of family-based and patient-based behavioural management in obsessive–compulsive disorder. *British Journal of Psychiatry, 157,* 133–135.

Menzies, L., Chamberlain, S. R., Laird, A. R., Thelen, S. M., Sahakian, B. J., & Bullmore, E. T. (2008). Integrating evidence from neuroimaging and neuro-psychological studies of obsessive-compulsive disorder: The orbitofronto-striatal model revisited. *Neuroscience & Biobehavioral Reviews, 32,* 525–549.

Nestadt, G., Samuels, J., Riddle, M. A., Liang, K.-Y., Bienvenu, O. J., Hoehn-Saric, R., . . . Cullen, B. (2001). The relationship between obsessive-compulsive disorder and anxiety and affective disorders: Results from the Johns Hopkins OCD Family Study. *Psychological Medicine, 31,* 481–487.

Obsessive Compulsive Cognitions Working Group. (2005). Psychometric validation of the Obsessive Belief Questionnaire and Interpretation of Intrusions Inventory—Part 2: Factor analyses and testing of a brief version. *Behaviour Research and Therapy, 43,* 1527–1542.

Peter, H., & Hand, I. (1988). Patterns of patient–spouse interaction in agoraphobics: Assessment by Camberwell Family Interview (CFI) and impact on outcome of self-exposure treatment. In I. Hand & H.-U. Wittchen (Eds.), *Panic and phobias: 2. Treatments and variables affecting course and outcome* (pp. 240–251). Berlin, Germany: Springer-Verlag.

Piacentini, J., Bergman, R. L., Keller, M., & McCracken, J. (2003). Functional impairment in children and adolescents with obsessive-compulsive disorder. *Journal of Child and Adolescent Psychopharmacology, 13*(Suppl.), S61–S69.

Rachman, S. J., & de Silva, P. (1978). Abnormal and normal obsessions. *Behaviour Research and Therapy, 16,* 233–248.

Rasmussen, S. A., & Eisen, J. L. (1992). The epidemiology and clinical features of obsessive compulsive disorder. *Psychiatric Clinics of North America, 15,* 743–758.

Renshaw, K. D., Chambless, D. L., Rodebaugh, T. L., & Steketee, G. (2000). Living with severe anxiety disorders: Relatives' distress and reactions to patient behaviors. *Clinical Psychology and Psychotherapy, 7,* 190–200.

Renshaw, K. D., Chambless, D. L., & Steketee, G. (2006). The relationship of relatives' attributions to their expressed emotion and to patients' improvement in treatment for anxiety disorders. *Behavior Therapy, 37,* 159–169.

Renshaw, K. D., Steketee, G., & Chambless, D. L. (2005). Involving family members in the treatment of OCD. *Cognitive Behaviour Therapy, 34,* 164–175.

Riggs, D. S., Hiss, H., & Foa, E. B. (1992). Marital distress and the treatment of obsessive compulsive disorder. *Behavior Therapy, 23,* 585–597.

Saxena, S., Brody, A. L., Schwartz, J. M., & Baxter, L. R. (1998). Neuroimaging and frontalsubcortical circuitry in obsessive–compulsive disorder. *British Journal of Psychiatry, 173*(Suppl. 35), 26–37.

Shafran, R., Ralph, J., & Tallis, F. (1995). Obsessive–compulsive symptoms and the family. *Bulletin of the Menninger Clinic, 59*, 472–479.

Simmons, R. A., Gordon, P. C., & Chambless, D. L. (2005). Pronouns in marital interaction: What do "you" and "I" say about mental health? *Psychological Science, 16*, 932–936.

Spanier, G. B. (1976). Measuring dyadic adjustment: New scales for assessing the quality of marriage and similar dyads. *Journal of Marriage and the Family, 38*, 15–28.

Steketee, G. (1993). Social support and treatment outcome of obsessive compulsive disorder at 9-month follow up. *Behavioural Psychotherapy, 21*, 81–95.

Steketee, G. (1997). Disability and family burden in obsessive–compulsive disorder. *Canadian Journal of Psychiatry, 42*, 919–928.

Steketee, G. S., Grayson, J. B., & Foa, E. B. (1985). Obsessive–compulsive disorder: Differences between washers and checkers. *Behaviour Research and Therapy, 23*, 197–201.

Steketee, G., & Pruyn, N. A. (1998). Families of individuals with obsessive–compulsive disorder. In R. P. Swinson, M. M. Antony, S. Rachman, & M. A. Richter (Eds.), *Obsessive–compulsive disorder: Theory, research, and treatment* (pp. 120–140). New York, NY: Guilford Press.

Steketee, G., & White, K. (1990). *When once is not enough: Help for obsessions and compulsions.* Oakland, CA: New Harbinger Press.

Stengler-Wenzke, K., Trosbach, J., & Dietrich, S. (2004). Experience of stigmatization by relatives of patients with obsessive compulsive disorder. *Archives of Psychiatric Nursing, 18*, 88–96.

Storch, E. A., Geffken, G. R., & Merlo, L. J. (2007). Family-based cognitive–behavioral therapy for pediatric obsessive-compulsive disorder: Comparison of intensive and weekly approaches. *Journal of the American Academy of Child & Adolescent Psychiatry, 46*, 469–478.

Thorgusen, S., Renshaw, K. D., & Chambless, D. L. (2008, November). *Patients whose relatives attribute non-disorder related events to their anxiety disorder benefit less from exposure therapy.* Poster session presented at the annual meeting of the Association of Behavior and Cognitive Therapies, Orlando, FL.

Toro, J., Cervera, M., & Osejo, E. (1992). Obsessive-compulsive disorder in childhood and adolescence: A clinical study. *Journal of Child Psychology and Psychiatry, 33*, 1025–1037.

Tynes, L. L., Salins, C., & Winstead, D. K. (1990). Obsessive–compulsive patients: Familial frustration and criticism. *Journal of the Louisiana State Medical Society, 142*, 24–29.

Van Noppen, B. L., Rasmussen, S. A., Eisen, J., & McCartney, L. (1991). A multi-family group approach as an adjunct to treatment of obsessive compulsive disorder. In M. T. Pato & J. Zohar (Eds.), *Current treatments of obsessive compulsive disorder* (pp. 115–134). Washington, DC: American Psychiatric Press.

Van Noppen, B., Steketee, G., McCorkle, B. H., & Pato, M. (1997). Group and multi-family behavioral treatment for obsessive compulsive disorder: A pilot study. *Journal of Anxiety Disorders, 11*, 431–446.

Wever, C., & Rey, J. M. (1997). Juvenile obsessive-compulsive disorder. *Australian and New Zealand Journal of Psychiatry, 31*, 105–113.

Whisman, M. A. (2001). The association between marital dissatisfaction and depression. In S. R. H. Beach (Ed.), *Marital and family processes in depression: A scientific foundation for clinical practice* (pp. 2–24). Washington, DC: American Psychological Association.

Zinbarg, R. E., Lee, J. E., & Yoon, K. L. (2007). Dyadic predictors of outcome in a cognitive-behavioral program for patients with generalized anxiety disorder in committed relationships: A "spoonful of sugar" and a dose of non-hostile criticism may help. *Behaviour Research and Therapy, 45*, 699–713.

7

POSTTRAUMATIC STRESS DISORDER IN AN INTERPERSONAL CONTEXT

CANDICE M. MONSON, STEFFANY J. FREDMAN, AND RACHEL DEKEL

Posttraumatic stress disorder (PTSD) is a relatively common mental health condition that can occur after exposure to a traumatic event. The lifetime prevalence of the disorder in the general population is about 8%, with a 2:1 prevalence of the disorder in women (10%) compared with men (5%; Kessler, Sonnega, Bromet, Hughes, & Nelson, 1995). Although a range of traumatic stressors may cause PTSD, the genesis of most PTSD cases are man-made traumas (Norris, 1992), portending the inherently interpersonal phenomenology and consequences of the disorder. Nonetheless, there have been limited efforts to understand PTSD through an interpersonal lens, despite compelling evidence establishing an association between PTSD and relationship problems. In this chapter, we describe PTSD and its manifestation in adult close relationships, review the empirical literature documenting an association between PTSD and close relationship problems, discuss theoretical constructs and models explaining the association, present various interpersonally oriented PTSD treatment efforts, and consider future directions for research.

CLINICAL PRESENTATION OF PTSD AND COMMON COMORBID CONDITIONS WITHIN CLOSE RELATIONSHIPS

According to the *Diagnostic and Statistical Manual of Mental Disorders* (4th ed., text rev; American Psychiatric Association, 2000), to be diagnosed with PTSD, a person must have been exposed to a traumatic event in which the person (a) experienced, witnessed, or was confronted with an event or events that involved actual or threatened death or serious injury or a threat to the physical integrity of self or others and (b) responded with intense fear, helplessness, or horror. In addition, the person must present with symptoms of each of the three different clusters of PTSD symptoms: reexperiencing, avoidance, and hyperarousal symptoms. *Reexperiencing symptoms* are characterized by intrusive memories, nightmares, flashbacks, and psychological and physiological reactivity when encountering trauma cues. *Avoidance symptoms* consist of avoiding thoughts and activities associated with traumatic experiences, inability to recall aspects of the traumatic event, diminished interest, emotional detachment, restricted affect, and a sense of foreshortened future. *Hyperarousal symptoms* of PTSD include sleep disturbance, irritability or anger, difficulty concentrating, hypervigilance, and an exaggerated startle response.

The symptoms of PTSD alone can adversely affect interpersonal relationships. For example, sleep disturbance and nightmares can cause intimate partners to avoid sleeping together because of the sleep disturbance caused to significant others by awakening or significant others' concerns about the potential for physical harm while sleeping (e.g., partner has combat-related nightmares involving aggression). Significant others also report distress, confusion, and concerns for their own safety during their loved ones' altered states of consciousness involved in flashbacks. The behavioral avoidance symptoms of PTSD can make engaging in routine pleasurable activities with romantic and nonromantic significant others less routine or nonexistent. Emotional numbing directly relates to the ability of those with PTSD to experience and express positive feelings within the range of close relationships. Finally, hyperarousal symptoms can have significant effects on close relationships. Irritability and anger can add tension and stress to close relationships, with surrounding others reporting that they walk on eggshells because of fear of upsetting their loved one with PTSD or provoking an angry outburst (Maloney, 1988).

It is critical to note that PTSD likely affects the interpersonal network of those with the disorder and is also affected by the nature and quality of the relationships in that network. Optimally, interpersonal relationships might facilitate recovery and prevent PTSD or improve the course of PTSD if it is diagnosed. In contrast, a negative, conflictual interpersonal environment may raise the stress level of the traumatized individual and make recovery more difficult. We want to emphasize the potential bidirectional relationship between

PTSD and interpersonal relationships. The way intimate partners, family members, and close friends react to a loved one with PTSD and vice versa may affect the health and well-being of these individuals and their relationships.

EMPIRICAL RESEARCH ON PTSD AND CLOSE RELATIONSHIPS

Much of the research on PTSD and close relationships has been descriptive in nature. For instance, epidemiological research has revealed that individuals with PTSD are as likely to marry as those without the disorder but are between three and six times more likely to divorce than those without PTSD (J. R. Davidson, Hughes, Blazer, & George, 1991; Kessler et al., 1995). A large community study of nearly 5,000 couples in Canada investigated the association between nine mental health diagnoses and the presence or absence of marital distress (Whisman, Sheldon, & Goering, 2000). A diagnosis of PTSD was associated with a 3.8 times greater likelihood of having relationship discord, second only to the 5.7 times greater likelihood of relationship distress with a dysthymia diagnosis. PTSD was on par with the strong associations between relationship distress and major depression, panic disorder, and generalized anxiety disorder.

Research with natural disaster victims has suggested that being married generally functions as a protective factor in men's individual postdisaster mental health, including PTSD symptoms, and as a risk factor for women's mental health (e.g., Brooks & McKinlay, 1992; Fullerton, Ursano, Kao, & Bharitya, 1999; Gleser, Green, & Winget, 1981; S. D. Solomon, 2002; Ursano, Fullerton, Kao, & Bhartiya, 1995). Interestingly, S. D. Solomon (2002) found that women who perceived themselves to have excellent spouse support were more vulnerable to mental health problems than were women with weaker spouse support. She noted that the social ties and obligations that accompany spouse support can serve as a source of stress for married women.

Three cross-sectional studies have assessed both members of heterosexual dyads after disasters to examine the association of their individual postdisaster mental health. In Vila et al.'s (2001) study of families affected by an industrial accident in France, husbands' and wives' individual postdisaster symptoms were correlated with each other. Gleser et al. (1981), studying the dam collapse in Buffalo Creek, West Virginia, found that husbands' mental health symptoms predicted their wives' mental health symptoms, and vice versa, after the severity of trauma exposure and other demographic variables were controlled. However, husbands' symptoms were more strongly predictive of their wives' symptoms than the other way around. This finding is consistent with the literature on the differential influence of intimate relationships on women's versus men's mental health problems in general (e.g., Dawson, Grant, Chou, & Stinson, 2007; Steelman, 2007). In a sample of hetero-sexual couples who experienced a severe flood, Monson, Gradus, La Bash, and Resick (in press) found that husbands' assumptions about the benevolence of the world moderated the association between wives' benevolent world assumptions and their PTSD symptoms. Specifically, when wives were married to husbands with fewer benevolent world assumptions, the expected inverse association between wives' benevolent world assumptions and PTSD symptoms emerged. Conversely, when husbands held more positive assumptions about the benevolence of the world, there was no association between the wives' assumptions and their PTSD symptoms. These findings suggest that cognitions held by significant others in a couple may serve to potentiate or attenuate the association between negative trauma-related beliefs and PTSD symptoms.

The balance of what is currently known about the intersection of PTSD, close relationship functioning, and significant others' adjustment has been derived mostly from research on male American Vietnam War veterans and their female intimate partners and, to a lesser extent, other countries' male veterans (e.g., Australia, Netherlands, Israel). These studies have consistently revealed that veterans diagnosed with PTSD and their partners report more numerous and severe relationship problems, more parenting problems, and generally poorer family adjustment than trauma-exposed veterans without PTSD and their partners (Jordan et al., 1992). Male veterans with PTSD have been found to be less self-disclosing and emotionally expressive with their partners (Carroll, Rueger, Foy, & Donahoe, 1985) and to have greater anxiety related to intimacy (Riggs, Byrne, Weathers, & Litz, 1998) compared with veterans without PTSD. Male veterans diagnosed with PTSD, compared with those without PTSD, are more likely to perpetrate verbal and physical aggression against their partners and children (Carroll et al., 1985; Glenn et al., 2002; Jordan et al., 1992; Verbosky & Ryan, 1988), with rates as high as 63% for some act of physical violence in the past year (Byrne & Riggs, 1996). The severity of violent behavior has been shown to be positively correlated with PTSD symptom severity (Byrne & Riggs, 1996; Glenn et al., 2002). In addition, research has documented sexual dysfunction across the sexual response cycle in those with PTSD, and especially in those who have been sexually traumatized (Becker & Skinner, 1983; Becker, Skinner, Abel, & Treacy, 1982; Bhugra, 2002; Cosgrove et al., 2002; Kilpatrick et al., 1998; Lee, Gavriel, Drummond, Richards, & Greenwald, 2002; McGuire & Wagner, 1978).

There have been a few attempts to explicate mechanisms accounting for these associations. For example, Jordan et al. (1992) found in the National Vietnam Veterans Readjustment Study that the veterans' PTSD symptoms accounted for variance in their intimate relationship distress above and beyond other factors known to be associated with intimate relationship dysfunction (e.g., childhood behavioral problems, low parental affection, parental violence and abuse). Riggs et al. (1998) found that of the PTSD symptom clusters, avoidance and numbing were most strongly associated with the ability of veterans diagnosed with PTSD to express emotions in their relationships. Their study suggested that emotional numbing symptoms, in particular, interfered with intimacy, contributing to problems in building and maintaining positive intimate relationships. However, in a sample of male veterans recently returned from Iraq, Nelson Goff, Crow, Reisbig, and Hamilton (2007) found that the veterans' sleep problems, dissociation, and sexual problems were the problems most strongly related to relationship dissatisfaction in both members of the couple.

Several studies have supported the role of cognitive processes in the association between veterans' PTSD and romantic relationship functioning. Using a modified Stroop methodology, Miterany (2004) found that priming with positive interpersonally oriented words (e.g., *love*) lowered the reaction time to trauma-relevant words among participants with PTSD symptoms, suggesting that evoking positive, interpersonally oriented cognitions or emotions might facilitate an individual's ability to filter out or temper threat-relevant cues. Studying cognitive variables at the dyadic level, Renshaw, Rodrigues, and Jones (2008) investigated the moderating role of wives' beliefs about their husbands' combat experiences. When wives believed that their husbands who had served in the National Guard in Iraq had experienced lower levels of combat exposure and their husbands reported high levels of PTSD symptoms, the wives reported the highest levels of relationship distress. Renshaw et al. interpreted these findings as an indication that partners' attributions about trauma-related symptoms contribute meaningfully to their feelings about the relationship. Given that relationship distress can serve as a general stressor that aggravates the course of PTSD, psychoeducation about trauma and its effects, in conjunction with disclosure to promote a shared understanding of traumatic experiences, offers the potential to facilitate recovery from PTSD.

Relatively more work has been done on factors accounting for the association between PTSD and intimate aggression perpetration. Using data from the National Vietnam Veterans Readjustment Study, Savarese, Suvak, King, and King (2001) found that veterans' self-reported hyperarousal symptom severity was particularly associated with partners' reports of psychological and physical violence victimization. Orcutt, King, and King (2003) used structural equation modeling with National Vietnam Veterans Readjustment Study data and found that PTSD had a direct relationship to the male veterans' perpetration of physical violence against their female partners. Factors previously established to be associated with intimate aggression perpetration, such as early family stressors and childhood antisocial behavior, were indirectly related to violence perpetration through their contribution to the likelihood of having PTSD. Interestingly, after the association between combat trauma exposure and PTSD was taken into account, higher trauma exposure was associated with less intimate violence perpetration. It appears that PTSD versus trauma exposure is unique in potentiating intimate aggression. Moreover, this research suggested that prior traumatic experiences without consequent PTSD may decrease the likelihood of perpetrating trauma against an intimate partner.

PTSD without at least one comorbid condition is the exception versus the rule (Kessler et al., 1995). The most commonly occurring comorbidities are depression, substance use disorders, and personality disorders. There are well-established literatures documenting the interpersonal aspects of each of these common comorbidities with regard to the onset, course, and treatment of the disorders (O'Farrell & Fals-Stewart, 2006; O'Leary & Beach, 1990). A few studies have examined the shared and unique associations among PTSD, any of these conditions, and interpersonal variables. Savarese et al.'s (2001) study on the association between PTSD and perpetration of intimate aggression in Vietnam veterans is one example. As noted earlier, hyperarousal symptoms were specifically associated with intimate aggression perpetration, but this relationship was moderated by alcohol use patterns. More frequent alcohol use, but in smaller quantities, diminished the association between hyperarousal symptoms and PTSD. Larger quantities of alcohol paired with more frequent use strengthened the association between hyperarousal symptoms and PTSD. Two studies with different types of trauma samples have examined the role of depression in the association between PTSD and relationship problems. Taft, Vogt, Marshall, Panuzio, and Niles (2007), examining a sample of male combat veterans seeking diagnostic assessment of PTSD, found that dysphoria was directly, and through PTSD, associated with the veterans' perpetration of aggressive behavior. Investigating a sample of predominantly female motor vehicle accident survivors, Beck, Grant, Clapp, and Palyo (2009) used hierarchical multiple regression to investigate the relative contribution of depression and PTSD symptoms in predicting interview-rated interpersonal functioning and self-reported social support. They found that depression, and not PTSD, predicted overall interpersonal functioning. Both the emotional numbing symptoms of PTSD and depression generally predicted social support. These studies highlighted potential sample differences (e.g., gender, type of trauma) and differences on the basis of assessment methodology. Additional research teasing out the role of comorbid conditions in the association between PTSD and interpersonal relationship problems is needed.

THEORETICAL CONSTRUCTS AND MODELS ACCOUNTING FOR PTSD AND CLOSE RELATIONSHIP PROBLEMS

Several constructs and theories have been put forth to account for the associations among trauma exposure, PTSD, and close relationship functioning. We organize these constructs and theories by the generally presumed direction of causality among the significant other, the individual who has been traumatized or has PTSD, and their close relationship functioning. We begin with those addressing the effect of close others on people who have been traumatized or have PTSD. Next, we review constructs positing a deleterious effect of PTSD on others in close relation to an individual with PTSD, and finally, we describe theories that posit reciprocal effects between significant others, the person with PTSD, and the shared influence of their relationship functioning.

Effect of Close Others on Trauma Recovery and PTSD

There have been relatively fewer constructs put forth presuming a causal pathway from close relationship functioning to individual posttraumatic symptom expression. The roles of social support and adult attachment are two such notions.

Social Support

Of the numerous factors that have been associated with the development and maintenance of PTSD, social support has emerged as one of the most robust constructs. According to meta-analysis, social support is among the variables most consistently and strongly associated with PTSD (Brewin, Andrews, & Valentine, 2000; Ozer, Best, Lipsey, & Weiss, 2003). Two consistent findings regarding the qualities of social support and PTSD are that perceived support is more important than objective support and that negative support is more powerful as a risk factor than positive support is as a protective factor (for a review, see Charuvastra & Cloitre, 2008).

Although the research establishing an association between social support and PTSD is well developed, the specific aspects of social support that account for its association with PTSD symptoms are not as fully understood. According to Joseph, Williams, and Yule (1997), significant others' appraisals of traumatic events positively or negatively influence survivors' own appraisals of traumatic events and, consequently, have an impact on the survivors' PTSD symptoms. For example, significant others might normalize a survivor's freezing response in an inescapable traumatic event and correct appraisals that alternative courses of actions would have led to positive outcomes. Williams and Joseph (1999) also argued that social support affects survivors' emotional states and coping strategies, which directly and indirectly facilitate recovery.

Although originally construed as a close relationship factor acting on the traumatized individual, there is evidence that chronic stress and chronic PTSD can, in fact, diminish the availability and quality of social support. Several researchers have found that certain types of chronic traumatic stressors (e.g., natural disasters) can erode social support, independent of PTSD symptoms

(Kaniasty & Norris, 1993; Lepore, Evans, & Schneider, 1991). The symptoms of PTSD can also erode social support. For example, a longitudinal study of more than 2,000 veterans who served in the first Gulf War revealed that PTSD symptoms 18 to 24 months after return from service were negatively associated with social support 5 years later. However, social support at the first assessment was not associated with PTSD symptoms 5 years later (King, Taft, King, Hammond, & Stone, 2006). Our clinical experience is that the symptoms of PTSD can burn out social support providers. In the course of working with couples in which one member has PTSD, one of us encountered a wife who was very reluctant to be emotionally supportive of her husband after living with his PTSD-related anger and irritability during their nearly 30 years of marriage.

Adult Attachment

Attachment theory, as originated by Bowlby (e.g., 1982), is primarily focused on understanding the effect of caregivers' responsiveness and attentiveness on the socioemotional health of infants and children. Hazan and Shaver (1994) were two of the first researchers to extend Bowlby's notions to adult intimate relationships. They argued that security in intimate relationships, like that found in healthy caregiver–child relationships, facilitates emotion regulation, effective cognitive processing of information, and clear communication.

The contribution of adult attachment theory to explain the effects of PTSD on others is related to two groups of questions: (a) the contribution of adult attachment to coping with traumatic events and (b) the effects of trauma on attachment and interpersonal relations. In relation to the former, insecure attachment developed in childhood and extending into adulthood is considered to be a risk factor that reduces resilience in times of stress, fosters negative affectivity, and contributes to emotional problems, maladjustment, and psychopathology when presented with stress (Mikulincer, Shaver, & Horesh, 2006). Regarding the latter, trauma increases the need for protective attachments and, at the same time, undermines the ability to trust and, therefore, to build such attachments (S. M. Johnson & Makinen, 2003). The negative impact of these interpersonal difficulties produces a relational cycle of mutual distance and disconnection between partners, reducing the secure attachment necessary for healthy functioning (S. M. Johnson, 2002).

Several cross-sectional studies of adults have found positive correlations among self-reported adult attachment insecurity, difficulties coping with traumatic events, and PTSD (e.g., Dieperink, Leskela, Thuras, & Engdahl, 2001; Z. Solomon, Ginzburg, Mikulincer, Neria, & Ohry, 1998). However, a recent longitudinal study has called into question the notion of adult attachment problems as a risk factor for PTSD symptoms. In a sample of Israeli prisoners of war, PTSD and attachment dimensions were assessed on two occasions.

PTSD symptoms at initial assessment predicted later attachment patterns better than vice versa (Z. Solomon, Dekel, & Mikulincer, 2008). These findings are consistent with prior studies showing relative instability in attachment patterns over time (Fraley, 2002) and also suggest that PTSD symptoms may be equally or more likely to negatively affect attachment within intimate relationships than the converse. Additional empirical research is needed to clarify the directionality of the associations among attachment, trauma, PTSD, and interpersonal relationships.

Effect of PTSD on Close Others

Various authors have described PTSD symptomatology to have a deleterious effect on close others and intimate relationship functioning. Secondary or vicarious traumatization, caregiver burden, ambiguous loss, and the intergenerational transmission of PTSD have been put forth to describe this way of conceptualizing the PTSD–close relationship association.

Secondary or Vicarious Traumatization

Several authors have discussed the secondary effects of trauma-related symptoms, including PTSD, on close others, including intimate partners, children, close friends, and therapists (e.g., McCann & Pearlman, 1990b; Z. Solomon et al., 1992). According to Figley (1989), the process of secondary traumatization starts with close others' efforts to emotionally support their troubled loved ones, which leads to attempts to understand their feelings and experiences and, from there, to empathize with them. In the process of gathering information about their suffering, significant others can take on the traumatized person's feelings, experiences, and even memories as their own— and, hence, their symptoms. In this conceptualization, those who are close to the trauma survivor can overidentify with him or her (Catherall, 1992; Figley, 1995) and develop symptoms that mimic the trauma symptoms in the survivor (Maloney, 1988; Z. Solomon et al., 1992). Others have considered a wide range of manifestations of distress, in addition to those that mimic posttraumatic symptoms, to constitute secondary or vicarious trauma (Dekel & Solomon, 2006).

Cross-sectional research has documented an association between PTSD in one partner and mental health problems and compromised life satisfaction in the other partner. Most of this research has been done with male combat veterans and their female partners. Using the instructions given to the identified partner with PTSD, female partners of those with PTSD reported symptoms specific to their partner's identified traumas. Others have not anchored the female partner's report of symptoms to her partner's trauma(s), making it difficult to determine whether the woman responded on the basis of her own history of trauma exposure or nontraumatic stressors or without a particular index event that she or her partner experienced. Using a broader definition of secondary or vicarious traumatization, female partners of veterans with PTSD, compared with female partners of veterans without PTSD, have reported more mental health symptoms (e.g., depression, anxiety), markedly reduced quality of life, greater feelings of demoralization, and more impaired and unsatisfying social relations (Jordan et al., 1992; Waysman, Mikulincer, Solomon, & Weisenberg, 1993; Westerink & Giarratano, 1999).

Caregiver Burden

Caregiver burden is defined as the extent to which caregivers perceive their emotional or physical health, social life, or financial status to be affected by their caring for an impaired relative (Zarit, Todd, & Zarit, 1986). This construct emerged in the literature on caregivers of chronically physically ill and mentally ill individuals (Chakrabarti & Kulhara, 1999; Cuijpers & Stam, 2000; Loukissa, 1995; Piccinato & Rosenbaum, 1997) and has been applied to female romantic partners of combat veterans with PTSD.

Several studies have shown an association between wives' perceived caregiving burden and their husbands' combat-related PTSD, as well as a relationship between caregiving burden and wives' level of individual distress (Beckham, Lytle, & Feldman, 1996; Ben Arzi, Solomon, & Dekel, 2000; Calhoun, Beckham, & Bosworth, 2002; Dekel, Solomon, & Bleich, 2005; Manguno-Mire et al., 2007).

Ambiguous Loss

This model suggests that two different experiences of perceived loss are associated with ambiguity. The first is in cases in which there is a physical absence with psychological presence, and the second is when there is a psychological absence with physical presence (Boss, 1999, 2007). PTSD in a relationship has been considered to fit the second type of ambiguous loss (Dekel, Goldblatt, Keidar, Solomon, & Polliack, 2005). According to this theory, the uncertainty or lack of information about the whereabouts or status of a loved one as absent or present is difficult for most individuals, couples, and families. The ambiguity freezes the grief process and prevents cognitive processing, thus blocking coping and decision-making processes (Boss, 1999).

As a result of the ambiguity regarding the loss of a loved one, significant others may experience symptoms of depression, anxiety, guilt, and distressing dreams. In addition, family members are uncertain in their perception of who is in or out of the family and who is performing what roles and tasks within the family system. This could result in immobilization of the family, such that decisions are put on hold or that more tasks are taken on by the "healthier" partner or by children taking on roles that are beyond their capacity (Boss, 1999).

A qualitative study of wives of Israeli veterans with PTSD has provided some support for ambiguous loss associated with PTSD. Wives' concerns included questions about whether the spouse is a husband or another child and, relatedly, whether he is an independent adult or a dependent person who needs constant care. This ambiguity was associated with psychological distress in the women (Dekel et al. 2005).

Intergenerational Transmission of PTSD

The notion that PTSD in one family generation or proband can translate into risk of PTSD in subsequent generations was originally raised with regard to Holocaust survivors and their families. Many of the studies in this population did not examine risk on the basis of PTSD status but rather on the basis of exposure to Holocaust experiences. A meta-analysis of studies involving more than 4,000 participants revealed minimal evidence that parents' traumatic Holocaust experiences alone were associated with PTSD symptomatology in their offspring (Van IJzendoorn, Bakermans-Kranenburg, & Sagi-Schwartz, 2003). Studies of PTSD specifically have revealed that parental PTSD (Kellerman, 2007), and especially maternal PTSD (Yehuda, Bell, Bierer, & Schmeidler, 2008), in Holocaust survivors has been associated with general mental health problems in their offspring. A few studies have also attempted to identify cross-generational biological markers associated with PTSD in this population. Studies have shown that the offspring of Holocaust survivors who have PTSD tend to have lower cortisol levels, for example (Yehuda et al., 2000; Yehuda, Blair, Labinsky, & Bierer, 2007; Yehuda, Halligan, & Bierer, 2002).

Studies on the intergenerational transmission of combat veterans' PTSD to their offspring have revealed inconsistent findings. For example, J. R. Davidson, Smith, and Kudler (1989) found that children of male veterans with PTSD had received more mental health treatment, had more eating and communication disorders, and had more academic and behavior problems than children in a control group of fathers without PTSD. Ahmadzadeh and Malekian (2004) found higher rates of aggression and anxiety among Iranian children whose fathers were veterans with PTSD in comparison with children of nonveteran fathers. In a sample of help-seeking veterans with PTSD, Beckham et al. (1997) found that these veterans' children reported high levels of illegal drug use, behavioral problems, PTSD symptoms, and hostility. Other studies of the children of veterans with PTSD have found no differences in emotional distress (A. C. Davidson & Mellor, 2001; Souzzia & Motta, 2004; Westerink & Giarratano, 1999), social development (Ahmadzadeh & Malekian,

2004), or self-esteem (A. C. Davidson & Mellor, 2001; Westerink & Giarratano, 1999) compared with children from various control groups.

Research on the intergenerational transmission of PTSD has yet to advance to using more sophisticated behavioral genetic methods designed to disentangle the environmental and genetic factors at work to place someone at risk for PTSD. Moreover, this work has tended to identify nonspecific mental health problems in offspring versus the specific conferred risk of PTSD intergenerationally. Thus, it is difficult to ascertain whether the possible intergenerational risk of PTSD is related to an increased likelihood of traumatic exposure in these families, psychological factors reviewed earlier and others that have yet to be identified, shared genetic risk, or an interaction of these factors.

Reciprocal Influences of PTSD and Close Relationship Functioning

The field is beginning to appreciate the likely reciprocal causal association between PTSD and close relationship functioning. Two systemic models have been put forth to date.

Couple Adaptation to Traumatic Stress

The couple adaptation to traumatic stress (Nelson Goff & Smith, 2005) model provides a systemic description of how individuals and couples are affected when trauma occurs. The model proposes that adaptation to traumatic stress in the couple is dependent on the systemic interaction of three factors: individual level of functioning of each of the partners, predisposing factors and resources, and couple functioning.

The model assumes that a survivor's level of functioning or trauma symptoms will set in motion a systemic response with the potential to result in secondary traumatic stress symptoms in the partner. However, because the model is bidirectional, partners' symptoms may intensify trauma-related symptoms in the survivor. Individual and couple functioning are determined by predisposing factors and resources (McClubbin & Patterson, 1982), which refer to individual characteristics or unresolved stress experienced by either partner before the trauma. Last, in between the individual and predisposition layers, there is the "couple functioning" component, which relates to the level and quality of variables such as relationship satisfaction, support or nurturance, intimacy, communication, and conflict, which are described as mutually influential components of the dyad system.

Cognitive–Behavioral Interpersonal Theory of PTSD

Monson, Stevens, and Schnurr (2004, 2006) have previously outlined a cognitive–behavioral theory accounting for the association between intimate relationship problems and PTSD. In this chapter, we expand this theory to include nonromantic close others. We present the model as applied to romantic dyads for greater ease in describing the model; however, the mechanisms described in the model could be applied and tested in groups or networks of close others more broadly (e.g., family members). As illustrated in the model depicted in Figure 7.1, we postulate that behavioral, cognitive, and emotional variables dynamically interact within each individual. In turn, these factors in each individual interact at the dyadic level to influence the relationship milieu shared by the dyad, as well as the components acting within each individual. In other words, there are within- and between-individual cognitive, behavioral, and affective interactions that influence the individuals involved and the relationship that they share.

In behavioral conceptualizations of PTSD, classical conditioning processes account for why certain stimuli associated with trauma later provoke the anxiety response; operant conditioning, and specifically the negative reinforcing value of avoidance, accounts for the maintenance of the anxiety response (Mowrer, 1960). At the dyadic level, significant others' well-intended caretaking behaviors (e.g., running interference with extended family members)

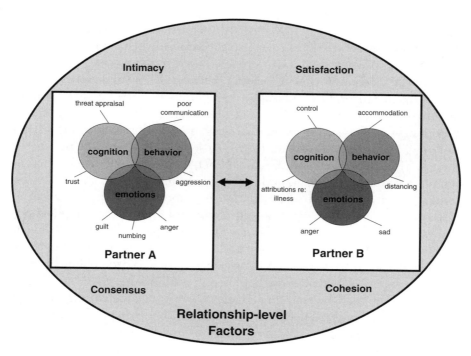

Figure 7.1. Cognitive–behavioral interpersonal theory of posttraumatic stress disorder.

can sometimes serve to promote or maintain avoidant behavior. In this way, the significant others' behavior "accommodates" the disorder. An example of behavioral accommodation that we have encountered is of a husband who drove his wife everywhere after her motor vehicle accident. We also worked with a couple in which the wife took over all shopping-related chores because grocery stores, malls, and other crowded venues served as PTSD-related triggers secondary to her husband's combat experiences. In some couples, partners may view these types of behaviors as opportunities to show care and concern for a loved one in distress; in others, partners may feel angry or resentful about taking on extra responsibilities that feel burdensome to them. However, regardless of partners' intentions, such behaviors can inadvertently reinforce the traumatized individual's avoidance and interfere with his or her recovery from PTSD.

Behavioral accommodation can also diminish close relationship satisfaction through less engagement in mutually reinforcing activities (e.g., dining out), constriction of affective expression, and limited self-disclosure, including trauma-related disclosure. Poor communication and conflict management, in tandem with avoidance, decrease the likelihood of effective trauma disclosure. Trauma disclosure in an encouraging and supportive environment can lead to the development of a more cogent trauma narrative and emotional processing of traumatic memories. Limited conflict management and problem-solving skills are also theorized to mediate the relationship between the hyperarousal symptoms of PTSD and aggressive relationship behavior.

We theorize that there are interrelated cognitive processes and thematic content that account for the association between PTSD and close relationship problems. Individual and dyadic dysfunction are theorized to arise from reliance on enduring, rigid, and maladaptive schemas in making meaning of experiences and the environment (Young, 1994). Borrowing from earlier work by McCann and Pearlman (1990a) also found in cognitive processing therapy (Resick, Monson, & Chard, 2007), we posit that themes such as safety, trust, power, esteem, and intimacy are disrupted as a result of the trauma and are pertinent to close relationship functioning. An example of an interpersonally oriented cognition with significant interpersonal implications comes from a veteran who served as a medic in Vietnam. His traumatic event involved the death of a Vietnamese child in his arms whom he believed he should have been able to save. As a consequence, he avoided holding his children or grandchildren, believing "children in my arms die."

We assert that the emotional disturbances associated with traumatization go beyond anxiety. There is strong evidence that individuals with PTSD experience disruption in a range of emotions in addition to fear, including guilt, shame, anger, grief, and sadness (e.g., Kubany & Watson, 2002; Novaco & Chemtob, 2002). In addition, avoidance can also generalize to the experience and expression of emotions in PTSD (Boeschen, Koss, Figueredo, & Coan, 2001). Emotional process disturbances such as alexithymia and difficulties with identifying and expressing emotions have also been associated with PTSD (Price, Monson, Callahan, & Rodriguez, 2006). These emotional content and process disturbances are suspected to contribute to emotional communication deficits and their related relationship impairments.

INTERPERSONALLY ORIENTED PTSD TREATMENT EFFORTS

Meta-analyses have revealed that the existing psychotherapies for PTSD result in substantial improvements in PTSD symptoms for many (Bradley, Greene, Russ, Dutra, & Westen, 2005; Van Etten & Taylor, 1998). Moreover, these treatments have been shown to improve overall social functioning in patients with PTSD (e.g., Foa et al., 1999; Galovski, Sobel, Phipps, & Resick, 2005). However, these gains do not necessarily translate to improvements in interpersonal relationship functioning. For example, in Monson, Macdonald, et al.'s (2006) randomized trial of cognitive processing therapy for veterans with military-related PTSD, participants experienced statistically significant improvements in overall social adjustment by the end of treatment, but there were no significant improvements in the interpersonal realms of functioning (e.g., spousal and family relations) from pre- to posttreatment (Monson, Macdonald, et al., 2006). Thus, to improve intimate relationship functioning, more interpersonally oriented treatments are indicated. In the next section, we review treatments for PTSD that target intimate relationship functioning, either through conjoint treatment with a significant other or through individually delivered treatment with an explicit interpersonal focus. We also review what is known about the contribution of interpersonal variables to outcomes in the context of individually delivered cognitive–behavioral therapies for PTSD.

Controlled Trials of Conjoint Therapies for PTSD

Only two randomized clinical trials have investigated conjoint therapy for PTSD, and both were conducted with samples of male combat veterans and their female partners. In an early small trial, Sweany (1987) compared general group behavioral couple therapy consisting of eight weekly 2-hour sessions focused on increasing positivity, improving communication and problem solving, and enhancing intimacy to a waiting-list control with a sample of combat veterans. Compared with those on the waiting list, those receiving behavioral couple therapy experienced significant self-reported improvements in PTSD symptoms, relationship satisfaction, and depression.

In a larger controlled study, Glynn et al. (1999) randomized Vietnam veterans with combat-related PTSD to (a) 18 sessions of twice-weekly individual directed therapeutic exposure (DTE) focused on repeated review and cognitive restructuring of two traumatic memories; (b) 18 sessions of twice-weekly individual DTE followed by 16 sessions of behavioral family therapy (DTE + BFT) consisting of psychoeducation about PTSD and available mental health services, communication skills training, anger management, and problem-solving; or (c) a waiting list. Most family members were intimate partners (89%). Compared with those on the waiting list, both active treatment groups demonstrated significant improvements in what the authors defined as the *positive* symptoms of PTSD (reexperiencing and hyperarousal) but not the *negative* symptoms (avoidance and numbing) or social adjustment. Although the two treatment groups did not differ statistically from each other at posttreatment or at follow-up with regard to PTSD symptoms, the change in positive symptoms was approximately twice as large in the DTE + BFT condition as in the DTE-alone condition. In addition, participants who received BFT demonstrated significantly more improvements in problem solving than did those who did not receive BFT. It is of note that roughly one third of the participants who were randomized to DTE + BFT dropped out of the condition after they received DTE but before they received BFT. Glynn et al. attributed this relatively high rate of dropout to remaining PTSD avoidance and numbing symptoms and the fragility of the veterans' relationships. Because of the serial design of this additive treatment study, it is difficult to determine the potential role of the veterans' couple or family member in facilitating DTE. Nevertheless, this is one of the few early studies showing any improvements in veterans' PTSD using a conjoint family format.

There have been four uncontrolled trials of conjoint therapy for PTSD with veterans; three of them used general behavioral couple therapy delivered in a group, and one used a cognitive–behavioral conjoint therapy developed specifically for PTSD delivered to individual couples. Cahoon (1984) reported the results of a 7-week group behavioral couple therapy focused on communication and problem-solving training for combat veterans and their female partners. Group leaders reported statistically significant improvements in veterans' PTSD symptoms and coping abilities, and female partners reported significant improvements in marital satisfaction and problem-solving communication. The veterans did not report improvements in problem-solving or emotional communication skills.

Devilly (2002) described the results of an uncontrolled study of Australian combat veterans and their partners who participated in an intensive week-long residential group intervention known as a Lifestyle Management Course. Topics included psychoeducation about PTSD, relaxation, meditation, self-care, diet and nutrition, alcohol, stress management, anger management, communication, and problem solving. At follow-up assessments, both veterans and their partners reported small, but significant, reductions in anxiety, depression, and stress; veterans reported a significant reduction in PTSD symptoms. Small improvements were also observed for anger and quality of life but not for relationship satisfaction. Another program for veterans with PTSD and their partners was the K'oach program (Rabin & Nardi, 1991). This cognitive–behavioral program included psychoeducation about PTSD and communication and problem-solving skills training. Minimal outcome data were reported on this intervention; however, 68% of the men and their wives reported relationship improvements. No decrease in veterans' PTSD symptoms was observed.

Cognitive–behavioral conjoint therapy for PTSD (Monson, Fredman, & Stevens, 2008) is a PTSD-specific conjoint treatment that has shown promise in simultaneously addressing both individual PTSD symptoms and relationship problems. This 15-session treatment consists of three modules: (a) psychoeducation about the dynamic interplay between PTSD and relationship functioning, exercises to promote positivity, and a shared sense of safety; (b) behavioral interventions that increase approach behaviors, enhance relationship satisfaction, and promote communication skills; and (c) cognitive interventions designed to address maladaptive thinking patterns that maintain both PTSD symptoms and relationship distress. Monson, Schnurr, et al. (2004) reported the results of an uncontrolled pilot study of cognitive–behavioral conjoint therapy for PTSD designed to evaluate this treatment in a small sample of Vietnam veterans with combat-related PTSD and their wives. From pre- to posttreatment, there were large and statistically significant improvements in clinicians' and partners' ratings of veterans' PTSD symptoms. The veterans reported moderate improvements in PTSD and statistically significant and large effect size improvements in depression, anxiety, and social functioning. Wives reported large effect size improvements in relationship satisfaction, general anxiety, and social functioning (Monson, Stevens, & Schnurr, 2004). Since the results of this study have been published, the treatment has been modified to be more trauma focused in nature, to have a greater emphasis on decreasing couple-level avoidance, and to focus more on promoting acceptance of traumatic events and couple-level posttraumatic growth (for a review of these changes, see Monson, Fredman, & Adair, 2009).

There have been several other applications of conjoint or family therapies to trauma survivors, but no outcome data have yet been published to support their efficacy. S. M. Johnson (2002) published a book on emotion-focused couple therapy for trauma survivors that includes case examples of the therapy's application. Leonard, Follette, and Compton (2006) described the application of behaviorally oriented principles, such as functional analysis and contingent responding, in combination with acceptance strategies, to assist couples affected by trauma. Other couple- or family-based approaches to the treatment of PTSD include family systems therapy (Figley, 1989), in which therapists work with families to help members communicate and solve problems; critical interaction therapy for veterans (D. R. Johnson, Feldman, & Lubin, 1995), in which couples are assisted with identifying trauma-related maladaptive interactional patterns and generating more constructive communication and problem-solving strategies; and the Support and Family Education (S.A.F.E) Program (Sherman, 2003), a family psychoeducational program for families in which one member suffers from a mental illness.

The interventions reviewed here have included significant others in the treatment to facilitate patients' recovery. However, there has been limited exploration of variables that predict whether significant others of an individual with PTSD will participate in the treatment process. One exception is Sautter et al.'s (2006) work to identify predictors of partner engagement in PTSD treatment. Through a telephone survey of cohabitating female partners of male Vietnam combat veterans with PTSD, Sautter et al. found that lower income, higher partner involvement in patients' lives (i.e., general emotional involvement, as well as specific behavioral involvement through shared activities), and greater partner caregiver burden for the veteran predicted higher levels of partners' engagement in treatment.

Interpersonal Influences on Individually Delivered PTSD Treatment Outcomes

A commonly used construct for evaluating the family environments of individuals with psychopathology is expressed emotion (Leff & Vaughn, 1985). *Expressed emotion* is defined as the extent to which the relatives of a psychiatric patient display criticism, hostility, or emotional overinvolvement in regard to the patient. In their study of imaginal exposure and cognitive therapy for PTSD, Tarrier, Sommerfield, and Pilgrim (1999) found that patients from families high in expressed emotion at pretreatment displayed less improvement in PTSD symptoms, depressive symptoms, and general anxiety after treatment than did patients from families low in expressed emotion. Additional analyses revealed that relatives' critical and hostile attitudes were associated with relatives attributing patients' behaviors to factors under the patients' control (Barrowclough, Gregg, & Tarrier, 2008). Specifically, deficits in normal behavior (negative symptoms), such as avoidance and restricted affect, were perceived as more controllable, internal, and stable than were the more obvious signs of PTSD (positive symptoms), such as hypervigilance and nightmares. Anger and irritability on the part of the patient were perceived as the most controllable PTSD symptoms. Although controllability attributions were associated with critical and hostile attitudes by relatives, they were not predictive of treatment outcome.

Monson, Rodriguez, and Warner (2005) studied the role of pretreatment interpersonal relationship variables in two forms of group cognitive–behavioral therapy for veterans with PTSD (trauma vs. skills focused). Although there were no differences in the PTSD outcomes of the two forms of treatment, there was a stronger inverse relationship between pretreatment intimate relationship functioning and violence perpetration outcomes in the trauma-focused group than in the skills-focused group. That is, greater intimate relationship adjustment at pretreatment was associated with lower levels of violence perpetration at follow-up for veterans who received trauma-focused versus skills-focused treatment.

Individual Interpersonal Psychotherapy for PTSD

Recognizing the interpersonal dimensions of PTSD and the success of interpersonal psychotherapy for depression (Klerman, Weissman, Rounsaville, & Chevron, 1984), Bleiberg and Markowitz (2005) applied interpersonal psychotherapy to the treatment of PTSD in a pilot study of patients who had experienced a range of traumatic events. The 14-week treatment focused on the interpersonal sequelae of trauma, such as interpersonal hypervigilance, difficulty trusting others, and impediments in social functioning as a result of avoidance. Bleiberg and Markowitz reported a low incidence of dropout from treatment (13 of 14 patients completed therapy) and significant reductions in PTSD and other comorbid conditions. At posttreatment assessment, 12 of 14 patients no longer met diagnostic criteria for PTSD, and 13 of 14 patients reported decreases across all three symptom clusters. Significant improvements were also observed in depression, anger, and interpersonal functioning.

CONCLUSIONS AND FUTURE DIRECTIONS

A growing body of evidence has substantiated the notion that PTSD exists within an interpersonal context that affects and is affected by close relationships. Although we have highlighted the likely bidirectional associations between PTSD and interpersonal variables, the empirical foundation of this assumption is not yet well established. With very few exceptions, almost all of the studies to date have been cross-sectional and, therefore, cannot speak with much certainty to the directionality of the various associations that have been found. Further prospective and longitudinal studies are sorely needed to understand the causal pathways of these variables.

As revealed in this chapter, much of what is known about PTSD and adult interpersonal relationships, with the exception of the role of social support in trauma recovery, relates to romantic relationships. Less knowledge is available about the association between PTSD and problems in other significant adult relationships (e.g., parents, close friends). Moreover, much of the knowledge in this area stems from studies on male veterans with PTSD. The association between interpersonal problems and PTSD in other trauma populations, and the potential for gender differences in these associations, has not been fully examined. It is also important to add that although this chapter focuses on adult close relationships, the effects of PTSD on parenting is an important issue in need of further empirical investigation (for a review, see Dekel & Goldblatt, 2008).

In this chapter, we presented several theories that seek to explain the interpersonal risk and resilience factors and consequences of PTSD. Yet, we are left wanting more research to support them. It is time to move beyond a description of the interpersonal problems associated with PTSD toward theory-driven research that can begin to elucidate the mechanisms accounting for the associations. For example, further longitudinal research on the association between adult attachment and PTSD would help to clarify the processes through which attachment style is both affected by and moderates the association between trauma exposure and the development and course of PTSD. The field would also profit from research that considers the developmental aspects of intimate relationships and PTSD. For instance, how do family life-cycle issues, such as rearing children, caring for aging parents, and contemplating one's own and one's partner's changing health status interact with the presence of PTSD in a couple? How does the length of time that the couple has been together with or without the presence of PTSD in the relationship affect these issues? Are the interpersonal variables associated with the development of PTSD different from those associated with its maintenance?

We have focused on the dynamic interplay between individual psychological functioning and interpersonal functioning. It is important to note that these spheres of functioning interact in the context of a range of biological factors (e.g., neurohormones, brain structures) that have been linked to PTSD (Southwick et al., 2007). In addition, a wider sociocultural milieu envelops and influences the individuals who live within that culture. For example, the rate of divorce among veterans with PTSD in Israel is lower than that found in the general Israeli population (Dekel, Goldblatt, et al., 2005), which is in contrast to the earlier reviewed heightened risk of divorce among veterans with PTSD in the United States. The perception of trauma and its effects and the importance of marriage and close others in various cultures should be better understood and taken into consideration when analyzing the interpersonal nature of PTSD. We hope that future research might take into account this larger biopsychosocial understanding of PTSD and the recursive relationships among these different levels of functioning. Kilpatrick et al.'s (2007) study of the interaction among trauma exposure, the serotonin transporter gene polymorphism, and social support in a sample of hurricane survivors in the southern United States illustrates the larger biopsychosocial approach to PTSD we want to promote.

Greater understanding of the interpersonal nature of PTSD, the longitudinal course of the PTSD–close relationship association, and the mechanisms that account for the association will ultimately be of value to refining and developing interpersonally oriented PTSD prevention and treatment strategies. Although social support appears to be one of the most important resilience factors in warding off PTSD, no efforts have been made to capitalize on this factor in prevention efforts. It may be very beneficial to help traumatized persons martial social support, use it effectively, and prevent burnout of their support network to prevent PTSD. In addition, application of the existing conjoint treatments to nonromantic significant others is another important avenue to pursue to reach the widest number of patients and their loved ones with PTSD. Finally, it is important to consider how technology (e.g., websites, teletherapy) might be used to incorporate significant others who are otherwise unwilling or unable to participate in the existing treatments but who could greatly facilitate their significant other's PTSD treatment. These interventions have the added benefit of addressing a range of barriers to care (e.g., stigma, transportation, proximity to health care settings with expertise in these interventions).

We are delighted to see more appreciation of the interpersonal nature of PTSD and efforts to capitalize on these interpersonal aspects to innovate and improve treatment. It is exciting to consider where these efforts will take the study and treatment of PTSD and the ultimate benefits of these advancements for traumatized individuals and their loved ones.

REFERENCES

Ahmadzadeh, G., & Malekian, A. (2004). Aggression, anxiety, and social development in adolescent children of war veterans with PTSD versus those of nonveterans. *Journal of Research in Medical Sciences, 9,* 33–36.

American Psychiatric Association. (2000). *Diagnostic and statistical manual of mental disorders* (4th ed., text rev.). Washington, DC: Author.

Barrowclough, C., Gregg, L., & Tarrier, N. (2008). Expressed emotion and causal attributions in relatives of post-traumatic stress disorder patients. *Behaviour Research and Therapy, 46,* 207–218.

Beck, J. G., Grant, D. M., Clapp, J. D., & Palyo, S. A. (2009). Understanding the interpersonal impact of trauma: Contributions of PTSD and depression. *Journal of Anxiety Disorders, 23,* 443–450.

Becker, J. V., & Skinner, L. J. (1983). Assessment and treatment of rape-related sexual dysfunctions. *Clinical Psychologist, 36,* 102–105.

Becker, J. V., Skinner, L. J., Abel, G. G., & Treacy, E. C. (1982). Incidence and types of sexual dysfunctions in rape and incest victims. *Journal of Sex and Marital Therapy, 8,* 65–74.

Beckham, J. C., Braxton, L. E., Kudler, H. S., Feldman, M. E., Lytle, B. L., & Palmer, S. (1997). Minnesota Multiphasic Personality Inventory profiles of Vietnam combat veterans with posttraumatic stress disorder and their children. *Journal of Clinical Psychology, 53,* 847–852.

Beckham, J. C., Lytle, B. L., & Feldman, M. E. (1996). Caregiver burden in partners of Vietnam War veterans with posttraumatic stress disorder. *Journal of Consulting and Clinical Psychology, 64,* 1068–1072.

Ben Arzi, N., Solomon, Z., & Dekel, R. (2000). Secondary traumatization among wives of PTSD and post-concussion casualties: Distress, caregiver burden and psychological separation. *Brain Injury, 14,* 725–736.

Bhugra, D. (2002). Literature update: A critical review. *Sexual and Relationship Therapy, 17,* 207–213.

Bleiberg, K. L., & Markowitz, J. C. (2005). A pilot study of interpersonal psychotherapy for posttraumatic stress disorder. *American Journal of Psychiatry, 162,* 181–183.

Boeschen, L. E., Koss, M. P., Figueredo, A. J., & Coan, J. A. (2001). Experiential avoidance and post-traumatic stress disorder: A cognitive mediational model of rape recovery. *Journal of Aggression, Maltreatment and Trauma, 4,* 211–245.

Boss, P. (1999). *Ambiguous loss: Learning to live with unresolved grief.* Cambridge, MA: Harvard University Press.

Boss, P. (2007). Ambiguous loss theory: Challenges for scholars and practitioners. *Family Relations, 56,* 105–111.

Bowlby, J. (1982). Attachment and loss: Retrospect and prospect. *American Journal of Orthopsychiatry, 52,* 664–678.

Bradley, R., Greene, J., Russ, E., Dutra, L., & Westen, D. (2005). A multidimensional meta-analysis of psychotherapy for PTSD. *American Journal of Psychiatry, 162,* 214–227.

Brewin, C. R., Andrews, B., & Valentine, J. D. (2000). Meta-analysis of risk factors for posttraumatic stress disorder in trauma-exposed adults. *Journal of Consulting and Clinical Psychology, 68,* 748–766.

Brooks, N., & McKinlay, W. (1992). Mental health consequences of the Lockerbie disaster. *Journal of Traumatic Stress, 5,* 527–543.

Byrne, C. A., & Riggs, D. S. (1996). The cycle of trauma: Relationship aggression in male Vietnam veterans with symptoms of posttraumatic stress disorder. *Violence and Victims, 11,* 213–225.

Cahoon, E. P. (1984). *An examination of relationships between post-traumatic stress disorder, marital distress, and response to therapy by Vietnam veterans.* Unpublished doctoral dissertation, University of Connecticut, Storrs.

Calhoun, P. S., Beckham, J. C., & Bosworth, H. B. (2002). Caregiver burden and psychological distress in partners of veterans with chronic posttraumatic stress disorder. *Journal of Traumatic Stress, 15,* 205–212.

Carroll, E. M., Rueger, D. B., Foy, D. W., & Donahoe, C. P. (1985). Vietnam combat veterans with posttraumatic stress disorder: Analysis of marital and cohabitating adjustment. *Journal of Abnormal Psychology, 94,* 329–337.

Catherall, D. R. (1992). *Back from the brink: A family guide to overcoming traumatic stress.* New York, NY: Bantam.

Chakrabarti, S., & Kulhara, P. (1999). Family burden of caring for people with mental illness. *British Journal of Psychiatry, 174,* 463.

Charuvastra, A., & Cloitre, M. (2008). Social bonds and posttraumatic stress disorder. *Annual Review of Psychology, 59,* 301–328.

Cosgrove, D., Gordon, Z., Bernie, J., Hami, S., Montoya, D., Stein, M. B., & Monga, M. (2002). Sexual dysfunction in combat veterans with post-traumatic stress disorder. *Urology, 60,* 881–884.

Cuijpers, P., & Stam, H. (2000). Burnout among relatives of psychiatric patients attending psychoeducational support groups. *Psychiatric Services, 51,* 375–379.

Davidson, A. C., & Mellor, D. J. (2001). The adjustment of children of Australian Vietnam veterans: Is there evidence for the transgenerational trasmission of war-related trauma? *Australian and New Zealand Journal of Psychiatry, 35,* 345–351.

Davidson, J. R., Hughes, D., Blazer, D. G., & George, L. K. (1991). Post-traumatic stress disorder in the community: An epidemiological study. *Psychological Medicine, 21,* 713–721.

Davidson, J. R., Smith, R., & Kudler, H. (1989). Familial psychiatric illness in chronic posttraumatic stress disorder. *Comprehensive Psychiatry, 30,* 339–345.

Dawson, D. A., Grant, B. F., Chou, S. P., & Stinson, F. S. (2007). The impact of partner alcohol problems on women's physical and mental health. *Journal of Studies on Alcohol and Drugs, 68,* 66–75.

Dekel, R., & Goldblatt, H. (2008). Is there intergeneration transmission of trauma? The case of combat veterans' children. *American Journal of Orthopsychiatry, 78,* 281–289.

Dekel, R., Goldblatt, H., Keidar, M., Solomon, Z., & Polliack, M. (2005). Being a wife of a veteran with posttraumatic stress disorder. *Family Relations, 54,* 24–36.

Dekel, R., & Solomon, Z. (2006). Secondary traumatization among wives of Israeli POWs: The role of POWs' distress. *Social Psychiatry and Psychiatric Epidemiology, 41,* 27–33.

Dekel, R., Solomon, Z., & Bleich, A. (2005). Emotional distress and marital adjustment of caregivers: Contribution of level of impairment and appraised burden. *Anxiety, Stress, and Coping, 18,* 71–82.

Devilly, G. J. (2002). The psychological effects of a lifestyle management course on war veterans and their spouses. *Journal of Clinical Psychology, 58*, 1119–1134.

Dieperink, M., Leskela, J., Thuras, P., & Engdahl, B. (2001). Attachment style classification and posttraumatic stress disorder in former prisoners of war. *American Journal of Orthopsychiatry, 71*, 374–378.

Figley, C. R. (1989). *Helping traumatized families.* San Francisco: Jossey-Bass.

Figley, C. (1995). Compassion fatigue as secondary traumatic stress disorder: An overview. In C. Figley (Ed.), *Compassion fatigue: Coping with secondary traumatic stress disorder in those who treat the traumatized* (pp. 1–20). New York, NY: Brunner/Mazel.

Foa, E. B., Dancu, C. V., Hembree, E. A., Jaycox, L. H., Meadows, E. A., & Street, G. P. (1999). A comparison of exposure therapy, stress inoculation training, and their combination for reducing posttraumatic stress disorder in female assault victims. *Journal of Consulting and Clinical Psychology, 67*, 194–200.

Fraley, C. R. (2002). Attachment stability from infancy to adulthood: Meta-analysis and dynamic modeling of developmental mechanisms. *Personality and Social Psychology Review, 6*, 123–151.

Fullerton, C. S., Ursano, R. J., Kao, T. C., & Bharitya, V. R. (1999). Disaster-related bereavement: Acute symptoms and subsequent depression. *Aviation, Space, and Environmental Medicine, 70*, 902–909.

Galovski, T., Sobel, A. A., Phipps, K. A., & Resick, P. A. (2005). Trauma recovery: Beyond posttraumatic stress disorder and other Axis I symptom severity. In T. A. Corales (Ed.), *Trends in posttraumatic stress disorder research* (pp. 207–227). Hauppauge, NY: Nova Science.

Glenn, D. M., Beckham, J. C., Feldman, M. E., Kirby, A. C., Hertzberg, M. A., & Moore, S. D. (2002). Violence and hostility among families of Vietnam veterans with combat-related posttraumatic stress disorder. *Violence and Victims, 17*, 473–489.

Gleser, G. C., Green, B. L., & Winget, C. N. (1981). *Prolonged psychological effects of disaster: A study of Buffalo Creek.* New York, NY: Academic Press.

Glynn, S. M., Eth, S., Randolph, E. T., Foy, D. W., Urbaitis, M., Boxer, L., . . . Crothers, J. (1999). A test of behavioral family therapy to augment exposure for combat-related posttraumatic stress disorder. *Journal of Consulting and Clinical Psychology, 67*, 243–251.

Hazan, C., & Shaver, P. R. (1994). Attachment as an organizational framework for research on close relationships. *Psychological Inquiry, 5*, 1–22.

Johnson, D. R., Feldman, S. C., & Lubin, H. (1995). Critical interaction therapy: Couples therapy in combat-related posttraumatic stress disorder. *Family Process, 34*, 401–412.

Johnson, S. M. (2002). *Emotionally focused couple therapy with trauma survivors: Strengthening attachment bonds.* New York, NY: Guilford Press.

Johnson, S. M., & Makinen, J. (2003). Posttraumatic stress. In D. K. Snyder & M. A. Whisman (Eds.), *Treating difficult couples* (pp. 308–329). New York: Guilford Press.

Jordan, B. K., Marmar, C. R., Fairbank, J. A., Schlenger, W. E., Kulka, R. A., Hough, R. L., . . . Weiss, D. S. (1992). Problems in families of male Vietnam veterans with posttraumatic stress disorder. *Journal of Consulting and Clinical Psychology, 60*, 916–926.

Joseph, S., Williams, R., & Yule, W. (1997). *Understanding posttraumatic stress*. New York: Wiley.

Kaniasty, K., & Norris, F. H. (1993). A test of the social support deterioration model in the context of natural disaster. *Journal of Personality and Social Psychology, 64*, 395–408.

Kellerman, N. (2007). Transgenerational effects of the Holocaust: The Israeli research perspective. In Z. Solomon & J. Chaitin (Eds.), *Childhood in the shadow of the Holocaust—Survived children and second generation* (pp. 286–303). Tel Aviv, Israel: Hakibbutz Hameuchad.

Kessler, R. C., Sonnega, A., Bromet, E., Hughes, M., & Nelson, C. B. (1995). Posttraumatic stress disorder in the National Comorbidity Survey. *Archives of General Psychiatry, 52*, 1048–1060.

Kilpatrick, D. G., Koenen, K. C., Ruggiero, K. J., Acierno, R., Galea, S., Resnick, H. S., Gelernter, J. (2007). The serotonin transporter genotype and social support and moderation of posttraumatic stress disorder and depression in hurricane-exposed adults. *American Journal of Psychiatry, 164*, 1693–1699.

Kilpatrick, D. G., Resnick, H. S., Freedy, J. R., Pelcovitz, D., Resick, P. A., Roth, S., . . . van der Kolk, B. (1998). Posttraumatic stress disorder field trial: Evaluation of the PTSD construct—Criteria A through E. In *DSM-IV sourcebook* (Vol. 4, pp. 803–844). Washington, DC: American Psychiatric Press.

King, D. W., Taft, C. T., King, L. A., Hammond, C., & Stone, E. R. (2006). Directionality of the association between social support and posttraumatic stress disorder: A longitudinal investigation. *Journal of Applied Social Psychology, 36*, 2980–2992.

Klerman, G. L., Weissman, M. M., Rounsaville, B. J., & Chevron, E. S. (1984). *Interpersonal psychotherapy of depression*. New York, NY: Basic.

Kubany, E. S., & Watson, S. B. (2002). Cognitive trauma therapy for formerly battered women with PTSD: Conceptual bases and treatment outlines. *Cognitive and Behavioral Practice, 9*, 111–127.

Lee, C., Gavriel, H., Drummond, P., Richards, J., & Greenwald, R. (2002). Treatment of PTSD: Stress inoculation training with prolonged exposure compared to EMDR. *Journal of Clinical Psychology, 58*, 1071–1089.

Leff, J., & Vaughn, C. (1985). *Expressed emotion in families: Its significance for mental illness*. New York, NY: Guilford Press.

Leonard, L. M., Follette, V. M., & Compton, J. S. (2006). A principle-based intervention for couples affected by trauma. In V. M. Follette & J. I. Ruzek (Eds.), *Cognitive-behavioral therapies for trauma* (pp. 364–387). New York, NY: Guilford Press.

Lepore, S. J., Evans, G. W., & Schneider, M. L. (1991). Dynamic role of social support in the link between chronic stress and psychological distress. *Journal of Personality and Social Psychology, 61*, 899–909.

Loukissa, D. A. (1995). Family burden in chronic mental illness: A review of research studies. *Journal of Advanced Nursing, 21*, 248–255.

Maloney, L. J. (1988). Post traumatic stresses on women partners of Vietnam veterans. *Smith College Studies in Social Work, 58*, 122–143.

Manguno-Mire, G., Sautter, F., Lyons, J. A., Myers, L., Perry, D., Sherman, M., . . . Sullivan, G. (2007). Psychological distress and burden among female partners of combat veterans with PTSD. *Journal of Nervous & Mental Disease, 195*, 144–151.

McCann, I. L., & Pearlman, L. A. (1990a). *Psychological trauma and the adult survivor: Theory, therapy, and transformation.* New York, NY: Brunner/Mazel.

McCann, L., & Pearlman, L. A. (1990b). Vicarious traumatization: A framework for understanding the psychological effects of working with victims. *Journal of Traumatic Stress, 3*, 131–149.

McClubbin, H. I., & Patterson, J. M. (1982). Family adaptation to crisis. In H. I. McClubbin, A. E. Cauble, & J. M. Patterson (Eds.), *Family stress, coping and social support* (pp. 26–47). Springfield, IL: Charles C Thomas.

McGuire, L. S., & Wagner, N. N. (1978). Sexual dysfunction in women who were molested as children: One response pattern and suggestions for treatment. *Journal of Sex and Marital Therapy, 4*, 11–15.

Mikulincer, M., Shaver, P. R., & Horesh, N. (2006). Attachment bases of emotion regulation and posttraumatic adjustment. In D. K. Snyder, J. A. Simpson, & J. N. Hughes (Eds.), *Emotion regulation in families: Pathways to dysfunction and health* (pp. 77–99). Washington, DC: American Psychological Association.

Miterany, D. (2004). *The healing effects of the contextual activation of the sense of attachment security: The case of posttraumatic stress disorder.* Unpublished master's thesis, Bar-Ilan University, Ramat-Gan, Israel.

Monson, C. M., Fredman, S. J., & Adair, K. C. (2009). Cognitive-behavioral conjoint therapy for PTSD: Application to Operation Enduring and Iraqi Freedom service members and veterans. *Journal of Clinical Psychology, 8*, 958–971.

Monson, C. M., Fredman, S. J., & Stevens, S. P. (2008). *Cognitive-behavioral conjoint therapy for posttraumatic stress disorder.* Unpublished manual.

Monson, C. M., Gradus, J. L., La Bash, H. A. J., & Resick, P. A. (in press). The role of couples' interacting world assumptions and relationship adjustment in women's post-disaster PTSD symptoms. *Journal of Traumatic Stress.*

Monson, C. M., Macdonald, A., Price, J. L., Schnurr, P. P., Resick, P. A., & Friedman, M. J. (2006, November). *Cognitive processing therapy for military-related PTSD: Secondary outcomes from a randomized controlled trial.* Paper presented at the annual conference of the Association of Behavioral and Cognitive Therapies, Chicago, Illinois.

Monson, C. M., Rodriguez, B. F., & Warner, R. (2005). Cognitive–behavioral therapy for PTSD in the real world: Do interpersonal relationships make a real difference? *Journal of Clinical Psychology, 61,* 751–761.

Monson, C. M., Schnurr, P. P., Stevens, S. P., & Guthrie, K. A. (2004). Cognitive–behavioral couple's treatment for posttraumatic stress disorder: Initial findings. *Journal of Traumatic Stress, 17,* 341–344.

Monson, C. M., Stevens, S. P., & Schnurr, P. P. (2004). Cognitive–behavioral couple's treatment for posttraumatic stress disorder. In T. A. Corales (Ed.), *Focus on posttraumatic stress disorder research* (pp. 251–280). Hauppauge, NY: Nova Science.

Monson, C. M., Stevens, S. P., & Schnurr, P. P. (2006). Kognitive Verhaltenstherapie fur Paare [Cognitive-behavioral couple's treatment for posttraumatic stress disorder]. In R. Rosner & A. Maercker (Eds.), *Psychotherapie der posttraumatischen belastungsstorungen* (pp. 102–115). Munich, Germany: Thieme.

Mowrer, O. A. (1960). *Learning theory and behavior.* New York, NY: Wiley.

Nelson Goff, B. S., Crow, J. R., Reisbig, A. M. J., & Hamilton, S. (2007). The impact of individual trauma symptoms of deployed soldiers on relationship satisfaction. *Journal of Family Psychology, 21,* 334–353.

Nelson Goff, B. S., & Smith, D. B. (2005). Systemic traumatic stress: The couple adaptation to traumatic stress model. *Journal of Marital and Family Therapy, 31,* 145–157.

Norris, F. H. (1992). Epidemiology of trauma: Frequency and impact of different potentially traumatic events on different demographic groups. *Journal of Clinical and Consulting Psychology, 60,* 409–418.

Novaco, R. W., & Chemtob, C. M. (2002). Anger and combat-related posttraumatic stress disorder. *Journal of Traumatic Stress, 15,* 123–132.

O'Farrell, T. J., & Fals-Stewart, W. (2006). *Behavioral couples therapy for alcoholism and drug abuse.* New York, NY: Guilford Press.

O'Leary, K. D., & Beach, S. R. H. (1990). Marital therapy: A viable treatment for depression and marital discord. *American Journal of Psychiatry, 147,* 183–186.

Orcutt, H. K., King, L. A., & King, D. W. (2003). Male-perpetrated violence among Vietnam veteran couples: Relationships with veterans' early life characteristics, trauma history, and PTSD symptomatology. *Journal of Traumatic Stress, 16,* 381–390.

Ozer, E. J., Best, S. R., Lipsey, T. L., & Weiss, D. S. (2003). Predictors of posttraumatic stress disorder and symptoms in adults: A meta-analysis. *Psychological Bulletin, 129,* 52–73.

Piccinato, J. M., & Rosenbaum, J. N. (1997). Caregiver hardiness explored within Watson's theory of human caring in nursing. *Journal of Gerontological Nursing, 23,* 32–39.

Price, J. L., Monson, C. M., Callahan, K., & Rodriguez, B. F. (2006). The role of emotional functioning in military-related PTSD and its treatment. *Journal of Anxiety Disorders, 20,* 661–674.

Rabin, C., & Nardi, C. (1991). Treating post-traumatic stress disorder couples: A psychoeducational program. *Community Mental Health Journal, 27*, 209–224.

Renshaw, K. D., Rodrigues, C. S., & Jones, D. H. (2008). Psychological symptoms and marital satisfaction in spouses of Operation Iraqi Freedom veterans: Relationships with spouses' perceptions of veterans' experiences and symptoms. *Journal of Family Psychology, 22*, 586–594.

Resick, P. A., Monson, C. M., & Chard, K. M. (2007). *Cognitive processing therapy: Veteran/military version.* Washington, DC: Department of Veterans Affairs.

Riggs, D. S., Byrne, C. A., Weathers, F. W., & Litz, B. T. (1998). The quality of the intimate relationships of male Vietnam veterans: Problems associated with posttraumatic stress disorder. *Journal of Traumatic Stress, 11*, 87–101.

Sautter, F., Lyons, J. A., Manguno-Mire, G., Perry, D., Han, X., Sherman, M., . . . Sullivan, G. (2006). Predictors of partner engagement in PTSD treatment. *Journal of Psychopathology and Behavioral Assessment, 28*, 123–130.

Savarese, V. W., Suvak, M. K., King, L. A., & King, D. W. (2001). Relationships among alcohol use, hyperarousal, and marital abuse and violence in Vietnam veterans. *Journal of Traumatic Stress, 14*, 717–732.

Sherman, M. D. (2003). The Support and Family Education (SAFE) Program: Mental health facts for families. *Psychiatric Services, 54*, 35–37.

Solomon, S. D. (2002). Gender differences in response to disaster. In G. Weidner, M. Kopp, & M. Kristenson (Eds.), *Heart disease: Environment, stress and gender* (pp. 267–274). Amsterdam, the Netherlands: IOS Press.

Solomon, Z., Dekel, R., & Mikulincer, M. (2008). Complex trauma of war captivity: A prospective study of attachment and post-traumatic stress disorder. *Psychological Medicine, 7*, 1–8.

Solomon, Z., Ginzburg, K., Mikulincer, M., Neria, Y., & Ohry, A. (1998). Coping with war captivity: The role of attachment style. *European Journal of Personality, 12*, 271–285.

Solomon, Z., Waysman, M., Levy, G., Fried, B., Mikulincer, M., Benbenishty, R., . . . Bleich, A. (1992). From front line to home front: A study of secondary traumatization. *Family Process, 31*, 289–302.

Southwick, S. M., Davis, L. L., Aikins, D. E., Rasmusson, A., Barron, J., & Morgan, C. A. (2007). Neurobiological alterations associated with PTSD. In S. J. Friedman, T. M. Keane, & P. A. Resick (Eds.), *Handbook of PTSD: Science and practice* (pp. 166–189). New York, NY: Guilford Press.

Souzzia, J. M., & Motta, R. (2004). The relationship between combat exposure and the transfer of trauma-like symptoms to offspring of veterans. *Traumatology, 10*, 17–37.

Steelman, J. R. (2007). Relationship dynamics: Understanding married women's mental health. *Advances in Nursing Science, 30*, 151–158.

Sweany, S. L. (1987). *Marital and life adjustment of Vietnam combat veterans: A treatment outcome study*. Unpublished doctoral dissertation, University of Washington, Seattle.

Taft, C. T., Vogt, D. S., Marshall, A. D., Panuzio, J., & Niles, B. L. (2007). Aggression among combat veterans: Relationships with combat exposure and symptoms of posttraumatic stress disorder, dysphoria, and anxiety. *Journal of Traumatic Stress, 20,* 135–145.

Tarrier, N., Sommerfield, C., & Pilgrim, H. (1999). Relatives' expressed emotion (EE) and PTSD treatment outcome. *Psychological Medicine, 29,* 801–811.

Ursano, R. J., Fullerton, C. S., Kao, T. C., & Bhartiya, V. R. (1995). Longitudinal assessment of posttraumatic stress disorder and depression after exposure to traumatic death. *Journal of Nervous and Mental Disease, 183,* 36–42.

Van Etten, M. L., & Taylor, S. (1998). Comparative efficacy of treatment for posttraumatic stress disorder: A meta-analysis. *Clinical Psychology and Psychotherapy, 5,* 126–144.

Van IJzendoorn, M. H., Bakermans-Kranenburg, M. J., & Sagi-Schwartz, A. (2003). Are children of Holocaust survivors less well-adapted? No meta-analytic evidence for secondary traumatization. *Journal of Traumatic Stress, 16,* 459–469.

Verbosky, S. J., & Ryan, D. A. (1988). Female partners of Vietnam veterans: Stress by proximity. *Issues in Mental Health Nursing, 9,* 95–104.

Vila, G., Witkowski, P., Tondini, M. C., Perez-Diaz, F., Mouren-Simeoni, M. C., & Jouvent, R. (2001). A study of posttraumatic disorders in children who experienced an industrial disaster in the Briey region. *European Child and Adolescent Psychiatry, 10,* 10–18.

Waysman, M., Mikulincer, M., Solomon, Z., & Weisenberg, M. (1993). Secondary traumatization among wives of posttraumatic combat veterans: A family typology. *Journal of Family Psychology, 7,* 104–118.

Westerink, J., & Giarratano, L. (1999). The impact of posttraumatic stress disorder on partners and children of Australian Vietnam veterans. *Australian & New Zealand Journal of Psychiatry, 33,* 841–847.

Whisman, M. A., Sheldon, C. T., & Goering, P. (2000). Psychiatric disorders and dissatisfaction with social relationships: Does type of relationship matter? *Journal of Abnormal Psychology, 109,* 803–808.

Williams, R., & Joseph, S. (1999). Conclusions: An integrative psychosocial model of PTSD. In W. Yule (Ed.), *PTSD: Concepts and theory* (pp. 297–314). Chichester, England: Wiley.

Yehuda, R., Bell, A., Bierer, L., & Schmeidler, J. (2008). Maternal, not paternal, PSTD is related to increased risk for PTSD in offspring of Holocaust survivors. *Journal of Psychiatric Research, 42,* 1104–1111.

Yehuda, R., Bierer, L. M., Schmeidler, J., Aferiat, D. H., Breslau, I., & Dolan, S. (2000). Low cortisol and risk for PTSD in adult offspring of Holocaust survivors. *American Journal of Psychiatry, 157,* 1252–1259.

Yehuda, R., Blair, W., Labinsky, E., & Bierer, L. M. (2007). Effects of parental PTSD on the cortisol response to dexamethansone administration in their adult offspring. *American Journal of Psychiatry, 164,* 163–166.

Yehuda, R., Halligan, S. L., & Bierer, L. (2002). Cortisol levels in adult offspring of Holocaust survivors: Relation to PTSD symptom severity in the parent and child. *Psychoneuroendocrinology, 27,* 171–180.

Young, J. E. (1994). *Cognitive therapy for personality disorders: A schema focused approach.* Sarasota, FL: Professional Resource Press.

Zarit, S. H., Todd, P. A., & Zarit, J. M. (1986). Subjective burden of husbands and wives as caregivers: A longitudinal study. *Gerontologist, 26,* 260–266.

8

INTERPERSONAL ASPECTS OF PANIC DISORDER AND AGORAPHOBIA

DIANNE L. CHAMBLESS

The experience of panic attacks is common. It is estimated that 28% of Americans will have one or more panic attacks during their lifetime (Kessler et al., 2006). Panic attacks are discrete episodes of very high anxiety that build rapidly and subside relatively quickly. The experience of panic differs for different people but often includes intense physical symptoms such as rapid heartbeat and breathlessness, perceptual experiences such as depersonalization and derealization, a strong sense of doom, and an overwhelming desire to flee. The attacks are particularly frightening when they appear to come out of nowhere, leaving the individual to try to make sense of an intense experience that seems to have no cause. No wonder that some believe they are dying or going insane.

Of those who experience panic attacks, some will develop panic disorder—approximately 5% of Americans in their lifetime (Kessler et al., 2006). Such individuals have experienced recurrent panic attacks that come out of the blue (and hence are not closely linked to phobic situations such as public speaking) and have become preoccupied with and apprehensive of future panic attacks (American Psychiatric Association, 1994). Many will begin to avoid situations or experiences that they fear will bring on a panic attack or from which they might have difficulty extracting themselves should an incapacitating panic attack come on. This avoidance may be relatively subtle—for example, the man with panic disorder who gives up running because his rapid heartbeat makes him feel like he is panicking or having a heart attack. Or it may be highly obvious—for example, the woman who becomes afraid to leave her home unless she is accompanied by a trusted person who will take care of her should she panic. When avoidance is significant, the person is said to have panic disorder with agoraphobia, for which the lifetime prevalence is about 1% (Kessler et al., 2006). Another 1% will have agoraphobia with panic attacks but will not meet full diagnostic criteria for panic disorder (Kessler et al., 2006); for example, they will not have had recurrent unexpected panic attacks. Much of the literature cited in this chapter was written before diagnostic distinctions between agoraphobia with and without panic disorder were made, and phenomenologically there is little difference to the patient between these disorders. I use the term *agoraphobia* to refer to both groups. Moreover, some more recent studies have focused on panic disorder without reference to whether there is associated agoraphobia. Thus, it is not always be possible to make distinctions between panic disorder with and without agoraphobia. When possible, I do so.

The social and health consequences of panic disorder are great. According to epidemiologic research, these include increased risk of alcohol and drug abuse, mood disorders, other anxiety disorders, subjectively poor health, poor social functioning, high use of health care services and emergency rooms, and financial dependence on disability and welfare payments (Kessler et al., 2006; Markowitz, Weissman, Ouellette, Lish, & Klerman, 1989). Disability is greatest for those who develop agoraphobia as a complication of panic disorder (Kessler et al., 2006). The more disabled patients become, the more likely they are to rely on family members for their daily functioning, posing a heavy burden on their intimate others. Reflecting not only agoraphobic patients' restricted lives but also the preponderance of women with the disorder—as many as 80% in clinical samples (Chambless & Mason, 1986)—an early synonym for agoraphobia was *housebound housewives*. Epidemiologic research has suggested that although women still predominate in the general population, the ratio of women to men with panic disorder and agoraphobia (about 2:1) is not as extreme as in clinical samples (Kessler et al., 2006).

The mass of research on interpersonal aspects of agoraphobia is substantially greater and older than that for the other anxiety disorders. No doubt this is because the role of the phobic companion in agoraphobia is so striking that the interpersonal context of the disorder could not be ignored. Marks (1970) estimated that 95% of people with agoraphobia are able to venture further into phobic situations or to enter phobic situations with less anxiety if accompanied by a trusted other. In laboratory research, Carter, Hollon, Carson, and Shelton (1995) demonstrated that patients with panic disorder with mild to moderate agoraphobia who were accompanied by their chosen safe person were significantly less physiologically and subjectively distressed by attempts to induce panic via carbon dioxide inhalations than were patients who were alone in the laboratory session, even though the safe person only sat quietly during the procedure.

MODELS

A variety of models for the onset and maintenance of panic disorder and agoraphobia have been proposed. Perhaps the simplest is that the strain of the disorder and its associated disability understandably lead to the development of marital and family problems. Alternatively, it has been proposed that panic and agoraphobia are in part the result of marital or family problems. This viewpoint comes in different varieties. In an early article, Fry (1962) described a family systems model developed on the basis of seven cases. He concluded that spouses were generally men whose own fears and anxieties were hidden by their wives' agoraphobia. The couples were unhappy but united by a compulsory marriage that, on the surface of things, neither spouse could leave because of the agoraphobic patient's disability. Fry observed that the patient's symptoms often began with a change in the spouse's life, for example, the spouse's taking a job in a new city. His interpretation was that the spouse experienced anxiety in the context of these changes but that this distress was expressed by the patient. This formulation would suggest that the system would resist change in the agoraphobic partner or that the supposedly healthy partner would become symptomatic if the person with agoraphobia improved. The systems approach was influential in the work of Hafner (e.g., 1977, 1984), which is described in subsequent sections.

Goldstein and Chambless (1978) proposed that for a subset of people with agoraphobia, those whom they labeled as having *complex agoraphobia*, interpersonal conflict was the most common antecedent of the onset of panic attacks and agoraphobia, although other types of stressors might be critical for some patients. They believed that people who eventually become agoraphobic are particularly vulnerable to experiencing high levels of stress in the face of marital or family conflict for two reasons: First, they tend to ignore the actual causes of their distress (and thus fail to solve interpersonal problems); instead, they focus on external situations as the cues for their anxiety. Second, they feel insufficiently self-sufficient to function on their own if they were to leave the conflictual relationship. As agoraphobic patients become more disabled, they become more dependent on the very people with whom they have conflict, thereby increasing their internal struggle. Goldstein and Chambless also assigned a minor role to secondary gain, in which patients are reinforced for their dependency by attention from an otherwise inattentive spouse or are negatively reinforced by being able to withdraw from unpleasant situations (e.g., visiting a disliked mother-in-law) because their phobia renders them incapable of going.

As support for this approach, Goldstein and Chambless (1978) presented data showing that agoraphobic patients described themselves as less emotionally mature and less self-sufficient and were rated by their therapists or a chart reviewer as less assertive (see also Chambless, Hunter, & Jackson, 1982) and as having poorer coping skills than patients with specific phobias. However, because these data were collected years after the onset of the disorder, it is quite plausible that these characteristics were the result of rather than a contributor to the development of agoraphobia. Data concerning the assertion that interpersonal conflict is a common contributor to development of agoraphobia are addressed in a later section.

More recent formulations of panic disorder and agoraphobia follow a stress-diathesis model, suggesting that interpersonal conflict is one of a number of stressors that contribute to the onset of these disorders or that interfere with treatment response in people who are vulnerable to panic by dint of biology or early life experience (Chambless & Steketee, 1999; Craske & Zoellner, 1995; Wade, Monroe, & Michelson, 1993). Finally, it is reasonable to suggest that the relationship of these disorders to marital and family conflict may be bidirectional, with the stress of conflict contributing to the onset and maintenance of the disorders and the consequences of the disorders leading to more stress and conflict. Evidence for the various models is examined in the sections that follow.

CONTEXT OF PANIC AND AGORAPHOBIA ONSET

It is clear that panic disorder is stress responsive, and a number of studies have demonstrated that the onset of panic attacks occurs during a time of heightened stress (e.g., Faravelli, 1985). The authors of three uncontrolled studies retrospectively assessed the type of stressors agoraphobic patients faced at the time of onset. For example, Kleiner and Marshall (1987) collected data from 50 agoraphobic patients using a structured, reliable interview to identify stressful events in the 12 months preceding the onset of their agoraphobia. Patients often identified multiple events. The most commonly reported stressors were prolonged conflict with a spouse or partner (84%) and prolonged family conflict (64%). Certainly other stressors, such as death of a loved one (22%) and financial problems, (12%) occurred. Although the specific percentages differ, the findings of the other two studies were similar in that relationship problems or separation from or loss of a spouse (Doctor, 1982; Last,

Barlow, & O'Brien, 1984) were the most common stressors, but other stressors, such as new responsibilities, birth, and miscarriage, were also represented. These studies support the proposition that interpersonal conflict, especially with a spouse or partner, is a highly common stressor preceding the onset of agoraphobia, but they did not include a control group. Do people with panic and agoraphobia experience such stressors before onset more often than at other times in their lives or more often than other people? To answer this question, I turn to the two controlled studies on this topic.

In an early investigation, Goldstein and Chambless (1978) examined case records or polled therapists of 32 patients with agoraphobia and 36 patients with specific phobias. Of the patients with agoraphobia, 83% were coded as having interpersonal conflict as the context for the onset of their disorder, whereas this was the case for only 6% of those with specific phobias—a highly significant difference. Although this study benefited from the use of a control group with anxiety disorders, it is open to investigator bias. One of the authors served as the coder, and there was no reliability rater. Pollard, Pollard, and Corn (1989) overcame this problem by administering a reliable, standardized questionnaire measure of stressful life events to 50 patients with agoraphobia at the time of their intake evaluation. In an ingenious design, they compared the occurrence of stressful life events in the 18 months surrounding the onset of panic attacks with (a) another 18-month period in the lives of these same 50 patients and (b) the same calendar period for a comparison group of 50 other patients with agoraphobia who may or may not have had their panic onset during this time. Significantly more stressful life events were reported in the time surrounding panic onset than in either of the two control conditions. The most common of these were loss, separation, or conflict (62% of index sample); new responsibility (54%); and illness (12%). Unfortunately, Pollard et al. did not separate conflict from loss and separation in their report.

ASSOCIATIONS WITH DIAGNOSTIC STATUS AND SYMPTOM SEVERITY

If the interpersonal context of people with panic disorder and agoraphobia is important, it seems reasonable to expect that measures reflecting this context will systematically differ between people who have these disorders and those who do not or that within this population, interpersonal measures will correlate with symptom severity. This has been an active area of inquiry for decades. The bulk of studies have concerned the marital adjustment of people with agoraphobia; however, a number of authors have focused on more specific aspects of interpersonal or marital functioning.

Diagnostic Status

Researchers have examined whether the diagnoses of panic disorder and agoraphobia are associated with interpersonal problems in, broadly speaking, two ways—by testing whether these patients differ from other groups in self-reported marital adjustment and by examining whether they differ on specific aspects of relationship functioning, such as problem solving.

Overall Marital Adjustment

In four investigations, the self-reported marital adjustment of people with agoraphobia who were recruited from clinic or support group samples was compared with that of normal or community control group samples. In all four cases (Arrindell & Emmelkamp, 1986; Chambless, Bryan, Aiken, Steketee, & Hooley, 2002; Epstein & Dutton, 1997; McCarthy & Shean, 1996), patients with agoraphobia were significantly less satisfied with their marriage than were the controls. The same was usually (Arrindell & Emmelkamp, 1986; Chambless et al., 2002) but not always true for their spouses (Epstein & Dutton, 1997). However, Arrindell and Emmelkamp (1986) also reported that women with agoraphobia and their husbands were significantly more satisfied with their marriages than were couples in other control groups—a maritally distressed control group and a control group of women with other psychiatric disorders and their husbands. Going beyond self-report measures, Chambless et al. (2002) also included behavioral observation of positive and negative behaviors tied to marital maladjustment. Couples in which the wife had agoraphobia were significantly more nonverbally negative than control couples and had longer chains of reciprocated negative behavior. However, these differences and those on the self-report measure of global marital satisfaction were no longer significantly different when comorbidity with depression was statistically controlled. Because depression is known to be associated with marital dissatisfaction and maladaptive behaviors during marital interaction (Whisman, 2001), establishing that agoraphobia has a specific relationship with marital problems apart from its comorbidity with depression is important.

Clinic and support group samples might be different from people with panic disorder and agoraphobia in the general population on marital adjustment, in that it is possible that those who are most unhappy in their relationships seek the support of treatment. For this reason, three epidemiologic studies are particularly useful. Markowitz et al. (1989) compared people with panic disorder in the Epidemiologic Catchment Area study with those with major depression and with neither major depression nor panic disorder. The panic disorder participants were significantly more likely to report that the quality of their marriage was negative than was the group without these two disorders and were equivalent in this regard to those with major depression. In a probability sample of suburban Detroit couples, McLeod (1994) found that when she controlled for comorbidity with depression, other anxiety disorders, and alcohol and substance use disorders, husbands of women with panic disorder were more negative about their marriages than husbands of women without panic disorder, but the wives' reports were not significantly different from those of women without panic disorder. Finally, Whisman (2007) analyzed data from the National Comorbidity Study Replication. Surprisingly, he found that marital distress was related to all diagnoses of anxiety disorder except panic disorder. Because this was the largest and most representative sample of any of the three epidemiologic studies included here, and the assessment of marital adjustment was more extensive in this study than in the other two, these findings are noteworthy.

Focused Relationship Measures

Arguing that general measures of marital adjustment may be less important than specific relationship aspects, some researchers have advocated examining more focused measures of the relationships between panic and agoraphobia patients and their spouses (e.g., Chambless et al., 2002; Daiuto, Baucom, Epstein, & Dutton, 1998). Given the amount of assistance people with agoraphobia require because of their work, family, and financial disability, it is surprising that more researchers have not examined social support in their marital relationships (Fokias & Tyler, 1995). The authors of two studies examined questionnaire measures of social support completed by members of agoraphobia support groups (almost entirely female) versus control samples. In both cases, people with agoraphobia reported their spouses to be less supportive than did those in the control groups (McCarthy & Shean, 1996; Pyke & Roberts, 1987). There are two difficulties with interpreting these data: First, it is possible that people who attend support groups do so precisely because they get insufficient support at home, thus biasing the results. Second, these authors did not distinguish between emotional and instrumental support. These are rather different constructs, and because of their difficulties people with agoraphobia require substantial instrumental support. Hence, it is possible that a perceived shortfall in instrumental support might have less to do with the absolute amount of support supplied by the spouse than with a discrepancy between the amount desired or needed and that provided.

Two observational studies are relevant in that the constructs assessed pertain to emotional support. Agoraphobic participants were recruited from clinical samples. In an early controlled study, Buglass, Clarke, Henderson, Kreitman, and Presley (1977) interviewed agoraphobic women and their husbands as well as control subjects. The interviews were later rated for the amount of affection the spouses showed toward one another. Husbands of women with agoraphobia were reported to be as affectionate toward their wives as were control husbands. Unfortunately, no interrater reliability for the ratings and little information on the nature of the rating scale were provided. Much later, Chambless et al. (2002) observed and rated women with agoraphobia and their husbands and control women and their husbands during a 10-minute problem-solving interaction. Husbands of women with agoraphobia were no less empathic with their wives than were control husbands. However, problem-solving interactions are ill-suited to adequate assessment of social support. Hence, additional research using interactions designed to elicit social support and using specific social support coding systems is desirable. Unfortunately neither Buglass et al. nor Chambless et al. collected self-report measures of social support. Accordingly, it is not possible to discern whether the discrepancies between the self-report and observational studies reflect measurement or sample differences.

Perhaps the antithesis of emotional support is criticism. Chambless et al. (2002) compared agoraphobic and control participants' ratings of perceived criticism by their spouses and counted the frequency of the husbands' criticisms during a problem-solving interaction. Wives with agoraphobia described their husbands as more critical of them than did women in the control group, and these descriptions were borne out by the observational data. The effect size was medium in the case of patient-report data and large for observational data. Controlling for a diagnosis of depression reduced the finding for observed criticism to a medium effect size, which was no longer statistically significant with the modest sample size of this study.

The greatest number of studies on specific aspects of marital relationships have focused on problem solving. Compared with control participants and according to their reports on questionnaires, people with panic disorder and agoraphobia have been found to eschew problem-focused coping in favor of self-blame, cognitive avoidance, avoidance of communication, wishful thinking, and pursuit of social support (Arrindell & Emmelkamp, 1986; Roy-Byrne et al., 1992; Vitaliano et al., 1987; Vollrath & Angst, 1993). This is problematic because use of problem-focused coping is generally related to lower psychological distress than are the panic patients' preferred strategies (Lazarus & Folkman, 1984; Roy-Byrne et al., 1992). Indeed, Marcaurelle, Bélanger, Marchand, Katerelos, and Mainguy (2005) found that the less patients with agoraphobia reported confidence in their problem-solving abilities and the less their involvement in problem-solving activities, the more severe their panic disorder and agoraphobia and their depression. If people with agoraphobia are deficient in problem solving or reluctant to engage in problem solving, interpersonal and other problems may fester, leading to greater stress and ultimately to greater symptom severity.

Is there objective evidence to suggest that people with agoraphobia are poor problem solvers? Research by Brodbeck and Michelson (1987) has indicated they are as capable as control women of solving cognitive problems (anagrams) but that when standardized descriptions of interpersonal problems were posed, women with agoraphobia generated fewer effective solutions, were disinclined to use effective solutions, and preferred avoidant responses compared with control women. The latter two differences remained significant when the contribution of depression was statistically controlled. In observations of women with agoraphobia and their husbands discussing the top problems in their relationships, Chambless et al. (2002) found that both husbands and wives were less likely to generate positive problem solutions than the control couples. The effect size was large and remained so even when the contribution of a diagnosis of depression was statistically controlled. Because half of the couples with a partner with agoraphobia talked about her anxiety disorder as the problem to be resolved, it is possible that these results are exaggerated. Almost by definition, people seek treatment when their own efforts at problem resolution have failed. Note, however, that Brodbeck and Michelson's results were based on standardized descriptions of problems rather than the patients' own, which suggests that these results are not peculiar to discussions about agoraphobia. Nonetheless, additional observational research on problem-solving abilities of people with panic disorder and agoraphobia in which the person's disorder is not the topic under discussion would be highly desirable.

Symptom Severity

Research on the relationship between symptom severity and marital adjustment is relatively sparse and difficult to interpret. Patients in treatment studies are often selected to meet certain criteria for the severity of the disorder, thus restricting the range of symptom severity and making it difficult to discern correlations. Bland and Hallam (1981) conducted the earliest research in this vein and reported that patients with agoraphobia in poorer marriages (according to a median split on a self-report questionnaire) rated themselves as more fearful of agoraphobic situations than those in better marriages. In contrast, Chambless et al. (2002) concluded there was no relationship between their agoraphobic patients' symptom severity and their relationship scores: Although there were a few significant results, these were hardly more than would have been expected by chance in light of the number of correlations computed. Finally, Marcaurelle et al. (2005) obtained mixed results, finding that phobic severity per se was not related to marital adjustment in their sample, but measures of fear of anxiety (catastrophic thinking about panic symptoms and fear of bodily sensations associated with panic) were higher in those who were less satisfied with their marriages. No consistent picture emerges from this set of studies.

TREATMENT'S EFFECTS ON THE MARRIAGE AND THE SPOUSE

In the 1970s, Hafner and others (e.g., Hafner, 1977; Hand & Lamontagne, 1976) presented dramatic case studies, reporting that a number of husbands of women with agoraphobia treated with rapid in vivo exposure had a crisis when their wives improved, for example, attempting suicide or developing paranoid ideation. They theorized that such rapid improvement on the heretofore dependent wives' part was too stressful for the marital system, particularly if the wife's disorder served to hide the husband's own weaknesses. Hafner (1984) suggested that husbands be involved in wives' treatment to give them an increased sense of control and perhaps that treatment be conducted more slowly to give the husband time to adjust to his wife's increased autonomy. Otherwise, wives might relapse to return the system to its former stability.

Certainly one sees such dramatic cases from time to time, but how typical are these findings? Does including spouses in treatment prevent deterioration of the marriage? A number of investigations have been conducted to examine these questions in a controlled fashion. Arrindell, Emmelkamp, and Sanderman (1986) identified women with agoraphobia who showed clinically significant change after prolonged group exposure (i.e., they had significantly improved and were within the normal range on the outcome measure). Spouses were not involved in treatment. According to the family systems model, the marriages of the women who had shown such strong improvement should be vulnerable. However, on standardized measures of marital functioning, neither husbands nor wives showed any significant deterioration. Interviewers also rated marital quality for these patients and thought the quality of the improved patients' marriages had declined. However, this was no different than the deterioration the interviewers also perceived in the marriages of the patients who did not improve, and the marriages of unimproved patients were significantly more likely to be rated as disturbed after treatment than those of the successful patients. These findings, which are contrary to the predictions from systems theory, point out the importance of a control group for interpretation of clinical data.

In a second study in which spouses were not included in the treatment, Monteiro, Marks, and Ramm (1985) reported that regardless of the initial status of the marriage on a self-report measure of marital adjustment, neither patients nor their spouses reported any deterioration in the quality of their marital relationship after treatment, although on the whole the treatment was successful for this group of patients. Note that in both of these studies, exposure treatment was spread out over a number of weeks rather than being brief and concentrated as was the case for authors reporting dramatic deterioration.

Having randomly assigned patients with agoraphobia to spouse-assisted versus patient-alone home-based exposure treatment, Cobb, Mathews, Childs-Clarke, and Blowers (1984) reported that regardless of group assignment, measures of marital quality generally improved from before to after treatment, with the changes being significant on some but not all measures. Subsequent studies of spouse-assisted versus patient-alone exposure yielded somewhat similar findings. Emmelkamp et al. (1992) found no differences between groups for marital measures or change over time in this regard for patients. However, husbands reported improved communication quality, whether they were in the spouse-assisted or patient-alone treatment condition. Himadi, Cerny, Barlow, Cohen, and O'Brien (1986) found that ratings of family functioning improved regardless of group assignment. Marital happiness increased for those patients who were treatment responders and was unchanged for those who had poor treatment outcome. Using the brief, intensive treatment format, Milton, Ward, and Hafner (1981) reported improvement in marital satisfaction by 6-month follow-up in those patients who were originally happier in their marriages, with no change in patients who began treatment more dissatisfied with their marriages. Regardless of their wives' initial marital satisfaction, husbands neither improved nor deteriorated on their marital measures. Assignment to spouse-assisted exposure in this case was not random; rather, spouses were invited to join the treatment when marital difficulties were prominent. In contrast to the findings on standardized measures, Milton et al. reported clinical observations that changes in treatment led to negative reactions such that nine of 15 couples on whom they had reports experienced increased marital dissatisfaction.

In several studies, authors looked specifically at the effects of treatment on the spouses' psychological functioning. Himadi et al. (1986) found no evidence of deterioration on standardized measures of depression for spouses regardless of their inclusion in the patients-only or spouse-assisted exposure conditions. Similarly, Oatley and Hodgson (1987) found that husbands' anxiety and depression on standardized measures remained low from pretest to posttest regardless of whether their wives were assigned to the spouse-assisted or friend-assisted treatment condition. Results of Milton et al.'s (1981) study are more difficult to interpret. They reported that compared with husbands whose wives were more satisfied with their marriages before treatment, husbands whose wives were unhappier in their marriages at pretest fared significantly worse on a standardized measure of psychopathology at one of three time points after treatment, that being the 6-month follow-up. However, these analyses do not take into account the apparent differences between husbands in these two groups before treatment began, and Milton et al. conducted a very large number of statistical analyses without any control of Type I error, making it very possible that this obtained effect was the result of chance.

With little exception, these studies indicated that exposure treatment is either neutral or positive for agoraphobic patients' marriages and that spouses do not suffer ill effects from their partners' improvement. How can these findings be reconciled with the clinical observations of extreme negative reactions to rapid changes with exposure? It is possible that as suggested by Hafner (1984) and Barlow, O'Brien, and Last (1984), the intensive treatment format poses more likelihood of iatrogenic effects. Indeed, the only case of marked deterioration in a spouse I have seen in 35 years of research on agoraphobia was the husband of a woman who improved radically with intensive treatment that did not involve her husband. It is also possible that these findings are the result of chance occurrences in uncontrolled studies with small samples of patients and reliance on unsystematic clinical observation. Changes in group means, such as reported by most authors discussed in this section, are not entirely satisfactory as a marker of deterioration or its absence in individual cases, particularly if they are as rare as they have been in my experience. It may be useful for authors to examine rates of negative impact on spouses using statistics such as Jacobson's reliable change index (Jacobson & Truax, 1991), which is designed to be applied to individual cases. Although this index is typically used to identify statistically reliable improvement, it can just as easily be used to mark statistically reliable deterioration.

TREATMENT

The interplay of interpersonal relationships and treatment of agoraphobia has been examined in several different ways, including whether relationship variables predict treatment outcome, whether involving spouses as assistants in exposure treatment is helpful, and whether a couple intervention facilitates response to individual treatment for agoraphobia.

Prediction of Outcome of Exposure Treatment for Agoraphobia

A number of authors have been interested in the question of the relationship between the quality of the marital relationship before treatment and the degree to which patients improve in exposure treatment for agoraphobia. If the stress from marital conflict appears to contribute to the onset of panic and agoraphobia, it is reasonable to posit that such conflict would interfere with progress in treatment. In most of these studies, the authors looked at the effects of global measures of marital adjustment or satisfaction.

The results of this research have been mixed. In five studies (Arrindell et al., 1986; Cobb et al., 1984; Emmelkamp, 1980; Emmelkamp et al., 1992; Himadi et al., 1986), no significant relationship was obtained between pretreatment global marital measures and improvement on measures of agoraphobia, whether patients were treated in spouse-assisted or patient-alone conditions. Moreover, Carter, Turovsky, Sbrocco, Meadows, and Barlow (1995) examined whether patients in spouse-assisted exposure were more likely to drop out of treatment if they were maritally dissatisfied. This proved not to be the case. In contrast, three other studies yielded different results. Monteiro et al. (1985) reported that patients who were initially happier in their marriages improved more in treatment, with this difference being significant at posttest. However, they added that this prediction was not unique to the marital happiness. For example, patients' satisfaction with their work was of equal importance, leading Monteiro et al. to suggest that patients' general adjustment was the important factor. Bland and Hallam (1981) and Milton et al. (1981) found that pretreatment marital satisfaction predicted better outcome on measures of agoraphobia either at follow-up (Milton et al., 1981) or at posttest and follow-up (Bland & Hallam, 1981). It is difficult to know what to make of these results in that the authors did not control for apparent pretest differences in agoraphobia severity in their analyses of posttest and follow-up data. Although the pretest differences may not have been significant at conventional alpha levels, there was little power to test the significance of these differences with only eight or nine patients per group. Consequently, it would still have been important to control for these pretest differences in the statistical analyses.

Much of this literature was synthesized in two meta-analyses (Daiuto et al., 1998; Dewey & Hunsley, 1990). Meta-analyses are particularly helpful when sample sizes are small and results may be contradictory because of low statistical power. Daiuto et al. (1998) and Dewey and Hunsley (1990) both concluded that effect sizes (expressed as d or its close relative g) for the relationship of pretreatment marital satisfaction and treatment outcome for phobia were small, in the range of 0.20 to 0.33, with dissatisfied patients having somewhat poorer outcome. Perhaps because their set of studies did not fully overlap and their statistical approaches may have differed, the authors obtained different findings as to whether these effects were statistically significant. In these meta-analyses, the authors did not code for and control for the effects of methodological quality of the research. Consequently, it is important to note that on the whole, those studies with larger effect sizes were generally methodologically poorer than those in which smaller effects were found.

Some authors (e.g., Daiuto et al., 1998) have argued that global marital satisfaction may be less important in predicting treatment outcome than specific aspects of the relationship between patients with agoraphobia and their spouses. Given findings reported earlier about the difficulties in communication reported by or observed in patients with agoraphobia and their spouses, one would expect that the relationship between communication skills and treatment response would be investigated. Yet there has been surprisingly little research on this topic. Emmelkamp et al. (1992) reported a trend for avoidance of communication on a questionnaire measure to predict poorer treatment outcome. This measure was an overall measure of marital communication quality.

Carter, Turovsky, et al. (1995) tested whether communication specifically about the patient's agoraphobia was important and found that when patients rated their spouses as better able to communicate about their agoraphobia before treatment, they were more likely to complete treatment than those who rated their partners as less proficient in this regard. Studying this same sample of patients, Craske, Burton, and Barlow (1989) reported that patients' ratings of their spouses' ability to communicate about their agoraphobia predicted treatment response. However, this was because patients who rated their spouses as better communicators were already less phobic before treatment rather than because they changed more during treatment than those who rated their spouses as less effective in such communication. Because Carter, Turovsky, et al. and Craske et al. conducted a great many statistical tests without correction for Type I error, these results should be considered as heuristic for future research rather than as solid findings.

In an intriguing study, Thomas-Peter, Jones, Sinnott, and Scott Fordham (1983) conducted interviews with patients' spouses before treatment on the basis of which they reliably rated how effective the spouses were at managing the patient's illness. These ratings proved to be strongly related to patients' severity of agoraphobia after treatment, with pretreatment severity controlled. Given the size of their effects (partial correlations in the .5 to .6 range), it is especially unfortunate that Thomas-Peter et al. provided little information about what constituted effective management and that others have not pursued their findings. Perhaps the closest finding is that of Chambless and Steketee (1999), who reported that patients[1] were more likely to drop out of treatment if their relatives were emotionally overinvolved. These authors hypothesized that such relatives would be less likely to push patients to endure the rigors of exposure treatment and would be too emotionally overreactive to respond calmly to the patients' episodes of panic and anxiety.

Given that expressed emotion has proved to be an important predictor of treatment outcome in other psychiatric disorders (Butzlaff & Hooley, 1998), Chambless and Steketee (1999) also examined whether expressed

---

[1]Patients in Chambless and Steketee's (1999) trial had a diagnosis of panic disorder with agoraphobia or obsessive–compulsive disorder. Although the two groups were combined for analysis to increase statistical power, the data were only pooled after it was demonstrated that diagnosis did not interact with the predictors of interest.

emotion predicted outcomes for patients with panic disorder with agoraphobia (see Footnote 1). Measures of expressed emotion include ratings of relatives' emotional overinvolvement, criticism, and hostility toward a psychiatric patient, as expressed in an interview conducted in the patient's absence (Leff & Vaughn, 1985). When relatives were rated as hostile on the basis of a pretreatment interview, patients were more likely to drop out of treatment or to improve less in treatment if they remained than were patients whose relatives were not hostile. *Hostility* is defined as a virulent form of criticism in which the relative criticizes not specific behaviors but the patient as a person, the relative makes statements clearly rejecting the patient, or both. In addition, Chambless and Steketee asked patients to rate the degree to which their relative (typically a spouse) was critical of them. These ratings proved an even stronger predictor of poor treatment outcome than the interview-based measure. Applying a stress-diathesis model, Chambless and Steketee hypothesized that hostility and perceived criticism from the relative serve as stressors that increase anxious patients' vulnerability to symptom exacerbation and thus interfere with treatment. See Steketee, Lam, Chambless, Rodebaugh, and McCullough (2007) for an exploratory test of this hypothesis.

Also positing that stress during treatment interferes with the improvement to be gained from exposure for patients with agoraphobia, Wade et al. (1993) obtained interview measures of stressful life events in the 12 months before treatment and during the time the patient was in treatment. Information about these stressors gathered before and at the end of treatment was later amplified in follow-up interviews 3 to 5 years after treatment. Eliminating stressors directly caused by the patient's agoraphobia, Wade et al. focused on moderate to severe chronic stressors that would be agreed to be a problem by most people. The most common stressor identified proved to be interpersonal stress (most frequently marital difficulties), and such stress was related to less improvement in treatment. However, interpersonal stress was not uniquely related to treatment outcome: Other stressors, when present, were equally as likely to predict poor treatment response. Because of the retrospective nature of the follow-up interviews, these findings have to be taken with caution. However, they are in keeping with the notion that agoraphobic patients' interpersonal problems are an important source of stress in their lives and that this stress may be involved not only in the onset of panic attacks but also in poor treatment response. Hence, this important research needs replication.

Spouse-Assisted Exposure

In the 1970s, Mathews, Teasdale, Mumby, Johnston, and Shaw (1977) developed a home-based exposure treatment program for people with agoraphobia, which involved the spouse as a sort of cotherapist. The goals included decreasing the amount of professional help required to make treatment cost effective but also increasing the effectiveness of treatment by soliciting the support of the spouse for exposure exercises. Recall that Hafner (e.g., 1984) advocated including the spouse on the basis of a systems approach, with the belief that the spouse would react less negatively to changes in treatment if he was included in the process and felt more of a sense of control over his wife's improvement. For a time, this was a very active area of research, with six outcome trials conducted to test the efficacy of spouse-assisted exposure versus treatment of the patient alone. In one additional study, the contrast for spouse-assisted exposure was friend-assisted exposure (Oatley & Hodgson, 1987).

The results of this research are almost entirely uniform. In six studies reviewed (Cobb et al., 1984; Emmelkamp et al., 1992; Marchand, Boisvert, Beaudry, Bérard, & Gaudette, 1985; Marchand & Comeau, 1992; Marchand, Todorov, Borgeat, & Pelland, 2007; Oatley & Hodgson, 1987), spouse-assisted exposure was not significantly more efficacious for agoraphobic symptoms than exposure for the patient without the spouse. These studies were largely clinic based, but two were home based (Cobb et al., 1984; Oatley & Hodgson, 1987). The sole exception to this pattern of results is the study by Barlow and colleagues (Barlow et al., 1984; Cerny, Barlow, Craske, & Himadi, 1987). There was no clear advantage of spouse-assisted exposure at posttest,[2] but by 1- or 2-year follow-up (at which time power had been increased by almost doubling the size of the spouse-assisted group), the spouse-assisted group was better on one (2-year) or two (1-year) of the major outcome measures.

The follow-up findings of Barlow's group (Cerny et al., 1987) are somewhat difficult to interpret because of the large amount of missing data and because the study was conducted before currently acceptable methods for handling missing data became widely used in clinical psychology. Moreover, no information was provided on additional treatment patients might have received during the prolonged follow-up interval. Finally, the follow-up study design was quasi-experimental in that additional patients were assigned to the spouse-assisted group without random assignment. Nonetheless, these data suggest that the Barlow group's outcome may be different from the other trials published. One factor that differentiates this study is that it appears that there was some focus in the spouse-assisted groups on communication about the

---

[2]Barlow et al. (1984) reported no significant differences in change for the spouse-assisted versus patient-alone exposure groups on the continuous measures of treatment outcome. They devised a measure of treatment response defined as 20% improvement on three of five outcome measures and reported that patients in the spouse-assisted group were more likely to be categorized as responders than those in the patient-alone group. Because it is highly unusual for categorical variables to yield significant effects when continuous measures do not (usually the opposite occurs because categorical measures lose statistical power) and because the authors presented no data to confirm that a 20% change is statistically reliable, the reported results on responder status may simply be a chance finding.

patient's fear and avoidance. As is apparent in the next section, helping patients and spouses communicate better about the disorder may have beneficial effects. In addition, the follow-up period in this project was substantially longer than those of other studies. Perhaps differences are only apparent after patients have been out of treatment a year or more.

Almost all of the studies included in this section suffer from low power, which might obscure better treatment effects for the spouse-assisted group. This does not appear to be the case. In the meta-analyses described in the Prediction of Outcome of Exposure Treatment for Agoraphobia section, Daiuto et al. (1998) and Dewey and Hunsley (1990) also synthesized the results of a number of the studies described in this section. Both sets of authors concluded that the effect sizes (d or g) were small (-0.190 to 0.10 at posttest and -0.21 to 0.10 at follow-up) and not statistically significant. Indeed, in Daiuto et al.'s meta-analysis, the results for spouse-assisted exposure were (nonsignificantly) worse than those for exposure without involvement of the spouse.

ADDRESSING MARITAL ISSUES IN THE CONTEXT OF EXPOSURE

In light of all the speculation on the importance of marital conflict for the development of agoraphobia and for its treatment response, it is surprising that little research has been accomplished on the contribution of frankly marital interventions along with cognitive–behavioral treatment for panic disorder and agoraphobia. As noted earlier, it appears that Barlow et al. (1984) touched on communications issues in their treatment insofar as these pertained to planned exposures.

Jones, Sinnott, and Scott Fordham (1980) compared group exposure for the agoraphobic patient alone with group exposure plus counseling of significant others. Spouses were not involved in treatment with the patients but were invited to separate sessions for discussion of the role of avoidance in agoraphobia and the relationship of excessive dependency and secondary gain to maintenance of phobia. There were no significant differences between groups at posttest or 3-month follow-up; however, with four to six patients per condition, effects would have to have been extremely large to achieve statistical significance. Inspection of group means suggests that patients in the group that included counseling for significant others improved substantially more than those in the exposure-alone group but that this difference had diminished by follow-up.

Only Arnow, Taylor, Agras, and Telch (1985) tested a treatment that combined exposure for agoraphobia with a true couples intervention. All patients first received therapist-conducted in vivo exposure followed by group spouse-assisted exposure conducted with homework assignments. After this initial phase of exposure treatment, patients were randomly assigned to either couples communication and problem-solving training or to a control condition of couples relaxation training. Both couples interventions were described as ways to reduce stress of change from exposure treatment. The couples therapy was specifically focused on changing communications patterns and increasing problem-solving skills pertaining to the patients' disorder. Spouse-assisted exposure continued for both groups during the second phase of treatment.

The treatment was effective in changing communications patterns in that the communication and problem-solving group was significantly more positive and less negative after treatment than the control group according to behavioral observation of a problem-solving interaction. However, the groups did not differ on fostering patient autonomy as assessed by a structured interview. In terms of change on measures of agoraphobia, patients in the communications and problem-solving group improved significantly more than patients in the control group on self-report and behavioral measures of agoraphobia, although not on frequency of panic attacks. Attrition and lack of information on any intervening treatment patients might have received at 8-month follow-up make these data difficult to interpret. Differences remained significant on behavioral but not on self-report measures. However, with only five or six patients per group at this point, statistical power was very low, and nonsignificant differences in favor of the communication and problem-solving group on the self-report measure are apparent. On the whole, this carefully conducted study indicated that addressing marital interaction is likely to be beneficial in treatment of agoraphobia, but surprisingly in the more than 20 years since its publication, this study has yet to be replicated.

CONCLUSION

In keeping with Goldstein and Chambless's (1978) model, the body of available data, on the whole, has indicated that panic and agoraphobia often begin in a climate of interpersonal conflict. However, other stressors also play an important role. These findings are most consistent with the stress-diathesis model, in which a variety of stressors may serve as triggering events for vulnerable people, although interpersonal problems may be of the first order. Note, however, that all of the studies reviewed relied on retrospective reports, typically years after panic onset. Patients' memories can change with the passage of time and with attempts to make sense of what has happened to them—attempts that may be shaped by intervening psychotherapies. Prospective research would be highly desirable if a group at risk could be identified and followed over time.

As hypothesized by Goldstein and Chambless (1978), marital dissatisfaction is common in people with agoraphobia who seek treatment or attend support groups. However, given that it is far from ubiquitous, it appears this early model overemphasized this connection. For example, Chambless et al. (2002) found that only 32% of couples with an agoraphobic spouse scored in the maritally distressed range on a self-report measure. Moreover, panic disorder and agoraphobia are comorbid with a variety of conditions, including other anxiety disorders, alcohol abuse, and mood disorders. For example, fully half of the people with a lifetime diagnosis of panic disorder also meet criteria for a lifetime diagnosis of major depression (Kessler et al., 1998). It is possible that the comorbid disorder, such as major depression, accounts for observed relationships with marital satisfaction (see Chambless et al., 2002) or that only when panic and agoraphobia are complicated by comorbidity are they related to unhappy marriages. Finally, the picture left by the extant epidemiologic research is very unclear as to the relationship of panic disorder and agoraphobia with marital dissatisfaction in the general population. In sum, not only does marital dissatisfaction fail to cleanly distinguish those with agoraphobia from those without this disorder, marital dissatisfaction has not proved to be related to phenomena of interest, in particular, treatment outcome.

Although the literature is scattered and the number of replications is insufficient, there are reasons to hypothesize that it is more valuable to focus on specific aspects of the marital relationship than on global marital satisfaction. For example, authors using a variety of methodologies have found evidence that people with agoraphobia (and in at least one study [Chambless et al., 2002], their spouses) are poor at solving interpersonal problems relative to control groups, either because of a lack of skills or because of an avoidant style of coping with problems. Moreover, relatives who are hostile toward the agoraphobic patient (see Footnote 1) with whom they live have specifically been observed to be deficient in generating positive problem solutions when interacting with the patient, relative to nonhostile family members (Chambless et al., 2001). This finding is particularly salient in that in this same sample, hostility among relatives and patients' perceptions of criticism from these relatives were predictive of poor treatment response or discontinuation. Communication patterns are also implicated in a number of studies, with observational data indicating that husbands of women with agoraphobia are more critical of their wives during a problem-solving interaction than are husbands of women without agoraphobia and with self-report data suggesting that women are more likely to complete treatment and to succeed in treatment if their husbands communicate more effectively with them about their agoraphobia.

A systems theory approach would suggest that marriages of patients with agoraphobia should suffer if exposure treatment, especially without the inclusion of the spouse in treatment, should lead to treatment gains. Moreover, the system should resist change in the patient, such that treatment without spousal involvement should be less effective than treatment that includes the spouse. These assertions are largely refuted by the data reviewed here. Nonetheless, on the basis of case reports, it appears that there may well be individual cases in which change in the person with agoraphobia does destabilize the marriage, and clinicians need to be alert to this possibility, perhaps particularly in the case of rapid treatment approaches.

Taken as a whole, the studies reviewed in this chapter yield some suggestions for treatment that includes the spouse or other family members of people with agoraphobia. Treatment that addresses the need for improved problem solving with active rather than avoidant coping and the need for constructive rather than hostile communication about the patient's anxiety disorder might improve treatment outcomes. Indeed, this was the finding of the one study (Arnow et al., 1985) to include couples communications and problem-solving training along with exposure. Replication of this small study is a priority. Finally, it is unlikely that couples or family interventions would be required for all patients with panic disorder and agoraphobia. Thus, replicated research identifying markers as to which patients and which families require this adjunctive treatment is required if treatment is to be cost effective.

Little of the literature reviewed addressed interpersonal problems of people with panic disorder without agoraphobia, and none of the treatment studies did so. Although such people do not require phobic companions, this does not mean that their relationships are not burdened by their extreme anxiety or that they do not respond with panic to stresses in their relationships. Accordingly, interpersonally focused research on this group would be informative. An additional lacuna in the literature on interpersonal aspects of panic and agoraphobia is research on the effects of comorbidity on the interpersonal context. When comorbidity has been considered in this body of research, and this is rare, the focus has typically been on depression. This makes sense in that depression's link with marital dissatisfaction is well established (Whisman, 2001), and panic and depression are highly comorbid (Kessler et al., 1998). However, comorbidity with other conditions such as generalized anxiety disorder is also high (Brown & Barlow, 1992), and an emerging body of research has suggested that patients with generalized anxiety disorder are likely to have marital problems (Whisman, Sheldon, & Goering, 2000), even when the contribution of other forms of comorbidity is controlled. Accordingly, researchers in this area need to take greater care to consider the effects of comorbid conditions in future research if they are to elucidate specific relationships between panic, agoraphobia, and interpersonal problems.

REFERENCES

American Psychiatric Association. (1994). *Diagnostic and statistical manual of mental disorders* (4th ed.). Washington, DC: Author.

Arnow, B. A., Taylor, C. B., Agras, W. S., & Telch, M. J. (1985). Enhancing agoraphobia treatment outcome by changing couple communication patterns. *Behavior Therapy, 16,* 452–467.

Arrindell, W. A., & Emmelkamp, P. M. G. (1986). Marital adjustment, intimacy and needs in female agoraphobics and their partners: A controlled study. *British Journal of Psychiatry, 149,* 592–602.

Arrindell, W. A., Emmelkamp, P. M. G., & Sanderman, R. (1986). Marital quality and general life adjustment in relation to treatment outcome in agoraphobia. *Advances in Behaviour Research and Therapy, 8,* 138–185.

Barlow, D. H., O'Brien, G. T., & Last, C. G. (1984). Couples treatment of agoraphobia. *Behavior Therapy, 15,* 41–58.

Bland, K., & Hallam, R. S. (1981). Relationship between response to graded exposure and marital satisfaction in agoraphobics. *Behaviour Research and Therapy, 19,* 335–338.

Brodbeck, C., & Michelson, L. (1987). Problem-solving skills and attributional styles of agoraphobics. *Cognitive Therapy and Research, 11,* 593–610.

Brown, T. A., & Barlow, D. H. (1992). Comorbidity among anxiety disorders: Implications for treatment and *DSM–IV*. *Journal of Consulting and Clinical Psychology, 60,* 835–844.

Buglass, D., Clarke, J., Henderson, A. S., Kreitman, N., & Presley, A. S. (1977). A study of agoraphobic housewives. *Psychological Medicine, 7,* 73–86.

Butzlaff, R. L., & Hooley, J. M. (1998). Expressed emotion and psychiatric relapse: A meta-analysis. *Archives of General Psychiatry, 55,* 547–552.

Carter, M. M., Hollon, S. D., Carson, R., & Shelton, R. C. (1995). Effects of a safe person on induced distress following a biological challenge in panic disorder with agoraphobia. *Journal of Abnormal Psychology, 104,* 156–163.

Carter, M. M., Turovsky, J., Sbrocco, T., Meadows, E. A., & Barlow, D. H. (1995). Patient dropout from a couples' group treatment for panic disorder with agoraphobia. *Professional Psychology: Research and Practice, 26,* 626–628.

Cerny, J. A., Barlow, D. H., Craske, M. G., & Himadi, W. G. (1987). Couples treatment of agoraphobia: A two-year follow-up. *Behavior Therapy, 18,* 401–415.

Chambless, D. L., Bryan, A. S., Aiken, L. S., Steketee, G., & Hooley, J. M. (2001). Prediction of expressed emotion via structural equation modeling: A study with families of obsessive–compulsive and agoraphobic outpatients. *Journal of Family Psychology, 15,* 225–240.

Chambless, D. L., Fauerbach, J., Floyd, F. J., Wilson, K. A., Remen, A., & Renneberg, B. (2002). Marital interaction of agoraphobic women: A controlled, behavioral observation study. *Journal of Abnormal Psychology, 111,* 502–512.

Chambless, D. L., Hunter, K., & Jackson, A. (1982). Social anxiety and assertiveness in college students and agoraphobics. *Behaviour Research and Therapy, 20,* 403–404.

Chambless, D. L., & Mason, J. (1986). Sex, sex role stereotyping, and agoraphobia. *Behaviour Research and Therapy, 24,* 231–235.

Chambless, D. L., & Steketee, G. (1999). Expressed emotion and outcome for behavior therapy for agoraphobia and obsessive–compulsive disorder. *Journal of Consulting and Clinical Psychology, 67,* 658–665.

Cobb, J. P., Mathews, A. M., Childs-Clarke, A., & Blowers, C. M. (1984). The spouse as co-therapist in the treatment of agoraphobia. *British Journal of Psychiatry, 144,* 282–287.

Craske, M. G., Burton, T., & Barlow, D. H. (1989). Relationships among measures of communication, marital satisfaction and exposure during couples treatment of agoraphobia. *Behaviour Research and Therapy, 27,* 131–140.

Craske, M. G., & Zoellner, L. A. (1995). Anxiety disorders: The role of marital therapy. In N. S. Jacobson & A. S. Gurman (Eds.), *Clinical handbook of couples therapy* (pp. 394–410). New York, NY: Guilford Press.

Daiuto, A. D., Baucom, D. H., Epstein, N., & Dutton, S. (1998). The application of behavioral couples therapy to the assessment and treatment of agoraphobia: Implications of empirical research. *Clinical Psychology Review, 18,* 663–687.

Dewey, D., & Hunsley, J. (1990). The effects of marital adjustment and spouse involvement on the behavioral treatment of agoraphobia: A meta-analytic review. *Anxiety Research, 2,* 69–83.

Doctor, R. (1982). Major results of a large-scale pretreatment survey of agoraphobics. In R. L. DuPont (Ed.), *Phobia: A comprehensive summary of modern treatments* (pp. 203–214). New York, NY: Brunner/Mazel.

Emmelkamp, P. M. G. (1980). Agoraphobics' interpersonal problems: Their role in the effects of exposure in vivo therapy. *Archives of General Psychiatry, 37,* 1303–1306.

Emmelkamp, P. M. G., van Dyck, R., Bitter, M., Heins, R., Onstein, E. J., & Eisen, B. (1992). Spouse-aided therapy with agoraphobics. *British Journal of Psychiatry, 160,* 51–56.

Epstein, N., & Dutton, S. S. (1997, November). *Relationship characteristics of agoraphobics and their partners.* Paper presented at the meeting of the Association for Advancement of Behavior Therapy, Miami, FL.

Faravelli, C. (1985). Life events preceding the onset of panic disorder. *Journal of Affective Disorders, 9,* 103–105.

Fokias, D., & Tyler, P. (1995). Social support and agoraphobia: A review. *Clinical Psychology Review, 15,* 347–366.

Fry, W. F., Jr. (1962). The marital context of an anxiety syndrome. *Family Process, 1,* 245–252.

Goldstein, A. J., & Chambless, D. L. (1978). A reanalysis of agoraphobia. *Behavior Therapy, 9,* 47–59.

Hafner, R. J. (1977). The husbands of agoraphobic women and their influence on treatment outcome. *British Journal of Psychiatry, 131,* 289–294.

Hafner, R. J. (1984). Predicting the effects on husbands of behavioural therapy for wives' agoraphobia. *Behaviour Research and Therapy, 22,* 217–226.

Hand, I., & Lamontagne, Y. (1976). The exacerbation of interpersonal problems after rapid phobia-removal. *Psychotherapy: Theory, Research, and Practice, 13,* 405–411.

Himadi, W. G., Cerny, J. A., Barlow, D. H., Cohen, S., & O'Brien, G. T. (1986). The relationship of marital adjustment to agoraphobia treatment outcome. *Behaviour Research and Therapy, 24,* 107–115.

Jacobson, N. S., & Truax, P. (1991). Clinical significance: A statistical approach to defining meaningful change in psychotherapy research. *Journal of Consulting and Clinical Psychology, 59,* 12–19.

Jones, R. B., Sinnott, A., & Scott Fordham, A. (1980). Group in-vivo exposure augmented by the counselling of significant others in the treatment of agoraphobia. *Behavioural Psychotherapy, 8,* 31–35.

Kessler, R. C., Chiu, W. T., Jin, R., Ruscio, A. M., Shear, M. K., & Walters, E. E. (2006). The epidemiology of panic attacks, panic disorder, and agoraphobia in the National Comorbidity Survey replication. *Archives of General Psychiatry, 63,* 415–424.

Kessler, R. C., Stang, P. E., Wittchen, H. U., Ustun, T. B., Roy-Byrne, P. P., & Walters, E. E. (1998). Lifetime panic-depression comorbidity in the National Comorbidity Survey. *Archives of General Psychiatry, 55,* 801–808.

Kleiner, L., & Marshall, W. L. (1987). The role of interpersonal problems in the development of agoraphobia with panic attacks. *Journal of Anxiety Disorders, 1,* 313–323.

Last, C. G., Barlow, D. H., & O'Brien, G. T. (1984). Precipitants of agoraphobia: Role of stressful life events. *Psychological Reports, 54,* 567–570.

Lazarus, R. S., & Folkman, S. (1984). *Stress, appraisal, and coping.* New York: Springer.

Leff, J., & Vaughn, C. (1985). *Expressed emotion in families: Its significance for mental illness.* New York: Guilford Press.

Marcaurelle, R., Bélanger, C., Marchand, A., Katerelos, T. E., & Mainguy, N. (2005). Marital predictors of symptom severity in panic disorder with agoraphobia. *Journal of Anxiety Disorders, 19,* 211–232.

Marchand, A., Boisvert, J. M., Beaudry, M., Bérard, M., & Gaudette, G. (1985). Le traitement de l'agoraphobie en groupe avec ou sans partenaire [The treatment of agoraphobia in groups with or without partners]. *Revue Québecoise de Psychologie, 3,* 36–48.

Marchand, A., & Comeau, S. (1992). Une recherche clinique sur le traitement en groupe de l'agorphobie avec ou san partenaire [A clinical study on group treatment of agoraphobia with or without partners]. *Science et Comportement, 2,* 163–174.

Marchand, A., Todorov, C., Borgeat, F., & Pelland, M. E. (2007). Effectiveness of a brief cognitive behavioural therapy for panic disorder with agoraphobia and the impact of partner involvement. *Behavioural and Cognitive Psychotherapy, 35,* 1–17.

Markowitz, J. S., Weissman, M. M., Ouellette, R., Lish, J. D., & Klerman, G. L. (1989). Quality of life in panic disorder. *Archives of General Psychiatry, 46,* 984–992.

Marks, I. M. (1970). Agoraphobic syndrome (phobic anxiety state). *Archives of General Psychiatry, 23,* 538–553.

Mathews, A. M., Teasdale, J., Mumby, M., Johnston, D., & Shaw, P. (1977). A home-based treatment programme for agoraphobia. *Behavior Therapy, 8,* 915–924.

McCarthy, L., & Shean, G. (1996). Agoraphobia and interpersonal relationships. *Journal of Anxiety Disorders, 10,* 477–487.

McLeod, J. D. (1994). Anxiety disorders and marital quality. *Journal of Abnormal Psychology, 103,* 767–776.

Milton, F., Ward, K., & Hafner, J. (1981). The outcome of behaviour therapy for agoraphobia in relation to marital adjustment. *Archives of General Psychiatry, 36,* 807–812.

Monteiro, W., Marks, I. M., & Ramm, E. (1985). Marital adjustment and treatment outcome in agoraphobia. *British Journal of Psychiatry, 146,* 383–390.

Oatley, K., & Hodgson, D. (1987). Influence of husbands on the outcome of their agoraphobic wives' therapy. *British Journal of Psychiatry, 150,* 380–386.

Pollard, C. A., Pollard, H. J., & Corn, K. J. (1989). Panic onset and major events in the lives of agoraphobics: A test of contiguity. *Journal of Abnormal Psychology, 98,* 318–321.

Pyke, J., & Roberts, J. (1987). Social support and married agoraphobic women. *Canadian Journal of Psychiatry, 32,* 100–104.

Roy-Byrne, P. P., Vitaliano, P. P., Cowley, D. S., Luciano, G., Zheng, Y., & Dunner, D. L. (1992). Coping in panic and major depression: Relative effects of symptom severity and diagnostic comorbidity. *Journal of Nervous and Mental Disease, 180,* 179–183.

Steketee, G., Lam, J. L., Chambless, D. L., Rodebaugh, T. R., & McCullough, C. E. (2007). Effects of perceived criticism on anxiety and depression during behavioral treatment for anxiety disorders. *Behaviour Research and Therapy, 45,* 11–19.

Thomas-Peter, B. A., Jones, R. B., Sinnott, A., & Scott Fordham, A. (1983). Prediction of outcome in the treatment of agoraphobia. *Behavioural Psychotherapy, 11,* 320–328.

Vitaliano, P. P., Katon, W., Russo, J., Maiuro, R. D., Anderson, K., & Jones, M. (1987). Coping as an index of illness behavior in panic disorder. *Journal of Nervous and Mental Disease, 175,* 78–84.

Vollrath, M., & Angst, J. (1993). Coping and illness behavior among young adults with panic. *Journal of Nervous and Mental Disease, 181,* 303–308.

Wade, S. L., Monroe, S. M., & Michelson, L. K. (1993). Chronic life stress and treatment outcome in agoraphobia with panic attacks. *American Journal of Psychiatry, 150,* 1491–1495.

Whisman, M. A. (2001). The association between depression and marital dissatisfaction. In S. R. H. Beach (Ed.), *Marital and family processes in depression: A scientific foundation for clinical practice* (pp. 3–24). Washington, DC: American Psychological Association.

Whisman, M. A. (2007). Marital distress and *DSM–IV* psychiatric disorders in a population-based national survey. *Journal of Abnormal Psychology, 116,* 638–643.

Whisman, M. A., Sheldon, C. T., & Goering, P. (2000). Psychiatric disorders and dissatisfaction with social relationships: Does type of relationship matter? *Journal of Abnormal Psychology, 109,* 803–808.

9

GENERALIZED ANXIETY DISORDER

MICHELLE G. NEWMAN AND THANE M. ERICKSON

Generalized anxiety disorder (GAD) is characterized by a number of symptoms that are likely to affect interpersonal relationships. The central symptom is excessive, uncontrollable anxiety and worry about a number of events or activities, occurring more days than not for at least 6 months (American Psychiatric Association, 1994). Consistent with the proposed idea of a generalized anxious temperament that belongs on Axis II (Akiskal, 1998), most people diagnosed with GAD report having always been worriers and view this as part of their personality, which may explain low treatment seeking in GAD (Bland, Newman, & Orn, 1997).

Chronic worry may have a negative impact on significant others. For example, worry entails constantly anticipating potential future danger and therefore difficulty being in the present moment. Worrying is also associated with heightened need for reassurance (Masi et al., 2004), extended decision-making time (Metzger, Miller, Cohen, Sofka, & Borkovec, 1990), and interpreting events in the worst possible light. Thus, someone with GAD can seem focused on threats, distracted, pessimistic, unable to make decisions, and overly reassurance seeking.

Somatic symptoms of GAD, such as restlessness, being keyed up or on edge, fatigue, difficulty concentrating, irritability, muscle tension, and sleep disturbance (three of six are required for diagnosis), are also likely to make being in the presence of a worrier unpleasant. Anecdotally, such individuals can have intermittent outbursts of anger over seemingly minor events, such as depicted in a client's spontaneous self-description during a therapy session:

> I've felt that all my life I've had a lot of anger. For example, there is a neighborhood family with dogs, and this was like the third or fourth time a dog was loose. And these dogs come bounding after you . . . and I'm afraid to get bitten. Not that I ever have been bitten, but I sort of expect that kind of behavior from a dog I don't know. And this was extremely irritating because you're supposed to keep them in a fenced-in area or tied up or something. So I was really angry, and on top of that, this dog kept circling around and walking in front of me for about a quarter of a mile before one of the owners came jogging by and tried to take the dog back home. And he laughed it off. And I was so mad I was afraid I would say something that I would regret. But I kept telling myself . . . the fact that they don't want to do what is the right thing is not my responsibility. I want them to do the right thing . . . to keep their dog under control. And I'm actually considering if this happens one more time . . . calling the township and asking what recourse do I have . . . which for me would be an extreme step. I don't like to make waves but they're pushing me to do something that I would consider extreme. (Newman & Borkovec, 2002)

Worry interferes with effective problem solving (Borkovec, Robinson, Pruzinsky, & DePree, 1983). In our own experience, this entails a kind of rigidity toward resolving interpersonal problems. In the preceding anecdote, the client perceived only the extreme options of passively saying nothing versus yelling at the neighbor or calling the authorities rather than politely asking the neighbor whether he would mind keeping his dogs on a leash. Like other disorders, diagnosis of GAD requires impaired functioning. Although GAD has historically been viewed as a mild diagnosis, studies have estimated levels of disability in GAD as comparable to depression and other mood disorders (Grant et al., 2005; Wittchen, Carter, Pfister, Montgomery, & Kessler, 2000) or chronic medical illnesses (Fifer et al., 1994). In one epidemiological study, GAD was associated with disability status, unemployment (around 50%), low occupational work level, and earning less than $10,000 per year (Massion, Warshaw, & Keller, 1993). Making diminished financial contribution to a household may negatively affect interpersonal relationships.

In addition to the impact of GAD on other people, others may influence the development of GAD symptoms. Operant conditioning theories have suggested that positive reinforcement by family members may maintain the disorder by rewarding anxious behavior and facilitating avoidant behaviors (Ayllon, Smith, & Rogers, 1970). Anxious behavior may also be learned by modeling (Bandura & Menlove, 1968). Similarly, early attachment experiences may also play a role in GAD (reviewed later in this chapter). Important others may also influence the course of GAD symptoms. A poor marital relationship predicts the failure to remit from GAD (Yonkers, Dyck, Warshaw, & Keller, 2000), and low marital tension predicts maintained treatment gains and decreased likelihood of relapse from psychodynamic therapy or anxiety management therapy (Durham, Allan, & Hackett, 1997). Similarly, Zinbarg, Lee, and Yoon (2007) found that whereas pretreatment partner hostility predicted lower endstate functioning in response to psychotherapy, nonhostile criticism predicted higher functioning. Taken together, data suggest that GAD symptoms are likely to negatively affect close others and that the quality of relationships influence the development and course of GAD.

ETIOLOGICAL FORMULATIONS AND THEORETICAL MODELS

Given that the primary symptoms of GAD are intrapersonal (e.g., worry, muscle tension), the fact that few theoretical models of GAD or worry explicitly address interpersonal processes is understandable. Here, we briefly review noninterpersonal theoretical models of GAD for their interpersonal implications, as well as an evolving, integrative interpersonal model of GAD.

Noninterpersonal Models

Theoretical models of GAD emphasize intrapersonal factors contributing to the disorder. For instance, specific models posit factors that hypothetically maintain worry, including negative beliefs about, and worry about, worry (Wells, 1995); dispositional intolerance of uncertainty (Dugas, Buhr, & Ladouceur, 2004); perseverative generation of problem solutions and interpreting negative mood as input that goals have not been achieved (Davey, 2006); and worry itself as an emotion-avoidant mental strategy that may prevent individuals from understanding and coping with emotions (Borkovec, Alcaine, & Behar, 2004).

Despite distinctive elements, these theories share several common assumptions, which may bear interpersonal implications. First, several theories of GAD have posited a lack of perceived competence to cope with threats, including poor problem-solving ability, self-efficacy, and stress tolerance. Because interpersonal behavior is a means for regulating emotions (Rimé, 2007) and submissive behavior tends to reflect appeasement or perceived "defeat" in the face of threats rather than a sense of competence (Sloman & Gilbert, 2000), individuals with GAD may overuse submissive behaviors. Second, many theories have proposed that worriers believe worry to possess positive characteristics, including superstitious belief that worry prevents negative outcomes, worry as considering all options in goal pursuit, or worry as reflecting desirable personal characteristics such as high responsibility. In other words, worry may be represented in the mind of the worrier as a protective form of care about goals and outcomes, which may trigger excessive reassurance seeking (Wells, 1995). Such theories imply that worriers "care too much," suggesting that they might also believe they must exhibit caring or affiliative behaviors toward others or perhaps actually predominate in the use of such behaviors.

Last, several of the theories assume that worry serves strategic functions of both preparing for possible threat and suppressing unpleasant emotions. Orientation toward threat might take the interpersonal form of negative social cognitive biases toward others. Likewise, avoidance of emotion might take an interpersonal form. Whereas vulnerable disclosure of emotions contributes to positive relationship development (Collins & Miller, 1994), individuals with GAD appear to find strong emotions aversive and may therefore avoid their own and others' emotional disclosure (Newman, Castonguay, Borkovec, & Molnar, 2004), thereby slowing relationship development. Alternatively, people with GAD might engage in disclosure when required but experience it as threatening, perhaps vacillating in openness across situations. In any event, both interpersonal vigilance and avoidance may contribute to difficulty in accurately interpreting social interactions.

An Interpersonal Model

Whereas other research groups have largely emphasized intrapersonal processes in the development and maintenance of GAD, researchers at Pennsylvania State University have overtly integrated consideration of interpersonal processes into research and theory development. Although this work has involved clinical description (e.g., Newman, 2000), novel psychotherapy integration strategies (Newman et al., 2004), or exploratory empirical studies (see the Research Review section) rather than a systematized formal theory, recent theorizing informed by attachment perspectives has begun to crystallize an interpersonal model of etiology and maintenance.

Such a model begins with Bowlby's (1973) theory that infants form generalized, implicit mental representations (i.e., internal working models) of their caregivers with regard to their availability and care, as well as the ability of the self to handle challenges. According to Bowlby, caregivers failing to provide a secure base may decrease the likelihood that an infant will autonomously engage in exploration and gain self-confidence, potentially leading to insecure attachment and diffuse anxious states. GAD may arise, in part, from experiences in which caregivers are inconsistently available, creating negative working models and pulling the child into a developmentally premature state of needing to take care of the caregiver, him- or herself, or both. In this context, negative interpersonal working models, worry, and social behaviors (e.g., caretaking) may develop to help the infant or child cope with a potentially dangerous world while lacking consistent support. Therefore, worry and anxiety may be maintained not only by negative reinforcement (i.e., worry as an emotion avoidance strategy) but also by generalized negative social expectations and interpersonal strategies that fail to meet individuals' needs.

Interpersonal Theory as a Conceptual Framework

The foregoing models of GAD may be further systematized under the rubric of interpersonal theory, which asserts that interpersonal processes shape and maintain psychopathology (Horowitz, 2004), as well as the associated nomological framework of the interpersonal circumplex (IPC; Wiggins, 1982). The IPC organizes the interpersonal content of individuals' behavior or traits according to the orthogonal dimensions of dominance (vs. submission) and affiliation (vs. coldness–detachment). Also, any combination of these two dimensions may be assessed, yielding blends of social behaviors (e.g., warm–submission, cold–dominance). Constructs such as interpersonal control and influence pertain to the dominance dimension, whereas warmth and social connection map onto the affiliation dimension. IPC dimensions also capture information about attachment style (Bartholomew & Horowitz, 1991), with secure and insecure attachment relating most directly to the affiliation dimension (Pincus, Dickinson, Schut, Castonguay, & Bedics, 1999; see also Chapter 1, this volume).

The IPC serves as a framework on which to operationalize social developmental hypotheses. Although not denying the contribution of temperament or genetic factors, interpersonal theorists have contended that early relationships shape later self-definitions and expectations for others. Additionally, social behavior is thought to influence others via the process known as interpersonal complementarity: Specific social behaviors invite restricted sets of responses from others in a probabilistic fashion. Thus, perceived dominance invites another to submit, whereas perceived submission invites dominance; warmth invites warmth (closeness) and coldness, coldness (Sadler & Woody, 2003); warm–dominance pulls for warm–submission, and so forth. According to this principle, people viewing their parents as cold and dominant might assume a detached and yielding stance toward them; according to the sociodevelopmental "copy process" that Benjamin (2003) termed *recapitulation*, the youth might come to act as though significant others are still present, acting in this cold–submissive stance toward others. However, other patterns exist, such as *antithesis* (e.g., when one responds to coldness with affiliation to elicit a warmer response) or *identification* (e.g., imitating cold–dominance). In other words, complementarity is a "request" that may be denied, not a mechanistic process (Horowitz, 2004). Samples of one's behavior, rather than knowledge of parents' behavior, are necessary to predict interpersonal patterns (e.g., abused children may learn to expect others to be abusive, become abusers, take the opposite extreme of rigid affiliativeness, or none of these; Benjamin, 2003); thus, we expect some heterogeneity in the interpersonal styles of individuals with GAD.

In addition to developmental considerations, interpersonal theory speaks to the maintenance of psychopathology via interactional processes. Specifically, problematic social expectations or perceptions lead to dysfunctional behaviors (often in complementary fashion). In turn, behaviors affect others and elicit responses that confirm initial expectations in a self-fulfilling fashion. This bidirectional social influence between individuals underscores the notion of maladaptive feedback loops that maintain pathology (Carson, 1991; Safran & Segal, 1990).

Viewed from this framework, the previously mentioned noninterpersonal models and the attachment-based interpersonal model of GAD may jointly predict several processes, such as perceiving one's caregiver as being on the cold side of the circumplex (e.g., unavailable or inconsistent), subsequent chronic tendencies toward perceiving others as cold (and therefore inaccurate social cognition), and some form of social behavior that might elicit negative responses of others. These behaviors might alternatively take cold forms (according to the principle of interpersonal complementarity), yielding submission to avoid conflict or affiliative forms of caretaking behavior as a way to "pull" parents or others out of cold stances.

RESEARCH REVIEW FOR INTERPERSONAL ONSET AND MAINTENANCE OF GAD

For interpersonal processes to contribute to the onset and maintenance of GAD, we might expect to find the sort of systematic relations between family experiences, social perceptions, ensuing behaviors, and interpersonal consequences outlined earlier. Here, we review available research, starting with findings relevant to the interpersonal factors in the development of GAD.

Social Developmental Factors in GAD

Several studies have associated GAD with self-reported negative developmental experiences. For instance, chronic worry and GAD have been respectively linked to endorsing a history of traumatic events such as catastrophes to significant others (Roemer, Molina, Litz, & Borkovec, 1996) and loss of a parent before age 16 (Torgersen, 1986). Family conflict may contribute to GAD onset as well. In one study, parent-rated poor marital relationship predicted lifetime prevalence of GAD in the children (Wade, Bulik, & Kendler, 2001). A history of a disturbed home environment is particularly pronounced in GAD with onset before age 20 (Hoehn-Saric, Hazlett, & McLeod, 1993). Unstable home environments and loss of significant others may teach one that the world is unsafe and that bad things can happen unexpectedly.

With regard to memories about one's childhood relationship to parents, when compared with nonanxious control participants, children and adolescents with high worry, GAD, or both have reported perceiving their caregivers as more cold, rejecting, and neglectful (i.e., low affiliation), as well as more controlling and overprotective and as granting less autonomy (e.g., high dominance; Cassidy, Lichtenstein-Phelps, Sibrava, Thomas, & Borkovec, 2009; Eng & Heimberg, 2006; Hale, Engels, & Meeus, 2006; León & León, 1990). Although perceiving caregivers as high in "affectionless control" is not unique to GAD, there exists some evidence that the link to GAD may be stronger than for other disorders (e.g., panic disorder; Silove et al.,1991), and it holds even when accounting for most other disorders (Kendler et al., 2000). Also, mothers of children with GAD were viewed as more controlling and overprotective than mothers of children with oppositional defiant disorder (Nordahl, Ingul, Nordvik, & Wells, 2007). Individuals with GAD report insecure attachment (Eng & Heimberg, 2006), with some endorsing role reversal and enmeshment in their early relationships with caregivers, believing that they need to take responsibility for the needs of their parents (Cassidy, 1995). Another study found that an angry–dismissive attachment style, associated with excessive self-reliance, anger, and mistrust of others, predicted new onset of GAD episodes when compared with panic disorder, major depression, and social phobia (Bifulco et al., 2006). Thus, many individuals with GAD experienced their parents as unaffiliative and dominant–controlling in an IPC framework, but there appears to be heterogeneity in how they coped interpersonally in response (e.g., taking overly warm vs. dismissive stances).

The literature has built a cumulative case for the role of problematic childhood family experiences in the development of GAD. However, the fact that anxiety disorders in children were linked to high maternal involvement (i.e., dominance dimension) in Australia, but low maternal involvement in Korea (Oh, Shin, Moon, Hudson, & Rapee, 2002) suggests that the developmental implications of parent behavior may be moderated by whether one's upbringing takes place in an individualistic or a collectivistic culture.

Interpersonal Factors That May Maintain GAD

A model of GAD informed by interpersonal theory must incorporate not only dysfunctional social experiences during childhood but also the social cognition and concomitant interpersonal behaviors that may perpetuate maladaptive cycles and maintain or exacerbate symptoms. Ample evidence has documented such processes in adults with GAD or chronic worry.

In terms of social cognition, people with GAD worry predominantly about interpersonal concerns over other topics (Breitholtz, Johansson, & Öst, 1995; Roemer, Molina, & Borkovec, 1997), endorse heightened interpersonal sensitivity (Gasperini, Battaglia, Diaferia, & Bellodi, 1990; Hoehn-Saric et al., 1993; Mavissakalian, Hamann, Haidar, & de Groot, 1995; Nisita et al., 1990), and display negatively biased perceptions of social information (Mathews & MacLeod, 1985; Mogg, Mathews, & Eysenck, 1992). Similarly, trait worry has predicted a bias toward perceiving others' behaviors as cold (Erickson & Newman, 2009), and students with GAD symptoms perceived confederates during social interaction as less affiliative and more attacking, ignoring, and controlling than did control students (Erickson & Pincus, 2005).

Whereas a number of studies have demonstrated social cognition biased toward threatening meanings, one study found biases in students with GAD symptoms both toward and away from threatening perceptions. Relative to control students, students with GAD either over- or underestimated the extent of their negative (hostile–submissive) impact on others (Erickson & Newman, 2007a). It is unclear whether such biases reflect distinct subgroups of worriers who are vigilant versus naïve to negative impact on others or whether vigilance and avoidance occur within the same individual, with potential vacillation between these motivations. Whereas one study failed to find significant vacillation in worriers' social perceptions across a week of interactions (Erickson & Newman, 2009), another study found that students with GAD symptoms endorsed conflict between viewing interaction partners as controlling versus ignoring as well as between controlling themselves versus granting themselves autonomy (Erickson & Pincus, 2005).

According to an interpersonal cycle model of GAD maintenance, problematic social cognition would naturally lead to problematic interpersonal behaviors. Indeed, students with GAD symptoms (Eng & Heimberg, 2006; Erickson & Newman, 2009) and individuals diagnosed with GAD (Salzer et al., 2008) endorse high levels of interpersonal problems—extreme and rigid versions of normal behaviors (e.g., exploitability as extreme warm–submissiveness).

The majority of interpersonal problems in GAD occur on the warm half of the circumplex. For instance, about half of individuals with GAD in a U.S. sample were classified as having predominant warm problems with being intrusive (e.g., excessive caretaking and pleasing others) or exploitable (overly accommodating; Kasoff & Pincus, 2002); two thirds of a German GAD sample endorsed the same problems (Salzer et al., 2008). Relative to controls, students with self-reported GAD have endorsed more problems with being relatively self-sacrificing, overly accommodating, intrusive, and nonassertive (Eng & Heimberg, 2006); higher warm personality traits and lower dominant and arrogant/cold–dominant traits (cold–dominance; Erickson & Newman, 2009); and higher empathy for others' pain (Peasley, Molina, & Borkovec, 1994), and they have exhibited greater sad affect in response to others' emotional disclosure (Erickson & Newman, 2007a). Also, trait worry predicted higher affiliation and lower quarrelsomeness in naturalistic interactions (Erickson & Newman, 2009).

In contrast, those with GAD have also endorsed elevated anger and hostility (Nisita et al., 1990), as well as ongoing interpersonal conflicts (Judd et al., 1998), suggesting that despite excessively affiliative behavior, they may also display problematic cold behaviors. Similarly, a subset of GAD clients endorsed predominant interpersonal problems related to vindictiveness or coldness (Kasoff & Pincus, 2002; Salzer et al., 2008). Such findings have provided further evidence for interpersonal subgroups with GAD. However, the social behavior of individuals high in worry may also vacillate across situations; when participants were asked about most likely responses to a range of specific interpersonal situations, trait worry predicted variability (standard deviation scores) between affiliative and cold behavior (Erickson & Newman, 2007b). Anger often occurs in response to thwarted interpersonal goals (Horowitz, 2004), so these individuals may be easily angered when affiliation goals are blocked or when caretaking behavior is not reciprocated. We note also that a subset of GAD patients have reported excessive submissiveness or nonassertion (Kasoff & Pincus, 2002; Salzer et al., 2008). Available data have clearly attested to interpersonal problems in GAD, as have substantial rates of personality pathology in GAD (reviewed later in this chapter).

Available research has also indicated problems with intimate relationships (Newman, 2000). Although individuals with GAD are more likely to enter into a marriage or similar relationship (Yoon & Zinbarg, 2007), they are also more likely to be unmarried currently, to have experienced multiple divorces, and to endorse poor marital relationship quality and conflict compared with those from other psychiatric groups (Blazer, Hughes, George, Swartz, & Boyer, 1991; Hunt, Issakidis, & Andrews, 2002; Wittchen, Zhao, Kessler, & Eaton, 1994). Moreover, in a sample of 4,933 married couples, marital discord was independently and more strongly associated with GAD than with major depression, mania, dysthymia, social phobia, simple phobia, agoraphobia, panic, and alcohol dependence after controlling for demographic variables, comorbid disorders, and quality of other relationships (Whisman,

Sheldon, & Goering, 2000). Individuals with early-onset GAD are particularly likely to endorse marital dysfunction (Hoehn-Saric et al., 1993). Additionally, parents with GAD have higher rates of dysfunctional relationships with their spouses and children compared with parents without GAD (Ben-Noun, 1998). GAD also predicted a lack of close friendships (Whisman et al., 2000).

In sum, robust linkages have been found between GAD or worry and impaired interpersonal processes. Such impairment includes distress about relationships, biased social cognition, problematic social behavior (especially overnurturance and submissiveness, but also potential heterogeneity), personality pathology, and problems maintaining satisfying relationships.

INTERPERSONAL PROCESSES AND COMORBIDITY

Clearly, a wealth of studies buttress the case for a link between GAD, worry, and interpersonal dysfunction. However, the specificity of this link remains uncertain because of frequent psychiatric comorbidity. As such, we review data on the nature of comorbidity in GAD and discuss which interpersonal processes may be specific to GAD and chronic worry.

Comorbidity in GAD is quite high. For example, rates of concurrent anxiety disorder diagnoses can be as high as 83% (Yonkers, Warshaw, Massion, & Keller, 1996), most often with social phobia (e.g., Brown & Barlow, 1992; Newman, Przeworski, Fisher, & Borkovec, 2008). Mood disorders including unipolar and bipolar depression and dysthymic disorder are commonly comorbid as well (e.g., Garyfallos et al., 1999), with lifetime prevalence rates for comorbid mood disorder around 80% (Garyfallos et al., 1999; Judd et al., 1998). Moreover, personality disorders (prima facie indicators of interpersonal dysfunction) commonly co-occur with GAD, with rates ranging from 37% to 53% (Mavissakalian et al., 1995; Sanderson, Wetzler, Beck, & Betz, 1994); rates of personality pathology are higher in GAD compared with other anxiety disorders (Blashfield et al., 1994; Dyck et al., 2001; Reich et al., 1994; Sanderson, Beck, & McGinn, 1994). Moreover, Axis II pathology predicted greater odds of GAD in an epidemiological survey (Nestadt, Romanoski, Samuels, Folstein, & McHugh, 1992).

Because disorders linked to interpersonal problems are highly comorbid with GAD, the question of specificity of interpersonal processes to GAD becomes salient. Particular interpersonal processes may increase risk for onset of new comorbid diagnoses; conversely, new comorbid diagnoses may influence interpersonal processes. Although existing studies make disentangling these causal relations difficult, some exceptions exist, such as reassurance seeking as a risk factor for depression but not anxiety (Joiner & Schmidt,

1998). We found no studies that directly tested whether interpersonal processes in people with GAD influence the development of comorbidity. Furthermore, most studies have not investigated "pure" GAD or statistically controlled for symptoms related to commonly comorbid conditions.

Nonetheless, a few studies have spoken to the specificity of links between GAD and interpersonal processes. Whereas a significant number of individuals with GAD without secondary mood disorder endorse significant interpersonal conflicts, this percentage increases with the presence of comorbid depression and further with bipolar disorders (Judd et al., 1998). The link between GAD and marital discord remains even after accounting for comorbidity and quality of other relationships (Whisman et al., 2000). Also, GAD is more strongly linked to vigilance toward threatening faces (Mogg, Millar, & Bradley, 2000), interpersonal sensitivity, and anger–hostility (Nisita et al., 1990) than is depression.

Studies with nonclinical samples have also shown some interpersonal specificity. Erickson and Newman (2009) found that pathological worry, social anxiety, and depression symptoms all robustly correlated with most types of self-reported interpersonal problems. However, after controlling for social anxiety and depression, worry (a) correlated with problems of being exploitable, overly nurturant, or submissive; (b) correlated positively with warm interpersonal traits and inversely with arrogant and cold traits; (c) predicted greater affiliative behavior and less quarrelsome behavior during a week of naturalistic social interactions; (d) predicted a bias toward cold social perceptions; and (e) predicted modestly increased fluctuation on the affiliation dimension. Last, the link between pathological worry and inaccurate estimation of one's interpersonal impact on others appears to remain even when accounting for social anxiety (Erickson & Newman, 2007a).

Therefore, even without comorbidity, GAD symptoms are linked to specific interpersonal processes. To conjecture, perhaps many of these individuals are prone to affiliative caretaking behavior but become colder when such strategies fail to elicit desired responses. Childhood temperament factors such as behavioral inhibition and interpersonal sensitivity may also contribute to the use of submissive–nonassertive behavior to regulate discomfort with novel or stressful social interactions, contributing to the etiology of both GAD and social anxiety. Furthermore, the use of submissive behaviors likely places one at further risk for later depressive episodes because submission tends to reflect passive and unempowered states (vs. self-efficacy and assertiveness). These formulations are consistent with what is known about the chronic, traitlike, and early-onset symptoms of social and general anxiety, as well as their temporal precedence to depression. However, such notions remain speculative and await further tests, particularly given findings of interpersonal heterogeneity in social phobia (Kachin, Newman, & Pincus, 2001), depression (Blatt & Zuroff, 1992), and GAD (Salzer et al., 2008). Nonetheless, comorbid mood and anxiety disorders contribute additional distress and disability to the course of GAD (e.g., Judd et al., 1998; Mancuso, Townsend, & Mercante, 1993), although not universally (Yonkers et al., 2000).

GAD and its commonly comorbid Axis I disorders (e.g., major depression and social phobia) are also among the Axis I disorders with which personality disorders are most likely to occur (Dyck et al., 2001). As a result, sorting out unique interpersonal processes in this morass of comorbidity is intractable at present. Comorbid personality disorders predict decreased likelihood of remission in GAD (Massion et al., 2002; Yonkers et al., 2000), in some cases even after accounting for the effect of depression (Yonkers et al., 2000). If we consider that personality disorders simply reflect traitlike, excessive, and rigid interpersonal problems, specific interpersonal styles may predispose individuals with GAD to particular personality disorders. Particular personality disorders map onto specific interpersonal problems on the IPC (e.g., submissiveness with avoidant personality disorder; Soldz, Budman, Demby, & Merry, 1993). Because of links between social phobia and avoidant personality disorder (e.g., Dyck et al., 2001), it is unclear whether problems with submissiveness occur only in individuals with both GAD and social phobia, but not GAD alone. Alternatively, the traitlike constellations of symptoms in generalized anxiety, social phobia, and personality disorder may develop in tandem. Ultimately, it is likely that maladaptive interpersonal processes lead to additional forms of comorbidity in GAD, and comorbidity in turn likely contributes to further interpersonal problems (Judd et al., 1998), consistent with the transactional view of psychopathology described in interpersonal theory.

INTERPERSONAL PROCESSES AND IMPLICATIONS FOR TREATMENT

Cognitive–behavioral therapy (CBT) for GAD produces significant improvement maintained up to 2 years posttreatment, with effects stronger than no treatment, analytic psychotherapy, pill placebo, nondirective therapy, and placebo therapy (Borkovec & Newman, 1998). However, CBT is not efficacious for all clients and leads to the smallest percentage of high end-state functioning among CBT interventions for anxiety disorders (Brown, Barlow, & Liebowitz, 1994). One explanatory hypothesis is that CBT protocols have not included techniques to address factors maintaining GAD such as interpersonal problems.

Consistent with this hypothesis, data have suggested that current CBT protocols are limited in successfully addressing interpersonal issues in GAD. Interpersonal factors such as marital tension (Durham et al., 1997) and comorbid personality disorders (Mancuso et al., 1993; Massion et al., 2002; Sanderson, Wetzler, et al., 1994) have predicted negative CBT treatment outcomes, higher drop-out rates, or diminished likelihood of GAD remission. Also, Borkovec, Newman, Pincus, and Lytle (2002) found that CBT failed to make a significant change in six of eight Inventory of Interpersonal Problems—Circumplex scales at posttherapy, and most clients continued to score at least 1 standard deviation above normative levels on at least one Inventory of Interpersonal Problems—Circumplex subscale. In the same study, clients endorsing pretherapy interpersonal problems associated with dominance (e.g., domineering–controlling, intrusive–needy, vindictive–self-centered) responded least favorably to CBT, and such problems left untreated predicted failure to maintain follow-up gains. Such evidence warrants therapy techniques to specifically address interpersonal problems, including the client's contribution to maintaining maladaptive ways of relating with others.

We are aware of only two research groups that have examined the impact of interpersonally focused therapy on GAD outcome. Crits-Christoph, Crits-Christoph, Wolf Palacio, Fichter, and Rudick (1995) examined a psychodynamically informed brief therapy based on Luborsky's (1984) supportive–expressive therapy. Reasons for standardizing and testing a GAD treatment for psychodynamic practitioners included (a) the fact that dynamic therapy continues to be a commonly practiced form of treatment (Jensen, Bergin, & Greaves, 1990); (b) the goal to facilitate wider dissemination of efficacious GAD treatments; and (c) theories about anxiety in the writings of Freud, Sullivan, Klein, and Kohut.

These researchers tailored Luborsky's (1984) general supportive–expressive (SE) treatment explicitly to clients with GAD (Crits-Christoph et al., 1995). The goal of the treatment was to help clients understand their anxiety symptoms in the context of interpersonal conflicts. Therapists' interventions were based on their formulations of clients' interpersonal conflicts using the core conflictual relationship theme method, which involves uncovering clients' relationship patterns in current and past relationships as well as their relationship with the therapist. Clients thereby work through relationship conflicts influencing their anxiety symptoms and explore more adaptive coping strategies. This treatment also emphasizes the development and maintenance of a positive therapeutic alliance, discussion of impending treatment termination in the context of the patients' core conflictual relationship theme, interpretation of primitive wishes, interpretation of resistances and defenses, and working with issues related to past traumas (for more information on this therapy approach, see Crits-Christoph et al., 1995).

Crits-Christoph and colleagues conducted two preliminary studies of SE therapy for GAD. The first was an open trial of 26 GAD patients (Crits-Christoph, Connolly, Azarian, Crits-Christoph, & Shappell, 1996), which found significant improvements in GAD symptoms over 16 weeks, with treatment effect sizes on primary outcome measures comparable to studies of CBT for GAD ($d = 1.9$ for the Beck Anxiety Inventory). These promising results led to a follow-up study comparing interpersonally oriented dynamic therapy ($n = 15$) to a supportive listening therapy condition ($n = 16$) previously used by the Pennsylvania State University research group to control for time in therapy and contact with a therapist. The interpersonal approach was statistically and clinically superior to supportive therapy on Hamilton Anxiety Scale remission rates, but with substantial variability in outcomes (Crits-Christoph, Gibbons, Narducci, Schamberger, & Gallop, 2005). Moreover, within-group effect sizes for the interpersonal group (0.93 for the Beck Anxiety Inventory) were not impressive compared with average within-group effect sizes for CBT studies of GAD (typically about 2.0). Thus, SE therapy may work best for patients with interpersonal issues at the core of their GAD symptoms, whereas supportive therapy provides some minimal benefit to all patients.

Additional analyses examined whether interpersonal problems changed in response to SE therapy and whether there was a subgroup of clients who did better in interpersonally focused GAD therapy (Crits-Christoph et al., 2005). SE therapy led to only modest pretest to posttest changes in interpersonal problems (Inventory of Interpersonal Problems—Circumplex scales), not significantly different from the supportive therapy condition. Nonetheless, interpersonal problems predicted unique variance in outcome (Crits-Christoph et al., 2004). Also, problems of nonassertion and exploitability tended to change the most, whereas problems in dominant, cold, and vindictive domains changed least; changes in interpersonal problems were correlated with changes in GAD symptoms (Crits-Christoph et al., 2005). Thus, these researchers concluded that SE therapy provides some benefit for clients with GAD who have problems with being assertive or easily exploitable.

Our Penn State research group has adopted a different approach to a psychotherapy that targets interpersonal problems. We decided to develop an integrative therapy that would combine our previously tested CBT protocol (e.g., Borkovec & Costello, 1993; Borkovec et al., 2002) with additional techniques aimed at addressing interpersonal issues and emotional deepening (Newman et al., 2004).

Our intervention is based on Safran and Segal's (1990) focus on complex interpersonal issues within an integrative CBT perspective. Guided by theorists such as Sullivan, Kiesler, and Bowlby, Safran has argued that early relationships with caregivers create interpersonal schemata, which determine individuals' perception of others and guide interpersonal behaviors in self-confirming ways. Such a model provides an especially comprehensive and coherent integration of cognitive, interpersonal, and emotional issues. However, in tailoring this treatment to GAD, the interpersonal and emotional processing (I-EP) segment of therapy targets interpersonal problems and facilitates emotional deepening without direct integration of cognitive techniques. Cognitive techniques were not integrated into the treatment partly on the basis of research suggesting that verbal linguistic cognitive processes interfere with emotional processing (Vrana, Cuthbert, & Lang, 1986) and help people with GAD avoid emotions (Borkovec & Newman, 1998). We therefore assumed that the examination and challenge of worry during this segment would hinder fostering of emotional processing at the core of I-EP.

In fact, each session of the integrative treatment was composed of two separate components: a CBT segment, followed by an I-EP segment (each 55 minutes long). Separation of CBT from I-EP also permitted the use of an additive–dismantling research design to help us determine whether the efficacy of CBT could be improved for GAD (Newman, Castonguay, & Borkovec, 2002). We used an additive strategy to determine whether CBT and I-EP would provide a significant increment in efficacy over CBT plus supportive listening to control for common factors, permitting a rigorous test of the additive benefit of I-EP.

The CBT and I-EP sessions were kept separate but were both presented within a cognitive–behavioral framework to preserve a consistent rationale. For example, an emotional deepening intervention can be viewed as exposure to feared stimuli (i.e., feared emotions; CBT framework). Patients were informed of the separation and prompted to save discussion material for the respective portion of therapy. CBT always preceded I-EP because engaging in alliance rupture repair methods (an interpersonal intervention) was allowed only in the I-EP segments. Thus, if a rupture occurred during CBT, it could be repaired during the next hour, whereas the reverse order could have left a rupture unaddressed for a full week, with potential deleterious effects.

Patients were told that current interpersonal difficulties and failure to access primary emotions are involved in the generation of anxiety and worry. Consequently, the goals of this portion of therapy were (a) identification of interpersonal needs, past and current patterns of interpersonal behavior that attempt to satisfy those needs, and emotional experience that underlies all of these and (b) generation of more effective interpersonal behavior to better satisfy the needs. Therapy made use of four primary and interrelated domains to accomplish these goals: (a) current problems in interpersonal relationships, including the negative impact clients have on others; (b) interpersonal developmental origins (e.g., attachment and trauma experiences) of relationship difficulties; (c) interpersonal patterns and problems (including ruptures in the therapeutic alliance) that emerged in the relationship with the therapist; and (d) emotional processing in the here-and-now of affects associated with these domains. Focus on these four domains was guided by eight principles, including emphasis on phenomenological experience; therapists' use of their emotional experience to identify interpersonal markers; use of the therapeutic relationship to explore affective processes and interpersonal patterns, with therapists assuming responsibility for their role in the interactions; promotion of generalization via exploration of between-session events and provision of homework experiments; detection of alliance ruptures and provision of emotionally corrective experience in their resolution; processing of patients' affective experiencing in relation to past, current, and in-session interpersonal relationships; and use of skill training methods (e.g., assertion, problem solving, communication training, role-playing) to provide more effective interpersonal behaviors to satisfy needs. In I-EP, therapists explicitly identified disaffiliative emotions, attended to their own emotional reactions to patients, and attempted to encourage patients to openly communicate their feelings with a goal of repairing any ruptures.

As opposed to I-EP, the CBT segment was meant to target intrapersonal aspects of anxious experience by the following methods taken directly from Borkovec's past and current CBT protocol:

1. *Applied relaxation and self-control desensitization* involves presentation of the multiple coping-response CBT model and rationale; training in self-monitoring of environmental, somatic, affective, imaginal, and thought (especially worry) cues that trigger anxiety spirals with special emphasis on increasingly early cue detection; external and especially internal cue hierarchy development; slowed diaphragmatic breathing and progressive relaxation (modified over sessions from 16 muscle groups, four muscle groups, four group recall, and counting; Bernstein & Borkovec, 1973); training in cue-controlled and differential relaxation; applied relaxation training; development of coping self-statements to use in response to cues; and employment of self-statements and applied relaxation during formal self-control desensitization imagery for rehearsal of coping responses. Hierarchies for self-control desensitization are constructed from pretherapy assessment information, daily self-monitoring, and in-session discussion with the patient.

2. *Cognitive therapy* (Beck & Emery, 1985) involves presentation of the role of cognition in anxiety; training in self-monitoring of early worry and automatic thought occurrence; identification of cognitive predictions, interpretations, beliefs, assumptions, and core beliefs underlying the threatening nature of events or cues; logical analysis; examination of evidence; labeling of logical errors; decatastrophization; generation of alternative thoughts

and beliefs; early application of these alternatives to daily living; the creation of behavioral experiments to obtain evidence for new beliefs; and use of cognitive perspective shifts learned in cognitive therapy during self-control desensitization rehearsals. Patients also monitor worrisome predictions and their actual, eventual outcomes. Socratic method is emphasized throughout therapy. Information from the pretherapy daily self-monitoring is used to identify crucial thoughts and underlying themes and beliefs.

Our first step in examining the integrative treatment was to conduct an open trial feasibility study (Newman, Castonguay, Borkovec, Fisher, & Nordberg, 2008). Eighteen participants received 14 sessions of CBT plus I-EP therapy and 3 participants (for training and feasibility purposes) received 14 sessions of CBT plus supportive listening (SL). Results showed that the integrative therapy significantly decreased GAD symptomatology, with maintenance of gains up to 1 year after treatment and an effect size higher than the average effect size of CBT for GAD ($d = 3.15$ averaged across the three most commonly used outcome measures for GAD) as well as a previous CBT trial by Borkovec et al. (2002). Results also showed clinically significant change in GAD symptomatology and interpersonal problems with continued gains during the 1-year follow-up. On the basis of these promising results, we conducted a follow-up study, randomly assigning 69 participants to CBT + I-EP or CBT + SL. Results of this study showed significant differences between the two therapies in Dysfunctional Attitude Scale (Weissman, 1979) scores during the follow-up period favoring IEP + CBT (Newman, Castonguay, Fisher, & Borkovec, 2008). Although this scale was originally developed to measure dysfunctional cognitions in depressed participants, a number of studies have found that this scale also reflects the distorted cognitions of individuals diagnosed with Axis II disorders (e.g., Hill et al., 1989). This was consistent with our initial prediction that it would take some time before interpersonal changes would emerge. We are also currently examining treatment moderators to identify subgroups of people who receive greater benefit from our integrative therapy or CBT alone.

CONCLUSION

The clinical vignette presented early in this chapter depicted a man with GAD who generally preferred an interpersonal stance of passivity so as not to make waves; however, he endorsed a tendency to assume responsibility for others' actions (e.g., intrusiveness), leading to anger. In the vignette, he appeared to move from a warm baseline stance to a colder accusatory state in which he considered taking vindictive action but not the warm–dominant approach of assertive yet friendly communication. In our experience, this portrait of individuals with GAD as prone to maladaptive affiliation behaviors (e.g., intrusive caretaking, overly nurturant, or overly accommodating) leading intermittently to resentment and irritability is fairly representative. It also dovetails with the emergent research linking worry, GAD, or both to childhood experiences of premature caretaking resulting from inconsistently available or cold parents, worry about relationships, bias toward negative perceptions of others, problematic social behavior (often involving excessive affiliation), and disrupted close relationships. Although affiliation normally constitutes prosocial, adaptive behavior, excessive affiliation might be differentiated by the motivation involved, as when friendliness is motivated by a strategic, self-protective function rather than a genuine desire to contribute to others' good; the former is less likely to contribute to individual and relational well-being. Despite convergent findings about excessive affiliation, a range of different types of interpersonal problems occurs in GAD and diminishes psychotherapy efficacy, suggesting the need to tailor interventions to specific interpersonal problems. Further research must continue to elucidate interpersonal processes in GAD and refine evidence-based interventions that improve both interpersonal functioning and anxiety symptoms in the lives of people prone to uncontrollable worry.

REFERENCES

Akiskal, H. S. (1998). Toward a definition of generalized anxiety disorder as an anxious temperament type. *Acta Psychiatrica Scandinavica, 393*(Suppl.), 66–73.

American Psychiatric Association. (1994). *Diagnostic and statistical manual of mental disorders* (4th ed.) Washington, DC: American Psychiatric Association.

Ayllon, T., Smith, D., & Rogers, M. (1970). Behavioral management of school phobia. *Journal of Behavior Therapy and Experimental Psychiatry, 1*, 125–138.

Bandura, A., & Menlove, F. L. (1968). Factors determining vicarious extinction of avoidance behavior through symbolic modeling. *Journal of Personality and Social Psychology, 8*, 99–108.

Bartholomew, K., & Horowitz, L. M. (1991). Attachment styles among young adults: A test of a four-category model. *Journal of Personality and Social Psychology, 61*, 226–244.

Beck, A. T., & Emery, G. (1985). *Anxiety disorders and phobias: A cognitive perspective.* New York, NY : Basic Books.

Benjamin, L. S. (2003). *Interpersonal reconstructive therapy: Promoting change in nonresponders.* New York, NY: Guilford Press.

Ben-Noun, L. (1998). Generalized anxiety disorder in dysfunctional families. *Journal of Behavior Therapy and Experimental Psychiatry, 29,* 115–122.

Bernstein, D. A., & Borkovec, T. D. (1973). *Progressive relaxation training.* Champaign, IL: Research Press.

Bifulco, A., Kwon, J., Jacobs, C., Moran, P. M., Bunn, A., & Beer, N. (2006). Adult attachment style as mediator between childhood neglect/abuse and adult depression and anxiety. *Social Psychiatry and Psychiatric Epidemiology, 41,* 796–805.

Bland, R. C., Newman, S. C., & Orn, H. (1997). Help-seeking for psychiatric disorders. *Canadian Journal of Psychiatry, 42,* 935–942.

Blashfield, R., Noyes, R., Reich, J., Woodman, C., Cook, B. L., & Garvey, M. J. (1994). Personality disorder traits in generalized anxiety and panic disorder patients. *Comprehensive Psychiatry, 35,* 329–334.

Blatt, S. J., & Zuroff, D. C. (1992). Interpersonal relatedness and self-definition: Two prototypes for depression. *Clinical Psychology Review, 12,* 527–562.

Blazer, D. G., Hughes, D. C., George, L. K., Swartz, M. S., & Boyer, R. (1991). Generalized anxiety disorder. In L. N. Robins & D. A. Regier (Eds.), *Psychiatric disorders in America: The Epidemiologic Catchment Area study* (pp. 180–203). New York, NY: Free Press.

Borkovec, T. D., Alcaine, O., & Behar, E. S. (2004). Avoidance theory of worry and generalized anxiety disorder. In R. Heimberg, D. Mennin, & C. Turk (Eds.), *Generalized anxiety disorder: Advances in research and practice* (pp. 77–108). New York, NY: Guilford Press.

Borkovec, T. D., & Costello, E. (1993). Efficacy of applied relaxation and cognitive–behavioral therapy in the treatment of generalized anxiety disorder. *Journal of Consulting and Clinical Psychology, 61,* 611–619.

Borkovec, T. D., & Newman, M. G. (1998). Worry and generalized anxiety disorder. In A. S. Bellack & M. Hersen (Series Eds.), & P. Salkovskis (Vol. Ed.), *Comprehensive clinical psychology: Vol. 6. Adults: Clinical formulation and treatment* (pp. 439–459). Oxford, England: Pergamon Press.

Borkovec, T. D., Newman, M. G., Pincus, A. L., & Lytle, R. (2002). A component analysis of cognitive–behavioral therapy for generalized anxiety disorder and the role of interpersonal problems. *Journal of Consulting and Clinical Psychology, 70,* 288–298.

Borkovec, T. D., Robinson, E., Pruzinsky, T., & DePree, J. A. (1983). Preliminary exploration of worry: Some characteristics and processes. *Behaviour Research and Therapy, 21,* 9–16.

Bowlby, J. (1973). *Attachment and loss: Vol. 2. Separation.* New York, NY: Basic Books.

Breitholtz, E., Johansson, B., & Öst, L. G. (1995). Cognitions in generalized anxiety disorder and panic disorder patients: A prospective approach. *Behaviour Research and Therapy, 37,* 533–544.

Brown, T. A., & Barlow, D. H. (1992). Comorbidity among anxiety disorders: Implications for treatment and DSM–IV. *Journal of Consulting and Clinical Psychology, 60*, 835–844.

Brown, T. A., Barlow, D. H., & Liebowitz, M. R. (1994). The empirical basis of generalized anxiety disorder. *American Journal of Psychiatry, 151*, 1272–1280.

Carson, R. C. (1991). *The social-interactional viewpoint.* Elmsford, NY: Pergamon Press.

Cassidy, J. A. (1995). Attachment and generalized anxiety disorder. In D. Cicchetti & S. L. Toth (Eds.), *Emotion, cognition, and representation* (Rochester Symposium on Developmental Psychopathology, Vol. 6, pp. 343–370). Rochester, NY: University of Rochester Press.

Cassidy, J., Lichtenstein-Phelps, J., Sibrava, N. J., Thomas, C. L., & Borkovec, T. D. (2009). Generalized anxiety disorder: Connections with self-reported attachment. *Behavior Therapy, 40*, 23–38.

Collins, N. L., & Miller, L. C. (1994). Self-disclosure and liking: A meta-analytic review. *Psychological Bulletin, 116*, 457–475.

Crits-Christoph, P., Connolly, M. B., Azarian, K., Crits-Christoph, K., & Shappell, S. (1996). An open trial of brief supportive-expressive psychotherapy in the treatment of generalized anxiety disorder. *Psychotherapy, 33*, 418–430.

Crits-Christoph, P., Crits-Christoph, K., Wolf Palacio, D., Fichter, M., & Rudick, D. (1995). Brief supportive-expressive psychodynamic therapy for generalized anxiety disorder. In J. P. Barber (Ed.), *Dynamic therapies for psychiatric disorders: Axis I* (pp. 43–83). New York, NY: Basic Books.

Crits-Christoph, P., Gibbons, M. B. C., Losardo, D., Narducci, J., Schamberger, M., & Gallop, R. (2004). Who benefits from brief psychodynamic therapy for generalized anxiety disorder? *Canadian Journal of Psychoanalysis, 12*, 301–324.

Crits-Christoph, P., Gibbons, M. B. C., Narducci, J., Schamberger, M., & Gallop, R. (2005). Interpersonal problems and the outcome of interpersonally oriented psychodynamic treatment of GAD. *Psychotherapy: Theory, Research, Practice, Training, 42*, 211–224.

Davey, G. C. L. (2006). A mood-as-input account of perseverative worrying. In G. C. L. Davey & A. Wells (Eds.), *Worry and its psychological disorders: Theory, assessment and treatment* (pp. 217–237). Hoboken, NJ: Wiley.

Dugas, M., Buhr, K., & Ladouceur, R. (2004). The role of intolerance of uncertainty in etiology and maintenance. In R. Heimberg, D. Mennin, & C. Turk (Eds.), *Generalized anxiety disorder: Advances in research and practice* (pp. 143–163). New York, NY: Guilford Press.

Durham, R. C., Allan, T., & Hackett, C. A. (1997). On predicting improvement and relapse in generalized anxiety disorder following psychotherapy. *British Journal of Clinical Psychology, 36*, 101–119.

Dyck, I. R., Phillips, K. A., Warshaw, M. G., Dolan, R. T., Shea, M. T., Stout, R. L., . . . Keller, M. B. (2001). Patterns of personality pathology in patients with generalized anxiety disorder, panic disorder with and without agoraphobia, and social phobia. *Journal of Personality Disorders, 15*, 60–71.

Eng, W., & Heimberg, R. G. (2006). Interpersonal correlates of generalized anxiety disorder: Self versus other perception. *Journal of Anxiety Disorders, 20*, 380–387.

Erickson, T. M., & Newman, M. G. (2007a). Interpersonal and emotional processes in generalized anxiety disorder analogues during social interaction tasks. *Behavior Therapy, 38*, 364–377.

Erickson, T. M., & Newman, M. G. (2007b, March). *Predicting cross-situational dysregulation of social behavior: Differential effects of worry, social anxiety, and depressive symptoms.* Paper presented at the 27th annual meeting of the Anxiety Disorders Association of America, St. Louis, MO.

Erickson, T. M., & Newman, M. G. (2009). *Delineating interpersonal correlates of worry, social anxiety, and depressive symptoms.* Manuscript in preparation.

Erickson, T. M., & Pincus, A. L. (2005). Using structural analysis of social behavior (SASB) measures of self- and social perception to give interpersonal meaning to symptoms: Anxiety as an exemplar. *Assessment, 12*, 243–254.

Fifer, S. K., Mathias, S. D., Patrick, D. L., Mazonson, P. D., Lubeck, D. P., & Buesching, D. P. (1994). Untreated anxiety among adult primary care patients in a health maintenance organization. *Archives of General Psychiatry, 51*, 740–750.

Garyfallos, G., Adamopoulou, A., Karastergiou, A., Voikli, M., Milis, V., Donias, S., . . . Parashos, A. (1999). Psychiatric comorbidity in Greek patients with generalized anxiety disorder. *Psychopathology, 32*, 308–318.

Gasperini, M., Battaglia, M., Diaferia, G., & Bellodi, L. (1990). Personality features related to generalized anxiety disorder. *Comprehensive Psychiatry, 31*, 363–368.

Grant, B. F., Hasin, D. S., Stinson, F. S., Dawson, D. A., Chou, S. P., June Ruan, W., & Huang, B. (2005). Co-occurrence of 12-month mood and anxiety disorders and personality disorders in the US: Results from the National Epidemiologic Survey on Alcohol and Related Conditions. *Journal of Psychiatric Research, 39*, 1–9.

Hale, W. W., III, Engels, R., & Meeus, W. (2006). Adolescent's perceptions of parenting behaviours and its relationship to adolescent generalized anxiety disorder symptoms. *Journal of Adolescence, 29*, 407–417.

Hill, C. V., Oei, T. P., & Hill, M. A. (1989). An empirical investigation of the specificity and sensitivity of the Automatic Thoughts Questionnaire and Dysfunctional Attitudes Scale. *Journal of Psychopathology and Behavioral Assessment, 11*, 291–311.

Hoehn-Saric, R., Hazlett, R. L., & McLeod, D. R. (1993). Generalized anxiety disorder with early and late onset of anxiety symptoms. *Comprehensive Psychiatry, 34*, 291–298.

Horowitz, L. M. (2004). *Interpersonal foundations of psychopathology.* Washington, DC: American Psychological Association.

Hunt, C., Issakidis, C., & Andrews, G. (2002). DSM-IV generalized anxiety disorder in the Australian National Survey of Mental Health and Well-Being. *Psychological Medicine, 32*, 649–659.

Jensen, J. P., Bergin, A. E., & Greaves, D. W. (1990). The meaning of eclecticism: New survey and analysis of components. *Professional Psychology: Research and Practice, 21*, 124–130.

Joiner, T. E., Jr., & Schmidt, N. B. (1998). Excessive reassurance-seeking predicts depressive but not anxious reactions to acute stress. *Journal of Abnormal Psychology, 107*, 533–537.

Judd, L. L., Kessler, R. C., Paulus, M. P., Zeller, P. V., Wittchen, H. U., & Kunovac, J. L. (1998). Comorbidity as a fundamental feature of generalized anxiety disorders: Results from the National Comorbidity Study (NCS). *Acta Psychiatrica Scandanavica, 98*(Suppl. 393), 6–11.

Kachin, K. E., Newman, M. G., & Pincus, A. L. (2001). An interpersonal problem approach to the division of social phobia subtypes. *Behavior Therapy, 32*, 479–501.

Kasoff, M. B., & Pincus, A. L. (2002, August). *Interpersonal pathoplasticity in generalized anxiety disorder*. Paper presented at the 110th Annual Convention of the American Psychological Association, Chicago, IL.

Kendler, K. S., Myers, J., & Prescott, C. A. (2000). Parenting and adult mood, anxiety and substance use disorders in female twins: An epidemiological, multi-informant, retrospective study. *Psychological Medicine, 30*, 281–294.

León, C. A., & León, A. (1990). Panic disorder and parental bonding. *Psychiatric Annals, 20*, 503–508.

Luborsky, L. (1984). *Principles of psychoanalytic psychotherapy: A manual for supportive-expressive treatment*. New York, NY: Basic Books.

Mancuso, D. M., Townsend, M. H., & Mercante, D. E. (1993). Long-term follow-up of generalized anxiety disorder. *Comprehensive Psychiatry, 34*, 441–446.

Masi, G., Millepiedi, S., Mucci, M., Poli, P., Bertini, N., & Milantoni, L. (2004). Generalized anxiety disorder in referred children and adolescents. *Journal of the American Academy of Child & Adolescent Psychiatry, 43*, 752–760.

Massion, A. O., Dyck, I. R., Shea, M. T., Phillips, K. A., Warshaw, M. G., & Keller, M. B. (2002). Personality disorders and time to remission in generalized anxiety disorder, social phobia, and panic disorder. *Archives of General Psychiatry, 59*, 434–440.

Massion, A. O., Warshaw, M. G., & Keller, M. B. (1993). Quality of life and psychiatric morbidity in panic disorder and generalized anxiety disorder. *American Journal of Psychiatry, 150*, 600–607.

Mathews, A., & MacLeod, C. (1985). Selective processing of threat cues in anxiety states. *Behaviour Research and Therapy, 23*, 563–569.

Mavissakalian, M. R., Hamann, M. S., Haidar, S. A., & de Groot, C. M. (1995). Correlates of DSM–III personality disorder in generalized anxiety disorder. *Journal of Anxiety Disorders, 9*, 103–115.

Metzger, R. L., Miller, M. L., Cohen, M., Sofka, M., & Borkovec, T. D. (1990). Worry changes decision making: The effect of negative thoughts on cognitive processing. *Journal of Clinical Psychology, 46*, 78–88.

Mogg, K., Mathews, A., & Eysenck, M. (1992). Attentional bias to threat in clinical anxiety states. *Cognition & Emotion, 6*, 149–159.

Mogg, K., Millar, N., & Bradley, B. P. (2000). Biases in eye movements to threatening facial expressions in generalized anxiety disorder and depressive disorder. *Journal of Abnormal Psychology, 109*, 695–704.

Nestadt, G., Romanoski, A. J., Samuels, J. F., Folstein, M. F., & McHugh, P. R. (1992). The relationship between personality and *DSM–III* Axis I disorders in the population: Results from an epidemiological survey. *American Journal of Psychiatry, 149*, 1228–1233.

Newman, M. G. (2000). Recommendations for a cost-offset model of psychotherapy allocation using generalized anxiety disorder as an example. *Journal of Consulting and Clinical Psychology, 68*, 549–555.

Newman, M. G., & Borkovec, T. D. (2002). [Transcript of cognitive–behavioral therapy session with a client with generalized anxiety disorder.] Unpublished therapy transcript.

Newman, M. G., Castonguay, L. G., & Borkovec, T. D. (2002, June). *Integrating cognitive-behavioral and interpersonal/emotional processing treatments for generalized anxiety disorder: Preliminary outcome findings.* Paper presented at the 33rd annual meeting of the Society for Psychotherapy Research, Santa Barbara, CA.

Newman, M. G., Castonguay, L. G., Borkovec, T. D., Fisher, A. J., & Nordberg, S. S. (2008). An open trial of integrative therapy for generalized anxiety disorder. *Psychotherapy: Theory, Research, Practice, Training, 45*, 135–147.

Newman, M. G., Castonguay, L. G., Borkovec, T. D., & Molnar, C. (2004). Integrative psychotherapy. In R. G. Heimberg, C. L. Turk, & D. S. Mennin (Eds.), *Generalized anxiety disorder: Advances in research and practice* (pp. 320–350). New York, NY: Guilford Press.

Newman, M. G., Castonguay, L. G., Fisher, A. J., & Borkovec, T. D. (2008). A *randomized controlled trial of interpersonal and emotional processing focused treatment in generalized anxiety disorder.* Paper presented at the 39th annual meeting of the Society for Psychotherapy Research, Barcelona, Spain.

Newman, M. G., Przeworski, A., Fisher, A. J., & Borkovec, T. D. (2009). *Diagnostic comorbidity in adults with generalized anxiety disorder: Impact of comorbidity on psychotherapy outcome and impact of psychotherapy on comorbid diagnoses.* Manuscript submitted for publication.

Nisita, C., Petracca, A., Akiskal, H. S., Galli, L., Gepponi, I., & Cassano, G. B. (1990). Delimitation of generalized anxiety disorder: Clinical comparisons with panic and major depressive disorders. *Comprehensive Psychiatry, 31*, 409–415.

Nordahl, H. M., Ingul, J. M., Nordvik, H., & Wells, A. (2007). Does maternal psychopathology discriminate between children with *DSM–IV* generalised anxiety disorder or oppositional defiant disorder? The predictive validity of maternal Axis I and Axis II psychopathology. *European Child & Adolescent Psychiatry, 16*, 87–95.

Oh, K. J., Shin, Y. J., Moon, K. J., Hudson, J. L., & Rapee, R. M. (2002). Child-rearing practices and psychological disorders in children: Cross-cultural comparison of Korea and Australia. *Yonsei Medical Journal, 43*, 411–419.

Peasley, C. E., Molina, S., & Borkovec, T. D. (1994, November). *Empathy in generalized anxiety disorder*. Paper presented at the 28th annual meeting of the Association for Advancement of Behavior Therapy, San Diego, CA.

Pincus, A. L., Dickinson, K. A., Schut, A. J., Castonguay, L. G., & Bedics, J. (1999). Integrating interpersonal assessment and adult attachment using SASB. *European Journal of Psychological Assessment, 15*, 206–220.

Reich, J., Perry, J. C., Shera, D., Dyck, I., Vasile, R., Goisman, R. M., . . . Keller, M. B. (1994). Comparison of personality disorders in different anxiety disorder diagnoses: Panic, agoraphobia, generalized anxiety, and social phobia. *Annals of Clinical Psychiatry, 6*, 125–134.

Rimé, B. (2007). Interpersonal emotion regulation. In J. J. Gross (Ed.), *Handbook of emotion regulation* (pp. 466–485). New York, NY: Guilford Press.

Roemer, L., Molina, S., & Borkovec, T. D. (1997). An investigation of worry content among generally anxious individuals. *Journal of Nervous and Mental Disease, 185*, 314–319.

Roemer, L., Molina, S., Litz, B. T., & Borkovec, T. D. (1996). Preliminary investigation of the role of previous exposure to potentially traumatizing events in generalized anxiety disorder. *Depression and Anxiety, 4*, 134–138.

Sadler, P., & Woody, E. (2003). Is who you are who you're talking to? Interpersonal style and complementarity in mixed-sex interactions. *Journal of Personality and Social Psychology, 84*, 80–95.

Safran, J. D., & Segal, Z. V. (1990). *Interpersonal process in cognitive therapy*. New York, NY: Basic Books.

Salzer, S., Pincus, A. L., Hoyer, J., Kreische, R., Leichsenring, F., & Leibing, E. (2008). Interpersonal subtypes within generalized anxiety disorder. *Journal of Personality Assessment, 90*, 292–299.

Sanderson, W. C., Beck, A. T., & McGinn, L. K. (1994). Cognitive therapy for generalized anxiety disorder: Significance of comorbid personality disorders. *Journal of Cognitive Psychotherapy, 8*, 13–18.

Sanderson, W. C., Wetzler, S., Beck, A. T., & Betz, F. (1994). Prevalence of personality disorders among patients with anxiety disorders. *Psychiatry Research, 51*, 167–174.

Silove, D., Parker, G., Hadzi Pavlovic, D., Manicavasagar, V., & Blaszczynski, A. (1991). Parental representations of patients with panic disorder and generalised anxiety disorder. *British Journal of Psychiatry, 159*, 835–841.

Sloman, L., & Gilbert, P. (2000). *Subordination and defeat: An evolutionary approach to mood disorders and their therapy* (Vol. 245). Mahwah, NJ: Erlbaum.

Soldz, S., Budman, S., Demby, A., & Merry, J. (1993). Representation of personality disorders in circumplex and five-factor space: Explorations with a clinical sample. *Psychological Assessment, 5*, 41–52.

Torgersen, S. (1986). Childhood and family characteristics in panic and generalized anxiety disorders. *American Journal of Psychiatry, 143*, 630–632.

Vrana, S. R., Cuthbert, B. N., & Lang, P. J. (1986). Fear imagery and text processing. *Psychophysiology, 23*, 247–253.

Wade, T. D., Bulik, C. M., & Kendler, K. S. (2001). Investigation of quality of the parental relationship as a risk factor for subclinical bulimia nervosa. *International Journal of Eating Disorders, 30*, 389–400.

Weissman, A. N. (1979). The Dysfunctional Attitude Scale: A validation study. *Dissertation Abstracts International, 40*, 1389–1390.

Wells, A. (1995). Meta-cognition and worry: A cognitive model of generalized anxiety disorder. *Behavioural and Cognitive Psychotherapy, 23*, 301–320.

Whisman, M. A., Sheldon, C. T., & Goering, P. (2000). Psychiatric disorders and dissatisfaction with social relationships: Does type of relationship matter? *Journal of Abnormal Psychology, 109*, 803–808.

Wiggins, J. S. (1982). Circumplex models of interpersonal behavior in clinical psychology. In P. C. Kendall & J. N. Butcher (Eds.), *Handbook of research methods in clinical psychology* (pp. 183–221). New York, NY: Wiley.

Wittchen, H. U., Carter, R. M., Pfister, H., Montgomery, S. A., & Kessler, R. C. (2000). Disabilities and quality of life in pure and comorbid generalized anxiety disorder and major depression in a national survey. *International Clinical Psychopharmacology, 15*, 319–328.

Wittchen, H. U., Zhao, S., Kessler, R. C., & Eaton, W. W. (1994). DSM-III-R generalized anxiety disorder in the National Comorbidity Survey. *Archives of General Psychiatry, 51*, 355–364.

Yonkers, K. A., Dyck, I. R., Warshaw, M., & Keller, M. B. (2000). Factors predicting the clinical course of generalised anxiety disorder. *British Journal of Psychiatry, 176*, 544–549.

Yonkers, K. A., Warshaw, M. G., Massion, A. O., & Keller, M. B. (1996). Phenomenology and course of generalised anxiety disorder. *British Journal of Psychiatry, 168*, 308–313.

Yoon, K. L., & Zinbarg, R. E. (2007). Generalized anxiety disorder and entry into marriage or a marriage-like relationship. *Journal of Anxiety Disorders, 21*, 955–965.

Zinbarg, R. E., Lee, J. E., & Yoon, K. L. (2007). Dyadic predictors of outcome in a cognitive-behavioral program for patients with generalized anxiety disorder in committed relationships: A "spoonful of sugar" and a dose of non-hostile criticism may help. *Behaviour Research and Therapy, 45*, 699–713.

10

HEALTH ANXIETY AND HYPOCHONDRIASIS: INTERPERSONAL EXTENSIONS OF THE COGNITIVE–BEHAVIORAL PERSPECTIVE

PAULA G. WILLIAMS, TIMOTHY W. SMITH, AND KEVIN D. JORDAN

For some individuals, the status of their health is a source of preoccupation, emotional distress, and disability. In most instances, this concern and distress involves consequences and implications of serious medical conditions, such as when individuals face a chronic disease (Stanton, Revenson, & Tennen, 2007). However, in other cases, these reactions occur in the absence of objective indications of medical disease or disorder. In the current diagnostic system, this preoccupation and distress in the absence of an actual medical condition is characterized as *hypochondriasis*. Less severe presentations of these characteristics have been termed *hypochondriacal tendencies, illness worry*, or *health anxiety*. Hypochondriacal individuals use health care resources excessively, well beyond the effects of any psychiatric or medical comorbidities (Barsky, Orav, & Bates, 2005). Hence, the societal implications of these conditions are pressing as already burdensome health care costs continue to rise.

Current approaches to hypochondriasis and clinically significant but subthreshold levels of health anxiety emphasize the cognitive–behavioral perspective (Looper & Kirmayer, 2002; Marcus, Gurley, Marchi, & Bauer, 2007; Williams, 2004). Interventions based on this perspective are generally effective in reducing somatic preoccupation, emotional distress, and excessive health care use. Interpersonal aspects of hypochondriasis and health anxiety have received far less attention than cognitive features, but attention to these factors could further our understanding of these costly conditions and improve intervention outcomes. In this chapter, we provide an overview of research on the nature and management of hypochondriasis and health anxiety, including emerging perspectives that place these conditions in their social context. We also consider related conditions that share the common element of complaints about physical health in the absence of identifiable medical disease or disorder. In these conditions, relationships between physicians and patients are often strained, and the quality and cost of medical care can suffer. Hence, we discuss both the social context of personal relationships (e.g., marital and family factors) and the interpersonal context of health care. For both social contexts, hypochondriasis, health anxiety, and related conditions both influence and are influenced by interpersonal processes, providing opportunities for refined interventions.

OVERVIEW OF HYPOCHONDRIASIS AND HEALTH ANXIETY

In this section, current diagnostic criteria for hypochondriasis and common differential diagnoses are presented. Predominant etiological perspectives and approaches to treatment are also discussed.

Clinical Description, Diagnoses, and Comorbidities

The central feature of hypochondriasis is preoccupation with the belief that one has a serious disease, based on misinterpretation of bodily symptoms and occurring in the absence of known organic pathology and persisting despite appropriate medical evaluation and reassurance. Although the prevalence rates for clinical hypochondriasis are typically not high (e.g., Barsky, Wyshak, Klerman, & Latham, 1990; Escobar et al., 1998), transient health anxiety is relatively common (Looper & Kirmayer, 2001). The costs of this constellation of conditions and closely related disorders are enormous, including overuse of health services, unnecessary medical tests, missed work, and subjective distress (Barsky et al., 2005; Looper & Kirmayer, 2002).

There has been a long-standing controversy about both where hypochondriasis "belongs" in diagnostic classification systems and the adequacy of current criteria for differentiating hypochondriasis from other disorders. Hypochondriasis is included with the somatoform disorders, along with somatization disorder, somatoform pain disorder, body dysmorphic disorder, and conversion disorder. The shared focus of these diagnoses is a dysfunction in the perception of the body. The leading alternative is to move hypochondriasis to the anxiety disorders, based on shared features and comorbidity with other anxiety disorders (Noyes, 2001).

Common diagnostic differentials include distinguishing hypochondriasis from somatization disorder and anxiety disorders. Distinguishing hypochondriasis and somatization disorder has been challenging (Fink et al., 2004; Noyes, Stuart, Watson, & Langbehn, 2006). In current diagnostic criteria, somatization disorder is characterized by multiple unexplained physical symptoms of particular number and type, whereas there is no such specification of the number or nature of symptoms in hypochondriasis. Hypochondriasis and somatization disorder are common sources of *medically unexplained symptoms* (Brown, 2007), a term that refers to complaints patients present that are judged as having no identifiable physical basis.

Familial and interpersonal factors also inform this distinction. Family studies have shown high rates of antisocial personality disorder in male relatives of somatization patients (Lilienfeld, Van Valkenburg, Larntz, & Akiskal, 1986) and links between antisocial behavior and somatization in families of clinic-referred children (Frick, Kuper, Silverthorn, & Cotter, 1995). Hence, somatization disorder may be better categorized as a personality disorder. Whereas hypochondriasis is characterized by anxiety and reassurance seeking regarding a conviction of having a serious illness, somatization disorder is characterized by persistent demands for, but also rejection of, health-related care and concern from others (Noyes, Stuart, & Watson, 2008). Also, patients with somatization disorder are often diagnosed with comorbid personality disorders (Rost, Akins, Brown, & Smith, 1992; G. R. Smith, Golding, Kashner, & Rost, 1991).

Hypochondriasis and panic disorder share the catastrophic interpretation of bodily symptoms. As Warwick and Salkovskis (1990) noted, in panic the perceived catastrophe is immediate (e.g., "I'm having a heart attack") and related to autonomic arousal (e.g., racing heart, hyperventilation). In hypochondriasis, the catastrophic thinking is not immediate (e.g., "I have cancer and will die in the future"), and misperceived symptoms are typically not a consequence of autonomic arousal (e.g., distended abdomen, a lump). Indeed, catastrophic beliefs about the consequences of acquiring a feared illness are specific to hypochondriasis, distinguishing it from health concerns in both panic disorder and obsessive–compulsive disorder (OCD; Abramowitz, Olatunji, & Deacon, 2007). However, panic attacks do occur in some cases of hypochondriasis (Fava, Grandi, Saviotti, & Conti, 1990). Hence, these disorders are distinguishable diagnoses that may coexist (Barsky, Barnett, & Cleary, 1994; Deacon & Abramowitz, 2008). Illness-related fear is prominent in both hypochondriasis and illness phobia. However, these two diagnoses may be distinguished by determining whether the fear is related to exposure to or "catching" a disease (phobia) or the fear that one already has a disease (hypochondriasis).

Comparisons have also been drawn between hypochondriasis and OCD. Persistent intrusive thoughts about illness are central to hypochondriasis, and it is often accompanied by behaviors such as frequent body checking, seeking medical reassurance, and searching for medical information on the Internet. These behaviors may have a compulsive quality—serving to temporarily alleviate anxiety, much like compulsions that characterize OCD—setting up a pattern of negative reinforcement. Although there are clearly differences in the content and focus of obsessional thoughts and compulsive behaviors in OCD versus hypochondriasis, there does appear to be overlap in the presence of a broader cognitive distortion, intolerance of uncertainty (Deacon & Abramowitz, 2008).

Studies of comorbidities have indicated that hypochondriasis, somatization disorder, and medically unexplained symptoms commonly occur with clinically significant symptoms of emotional distress. Both hypochondriasis and somatization disorder tend to co-occur with anxiety and depression (Demopulos, Fava, McLean, & Alpert, 1996; Noyes et al., 1994). Indeed, across somatoform disorders and subthreshold levels of related conditions, anxiety and depression are quite common (Lieb, Meinlschmidt, & Araya, 2007), suggesting that interventions that address a range of anxiety, depressive, and somatic symptoms may be particularly useful in such patients.

Etiological Formulations

Although rigorous and definitive etiological research is lacking, much of the current research has suggested that vulnerability factors for the development of hypochondriasis may be similar to those for several of the anxiety disorders. For example, the personality factor Neuroticism is the five factor personality model trait most strongly associated with health anxiety and hypochondriasis, but it is also associated with most of the anxiety disorders, as well as depression and insomnia (see Williams, 2004, for review).

Cognitive models have been predominant in understanding the etiology of health anxiety and hypochondriasis. These models suggest that individuals with hypochondriacal tendencies misinterpret benign physical sensations as signs of disease (Barsky & Klerman, 1983; Barsky, Wyshak, Latham, & Klerman, 1990; Barsky, Wyshak, & Klerman, 1990; Marcus, 1999). For example, hypochondriacal patients consider more symptoms to be indicative of disease than do nonhypochondriacal patients (Barsky, Coeytaux, Sarnie, & Cleary, 1993), and individuals high in hypochondriacal tendencies provide higher probability ratings that a variety of symptoms are indicative of a serious illness, even when a broad range of mood and anxiety symptoms are controlled (Marcus & Church, 2003). Catastrophic thought content about physical symptoms is also accompanied by a ruminative cognitive style in health anxiety (Marcus, Hughes, & Arnau, 2008). These cognitive factors can form a self-exacerbating cycle in which disease fear and conviction prompt attention to somatic sensations, preoccupation and rumination about their implications, and the amplification of such symptoms; attention and amplification, in turn, can reinforce and heighten disease conviction (Barsky, Wyshak, Latham, & Klerman, 1990). This cognitive model is also applicable to the broader category of medically unexplained symptoms (Deary, Chalder, & Sharpe, 2007).

Current Approaches to Treatment and Management

The most well-supported treatment approach for hypochondriasis and health anxiety is cognitive–behavioral therapy (CBT; Looper & Kirmayer, 2002). The approach targets inaccurate or catastrophic cognition about the meaning of physical sensations and the amplification of symptoms. This cognitive restructuring involves monitoring illness-related thoughts and reappraisal of somatic experiences and is often combined with relaxation training and desensitization (Stuart, Noyes, Starcevic, & Barsky, 2008). Randomized trials have demonstrated that CBT reduces symptoms of hypochondriasis and health anxiety, other types of emotional distress (e.g., anxiety, depressive symptoms), functional disability levels, and health care use (e.g., Barsky & Ahern, 2004; Clark et al., 1998; Greevan et al., 2007). CBT produces similar benefits for patients with somatization disorder (Allen, Woolfolk, Escobar, Gara, & Hamer, 2006) and medically unexplained symptoms (Escobar et al., 2007) and hence has broad utility for somatoform disorders (Kroenke, 2007).

Hypochondriasis and somatization disorder can also be managed through interventions in the health care system. Psychiatric consultations followed by a letter outlining recommendations to the primary care physician can produce significant reductions in health care use and related costs for somatizing patients (Rost, Kashner, & Smith, 1994; G. R. Smith, Monson, & Ray, 1986; G. R. Smith, Rost, & Kashner, 1995). The combination of CBT and this type of consultation intervention has been found to be highly effective for hypochondriasis (Barsky & Ahern, 2004). Recommendations in the communications to primary care physicians include (a) instructions for the physician to shift the focus to improved coping with symptoms, rather than symptom elimination, as the goal of care; (b) uncoupling of medical visits and escalating anxiety over symptoms by implementation of regularly scheduled medical appointments versus patient-initiated appointments; (c) provision of appropriate reassurance, empathy, and support; and (d) adoption of a medically appropriate but conservative approach to diagnostic procedures and interventions.

INTERPERSONAL CONSIDERATIONS

The cognitive perspective on hypochondriasis, health anxiety, and related conditions might be usefully expanded to include interpersonal factors. Unlike the burgeoning literature on marital and family relationships in depression and anxiety disorders, little research to date has examined the role of these relationships in health anxiety and hypochondriasis. There have been few studies of associations of these symptom patterns with social support, expressed emotion, and conflict in personal relationships. Hence, a common approach in the literature on depression and anxiety in which marital and family functioning correlates are used to guide the development and implementation of alternative or additional relationship-focused therapies is simply missing from the literature on health anxiety and hypochondriasis. Yet, the cognitive model of health anxiety and hypochondriasis has been usefully extended to social processes, albeit in a preliminary manner. For example, in addition to sensitivity to illness threat, health anxiety is associated with bias toward social threat (Hitchcock & Mathews, 1992).

Rather than focusing on current marital and family relationships, the most well-developed interpersonal approach to health anxiety and hypochondriasis is a developmental perspective based in the attachment paradigm (Bowlby, 1973, 1979), in which early parent–child interactions give rise to either secure attachment or a variety of insecure attachment patterns involving anxiety and avoidance. These attachment patterns are hypothesized to shape interpersonal functioning over the course of development (Bowlby, 1973, 1979; Mikulincer & Shaver, 2007).

In applying attachment theory to hypochondriasis, Noyes et al. (2003) suggested that negative attachment histories result in interpersonal deficits—specifically, insecurity about personal relationships and poor skills in the expression of emotional needs. Hypochondriacal complaints, in turn, are used to manage underlying interpersonal insecurities and garner emotional support from others, both in the context of personal relationships and in interactions with medical professionals. Consistent with this view, measures of childhood separation anxiety are associated with hypochondriasis (Noyes et al., 2002). Noyes et al. (2003) suggested that separation anxiety may be considered an indirect measure of insecure attachment and is hypothesized to be a vulnerability factor for the development of psychopathology, broadly speaking, in adulthood. Measures of insecure attachment are consistently associated with hypochondriasis and somatization (Noyes et al., 2003; Waldinger, Schulz, Barsky, & Ahern, 2006). The role of temperament and personality in these findings is unclear; however, Noyes et al. (2003) reported that fearful attachment style is positively correlated with neuroticism, and when both are included in regression analyses, neuroticism is the stronger predictor of hypochondriasis. These findings suggest that attachment style may be a general vulnerability factor (i.e., not specific to hypochondriasis), although it may have direct bearing on the interpersonal expression (e.g., adverse interactions with medical professionals) of hypochondriasis. Furthermore, it is important to note that studies demonstrating associations between attachment styles and hypochondriasis or somatizing are cross-sectional; no studies to date have tested this model in longitudinal designs.

Whereas insecure attachment style may be a risk factor for a variety of forms of psychopathology, it has been suggested that childhood experience with significant illness is a specific antecedent of hypochondriasis (Barsky, Wool, Barnett, & Cleary, 1994). For example, Noyes et al. (2002) found that when presented with a list of traumatic childhood events, patients with hypochondriasis were more likely to report events such as having a serious illness or injury during childhood, a parent with a hazardous occupation, a family member with an alcohol or drug problem, a chronic illness in a family member, or serious illness in a close friend than were nonhypochondriacal individuals. That is, the events that differentiated hypochondriacal patients from nonhypochondriacal patients involved health-related threat to either self or close others. Noyes et al. (2002) also found modest correlations between hypochondriasis and measures of parental overconcern in relation to illness. Indeed, individuals with hypochondriacal concerns report more instrumental and vicarious learning experiences around bodily symptoms (Watts & Stewart, 2000). Moreover, in an examination of maternal factors that influence parental response to children's illness, mothers' own self-assessed health was a stronger predictor of more extreme caretaking behavior and encouragement of sick role behavior in their children than was maternal neuroticism (Scalzo, Williams, & Holmbeck, 2005).

In summary, prior research has suggested that illness- and injury-related events (either vicarious or directly experienced) and interpersonal learning experiences involving illness (either modeled or directly experienced) represent the specific social developmental factors that may make vulnerable children (i.e., high neuroticism, insecure attachment) begin a trajectory toward health anxiety (vs. other forms of psychopathology). Moreover, prior social learning experiences that lead to general attachment difficulties, as well as illness-specific learning experiences (e.g., parental overconcern about illness), may contribute to the interpersonal style thought to maintain hypochondriasis once it has begun.

Interpersonal Processes and Their Role in the Onset and Maintenance of Health Anxiety

The onset of a specific episode of health anxiety often occurs in response to a *trigger* involving a personal health scare, a health threat to a close other person, or media coverage of a disease or health threat (Salkovskis & Warwick, 2001). It is not clear whether personal or vicarious illness experiences in adulthood are sufficient to trigger hypochondriasis in the absence of the types of childhood experiences described earlier. In other words, it is clear that personal experience of a health scare or knowing someone with a serious illness as an adult may be a proximal precipitating factor for health anxiety or hypochondriasis; whether a learning history related to illness threat moderates this relationship awaits empirical investigation.

To receive a diagnosis of hypochondriasis, the belief that one has a serious illness must persist despite appropriate medical evaluation and reassurance from a health care provider. It is this latter aspect of hypochondriasis that is uniquely interpersonal. The inability to respond to reassurance often distinguishes an individual with transient health anxiety from one with diagnosable hypochondriasis. Although the diagnostic focus of hypochondriasis is on interactions with health care providers, a similar pattern of reassurance seeking may occur in other close relationships and may play a role in the maintenance of health anxiety. Some researchers have incorporated interpersonal aspects of hypochondriasis that are not specific to health care providers into assessment. For example, two subscales of the Multidimensional Inventory of Hypochondriacal Traits (Longley, Watson, & Noyes, 2005) are largely interpersonal in nature. The Hypochondriacal Alienation subscale includes items such as "Others do not seem sympathetic to my health problems," and the Hypochondriacal Reassurance subscale contains items such as "I like to be reassured when I feel sick." Longley et al. (2005) described these subscales as "cognitive" and "behavioral" components of hypochondriasis, but they illustrate interpersonal aspects of hypochondriacal tendencies.

To account for the maintenance of hypochondriasis, Warwick and Salkovskis (1990) hypothesized that a combination of a cognitive bias toward attending to information that confirms illness concerns and avoidance behaviors (e.g., medical consultations, bodily checking) serves to perpetuate health anxiety. The latter have been compared with compulsions in OCD in that the behaviors may initially, but only temporarily, alleviate anxiety. Thus, seeking medical reassurance, and perhaps the reassurance of close others, regarding health concerns likely serves to reduce anxiety in the short term; however, when illness worry returns, the behavior is repeated. Indeed, patients high in health anxiety recall medical reassurance as less certain in ruling out a serious health problem compared with patients low in health anxiety when obtaining medical consultation for unexplained symptoms (Lucock, White, Peak, & Morley, 1998).

The repeated nature of seeking reassurance may eventually strain relations with both close others and health care providers. The frustration on the part of family members and health care providers with their inability to successfully reassure the individual with health anxiety may become apparent, perhaps even leading to avoidance of or resentment toward the individual. This pattern may then serve to reinforce the hypochondriacal individual's interpersonal insecurities and further entrench attributions that others do not take their complaints seriously. This excessive reassurance seeking associated with health anxiety and hypochondriasis has an important parallel in research on depression, in which the insecurities of depressed people prompt reassurance seeking; despite short-term benefits, excessive reassurance seeking can strain relationships over time, thereby creating stressful and ultimately depression-exacerbating experiences (Joiner & Metalsky, 2001). However, it is important to note that this interpersonal process is more apparent in depression than in anxiety (Joiner & Schmidt, 1998).

Interpersonal Processes and Comorbidity

As described earlier, health anxiety often co-occurs with other disorders, including depression. The interpersonal consequences of health anxiety and hypochondriasis may represent vulnerability factors for the development of depression. Poorer self-assessed health, even without accompanying anxiety, predicts increases in depressive symptoms (Williams, Colder, Richards, & Scalzo, 2002), perhaps through the mechanism of functional disability (Lewinsohn, Seeley, Hibbard, Rohde, & Sack, 1996). Prior research has suggested that withdrawal from positive activities, particularly a lack of pleasurable engagement in social relationships, may be central to the onset and perpetuation of depressed mood (Joiner, Lewinsohn, & Seeley, 2002). Thus, to the extent that health anxiety results in strained interpersonal relations, withdrawal from supportive relations, or both, these individuals will be at risk of depression.

ELABORATING THE INTERPERSONAL MODEL

The attachment model of hypochondriasis and health anxiety (Noyes et al., 2003) is an example of the general interpersonal tradition in clinical psychology (Horowitz, 2004; Kiesler, 1996; Pincus & Ansell, 2003). Although emphasizing attachment as the foundation of adjustment and interpersonal functioning, this perspective includes additional concepts and methods that may be useful in the further understanding of social features of hypochondriasis and health anxiety. More important, this approach views personality and psychopathology as involving recurring patterns of social interaction (Sullivan, 1953). Hence, from a general perspective, interpersonal patterns will form core elements of hypochondriasis and health anxiety.

Within this perspective, interpersonal behavior varies along two basic dimensions: *affiliation* (i.e., warmth vs. hostility) and *control* (i.e., dominance vs. submissiveness). Together, affiliation and control make up the interpersonal circumplex (IPC), the basic structural model in this perspective (Kiesler, 1983; Leary, 1957; see Chapter 1, this volume). The IPC can be used to describe moment-by-moment social behavior, as well as more enduring characteristics of the social environment such as social support (Trobst, 2000) and personality traits (Trapnell & Wiggins, 1990). In the IPC, neuroticism, anxiety, and depressive symptoms are associated with an unfriendly and submissive interpersonal style (Schmidt, Wagner, & Kiesler, 1999; Wiggins & Broughton, 1991). Hence, to the extent that health anxiety and hypochondriasis are related to neuroticism, as well as to other aspects of anxiety and depression, these somatoform characteristics should also be associated with an unfriendly and submissive interpersonal style.

The IPC has been used as an integrative perspective and empirical tool in the study of patient–physician relationships and interactions (Kiesler & Auerbach, 2003). Generally speaking, warmth in such interactions is associated with improved care and patient satisfaction, whereas cold, unsupportive, or hostile interactions (e.g., criticism) are associated with negative outcomes. The correlates of variation in patient–physician interaction along the control axis are more varied, although overly directive, controlling, or task-focused physician behavior has been associated with negative outcomes in some studies (Kiesler & Auerbach, 2003).

The interpersonal style associated with health anxiety and hypochondriasis gains additional importance in light of another component of interpersonal theory—the principle of complementarity (Kiesler, 1996; Horowitz, 2004). In this view, the behavior of one individual tends to "pull, invite, or evoke restricted classes of responses from the other" (Pincus & Ansell, 2003, p. 215). The behavior that is "invited" or complementary is similar along the IPC affiliation axis and opposite along the control axis. That is, displays of warmth invite warm responses, whereas cold or hostile expressions invite hostility in return. Expressions of dominance invite submissiveness, whereas submissive behavior encourages dominance. A substantial body of research has supported the principle of complementarity (Fournier, Moskowitz, & Zuroff, 2008; Horowitz et al., 2006). If health-anxious individuals display an unfriendly and submissive interpersonal style, they would implicitly invite or evoke unfriendly and controlling responses from others. Given the strong reciprocity of interpersonal behavior along the IPC affiliation axis, these individuals would experience low levels of social support and interpersonal connection. If hypochondriasis reflects attachment insecurity, low support could exacerbate such concerns over time.

Complementarity and the recurring patterns of social interaction at the core of personality and psychopathology can be described as reflecting the transactional cycle (Carson, 1969; Kiesler, 1996), another core concept in the interpersonal perspective. In this perspective, aspects of an actor's internal experience (e.g., affect, expectations, appraisals of interaction partners, somatic sensations) guide that actor's expressive behavior, as when an anxious and mistrusting person is outwardly guarded or defensive. This expressive behavior restricts the range of likely reactions or experiences in the interaction partner. For example, the interaction partner might appraise the guarded and defensive actor as irritated or even hostile. Those internal reactions, in turn, lead the partner to be more likely to express behavior that is complementary to the actor's initial expectations, as when after the actor's guarded or defensive behavior, warmth from interaction partners becomes less likely and hostile reactions become more so. These transactional processes can shape the tone of social interactions across a variety of contexts, including close relationships (T. W. Smith & Glazer, 2006), although contexts involving structured roles (e.g., supervisor vs. supervisee) can alter complementarity, as when individuals refrain from responding in kind to their employer's hostile comments (Moskowitz, Ho, & Turcotte-Tremblay, 2007). The transactional cycle is quite consistent with a general assumption of reciprocal determinism common across many areas of psychology (Bandura, 1978; Buss, 1987; Caspi & Roberts, 1999; Mischel & Shoda, 1998); simply put, individuals both influence and are influenced by the social situations they encounter in an ongoing manner.

Two Transactional Cycles Associated With Health Anxiety

In hypochondriasis and health anxiety, transactional cycles are important in two distinct social contexts—relationships with family members and interactions with physicians and other health care providers. These two cycles are depicted in Figure 10.1. In the middle section of Figure 10.1, the two boxes depicting the internal experience and overt behavior of the identified patient are consistent with current intrapersonal cognitive behavioral models. Figure 10.1 further depicts the transactional cycles that would be hypothesized to occur, given the cognitive–behavioral characteristics of health anxiety. For both cycles, the early phases of ongoing relationships and interaction patterns may differ in important ways from the patterns that evolve over time.

In marital and family interactions (see lower portion of Figure 10.1), the internal experience of hypochondriacal individuals includes somatic preoccupation, anxiety, illness conviction, and symptom amplification, prompting worried expressions, somatic complaints, and expression of concerns, fears, or convictions about disease in interactions with close relationship partners or other family members. Initially, such behavior by the hypochondriacal

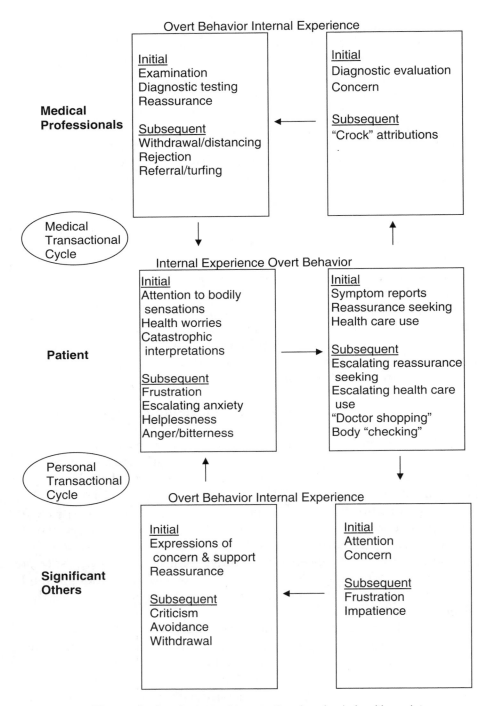

Figure 10.1. The medical and personal transactional cycles in health anxiety.

individual may evoke attention, concern, and sympathy as family members express support and offer advice or assistance in seeking medical care. Over time, however, expressions of health anxiety and somatic complaints to family members could lead to skepticism, reduced attention, avoidance, withdrawal of support, and even criticism. Hence, early transactions may be reassuring and comforting, thereby reinforcing the expression of somatic complaints. Later interactions, however, may be experienced as rejection and dismissal, prompting irritation and maintaining or even exacerbating anxiety. If insecurity in important relationships contributes to health anxiety and hypochondriasis, this dysfunctional cycle can be maintained over time. Strained and isolating personal relationships may also pose a risk for comorbid depression.

In the medical context (see the upper portion of Figure 10.1), health-anxious patients typically present their concerns to primary care physicians. Physicians can distinguish between medical symptom presentations by patients who are high versus low in neuroticism, a personality trait closely associated with hypochondriasis (Ellington & Wiebe, 1999). Specifically, health care providers perceive symptom presentations by patients high in neuroticism as less credible and less warranting of medical treatment. Yet, the physicians' typical response is to evaluate the symptoms through interviewing, physical examination, and diagnostic testing. When this process fails to identify a specific medical cause, physicians often provide appropriate reassurance. This can have a positive short-term effect on patients' anxiety and concerns, but health-anxious individuals may also leave such evaluations believing that a serious problem has escaped detection. Either way, recurring health anxiety may motivate additional health care seeking.

Over time, physicians come to recognize these patients as frequently presenting with medically unexplained symptoms and seeking excessive care. Process studies of patient–physician interactions for medically unexplained symptoms have indicated that these patients repeatedly seek support from the physician but are often met instead with criticism (Salmon, Humphris, Ring, Davies, & Dowrick, 2007). Physician criticism of patients is, in turn, associated with physician beliefs that emotional concerns are not legitimate topics for medical visits and with the physician view that patients share responsibility for managing medical problems rather than being passive recipients of care. The greater the focus is on physical symptoms and their medical cause in these visits, the more likely patients presenting medically unexplained symptoms are to receive somatic intervention—usually medication (Salmon, Wissow, et al., 2007). In contrast, the probability of somatic interventions for medically unexplained symptoms decreases as the focus of the consultation includes psychosocial concerns. Hence, maintaining a traditional medical focus during medical visits rather than including attention to psychosocial concerns can result in a continuing medical approach to managing what are actually emotional concerns and symptoms. In the course of such medical visits, patients presenting with medically unexplained symptoms often provide cues that psychosocial issues are relevant to the presenting concerns, but physicians typically ignore or at least fail to respond to such cues and may also demonstrate little empathic concern (Ring, Dowrick, Humphries, Davies, & Salmon, 2005).

This emerging description of patient–physician interaction regarding medically unexplained symptoms counters the conventional notion that somatizing or health-anxious patients demand medical treatment for obviously emotional concerns. Instead, such patients appear to provide evidence— perhaps unintentionally—that their somatic complaints and illness convictions are accompanied by psychosocial problems, such as anxiety and stressful life circumstances. Yet, the common failure by physicians to attend directly to these psychosocial issues during the visit and the default focus on a more strictly somatic conceptualization and agenda results in unnecessary diagnostic tests and medical treatments, as well as a missed opportunity to change the focus of patient management to include psychosocial concerns. More direct efforts by patients in this regard, such as seeking emotional support from physicians, may even be met with criticism. Physicians may also continue to permit patients who present with medically unexplained symptoms to schedule medical visits "on demand" in response to acute concerns (Anderson et al., 2008). This approach creates the possibility that an inappropriate medical focus of care will continue and that short-term anxiety reduction and attention from physicians will reinforce anxiety-driven health care seeking. Regularly scheduled visits that are not linked to acute complaints and that include physician support for patients concerns and coping efforts are more appropriate and effective (Nordin et al., 2006).

Over time, physicians may come to view somatizing and health-anxious patients as "crocks" with clearly inappropriate tendencies to misuse medical care. A cold and resistant interpersonal stance toward such patients may even be followed by "turfing"—referring the patient elsewhere with the hope of minimizing further contact. For patients, frustrating and even punishing interactions with physicians may lead to "doctor shopping" in an effort to obtain elusive reassurance and resolution of continuing health concerns. Obviously, this pattern can exacerbate patient frustration and lead to maintained and even escalating health anxiety.

Implications for Treatment

As noted previously, cognitive–behavioral approaches to the treatment of health anxiety and hypochondriasis have been predominant, typically focusing on altering cognitive distortions related to the experience of physical symptoms (Looper & Kirmayer, 2002). From the interpersonal perspective, these interventions can be seen as modifying key components of maladaptive transactional cycles. Additional aspects of the interpersonal approach to treatment may be a useful supplement to CBT (Stuart & Noyes, 2006).

The central role of health care providers suggests a unique interpersonal focus in the treatment of health anxiety and hypochondriasis compared with other anxiety disorders. Indeed, many researchers think this aspect of treatment is the most crucial element for successful outcome (Lipsitt, 2001). Because of the nature of health anxiety, establishing a trusting relationship with a health care provider increases the probability that the individual can be reassured about his or her health status. As depicted in Figure 10.1, individuals high in health anxiety often have higher rates of health care use (Barsky et al, 2005; Ciechanowski, Walker, Katon, & Russo, 2002) and may doctor shop (Fink, 1993), making reduction in inappropriate health care use a target for treatment. An important strategy in lowering unnecessary health care use is to enlist an identified primary care provider who manages the patient's medical treatment and referrals.

As described earlier, this involves establishing set appointments with the health care provider rather than allowing the high-use individual to make appointments under conditions of escalating anxiety. For example, if an individual with health anxiety is seeking medical consultation several times a month, a weekly appointment could be established and then gradually extended as the connection between anxiety and health-care seeking is extinguished. Also as described earlier, communication between mental health professionals and primary care physicians that includes suggestions for regularly scheduled appointments, suggestions that physicians provide support for patient concerns and encourage a coping approach to physical complaints rather than symptom elimination, and a medically appropriate but conservative approach to further diagnostic testing and medical treatment can be effective in reducing health care use. This consultation-based intervention interrupts the ongoing maladaptive transactional cycle between the health-anxious patient and his or her health care providers and replaces it with a more adaptive cycle that still maintains appropriate medical care.

Similarly, if there is a pattern of excessive reassurance seeking and strain or conflict in other interpersonal relationships, working with the identified patient and the spouse, for example, could substantially add to treatment gains (Watson & McDaniel, 2000; Woolfolk, Allen, & Tiu, 2007). Although this has been demonstrated with other anxiety disorders, the benefits of involving significant others in the treatment of hypochondriasis has not been investigated.

As described earlier, individuals with hypochondriacal tendencies may have trouble establishing satisfying relationships with others, perhaps because of a history of unreliable and inconsistent care giving. Current assessment research has suggested that these individuals do not feel their concerns are taken seriously by others (Longley et al., 2005), and their persistence in sharing health worries may be an attempt to reduce anxiety, garner support, and stay connected with others. Interpersonal psychotherapy with these individuals could involve examination of their attachment history, internal working models, interpersonal problems, and communication patterns (Stuart et al., 2008). Thus, a key goal of psychotherapy with hypochondriacal individuals is to encourage direct communication of needs to replace attempts to get interpersonal needs met via physical symptom complaints or expression of health worry. In an interpersonal approach, awareness of interpersonal style is increased, and clients move from automatic engagement in maladaptive interpersonal transactions to conscious attempts at assertive behavior.

Although there has been little research on interpersonal approaches to the treatment of health anxiety and hypochondriasis, there is supportive evidence from research on related disorders. Creed et al. (2008) found that patients with irritable bowel syndrome and comorbid high somatization tendencies responded well to brief interpersonal psychotherapy. Kashner, Rost, Cohen, Anderson, and Smith (1995) conducted a randomized controlled trial of brief group therapy on patients with somatization disorder, with positive results in the form of better self-reported mental and physical health over a 1-year period. Although their group therapy intervention was not interpersonal therapy per se, it did include a number of interpersonal elements such as learning to label and express emotion, getting along with others, and assertiveness training.

CONCLUSIONS AND FUTURE DIRECTIONS

The generally effective cognitive–behavioral approach to hypochondriasis and health anxiety could be usefully expanded to include interactions and relationships with family members and with health care providers. In both contexts, maladaptive transactional cycles can maintain and exacerbate a dysfunctional focus on medical concerns while simultaneously diverting attention from and exacerbating underlying emotional and interpersonal difficulties. Well-established CBT interventions modify key components of these interaction patterns but can be enhanced through relatively brief, cost-effective, and empirically supported consultation-based interventions with primary care physicians that modify the physician's unintended contribution to maladaptive transactions.

Assessment of marital and family relationship factors may identify worrisome levels of strain and waning support, although there has been surprisingly little empirical research on the marital and family context of health anxiety and hypochondriasis. Empirically supported relationship interventions could be adapted for health anxiety and hypochondriasis (Snyder, Castellani, & Whisman, 2006) to disrupt dysfunctional transactional cycles that lead to strain, reduced support, and even conflict in close relationships. Such efforts could not only reduce health anxiety but may also prevent and manage commonly comorbid conditions such as depression.

Despite their similarities, health anxiety and hypochondriasis differ in important ways from somatization and somatization disorder. The latter subthreshold condition and formal disorder may be less characterized by anxiety than by long-standing interpersonal dysfunction (Noyes et al., 2008). CBT and consultation–liaison interventions in the medical care system are empirically supported for somatization (Allen et al., 2006; Martin, Rauh, Fichter, & Rief, 2007; Rost et al., 1994; G. R. Smith et al., 1995), but the surrounding interpersonal context may differ in important ways. Those dysfunctional transactional cycles may be characterized by greater resistance to change and the patient's intentional manipulation of others through somatic complaints. Hence, if initial evaluation of individual patients suggests that somatization is a more accurate diagnosis than health anxiety, personality disorder symptoms should be included in further assessment, and interpersonal approaches to treatment might be usefully expanded to include those tailored for the chronic and more severe interpersonal dysfunctions typical of Axis II conditions (Benjamin, 2003). Also, ethnicity and culture are powerful forces shaping the experience and expression of physical symptoms and health care seeking. Hence, assessment and intervention in health anxiety and hypochondriasis should consider these aspects of diversity (Kirmayer & Sartorius, 2007), as should future research on related interpersonal concerns.

In future studies of hypochondriasis and health anxiety, the large body of research on interactional bases of anxiety and depression can provide valuable guidance, as can the similarly substantial literature on interpersonal aspects of medical problems such as chronic pain (Leonard, Cano, & Johansen, 2006; Mikail, 2003). Complaints and worries about physical health constitute compelling interpersonal communications, with potential for both adaptive and maladaptive consequences. Additional research on these aspects of health anxiety may lead to more effective approaches to management, an inviting prospect given the economic impact of unfounded medical complaints in the current climate of health care expenditures. The concepts and methods of the interpersonal approach (Horowitz, 2004; Kiesler, 1996; Pincus & Ansell, 2003) can facilitate such efforts by explicating the dynamic social contexts in which health anxiety and hypochondriasis are often tenaciously embedded.

REFERENCES

Abramowitz, J. S., Olatunji, B. O, & Deacon, D. J. (2007). Health anxiety, hypochondriasis, and the anxiety disorders. *Behavior Therapy, 38,* 86–94.

Allen, L. A., Woolfolk, R. L., Escobar, J. I., Gara, M. A., & Hamer, R. M. (2006). Cognitive-behavioral therapy for somatization disorder: A randomized controlled trial. *Archives of Internal Medicine, 166,* 1512–1518.

Anderson, M., Hartz, A., Nordin, T., Rosenbaum, M., Noyes, R., James, P., . . . Anderson, S. (2008). Community physicians' strategies for patients with medically unexplained symptoms. *Family Medicine, 40,* 111–118.

Bandura, A. (1978). The self-system in reciprocal determinism. *American Psychologist, 33,* 1175–1184.

Barsky, A. J., & Ahern, D. K. (2004). Cognitive behavior therapy for hypochondriasis: A randomized controlled trial. *JAMA, 291,* 1464–1470.

Barsky, A. J., Barnett, M. C., & Cleary, P. D. (1994). Hypochondriasis and panic disorder: Boundary and overlap. *Archives of General Psychiatry, 51,* 918–925.

Barsky, A. J., Coeytaux, R. R., Sarnie, M. K., & Cleary, P. D. (1993). Hypochondriacal patients' beliefs about good health. *American Journal of Psychiatry, 150,* 1085–1089.

Barsky, A. J., & Klerman, G. L. (1983). Overview: Hypochondriasis, bodily complaints, and somatic styles. *American Journal of Psychiatry, 140,* 273–283.

Barsky, A. J., Orav, E. J., & Bates, D. W. (2005). Somatization increases medical utilization and costs independent of psychiatric and medical comorbidity. *Archives of General Psychiatry, 62,* 903–910.

Barsky, A. J., Wool, C., Barnett, M. C., & Cleary, P. D. (1994). Histories of childhood trauma in adult hypochondriacal patients. *American Journal of Psychiatry, 151,* 397–401.

Barsky, A. J., Wyshak, G., & Klerman, G. L. (1990). Transient hypochondriasis. *Archives of General Psychiatry, 47,* 746–752.

Barsky, A. J., Wyshak, G., Klerman, G. L., & Latham, K. S. (1990). The prevalence of hypochondriasis in medical outpatients. *Social Psychiatry and Psychiatric Epidemiology, 25,* 89–94.

Barsky, A. J., Wyshak, G., Latham, K. S., & Klerman, G. L. (1990). The Somatosensory Amplification Scale and its relationship to hypochondriasis. *Journal of Psychiatry Research, 24,* 323–334.

Benjamin, L. S. (2003). *Interpersonal reconstructive therapy (IRT): Promoting change in nonresponders.* New York, NY: Guilford Press.

Bowlby, J. (1973). *Attachment and loss. Vol. 2: Separation: Anxiety and anger.* London, England: Hogarth Press.

Bowlby, J. (1979). *The making and breaking of affectional bonds.* London, England: Tavistock.

Brown, R. J. (2007). Introduction to the special issue on medically unexplained symptoms: Background and future directions. *Clinical Psychology Review, 27*, 769–780.

Buss, D. M. (1987). Selection, evocation, and manipulation. *Journal of Personality and Social Psychology, 53*, 1214–1221.

Carson, R. C. (1969). *Interaction concepts of personality.* Oxford, England: Aldine.

Caspi, A., & Roberts, B. W. (1999). Personality continuity and change across the life course. In L. A. Pervin & O. P. John (Eds.), *Handbook of personality: Theory and research* (2nd ed., pp. 300–326). New York, NY: Guilford Press.

Ciechanowski, P., Walker, E. A., Katon, W. J., & Russo, J. E. (2002). Attachment theory: A model for health care utilization and somatization. *Psychosomatic Medicine, 64*, 660–667.

Clark, D. M., Salkovskis, P. M., Hackmann, A., Wells, A., Fennell, M., Ludgate, J., . . . Gelder, M. (1998). Two psychological treatments for hypochondriasis: A randomized controlled trial. *British Journal of Psychiatry, 173*, 218–225.

Creed, F., Tomenson, B., Guthrie, E., Ratcliffe, J., Fernandes, L., Read, N., . . . Thompson, D. G. (2008). The relationship between somatization and outcome in patients with severe irritable bowel syndrome. *Journal of Psychosomatic Research, 64*, 613–620.

Deacon, B. J., & Abramowitz, J. S. (2008). Is hypochondriasis related to obsessive–compulsive disorder, panic disorder, or both? An empirical evaluation. *Journal of Cognitive Psychotherapy: An International Quarterly, 22*, 115–127.

Deary, V., Chalder, T., & Sharpe, M. (2007). The cognitive–behavioral model of medically unexplained symptoms: A theoretical and empirical review. *Clinical Psychology Review, 27*, 781–797.

Demopulos, C., Fava, M., McLean, N. E., & Alpert, J. E. (1996). Hypochondriacal concerns in depressed outpatients. *Psychosomatic Medicine, 58*, 314–320.

Ellington, L., & Wiebe, D. J. (1999). Neuroticism, symptom presentation, and medical decision making. *Health Psychology, 18*, 634–643.

Escobar, J. I., Gara, M. A., Diaz-Martinez, A., Interian, A., Warman, M., Allen, L. A., . . . Rodgers, D. (2007). Effectiveness of a time-limited cognitive behavior therapy–type intervention among primary care patients with medically unexplained symptoms. *Annals of Family Medicine, 5*, 328–335.

Escobar, J. I., Gara, M., Waitzkin, H., Cohen Silver, R., Holman, A., & Compton, W. (1998). DSM-IV hypochondriasis in primary care. *General Hospital Psychiatry, 20*, 155–159.

Fava, G. A., Grandi, S., Saviotti, F. M., & Conti, S. (1990). Hypochondriasis with panic attacks. *Psychosomatics, 31*, 351–353.

Fink, P. (1993). Admission patterns of persistent somatization patients. *General Hospital Psychiatry, 15*, 211–218.

Fink, P., Ornbol, E., Toft, T., Sparle, K. C., Frostholm, L., & Olesen, F. (2004). A new, empirically established hypochondriasis diagnosis. *American Journal of Psychiatry, 161,* 1680–1691.

Fournier, M. A., Moskowitz, D. S., & Zuroff, D.C. (2008). Integrating dispositions, signatures, and the interpersonal domain. *Journal of Personality and Social Psychology, 94,* 531–545.

Frick, P. J., Kuper, K., Silverthorn, P., & Cotter, M. (1995). Antisocial behavior, somatization, and sensation-seeking behavior in mothers of clinic-referred children. *Journal of the American Academy of Child & Adolescent Psychiatry, 34,* 805–812.

Greevan, A., van Balkom, A. J. L. M., Visser, S., Merkelbach, J. W., van Rood, Y. R., van Dyck, R., . . . Spinhoven, P. (2007). Cognitive behavior therapy and paroxetine in the treatment of hypochondriasis: A randomized controlled trial. *American Journal of Psychiatry, 164,* 91–99.

Hitchcock, P. B., & Mathews, A. (1992). Interpretation of bodily symptoms in hypochondriasis. *Behaviour Research and Therapy, 30,* 223–234.

Horowitz, L. M. (2004). *Interpersonal foundations of psychopathology.* Washington, DC: American Psychological Association.

Horowitz, L. M., Wilson, K. R., Turan, B., Zolotsev, P., Constantino, M. J., & Henderson, L. (2006). How interpersonal motives clarify the meaning of interpersonal behavior: A revised circumplex model. *Personality and Social Psychology Review, 10,* 67–86.

Joiner, T. E., Jr., Lewinsohn, P. M., & Seeley, J. R. (2002). The core of loneliness: Lack of pleasurable engagement—more so than painful disconnection—predicts social impairment, depression onset, recovery from depressive disorders among adolescents. *Journal of Personality Assessment, 79,* 472–491.

Joiner, T. E., Jr., & Metalsky, G. I. (2001). Excessive reassurance seeking: Delineating a risk factor involved in the development of depressive symptoms. *Psychological Science, 12,* 371–378.

Joiner, T. W., Jr., & Schmidt, N. B. (1998). Excessive reassurance seeking predicts depressive but not anxious reactions to acute stress. *Journal of Abnormal Psychology, 107,* 533–537.

Kashner, T. M., Rost, K., Cohen, B., Anderson, M., & Smith, G. R. (1995). Enhancing the health of somatization disorder patients: Effectiveness of short-term group therapy. *Psychosomatics, 36,* 462–470.

Kiesler, D. J. (1983). The 1982 interpersonal circle: A taxonomy for complementarity in human transactions. *Psychological Review, 90,* 185–214.

Kiesler, D. J. (1996). *Contemporary interpersonal theory and research.* New York: Wiley.

Kiesler, D. J., & Auerbach, S. M. (2003). Integrating measurement of control and affiliation in studies of physician-patient interaction: The interpersonal circumplex. *Social Science & Medicine, 57,* 1707–1722.

Kirmayer, L. J., & Sartorius, N. (2007). Cultural models and somatic syndromes. *Psychosomatic Medicine, 69*, 832–840.

Kroenke, K. (2007). Efficacy of treatment for somatoform disorders: A review of randomized controlled trials. *Psychosomatic Medicine, 69*, 881–888.

Leary, T. F. (1957). *Interpersonal diagnosis of personality*. New York, NY: Ronald.

Leonard, M. T., Cano, A., & Johansen, A. B. (2006). Chronic pain in a couples context: A review and integration of theoretical models. *Journal of Pain, 7*, 377–390.

Lewinsohn, P. M., Seeley, J. R., Hibbard, J., Rohde, P., & Sack, W. H. (1996). Cross-sectional and prospective relationships between physical morbidity and depression in older adolescents. *Journal of the Academy of Child & Adolescent Psychiatry, 35*, 1120–1129.

Lieb, R., Meinlschmidt, G., & Araya, R. (2007). Epidemiology of the association between somatoform disorder and anxiety and depressive disorders. *Psychosomatic Medicine, 69*, 860–863.

Lilienfeld, S. O., Van Valkenburg, C., Larntz, K., & Akiskal, H. S. (1986). The relationship of histrionic personality disorder to antisocial personality and somatization disorders. *American Journal of Psychiatry, 143*, 718–722.

Lipsitt, D. R. (2001). The patient–physician relationship in the treatment of hypochondriasis. In V. Starcevic & D. R. Lipsitt (Eds.), *Hypochondriasis: Modern perspectives on an ancient malady* (pp. 265–290). New York, NY: Oxford University Press.

Longley, S. L., Watson, D., & Noyes, R., Jr. (2005). Assessment of the hypochondriasis domain: The Multidimensional Dimensional Inventory of Hypochondriacal Traits (MIHT). *Psychological Assessment, 17*, 3–14.

Looper, K. J., & Kirmayer, L. J. (2001). Hypochondriacal concerns in a community population. *Psychological Medicine, 31*, 577–584.

Looper, K. J., & Kirmayer, L. J. (2002). Behavioral medicine approaches to somatoform disorders. *Journal of Consulting and Clinical Psychology, 70*, 810–827.

Lucock, M. P., White, C., Peake, M. D., & Morley, S. (1998). Biased perception and recall of reassurance in medical patients. *British Journal of Health Psychology, 3*, 237–243.

Marcus, D. K. (1999). The cognitive-behavioral model of hypochondriasis: Misinformation and triggers. *Journal of Psychosomatic Research, 47*, 79–91.

Marcus, D. K., & Church, S. E. (2003). Are dysfunctional beliefs about illness unique to hypochondriasis? *Journal of Psychosomatic Research, 54*, 543–547.

Marcus, D. K., Gurley, J. R., Marchi, M. M., & Bauer, C. (2007). Cognitive and perceptual variables in health anxiety: A systematic review. *Clinical Psychology Review, 27*, 127–139.

Marcus, D. K., Hughes, K. T., & Arnau, R. (2008). Health anxiety, rumination, and negative affect: A mediational analysis. *Journal of Psychosomatic Research, 64*, 495–501.

Martin, A., Rauh, E., Fichter, M., & Rief, W. (2007). A one-session treatment for patients suffering from medically unexplained symptoms in primary care: A randomized clinical trial. *Psychosomatics: Journal of Consultation Liaison Psychiatry, 48,* 294–303.

Mikail, S. F. (2003). Attachment and the experience of chronic pain: A couples perspective. In S. M. Johnson & V. E. Wiffen (Eds.), *Attachment processes in couple and family therapy* (pp. 366–385). New York, NY: Guilford Press.

Mikulincer, M., & Shaver, P. (2007). *Attachment in adulthood: Structure, dynamics, and change.* New York: Guilford Press.

Mischel, W., & Shoda, Y. (1998). Reconciling processing dynamics and personality dispositions. *Annual Review of Psychology, 49,* 229–258.

Moskowitz, D. S., Ho, M. R., & Turcotte-Tremblay, A. (2007). Contextual influences on interpersonal complementarity. *Personality and Social Psychology Bulletin, 33,* 1051–1063.

Nordin, T. A., Hartz, A. J., Noyes, R., Anderson, M. C., Rosenbaum, M. E., James, P. A., . . . Levy, B. T. (2006). Empirically identified goals for the management of unexplained symptoms. *Family Medicine, 38,* 476–482.

Noyes, R., Jr. (2001). Hypochondriasis: Boundaries and comorbidities. In G. J. G. Asmundson, S. Taylor, & B. J. Cox (Eds.), *Health anxiety: Clinical and research perspectives on hypochondriasis and related conditions* (pp. 132–160). New York: Wiley.

Noyes, R., Jr., Kathol, R. G., Fisher, M. M., Phillips, B. M., Suelzer, M. T., & Woodman, C. L. (1994). One-year follow-up of medical outpatients with hypochondriasis. *Psychosomatics, 35,* 533–545.

Noyes, R., Jr., Stuart, S., Langbehn, D. R., Happel, R. L., Longley, S. L., Muller, B. A., & Yagla, S. J. (2003). Test of an interpersonal model of hypochondriasis. *Psychosomatic Medicine, 65,* 292–300.

Noyes, R., Jr., Stuart, S., Langbehn, D. R., Happel, R. L., Longley, S. L., & Yagla, S. J. (2002). Childhood antecedents of hypochondriasis. *Psychosomatics, 43,* 282–289.

Noyes, R., Jr., Stuart, S., & Watson, D. (2008). A reconceptualization of the somatoform disorders. *Psychosomatics, 49,* 14–22.

Noyes, R., Stuart, S., Watson, D. B., & Langbehn, D. R. (2006). Distinguishing between hypochondriasis and somatization disorder: A review of the existing literature. *Psychotherapy and Psychosomatics, 75,* 270–281.

Pincus, A. L., & Ansell, E. B. (2003). Interpersonal theory of personality. In T. Millon & M. J. Lerner (Eds.), *Handbook of psychology: Vol. 5. Personality and social psychology* (pp. 209–229). New York, NY: Wiley.

Ring, A., Dowrick, C. F., Humphries, G. M., Davies, J., & Salmon, P. (2005). The somatizing effect of clinical consultation: What patients and doctors say and do not say when patients present with medically unexplained physical symptoms. *Social Science & Medicine, 61,* 1505–1512.

Rost, K. M., Akins, R. N., Brown, F. W., & Smith, G. R. (1992). The comorbidity of DSM–III–R personality disorders in somatization disorder. *General Hospital Psychiatry, 14,* 322–326.

Rost, K. M., Kashner, T. M., & Smith, G. R., Jr. (1994). Effectiveness of psychiatric intervention with somatization disorder patients: Improved outcomes at reduced costs. *General Hospital Psychiatry, 16,* 381–387.

Salkovskis, P. M., & Warwick, H. M. C. (2001). Making sense of hypochondriasis: A cognitive theory of health anxiety. In G. J. G. Asmundson, S. Taylor, & B. J. Cox (Eds.), *Health anxiety: Clinical and research perspectives on hypochondriasis and related conditions* (pp. 46–64). New York, NY: Wiley.

Salmon, P., Humphris, G. M., Ring, A., Davies, J. C., & Dowrick, C. F. (2007). Primary care consultations about medically unexplained symptoms: Patient presentations and doctor responses that influence probability of somatic intervention. *Psychosomatic Medicine, 69,* 571–577.

Salmon, P., Wissow, L., Carrol, J., Ring, A., Humphris, G., Davies, J., & Dowrick, C. (2007). Doctors' responses to patients with medically unexplained symptoms who seek emotional support: Criticism or confrontation? *General Hospital Psychiatry, 29,* 434–460.

Scalzo, C. A., Williams, P. G., & Holmbeck, G. N. (2005). Mothers' emotionality and self-assessed health predict maternal response to child illness. *Children's Health Care, 34,* 61–79.

Schmidt, J. A., Wagner, C. C., & Kiesler, D. J. (1999). Covert reactions to Big Five personality traits: The Impact Message Inventory and the NEO-PI-R. *European Journal of Personality Assessment, 15,* 221–232.

Smith, G. R., Golding, J. M., Kashner, T. M., & Rost, K. (1991). Antisocial personality disorder in primary care patients with somatization disorder. *Comprehensive Psychiatry, 32,* 367–372.

Smith, G. R., Monson, R. A., & Ray, D. C. (1986). Psychiatric consultation in somatization disorder: A randomized controlled study. *New England Journal of Medicine, 314,* 1407–1413.

Smith, G. R., Rost, K., & Kashner, T. M. (1995). A trial of the effect of a standardized psychiatric consultation on health outcomes and costs on somatizing patients. *Archives of General Psychiatry, 52,* 238–243.

Smith, T.W., & Glazer, K. (2006). Hostility, marriage, and the heart: The social psychophysiology of cardiovascular risk in close relationships. In D. R. Crane & E. S. Marshall (Eds.), *Handbook of families and health: Interdisciplinary perspectives* (pp. 19–39). Thousand Oaks, CA: Sage.

Snyder, D. K., Castellani, A. M., & Whisman, M. A. (2006). Current status and future directions in couple therapy. *Annual Review of Psychology, 57,* 317–344.

Stanton, A. L., Revenson, T. A., & Tennen, H. (2007). Health psychology: Psychological adjustment to chronic disease. *Annual Review of Psychology, 58,* 565–592.

Stuart, S., & Noyes, R., Jr. (2006). Interpersonal psychotherapy for somatizing patients. *Psychotherapy and Psychosomatics, 75,* 209–219.

Stuart, S., Noyes, R., Jr., Starcevic, V., & Barsky, A. (2008). An integrative approach to somatoform disorders combining interpersonal and cognitive-behavioral therapy and techniques. *Journal of Contemporary Psychotherapy, 38,* 45–53.

Sullivan, H. S. (1953). *The interpersonal theory of psychiatry.* New York, NY: Norton.

Trapnell, P., & Wiggins, J. S. (1990). Extension of the Interpersonal Adjective Scales to include the Big Five dimensions of personality. *Journal of Personality and Social Psychology, 59,* 781–790.

Trobst, K. K. (2000). An interpersonal conceptualization and quantification of social support transactions. *Personality and Social Psychology Bulletin, 26,* 971–986.

Waldinger, R. J., Schulz, M. S., Barsky, A. J., & Ahern, D. K. (2006). Mapping the road from childhood trauma to adult somatization: The role of attachment. *Psychosomatic Medicine, 68,* 129–135.

Warwick, H. M., & Salkovskis, P. M. (1990). Hypochondriasis. *Behaviour Research and Therapy, 28,* 105–117.

Watson, W. H., & McDaniel, S. H. (2000). Relational therapy in medical settings: Working with somatizing patients and their families. *Journal of Clinical Psychology, 56,* 1065–1082.

Watts, M. C., & Stewart, S. H. (2000). Anxiety sensitivity mediates the relationships between childhood learning experiences and elevated hypochondriacal concerns in young adults. *Journal of Psychosomatic Research, 49,* 107–118.

Wiggins, J. S., & Broughton, R. (1991). A geometric taxonomy of personality scales. *European Journal of Personality, 5,* 343–365.

Williams, P. G. (2004). The psychopathology of self-assessed health: A cognitive approach to health anxiety and hypochondriasis. *Cognitive Therapy and Research, 28,* 629–644.

Williams, P. G., Colder, C. C., Richards, M. H., & Scalzo, C. A. (2002). The role of self-assessed health in the relationship between gender and depressive symptoms among adolescents. *Journal of Pediatric Psychology, 27,* 509–517.

Woolfolk, R. L., Allen, L. A., & Tin, J. E. (2007). New directions in the treatment of somatization. *Psychiatric Clinics of North American, 30,* 621–644.

III

CONCLUSION

11

WHAT LIES AHEAD: STEPS IN UNDERSTANDING INTERPERSONAL PROCESSES IN THE ANXIETY DISORDERS

J. GAYLE BECK

As illustrated throughout this volume, understanding of interpersonal processes in the anxiety disorders is steadily growing. Although progress is uneven across various topical areas, a number of cross-cutting issues have emerged that speak to larger developments in this literature. Consideration of these issues can advance our progress in the conceptualization of interpersonal processes in the anxiety disorders.

WHAT EARLY LIFE FACTORS INFLUENCE THE DEVELOPMENT OF ANXIETY DISORDERS?

Several chapters in this volume discussed the developmental antecedents of anxiety disorders. As illustrated by Ollendick, Costa, and Benoit in Chapter 3; Davila, La Greca, Starr, and Landoll in Chapter 4; and Alden and Taylor in Chapter 5, consideration of attachment processes is a natural starting point. *Attachment* refers to the caretaker–child bond and represents the first interpersonal relationship that individuals form. Children with secure attachment explore their environment with confidence, trust their interactions with adults, and are able to separate appropriately from their caretaker (Bowlby, 1973). Moreover, mothers of securely attached children behave differently than those with insecurely attached children (e.g., Moss, Cyr, & DuBois-Comtois, 2004). In this volume, authors have speculated about the role of excessive parental control, criticism, and intrusiveness, suggesting that this subset of behaviors deserves greater attention as developmental antecedents. Given the interplay between parents and their children, examination of chains of behavior is essential for understanding how specific parenting behaviors interact with children's emotional responses and contribute to anxiety management difficulties.

Although the concept of attachment was originally developed with reference to infants and young children, Hazan and Shaver (1987) extended this notion to adult romantic relationships. In considering the importance of a "safe other" to many anxious adults, one wonders how childhood attachment plays forward in selecting a romantic partner, close friends, or both in adulthood and what factors influence this putative risk factor. Although the issue of what causes psychopathology is too broad to be a useful research heuristic, examination of linkages between childhood experiences and adult emotional problems could illuminate continuity and discontinuity within interpersonal relationships across anxiety problems. This type of research could expand our understanding of developmental processes within the anxiety disorders.

A related developmental issue concerns early influences on avoidance motivation; although avoidance forms one of the cornerstones of the anxiety disorders, it is unclear which factors contribute to this process. From a developmental standpoint, avoidance is one avenue that is used in emotion regulation when one is stressed, with other options including aggression and self-soothing (Sroufe, 1996). How do parental and peer behavior contribute to learning avoidance as an emotion regulation strategy in children and adolescents? Given sex differences in the prevalence of specific adult anxiety disorders (Kessler, Chiu, Demler, Merikangas, & Walters, 2005), one could wonder whether these interpersonal processes contribute in gender-specific ways.

Clearly, early life factors seem relevant when considering anxiety problems in children, adolescents, and adults. It is notable that the literature has etiological models for social anxiety disorder (SAD; Chap. 5, this volume) and generalized anxiety disorder (GAD; Chap. 9, this volume) that include developmental antecedents to adult anxiety pathology. Although some theoretical approaches downplay the saliency of early life factors in adult problems, other models include discussion of early learning history in interaction with biologically predisposed processes. This would appear to be a fruitful direction for future work.

FRIENDS, FAMILY, ROMANTIC PARTNER: DOES IT MAKE A DIFFERENCE?

Embedded within the interpersonal literature on anxiety disorders is an unspoken issue, namely, a lack of knowledge about specific types of close relationships. In considering adult anxiety disorders, most studies have focused on romantic relationships, examining topics such as the impact of symptoms on marital communication and satisfaction (e.g., Riggs, Byrne, Weathers, & Litz, 1998). In the child anxiety literature, emphasis is given to parent–child functioning, with topics subsuming parental overprotection and criticism (see Chap. 3, this volume). And yet, with the exception of very young children, most individuals have a number of interpersonal domains, including family, best friends, broader social circles, and, beginning in adolescence, romantic partners. At this point, we know very little about whether these various relationships exert similar influences on anxiety-disordered individuals. The information that we do possess is gleaned from a number of studies, often involving disparate methodology. For example, Alden and Taylor (Chap. 5, this volume) discussed how socially anxious individuals have been noted to be guarded with others. It is possible that the degree of perceived closeness can moderate this reticence in individuals with SAD. Two studies have noted that socially anxious individuals can display extremely negative behaviors when stressed in the company of a romantic partner, behavior that cannot be described as guarded (Beck, Davila, Farrow, & Grant, 2006; Wenzel, Graff-Dolezal, Macho, & Brendle, 2005). It is plausible that different types of relationships exert different influences on the anxiety-disordered individual. In particular, the role of criticism has been highlighted among families of anxiety-disordered people (e.g., Chaps. 6 and 8, this volume). One could examine the impact of criticism from different relationship domains in future studies. In recognition of the bidirectionality of relationships, it is equally as important to examine the impact of anxiety symptomatology on different types of relationships with close others (e.g., parent, close friend, sibling). Ideally, these issues could be examined over the life span to account for normal developmental shifts in the saliency of various relationships.

An interesting facet of this question is raised by Williams, Smith, and Jordan in Chapter 10 of this volume in their discussion of the role of the health care provider with people with health anxiety. Although the field typically focuses on personal relationships when addressing interpersonal processes, inclusion of more structured relationships is also worthy of study. As highlighted by Williams et al., relationship processes could easily be altered in structured versus unstructured relationships. Thus, a focus on relationships within the workplace might be revealing for anxiety-disordered individuals who are employed. Extending this research focus would help in distinguishing interpersonal features that are invariant across relationships from those that are not.

INTERPERSONAL PROCESSES AND THE ILLUSION OF CAUSALITY

Within psychology, we strive to determine causal factors wherever possible. When we discuss interpersonal influences, it often becomes impossible to designate one facet of a complex, interrelated set of processes as "the" cause. Many chapters in this volume discussed bidirectional influences in interpersonal contributions to the anxiety disorders and provided many examples of this bidirectionality. As researchers and clinicians, it can be both frustrating and challenging to decipher interactions in ways that increase our understanding of interpersonal influences without expressly targeting one individual's behavior as causal. For example, hostility, criticism, and emotional over-involvement have been identified as family processes that negatively affect treatment and increase the risk of relapse after intervention ends (Leff & Vaughn, 1985). Together, these negative communication styles are termed *expressed emotion*. Current thinking has suggested that hostility may be the essential negative influence for anxiety-disordered individuals (see Chap. 6, this volume). Detailed analysis such as this provides useful information that can guide clinical work with anxiety-disordered individuals and their families. Moreover, it opens the door for examination of the specific processes involved, such as cognitive self-schemas (e.g., Chap. 5) or a specific vulnerability to interpersonal stress (e.g., Chap. 8). It is important that Leff and Vaughn (1985) eschewed identifying expressed emotion as a cause or an effect of living with a family member with mental illness, illustrating how this concept can be useful in guiding our work without positing causation.

Beginning with Goldstein and Chambless (1978), recognition has grown that interpersonal processes are important within theories of anxiety disorders. Although no overarching models of interpersonal processes in the anxiety disorders have been postulated, a number of disorder-specific models have guided research and clinical work. As aptly reviewed by Whisman and Beach in Chapter 1 of this volume, conceptual tools are available in the larger literature that can be useful in developing available models. Ongoing work in this area has enormous potential. Ideally, our available theories can be tested, refined, and perhaps overhauled, depending on the kind and nature of empirical support. Theories that address the interplay between intrapersonal and interpersonal processes in the anxiety disorders seem particularly important. As noted by Alden and Taylor in Chapter 5, interpersonal processes can feed intrapersonal symptomatology, and vice versa. As models become more expansive, it is expected that they will include working hypotheses concerning specific symptoms that have notable interpersonal features. As discussed by Monson, Fredman, and Dekel in Chapter 7, individual symptoms of post-traumatic stress disorder are not created equally when one is considering interpersonal features. Thus, it will be interesting to watch the development of theories that link different facets of psychopathology with interpersonal processes to unite these two domains.

COMORBIDITY AND THE INTERPERSONAL WORLD OF ANXIETY-DISORDERED PATIENTS

Anxiety disorders rarely occur in isolation. As noted by Kessler et al. (2005) and Davila et al. in Chapter 4 of this volume, many adults and children with anxiety disorders have additional disorders. However, we have only begun to map out interpersonal processes associated with comorbidity in the anxiety disorders. Two general approaches to this issue have surfaced. In the first approach, comorbid disorders are considered factors that need to be controlled within statistical analyses. This makes good sense when one is unclear whether specific findings can be attributable to anxiety or to coexisting depression. Because depression exerts profoundly negative interpersonal effects, approaching comorbidity in this fashion in research studies helps to clarify the nature of interpersonal processes that are specific to anxiety. In Chapter 8, Chambless provided several examples of studies that have examined marital functioning in samples diagnosed with panic disorder with agoraphobia (PDA) and have controlled for depression. In Chapter 9, Newman and Erickson likewise reviewed studies within the GAD literature that have statistically controlled for depression and social anxiety. Within these efforts, both PDA and GAD have some specific interpersonal effects. Thus, statistical control for comorbid disorders allows for greater precision in defining interpersonal features of individual anxiety disorders.

A second approach to handling comorbidity has focused on associated disorders as a feature of a given disorder. As discussed by Alden and Taylor in Chapter 5's review of SAD, depressive disorders, GAD, and substance use disorders tend to be comorbid and are often preceded in time by SAD. Within this literature, investigators have looked for common linkages, examining features such as social development (e.g., Gibb, Chelminski, & Zimmerman, 2007) and specific interpersonal behavior (Grant, Beck, Farrow, & Davila, 2007). This approach is an effort to examine comorbidity as an intrinsic feature of a specific anxiety disorder. Certainly, both approaches are informative about interpersonal processes in the anxiety disorders.

In this context, special attention needs to be paid to the overlap between depression and anxiety. There is considerable knowledge about interpersonal facets of depression. For instance, support exists for the role of excessive reassurance seeking in interpersonal rejection among individuals with varying degrees of depression (Starr & Davila, 2008). Although much of this literature has involved college students, similar patterns have been noted with patient samples and with children, suggesting continuity in findings (Starr & Davila, 2008). Traditionally, there has not been much cross-talk between the literatures on depression and anxiety. However, greater dialogue would benefit both fields; for example, reassurance seeking can be conceptualized as an anxiety-based behavior (for a discussion of reassurance seeking in health anxiety, see Chap. 10, this volume). Given the comorbidity of anxiety problems in depressed samples, it is conceivable that some components of reassurance seeking are more closely related to anxiety than to depression. A greater focus on the specific function of selected interpersonal behaviors can help to unite these fields, particularly in going beyond the simple labels of anxiety or depression.

THROUGH WHICH LENS? ASSESSMENT ISSUES THAT MAKE A DIFFERENCE

In Chapter 2 of this volume, Snyder et al. provided a methodological overview of the assessment of interpersonal processes and anxiety disorders and highlighted a number of considerations within each area in an effort to bridge the two. In addition to the concerns outlined by Snyder et al., several other assessment-related issues have surfaced in this volume. To begin, one's choice of informant is salient when exploring interpersonal processes. As illustrated by Chambless's (Chap. 8) discussion of marital satisfaction in patients with PDA, informants do not always agree with each other. This holds true across relationships (e.g., romantic partners, parents, siblings) and reveals the inherent complexity involved in interpersonal processes. In this circumstance, one cannot ignore the psychological state of the relationship partner. For example, if the identified patient is married to an individual who is also highly anxious, the spouse's report of marital functioning could primarily reflect his or her anxiety. Similarly, when exploring parent versus youth reports, consideration of anxiety processes for both individuals is highly relevant. As summarized by Davila et al. in Chapter 4, anxious mothers are less responsive to their children and tend to react to their child's distress by becoming distressed themselves. This type of chained behavior highlights the importance of thorough assessment of all informants, whether identified as the patient or not.

A related assessment issue involves the contrast between observational and self-report measures. As Snyder et al. (Chap. 2) reminded us, multimodal assessment is preferable relative to reliance on one modality. Yet, the difficulty level in adopting this recommendation increases when considering assessment of interpersonal processes. For example, interpersonal behavior needs to be approached with a coding system, preferably one that is anchored within the larger literature. Differences in self-report are bound to occur between participants, and sophisticated statistical approaches are needed to account for the nonrandom "clustering" of participants within dyads (as exemplified by Barnett, Marshall, Raudenbush, & Brennan, 1993). Despite these difficulties, efforts to contrast observational and self-reported interpersonal functioning can be invaluable in advancing our efforts. Although researchers who work with marital and family processes are accustomed to this complexity (e.g., Jacobson et al., 1994), anxiety disorder researchers may not be. As such, this is an area in which collaboration between scholars in these two areas can be fruitful and productive.

INTERPERSONAL PROCESSES AND THE TREATMENT OF ANXIETY-DISORDERED PATIENTS

Among clinical psychologists, a focus on the role of interpersonal processes in treating anxious patients is natural. Although there has been speculation about whether and how to include close others, it has only been recently that empirical papers have examined interpersonal facets of treatment. In this literature, four types of questions have been raised, centering on different ways that interpersonal processes can be integrated into treatment.

First, significant others have been included in existing treatment protocols, such as spouse-assisted exposure for PDA (see Chap. 8) and teaching parents anxiety management protocols so they can assist in the treatment of their anxious child (see Chap. 3). In these efforts, emphasis is placed on facilitating use of specific interventions within the patient's environment, via provision of a trained supportive other who can serve as a coach and motivator. Some of the earliest research to appear in this literature falls in this category, with overall positive support for including a close other in treatment. As highlighted by Renshaw et al. in Chapter 6, sometimes psychoeducation needs to be included because family members may inadvertently be aggravating the identified patient's symptoms. These studies have supported the importance of including significant others in treatment, which is particularly salient when considering approaches to facilitate generalization of treatment gains.

The second domain in the treatment area in which interpersonal processes have been included are studies examining the impact of treatment on interpersonal functioning. These efforts have examined the radiating impact of cognitive–behavioral therapy (CBT) for specific disorders (e.g., posttraumatic stress disorder [Galovski, Sobel, Phipps, & Resick, 2005] and GAD [Borkovec, Newman, Pincus, & Lytle, 2002]). Although successful CBT typically results in improvements in overall social functioning, most of these reports have documented that these changes do not extend to improvements within specific close relationships (e.g., marital functioning). This literature has provided the rationale for developing specific treatments that target interpersonal deficits in anxiety-disordered patients, the third domain in this literature. As an example, in Chapter 9 Newman and Erickson described an integrative CBT that includes interpersonal and emotional processing components to target interpersonal problems among individuals with GAD. The interpersonal and emotional processing aspects of treatment emphasize identification of primary emotions and generation of adaptable interpersonal behavior with the goal of helping the patient with GAD to meet his or her needs. As well, traditional CBT interventions are included. This creative blend of treatment approaches has shown promise, although some differences in outcome emerged between studies (see Chap. 9). A similar treatment has been developed by Alden and Taylor (Chap. 5), targeting interpersonal facets of SAD alongside fear and avoidance.

In considering this facet of the treatment literature, it is notable that those treatments that solely target interpersonal functioning have shown mixed results. For example, within the child anxiety literature, there is no evidence of efficacy for attachment-based therapies (see Chap. 3), whereas in the adolescent literature, one trial has provided strong evidence that attachment-based therapy can be effective for anxious teenagers (see Chap. 4). This unevenness is puzzling but may reflect the fact that few such trials have been conducted and their methodological quality varies. This is an area that warrants more focused attention. As noted throughout this volume, expansion of empirically supported treatment options to include approaches that address interpersonal deficits may benefit our patients in ways that we can barely imagine. Because the anxiety disorders tend to be interpersonally disruptive, it is possible that some patients may prefer a treatment that directly focuses on their relationships with close others. The development of this literature will be interesting to watch in the upcoming future.

A fourth area in the treatment literature that has considered interpersonal processes has focused on clinical observations of anxiety patients' close relationships. The earliest example emerged from the PDA literature, based on the reflection that an agoraphobic wife's rapid improvement instigated a mental health crisis for her husband. In this instance, a clinical observation spawned a series of empirical studies examining the role of marital functioning during exposure treatment (for a review, see Chap. 8). Presently, researchers are focusing on the role of expressed emotion within families of anxiety-disordered patients to explore how communication patterns influence symptom severity and treatment response. This type of work helps to build a strong bridge between the science and the practice arms of our field. Although specific clinical observations may not always prove to be the rule when examined empirically, they can highlight specific interpersonal processes for closer scrutiny.

FINAL THOUGHTS

The past 25 years have produced enormous progress in understanding the psychopathology and treatment of anxiety disorders in children, adolescents, and adults. Widening our research and clinical lenses to include greater understanding of interpersonal processes has the potential to build on these gains, allowing us to develop treatments that address the full spectrum of disability that is produced by this set of disorders. By considering the interpersonal world of individuals with anxiety disorders, we have the ability to help them to become interdependent with other people in healthy ways.

REFERENCES

Barnett, R. C., Marshall, N. L., Raudenbush, S. W., & Brennan, R. T. (1993). Gender and the relationship between job experiences and psychological distress: A study of dual earner couples. *Journal of Personality and Social Psychology, 64*, 794–806.

Beck, J. G., Davila, J., Farrow, S., & Grant, D. (2006). When the heat is on: Romantic partner responses influence distress in socially anxious women. *Behaviour Research and Therapy, 44*, 737–748.

Bowlby, J. (1973). *Attachment and loss: Vol. 2. Separation anxiety and anger*. New York: Basic Books.

Borkovec, T. D., Newman, M. G., Pincus, A. L., & Lytle, R. (2002). A component analysis of cognitive–behavioral therapy for generalized anxiety disorder and the role of interpersonal problems. *Journal of Consulting and Clinical Psychology, 70*, 288–298.

Galovski, T., Sobel, A. A., Phipps, K. A., & Resick, P. A. (2005). Trauma recovery: Beyond posttraumatic stress disorder and other Axis I symptom severity. In T. A. Corales (Ed.), *Trends in posttraumatic stress disorder research* (pp. 207–227). Hauppauge, NY: Nova Science.

Gibb, B. E., Chelminski, I., & Zimmerman, M. (2007). Childhood emotional, physical, and sexual abuse and diagnoses of depressive and anxiety disorders in adult psychiatric outpatients. *Depression and Anxiety, 24*, 256–263.

Goldstein, A. J., & Chambless, D. L. (1978). A reanalysis of agoraphobia. *Behavior Therapy, 9*, 47–59.

Grant, D. M., Beck, J. G., Farrow, S. M., & Davila, J. (2007). Do interpersonal features of social anxiety influence the development of depressive symptoms? *Cognition & Emotion, 21*, 646–663.

Hazan, C., & Shaver, P. R. (1987). Romantic love conceptualized as an attachment process. *Journal of Personality and Social Psychology, 52*, 511–524.

Jacobson, N. S., Gottman, J. M., Waltz, J., Rushe, R., Babcock, J., & Holtzworth-Munroe, A. (1994). Affect, verbal content, and psychophysiology in the arguments of couples with a violent husband. *Journal of Consulting and Clinical Psychology, 62*, 982–988.

Kessler, R. C., Chiu, W. T., Demler, O., Merikangas, K. R., & Walters, E. E. (2005). Prevalence, severity, and comorbidity of 12-month DSM-IV disorders in the National Comorbidity Survey Replication. *Archives of General Psychiatry, 62*, 617–627.

Leff, J., & Vaughn, C. (1985). *Expressed emotion in families: Its significance for mental illness*. New York, NY: Guilford Press.

Moss, E., Cyr, C., & Dubois-Comtois, K. (2004). Attachment at early school age and developmental risk: Examining family contexts and behavior problems of controlling–care giving, controlling–punitive, and behaviorally disorganized children. *Developmental Psychology, 40*, 519–532.

Riggs, D. S., Byrne, C. A., Weathers, F. W., & Litz, B. T. (1998). The quality of the intimate relationships of male Vietnam veterans: Problems associated with posttraumatic stress disorder. *Journal of Traumatic Stress, 11*, 87–101.

Sroufe, L. A. (1996). *Emotional development: The organization of emotional life in the early years*. New York, NY: Cambridge University Press.

Starr, L. R., & Davila, J. (2008). Excessive reassurance seeking, depression, and interpersonal rejection: A meta-analytic review. *Journal of Abnormal Psychology, 117*, 762–775.

Wenzel, A., Graff-Dolezal, J., Macho, M., & Brendle, J. R. (2005). Communication and social skills in socially anxious and nonanxious individuals in the context of romantic relationships. *Behaviour Research and Therapy, 43*, 505–519.

INDEX

Cahoon, E. P., 194
Camberwell Family Interview (CFI), 18, 19, 47–48
Caputo, G. C., 52, 53
Caregiver burden, 188
Caregivers, 238–239, 241
Carson, R., 210–211
Carter, M. M., 210–211, 222
Cashman, L., 53
Caspi, A., 24, 26
Cassidy, J. A., 241
Castonguay, L. G., 249, 251
Causality, in anxiety disorders, 290–291
CBGT. *See* Cognitive–behavioral group therapy
CBT. *See* Cognitive–behavioral therapy
Cerny, J. A., 224–225
CFI (Camberwell Family Interview), 18, 19, 47–48
Chambless, D. L., 17–18, 21, 49, 52–53, 157–159, 163, 210–214, 216–217, 222–223, 226–227
Child abuse, 14–15
Child and Adolescent Psychiatric Assessment, 56–57
Child Anxiety Sensitivity Index, 57
Childhood, anxiety disorders in, 71–89
    developmental considerations, 76–83
        attachment, 78–79
        emotion regulation, 79–80
        parental behaviors, 81–83
        peer relationships, 80–81
        temperament, 77–78
    etiology of, 72
    and normative interpersonal development, 73–76
    and peer relations, 50
    prevalence of, 71–72
    treatment of, 83–88
Children's Anxiety Scale, 57
Chorpita, B. F., 57
Christensen, A., 42, 44
Chronic stress, 185–186
Chu, B. C., 85
Circumscribed social anxiety disorder, 126
Clapp, J. D., 184
Clark, D. M., 126–127, 141
Clark, L., 50

Clarke, J., 53, 215–216
Clinical interviews, 39
Clinical presentation
    of posttraumatic stress disorder, 180–181
    of social anxiety disorder, 126
Clinician-Administered Posttraumatic Stress Disorder Scale, 51
Cliques, 100
Close relationships, 294
    and anxiety disorders, 289–290
    in childhood, 129–130
    and levels of anxiety, 16–18
    and posttraumatic stress disorder, 180–193
        effects, 187–190
        empirical research, 181–184
        reciprocal influences, 190–193
        trauma recovery, 185–187
    and social anxiety disorder, 126
Coaches (for help with ERP tasks), 169–170
Cobham, V. E., 85
Coding systems, 40, 45–46
Cognitive–behavioral group therapy (CBGT), 84–85, 141
Cognitive–behavioral interpersonal theory, 190–193
Cognitive–behavioral therapy (CBT), 246–247, 294
    with children, 84–87
    conjoint, 195
    family-based, 112–113
    for generalized anxiety disorder, 248–251
    for health anxiety/hypochondriasis, 265, 274–275, 277
    interpersonal, 115
    for social anxiety disorder, 126–127, 142–143
Cognitive perspective, on OCD, 155
Cognitive representations, 130–131
Cognitive therapy, 141, 250–251
Cohabiting relationships, 17
Cohen, B., 21, 276
Coldness, 11, 239
Collica, T. J., 57
Combat veterans, 188–189, 193–196
Communication behaviors, 42

Discord, 17
Distressed dyads, 42–43
"Doctor shopping," 274, 275
Dominance, 11, 239
Donovan, C., 85–86
Doss, B. D., 44
Dowrick, C. F., 273, 274
DSM–IV. *See Diagnostic and Statistical Manual of Mental Disorders*
DSM–IV–TR. *See Diagnostic and Statistical Manual of Mental Disorders*
DTE (directed therapeutic exposure), 194
Dulcan, M. K., 56
Dyadic Adjustment Scale, 44, 159
Dyck, I. R., 246
Dysfunctional Attitude Scale, 251
Dysregulation, hedonic, 134

Early adolescence, 98
Early life factors, 287–288
Eating disorders, 111–112
EE. *See* Expressed emotion
Eisenberg, N., 76
Electrodermal activity, 55
Eley, T. C., 109
Elliott, S. N., 50
Emery, G., 250–251
Emmelkamp, P. M. G., 214, 218
Emotional competence, 75–76
Emotional numbing, 183
Emotional overinvolvement (EOI), 49
Emotion regulation, 74–75, 79–80
Emotion socialization, 75
Emotion suppression, 238
Endophenotypes, 23–24
Eng, W., 135
EOI (emotional overinvolvement), 49
Epigenetic regulation, 25
Epstein, N. B., 48, 52, 159
Erickson, T. M., 242, 245
Erkanli, A., 98
ERP. *See* Exposure and response prevention
Esman, A. H., 154
Essau, C. A., 110
Essex, M., 80
Ethnicity, 277
Exposure, situational, 113–114
Exposure and response prevention (ERP), 155, 157, 168–171

Exposure treatment, 220
Expressed emotion (EE), 290
and family processes, 18–19, 47–48
and OCD, 158, 163–164
and panic disorder/agoraphobia, 222–223
and PTSD, 196–197
self-report measures of, 48
Eysenck, M. W., 54

Fabes, R. A., 76
Family Adaptability and Cohesion Evaluation Scale, 48
Family Assessment Device, 48, 159
Family Attitude Scale, 48
Family-based cognitive–behavioral therapy, 112–113
Family-based exposure and response prevention, 168–171
Family environment, 128–129
Family Environment Scale, 48
Family functioning, 18, 48
Family interactions
with adolescents, 99–100
and health anxiety/hypochondriasis, 271–273, 277
observational measures of, 48–49
Family members
and OCD, 159–165, 171–172
and treatment outcome, 86
Family processes, 102–105
Family systems model, 211
Family therapy, 88, 112–113
Farrow, S. M., 133
Fear of Negative Evaluation Scales, 53
Fear Survey Schedule for Children—Revised, 57
Fear Survey Schedule—III, 54
Fichter, M., 247
Fields, J. M., 16–17
Figley, C. R., 187
Fincham, F. D., 45
First, M. B., 51
Fisher, A. J., 251
Fisher, P., 56, 114
5HTT, 23–24
5HTTLPR, 24
Fleisig, W., 57
Flexibility, 12
Foa, E. B., 52–54, 156, 159, 163

Obsessive–compulsive disorder (OCD),
  continued
    interpersonal model of, 156–159
    measures for, 54
    prevalence of, 153
    theoretical models of, 154–156
    treatment for, 165–172
Obsessive Compulsive Inventory—
    Revised, 54
OCD. *See* Obsessive–compulsive
    disorder
Oh, K. J., 241
Ollendick, T. H., 57, 84, 102
Olson, D. H., 41, 48
Orcutt, H. K., 183–184
Oregon Adolescent Depression
    Project, 98, 110
Orn, H., 235
Other-report measures, 39–40
Ought-other self, 131
Overbeck, G., 17
Overprotection, parental, 82
Overt compulsions, 157
Overt peer victimization, 106

Padua Inventory, 54
Palyo, S. A., 184
Panic Attack Questionnaire, 52
Panic control treatment, 113–114
Panic disorder and agoraphobia,
    209–228, 263
    consequences of, 210
    diagnostic status of, 214–217
    effects of, on marriage/spouse,
        218–220
    marital issues in, 225–226
    models of, 211–212
    onset of, 212–213
    self-report measures of, 52–53
    symptom severity, 217–218
    treatment of, 220–225
Parental anxiety, 104
Parental behaviors, 81–83
Parental overprotection, 82
Parental rejection–criticism, 82
Parent–child attachment, 73–74, 80–81
Parent–child relationship, 102–103
Parenting behaviors, 103–104, 129
Parker, J. D., 57
Pasch, L. A., 43

Pato, M., 168
Patterson, G. R., 46
Peer involvement (in treatment), 86
Peer relations
    in adolescence, 100–101, 105–107
    aversive–exclusionary, 106–107
    in childhood, 76, 80–81
    negative, 129
    and rejection, 106
Peer victimization (PV), 106–107
Penn State Worry Questionnaire, 54
Penn State Worry Questionnaire for
    Children, 57
Pepler, D. J., 50
Perceived criticism, 19, 223
Perry, K., 53
Personal transactional cycle, 272
Peterson, R. A., 52, 57
Phillips, N., 13
Phobias, 54. *See also* Social phobia
Physiological measures, 40–41, 57–58
Piacentini, J. C., 85
Pincus, A. L., 13, 242, 270
Play therapy, 88
Pollard, C. A., 213
Pollard, H. J., 213
Posttraumatic Diagnostic Scale, 53
Posttraumatic stress disorder (PTSD),
    179–199
    in adolescents, 99, 109
    clinical presentation of, 180–181
    and close relationships, 180–193
    empirical research on, 181–184
    future research directions, 197–199
    measures of, 53–54
    models of, 181–184
    treatment of, 193–197
Presley, A. S., 215–216
Primary care physicians. *See* Health care
    providers
Principle of complementarity, 128
Problem solving, 216–217
Psychodynamic-based therapy, 88
Psychoeducation, 167–168
Psychological control, 82
Psychological measures, 55
Psychopathology, 240
PTSD. *See* Posttraumatic stress disorder
PTSD Checklist, 53

Specific phobias, 54
Spence, S. H., 57, 85–86
Spielberger, C. D., 52
Spousal support, 21
Spouse-assisted treatment, 218–220, 223–226
Stallings, P., 57
Stanley, M. A., 53
Starr, L. R., 111
Startle response, 55
State–Trait Anxiety Inventory, 52
Steer, R. A., 51, 52
Steerneman, P., 57
Steketee, G., 49, 157–158, 162–163, 168, 222–223
Stevens, S. P., 190–191, 195
Stevenson, J., 109
Stone, E. R., 186
Stone, W. L., 57
Strange, C., 21
Strauman, T. J., 130–131
Straus, M. A., 45
Stress
    chronic, 185–186
    during treatment, 223
Stress-diathesis model, 212, 226
Stressful life events, 109, 212–213
Stress generation, 15–16
Strong link model, 41
Stroop methodology, 183
Structural Analysis of Behavior (SASB), 46–47
Stuart, S., 263
Submission, 239
Submissiveness, 11
Substance use, 112, 140–141
Sugarman, D. B., 45
Sullivan, H. S., 11, 13
Sullivan, K., 57
Suomi, S. J., 25
Support, 21. See also Social support
Support and Family Education (S.A.F.E.), 196
Supportive–expressive therapy (SE), 247–248
Suppression of emotions, 238
Symptom severity, 217–218
System for Coding Interactions and Family Functioning, 49

Taft, C. T., 186
Tallis, F., 54
Taxonomy of interpersonal behaviors, 11
Taylor, C. B., 225–226
Taylor, C. T., 22, 131, 142
Teacher Rating of Social Skills, 50
Teasdale, J., 19, 223–224
Telch, M. J., 225–226
Temperament, 77–78, 80–81
Test anxiety, 87
Testbusters, 87
Third National Incidence Study of Child Abuse and Neglect, 14–15
Thompson, R. A., 74
Tiesel, J. W., 48
Tracey, S. A., 57
Transactional cycles, 270–274, 277
Transactional model of obsessive–compulsive disorder, 158–159
Traumatization, 187–188. See also Posttraumatic stress disorder
Treatment(s), 293–295
    for adolescents, 112–115
    for children, 83–88
    delivery of, 165–172
    exposure, 220
    for generalized anxiety disorder, 246–251
    for health anxiety/hypochondriasis, 265, 274–276
    for obsessive–compulsive disorder, 165–172
    of panic disorder/agoraphobia, 220–225
    peer involvement in, 86
    for posttraumatic stress disorder, 193–197
    for social anxiety disorder, 141–143
    stress during, 223
Triggers, 267–268
Truax, P., 220
"Turfing," 274
Turner, S. M., 53, 57, 114
Turovsky, J., 222
Typological category, 12

ABOUT THE EDITOR

J. Gayle Beck, PhD, is the Lillian and Morrie Moss Chair of Excellence at the University of Memphis, Memphis, TN. During her doctoral training at the University at Albany, State University of New York, she worked with David Barlow on clinical research that changed the field's conceptualization of anxiety and anxiety-based disorders. After completing an internship at University of Medicine and Dentistry of New Jersey–Rutgers Medical School, Dr. Beck joined the faculty at the University of Houston and subsequently moved to the State University of New York–Buffalo. Over the years, Dr. Beck has conducted research on a variety of adult anxiety disorders, including panic disorder, anxiety in medical patients with nonorganic chest pain, generalized anxiety disorder in older adults, and most recently posttraumatic stress disorder. She has published numerous scientific articles, contributed many chapters, and authored a book on sexual psychophysiology. Her work has been funded by the National Institute of Mental Health, the American Heart Association, and various state and local agencies. Dr. Beck serves on numerous editorial boards and previously completed a term as editor of *Behavior Therapy*. As past president of the Association for Behavioral and Cognitive Therapies (formerly the Association for the Advancement of Behavior Therapy), Dr. Beck has striven to build conceptual bridges between various facets of clinical psychology and to encourage solid empirical work to inform the understanding and treatment of disordered behavior.